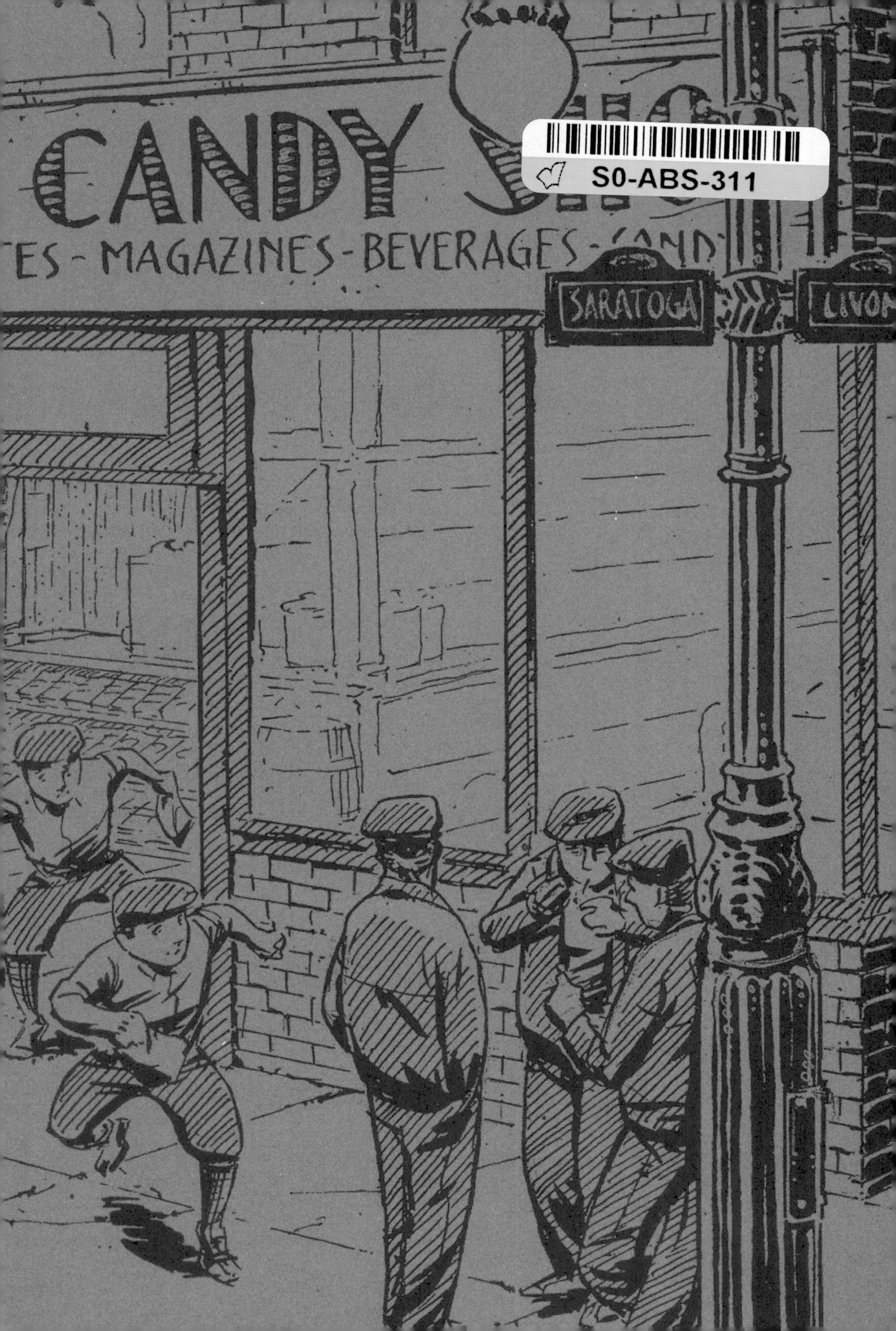
CANDY
ES - MAGAZINES - BEVERAGES -
SARATOGA
S0-ABS-311

BROWNSVILLE

brownsville

written by

illustrated by

neil kleid

jake allen

ISBN-10: 1-56163-458-1, hc.
ISBN-10:1-56163-459-X, pb.
ISBN-13: 978-1-56163-458-3, hc.
ISBN-13: 978-1-56163-459-0, pb.
© 2006 Neil Kleid & Jake Allen
Printed in China
3   2   1

Comicslit is an imprint
and trademark of

NANTIER · BEALL · MINOUSTCHINE
Publishing inc.
new york

For **Laurie,** love of my life; partner in crime. - Neil

Mom, this book wouldn't have been possible without your support. - Jake

Neil would also like to thank Mom, Dad, Aaron, Jill, Esti, Jose, Dovid, Noah and Hannah for teaching me about family; Jake for herculean efforts; Terry for believing in this; Dean Haspiel for going above and beyond; Carla Speed McNeil; Harvey Pekar; and everyone who supported us on the long road we began three years ago.

Jake would also like to thank Dad; Robyn; Chuck; Angie; Sashi; Matt; Jon; Charles; Terry and Neil.

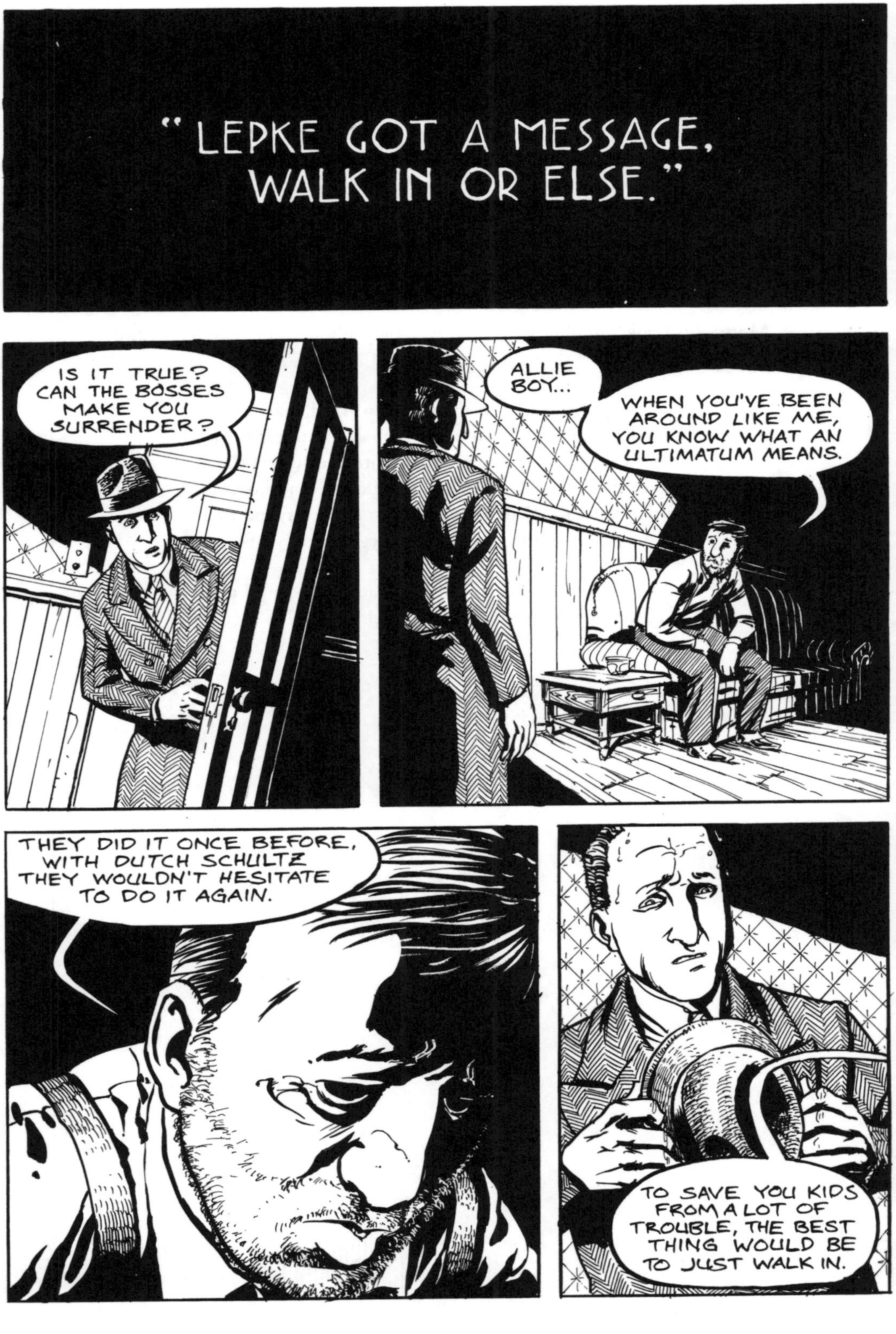
"LEPKE GOT A MESSAGE, WALK IN OR ELSE."
IS IT TRUE? CAN THE BOSSES MAKE YOU SURRENDER?
ALLIE BOY...
WHEN YOU'VE BEEN AROUND LIKE ME, YOU KNOW WHAT AN ULTIMATUM MEANS.
THEY DID IT ONCE BEFORE, WITH DUTCH SCHULTZ THEY WOULDN'T HESITATE TO DO IT AGAIN.
TO SAVE YOU KIDS FROM A LOT OF TROUBLE, THE BEST THING WOULD BE TO JUST WALK IN.

GOOD JEWISH BOYS

ALLIE

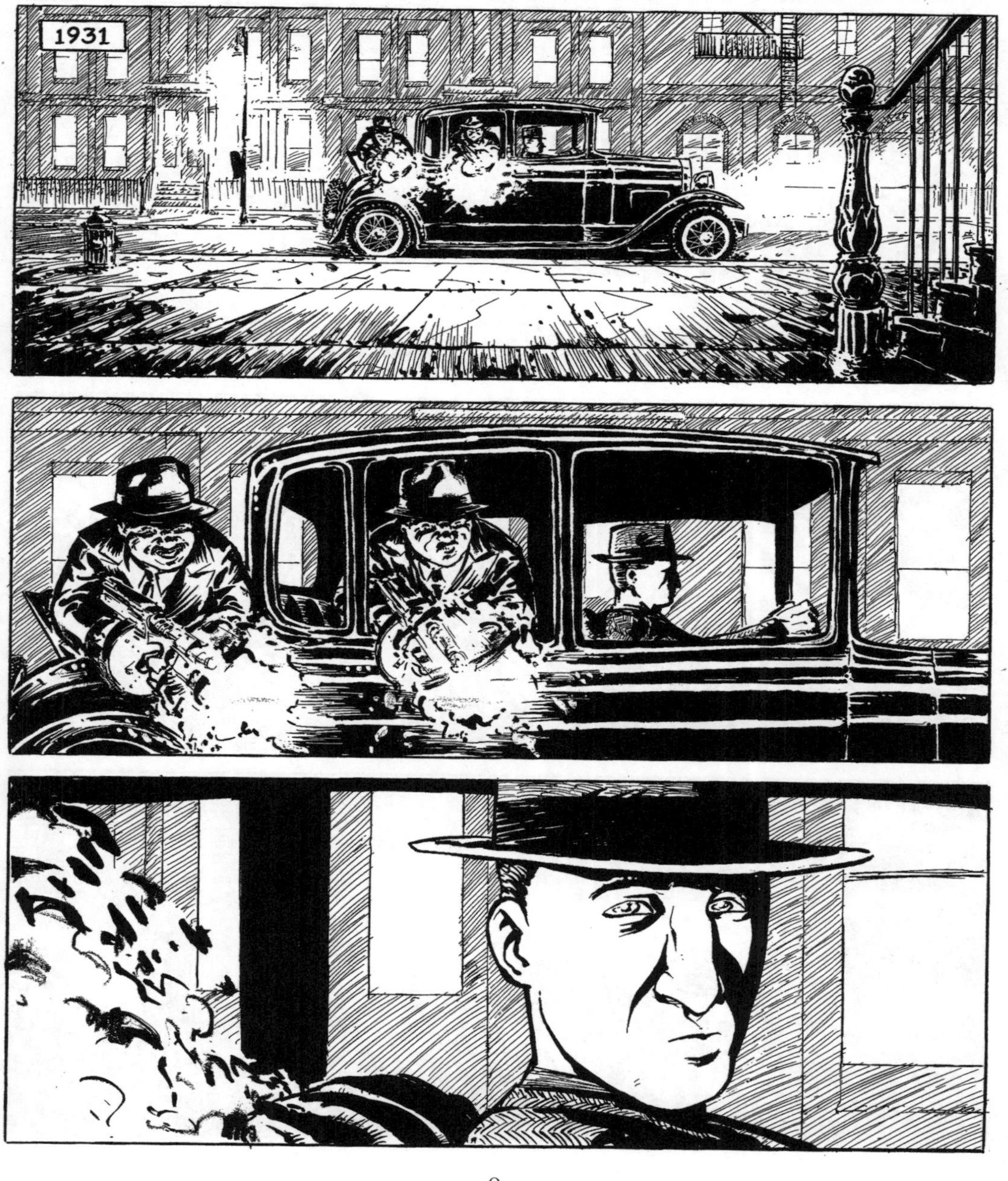
1931

LOCH SHELDRAKE COUNTRY CLUB 1925

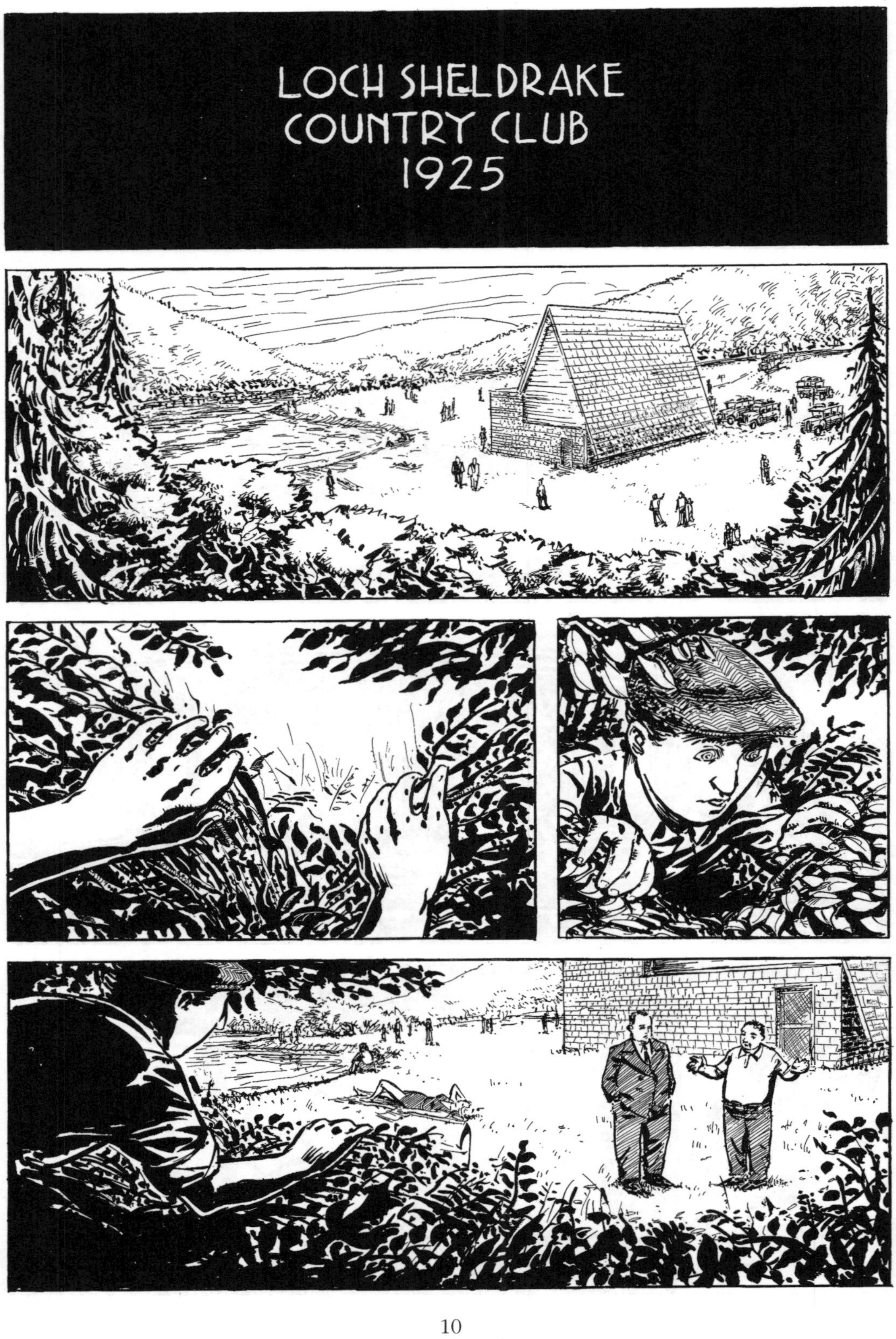

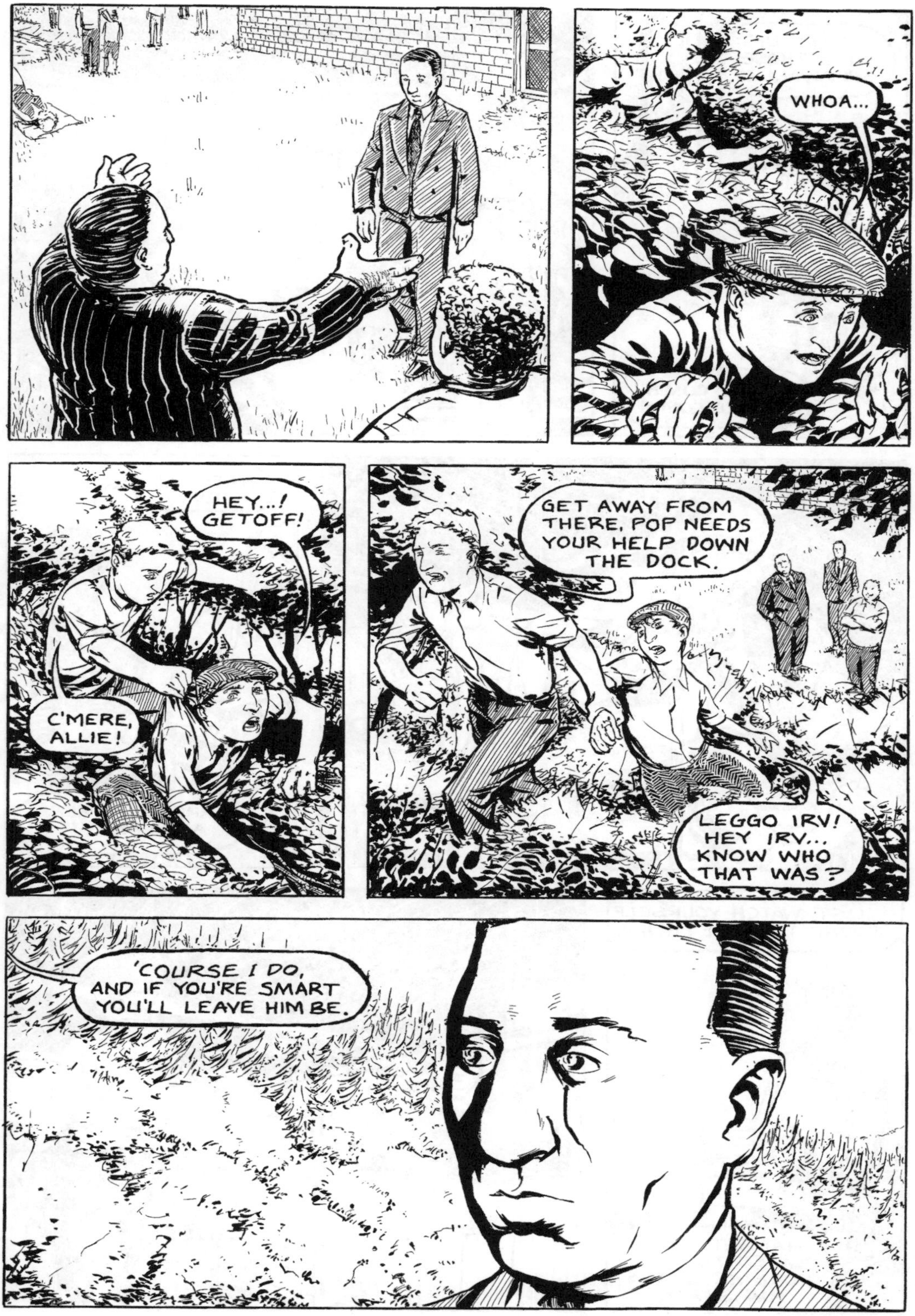
WHOA...
HEY...! GETOFF!
C'MERE, ALLIE!
GET AWAY FROM THERE, POP NEEDS YOUR HELP DOWN THE DOCK.
LEGGO IRV! HEY IRV... KNOW WHO THAT WAS?
'COURSE I DO, AND IF YOU'RE SMART YOU'LL LEAVE HIM BE.

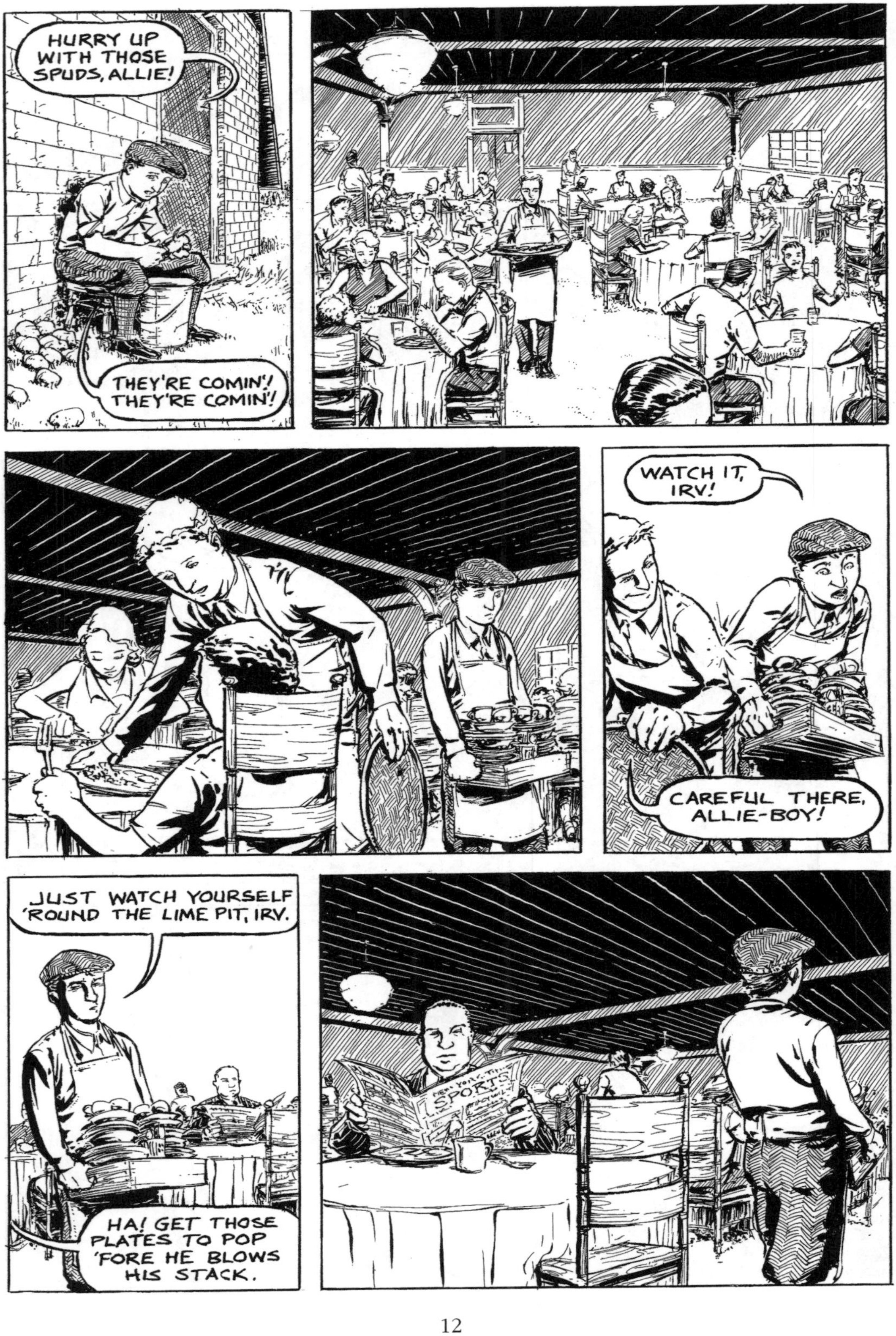
HURRY UP WITH THOSE SPUDS, ALLIE!
THEY'RE COMIN'! THEY'RE COMIN'!
WATCH IT, IRV!
CAREFUL THERE, ALLIE-BOY!
JUST WATCH YOURSELF 'ROUND THE LIME PIT, IRV.
HA! GET THOSE PLATES TO POP 'FORE HE BLOWS HIS STACK.
SPORTS

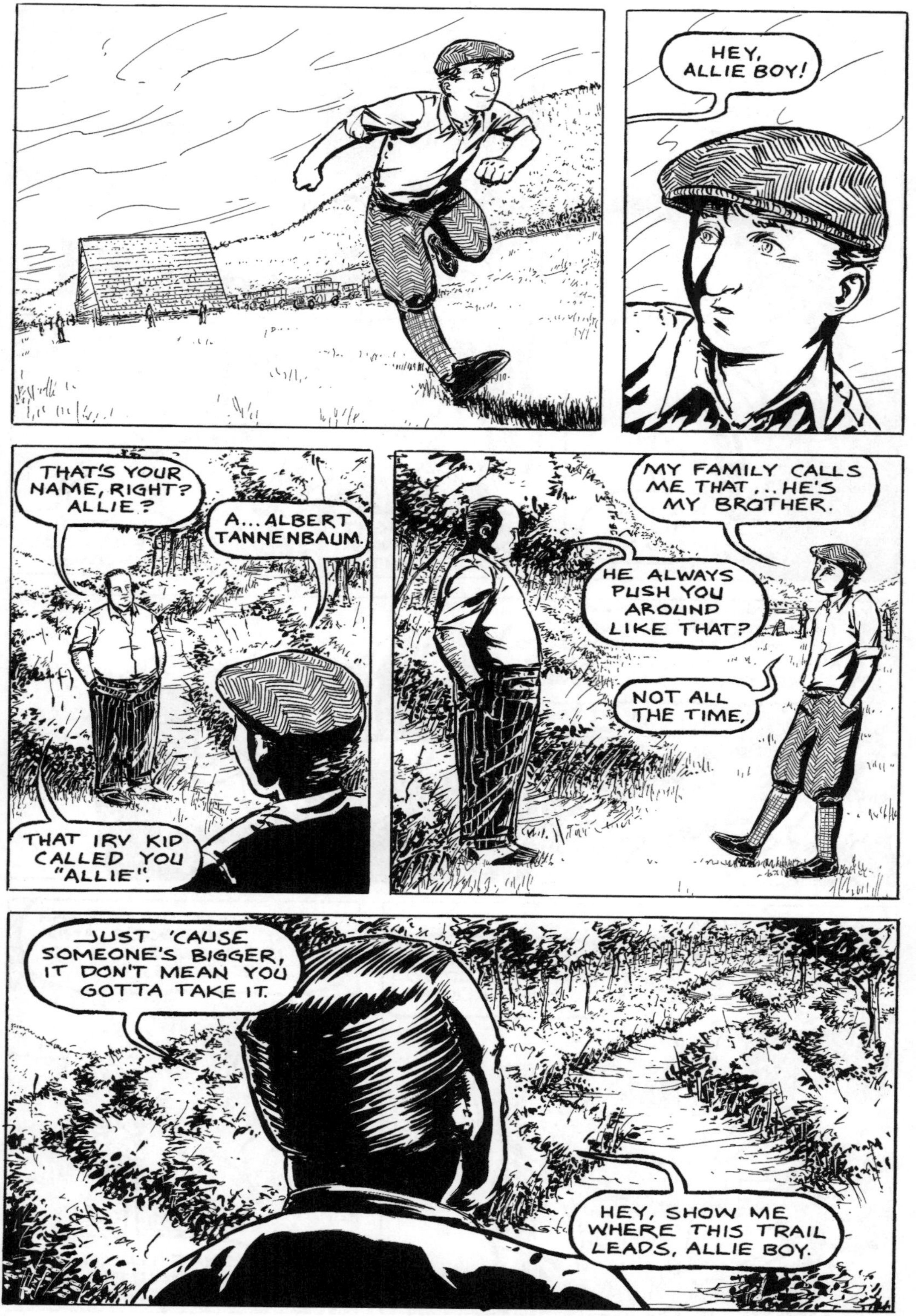
HEY, ALLIE BOY!
THAT'S YOUR NAME, RIGHT? ALLIE?
A... ALBERT TANNENBAUM.
THAT IRV KID CALLED YOU "ALLIE".
MY FAMILY CALLS ME THAT... HE'S MY BROTHER.
HE ALWAYS PUSH YOU AROUND LIKE THAT?
NOT ALL THE TIME.
JUST 'CAUSE SOMEONE'S BIGGER, IT DON'T MEAN YOU GOTTA TAKE IT.
HEY, SHOW ME WHERE THIS TRAIL LEADS, ALLIE BOY.

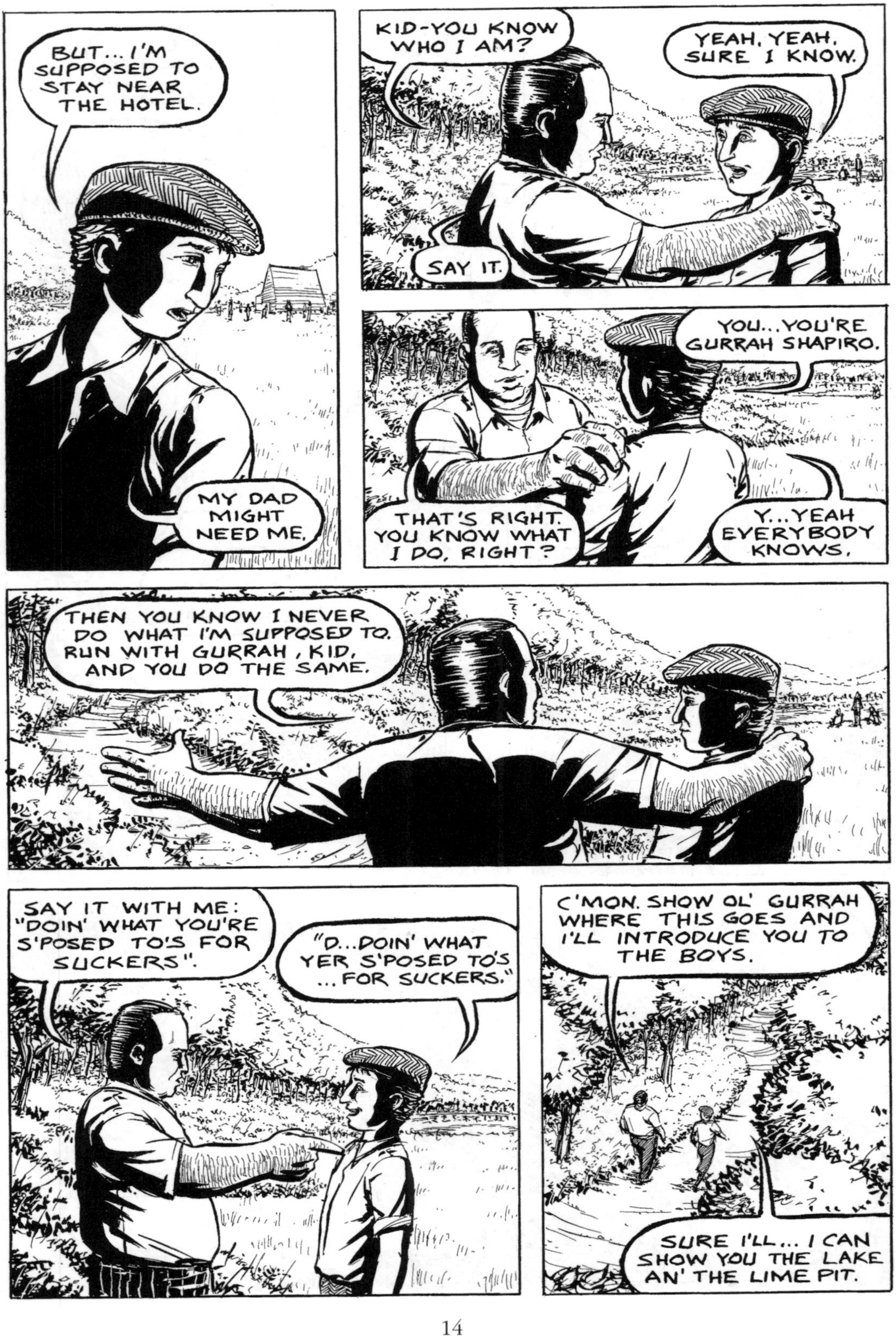
BUT... I'M SUPPOSED TO STAY NEAR THE HOTEL.
MY DAD MIGHT NEED ME.
KID-YOU KNOW WHO I AM?
YEAH, YEAH, SURE I KNOW.
SAY IT.
YOU... YOU'RE GURRAH SHAPIRO.
THAT'S RIGHT. YOU KNOW WHAT I DO, RIGHT?
Y...YEAH EVERYBODY KNOWS.
THEN YOU KNOW I NEVER DO WHAT I'M SUPPOSED TO. RUN WITH GURRAH, KID, AND YOU DO THE SAME.
SAY IT WITH ME: "DOIN' WHAT YOU'RE S'POSED TO'S FOR SUCKERS".
"D...DOIN' WHAT YER S'POSED TO'S ...FOR SUCKERS."
C'MON. SHOW OL' GURRAH WHERE THIS GOES AND I'LL INTRODUCE YOU TO THE BOYS.
SURE I'LL... I CAN SHOW YOU THE LAKE AN' THE LIME PIT.

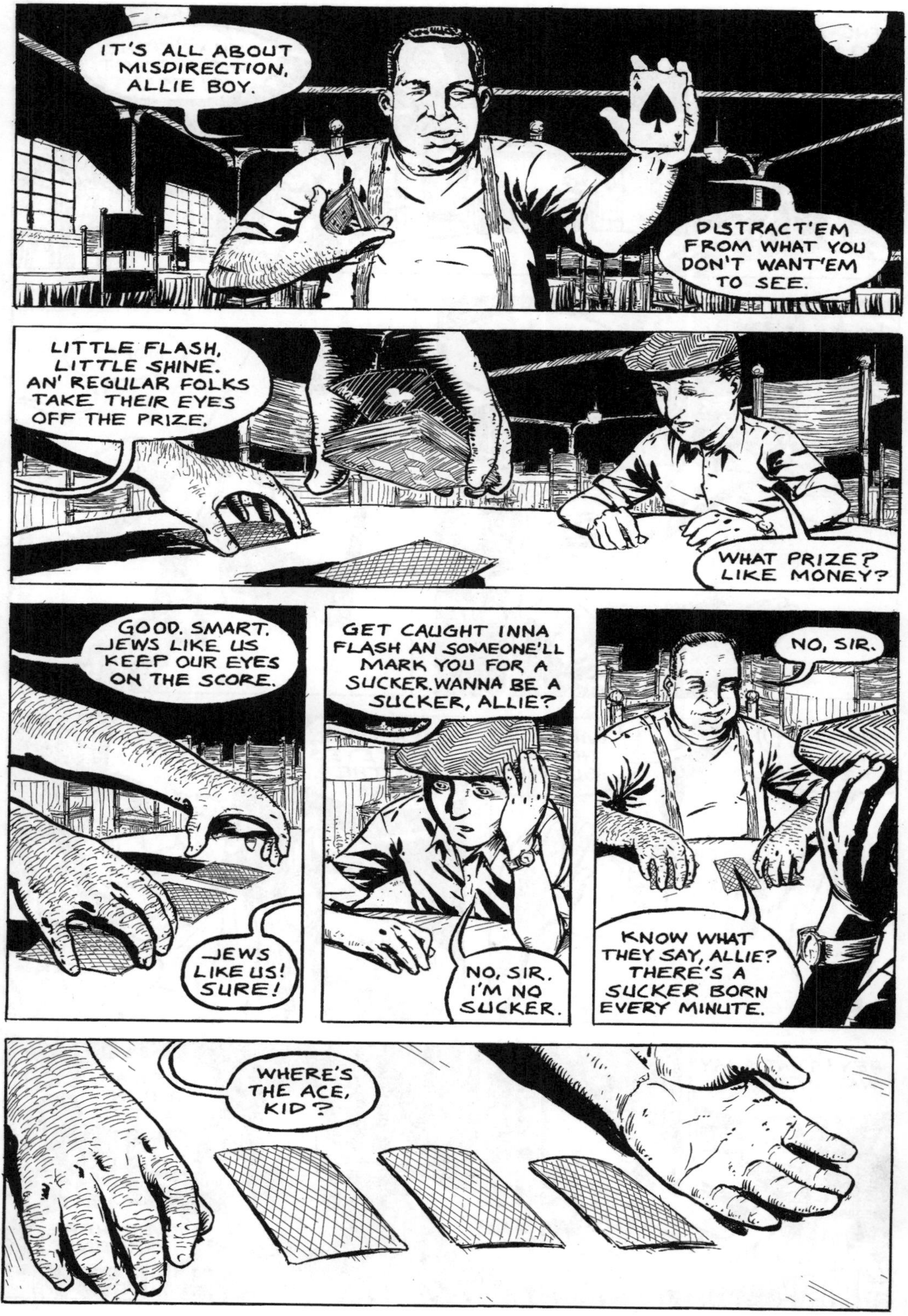
IT'S ALL ABOUT MISDIRECTION, ALLIE BOY.
DISTRACT'EM FROM WHAT YOU DON'T WANT'EM TO SEE.
LITTLE FLASH, LITTLE SHINE. AN' REGULAR FOLKS TAKE THEIR EYES OFF THE PRIZE.
WHAT PRIZE? LIKE MONEY?
GOOD. SMART. JEWS LIKE US KEEP OUR EYES ON THE SCORE.
JEWS LIKE US! SURE!
GET CAUGHT INNA FLASH AN SOMEONE'LL MARK YOU FOR A SUCKER. WANNA BE A SUCKER, ALLIE?
NO, SIR. I'M NO SUCKER.
NO, SIR.
KNOW WHAT THEY SAY, ALLIE? THERE'S A SUCKER BORN EVERY MINUTE.
WHERE'S THE ACE, KID?

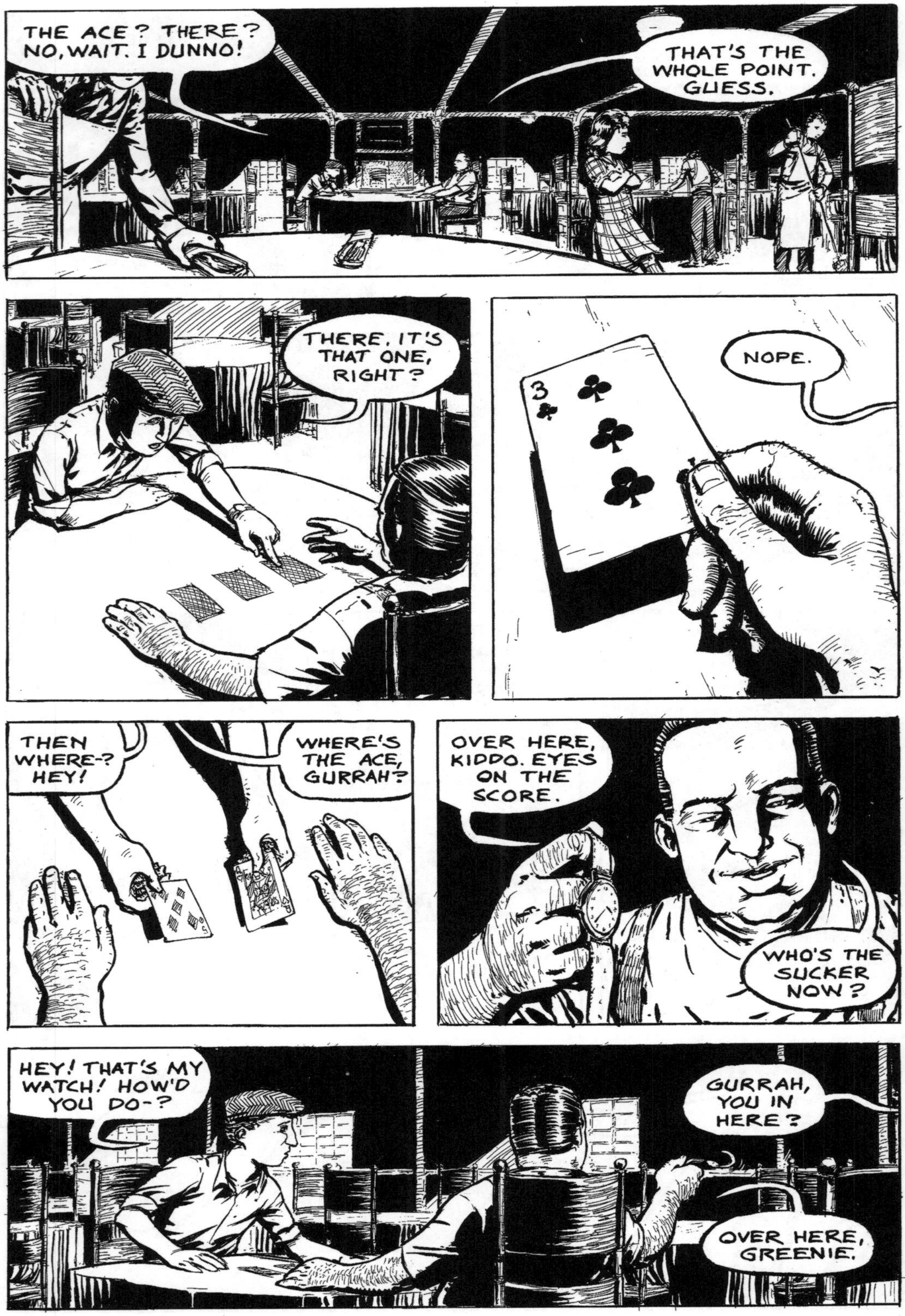
THE ACE? THERE? NO, WAIT. I DUNNO!
THAT'S THE WHOLE POINT. GUESS.
THERE, IT'S THAT ONE, RIGHT?
NOPE.
THEN WHERE-? HEY!
WHERE'S THE ACE, GURRAH?
OVER HERE, KIDDO. EYES ON THE SCORE.
WHO'S THE SUCKER NOW?
HEY! THAT'S MY WATCH! HOW'D YOU DO-?
GURRAH, YOU IN HERE?
OVER HERE, GREENIE.

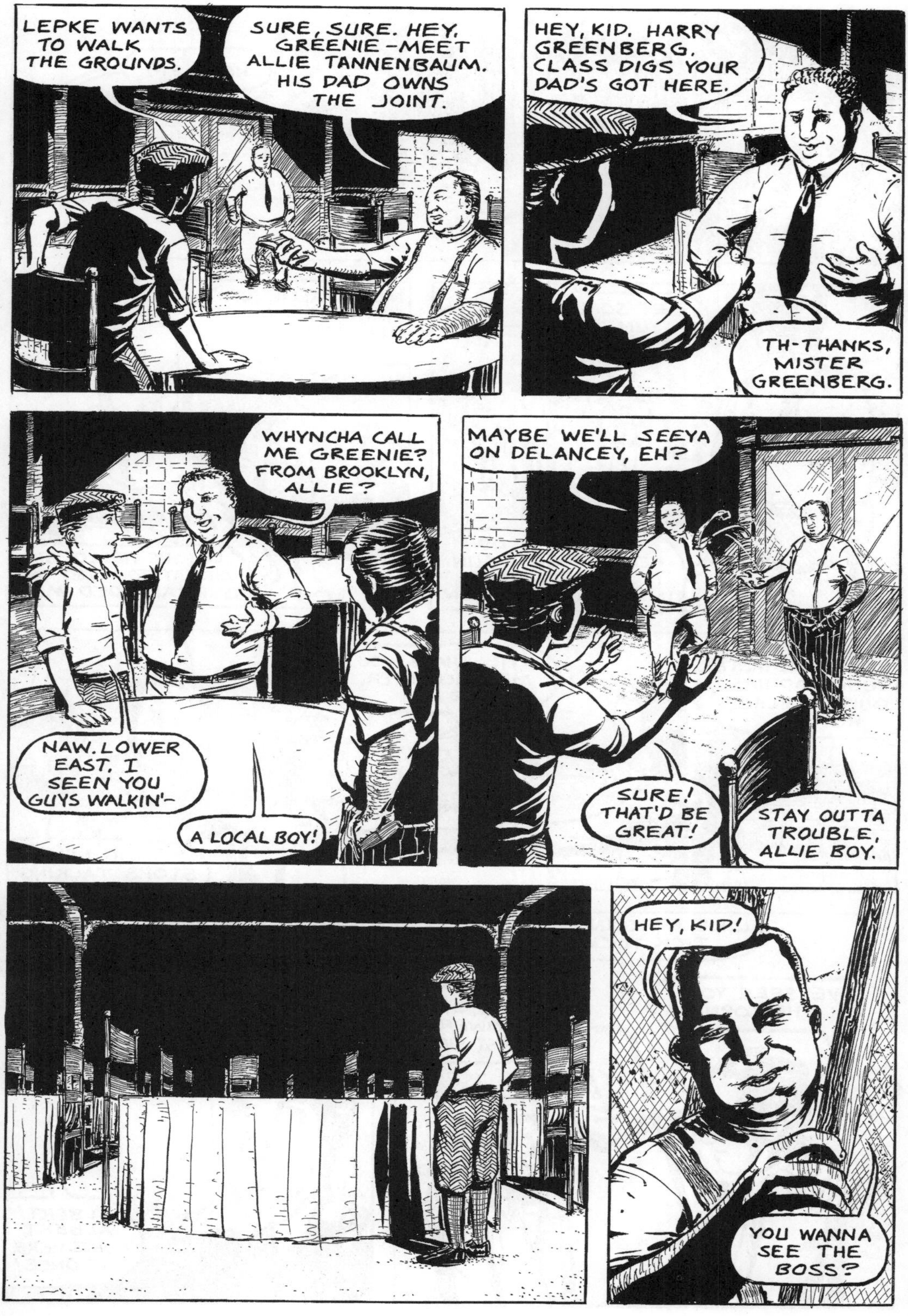
LEPKE WANTS TO WALK THE GROUNDS.
SURE, SURE. HEY, GREENIE - MEET ALLIE TANNENBAUM. HIS DAD OWNS THE JOINT.
HEY, KID. HARRY GREENBERG. CLASS DIGS YOUR DAD'S GOT HERE.
TH-THANKS, MISTER GREENBERG.
WHYNCHA CALL ME GREENIE? FROM BROOKLYN, ALLIE?
NAW. LOWER EAST. I SEEN YOU GUYS WALKIN'-
A LOCAL BOY!
MAYBE WE'LL SEEYA ON DELANCEY, EH?
SURE! THAT'D BE GREAT!
STAY OUTTA TROUBLE, ALLIE BOY.
HEY, KID!
YOU WANNA SEE THE BOSS?

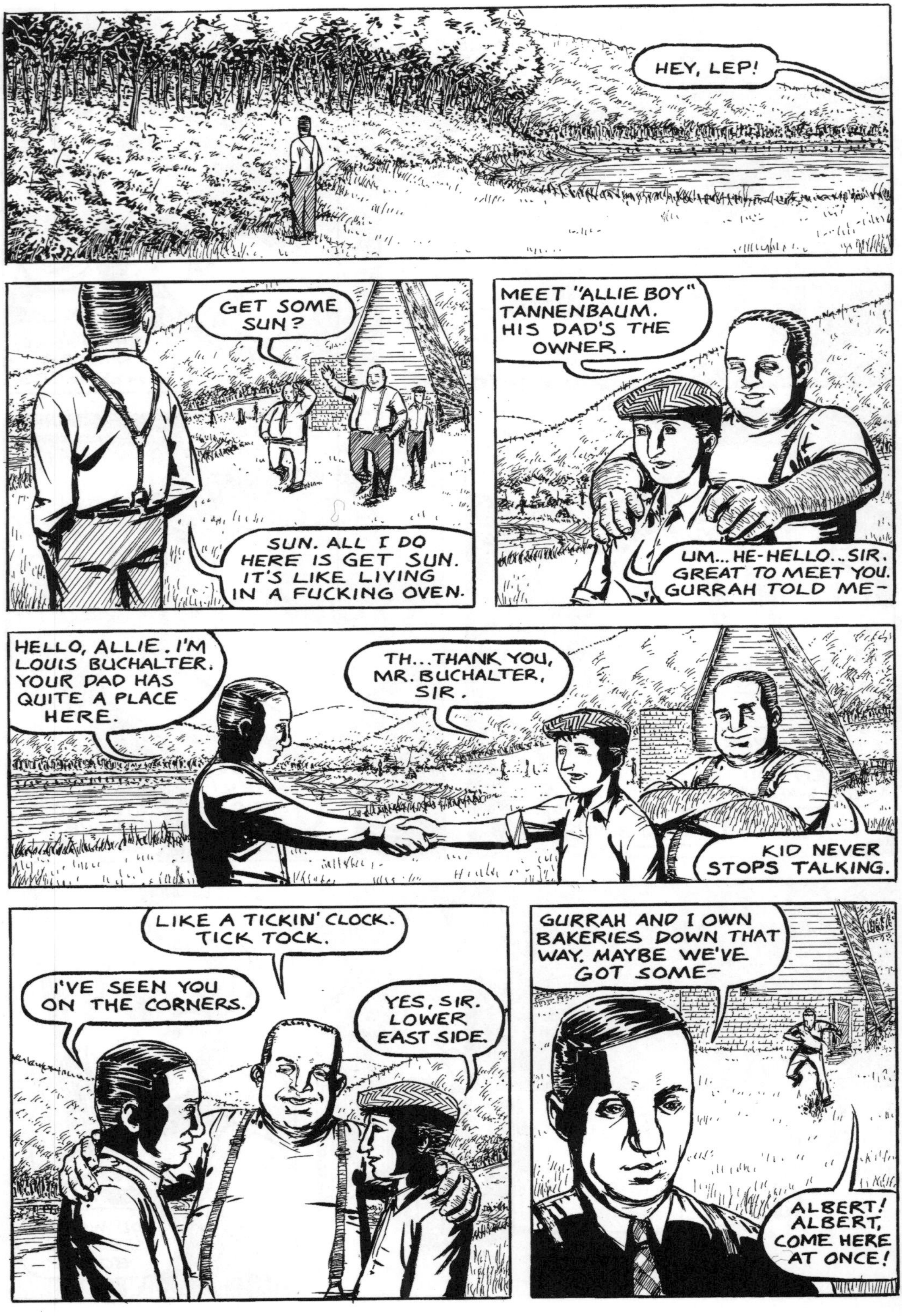
HEY, LEP!
GET SOME SUN?
SUN. ALL I DO HERE IS GET SUN. IT'S LIKE LIVING IN A FUCKING OVEN.
MEET "ALLIE BOY" TANNENBAUM. HIS DAD'S THE OWNER.
UM... HE-HELLO.. SIR. GREAT TO MEET YOU. GURRAH TOLD ME-
HELLO, ALLIE. I'M LOUIS BUCHALTER. YOUR DAD HAS QUITE A PLACE HERE.
TH... THANK YOU, MR. BUCHALTER, SIR.
KID NEVER STOPS TALKING.
LIKE A TICKIN' CLOCK. TICK TOCK.
I'VE SEEN YOU ON THE CORNERS.
YES, SIR. LOWER EAST SIDE.
GURRAH AND I OWN BAKERIES DOWN THAT WAY. MAYBE WE'VE GOT SOME-
ALBERT! ALBERT, COME HERE AT ONCE!

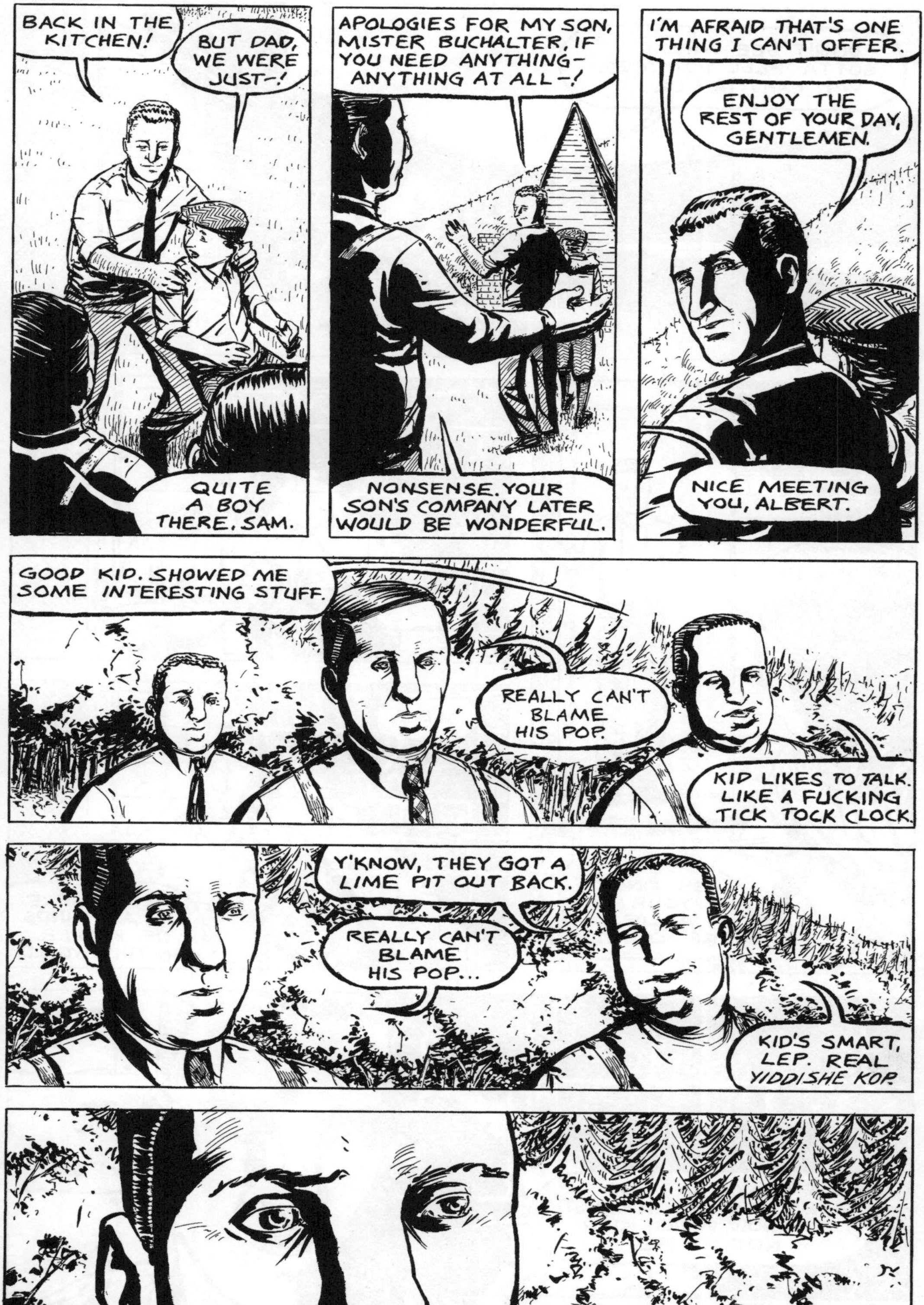
BACK IN THE KITCHEN!
BUT DAD, WE WERE JUST-!
QUITE A BOY THERE, SAM.
APOLOGIES FOR MY SON, MISTER BUCHALTER, IF YOU NEED ANYTHING- ANYTHING AT ALL-!
NONSENSE. YOUR SON'S COMPANY LATER WOULD BE WONDERFUL.
I'M AFRAID THAT'S ONE THING I CAN'T OFFER.
ENJOY THE REST OF YOUR DAY, GENTLEMEN.
NICE MEETING YOU, ALBERT.
GOOD KID. SHOWED ME SOME INTERESTING STUFF.
REALLY CAN'T BLAME HIS POP.
KID LIKES TO TALK. LIKE A FUCKING TICK TOCK CLOCK.
Y'KNOW, THEY GOT A LIME PIT OUT BACK.
REALLY CAN'T BLAME HIS POP...
KID'S SMART, LEP. REAL *YIDDISHE KOP.*

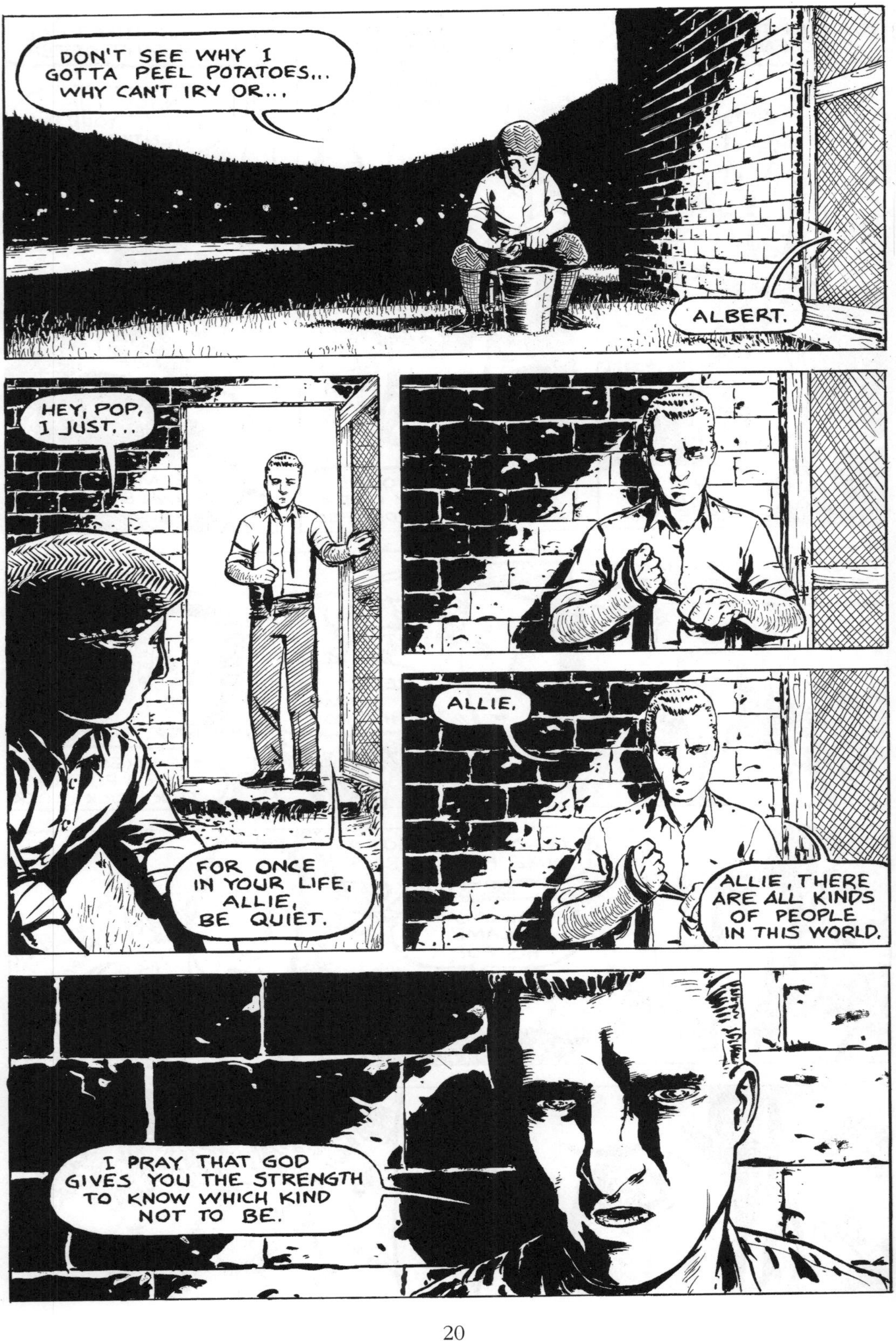
DON'T SEE WHY I GOTTA PEEL POTATOES... WHY CAN'T IRV OR...
ALBERT.
HEY, POP, I JUST...
FOR ONCE IN YOUR LIFE, ALLIE, BE QUIET.
ALLIE.
ALLIE, THERE ARE ALL KINDS OF PEOPLE IN THIS WORLD.
I PRAY THAT GOD GIVES YOU THE STRENGTH TO KNOW WHICH KIND NOT TO BE.

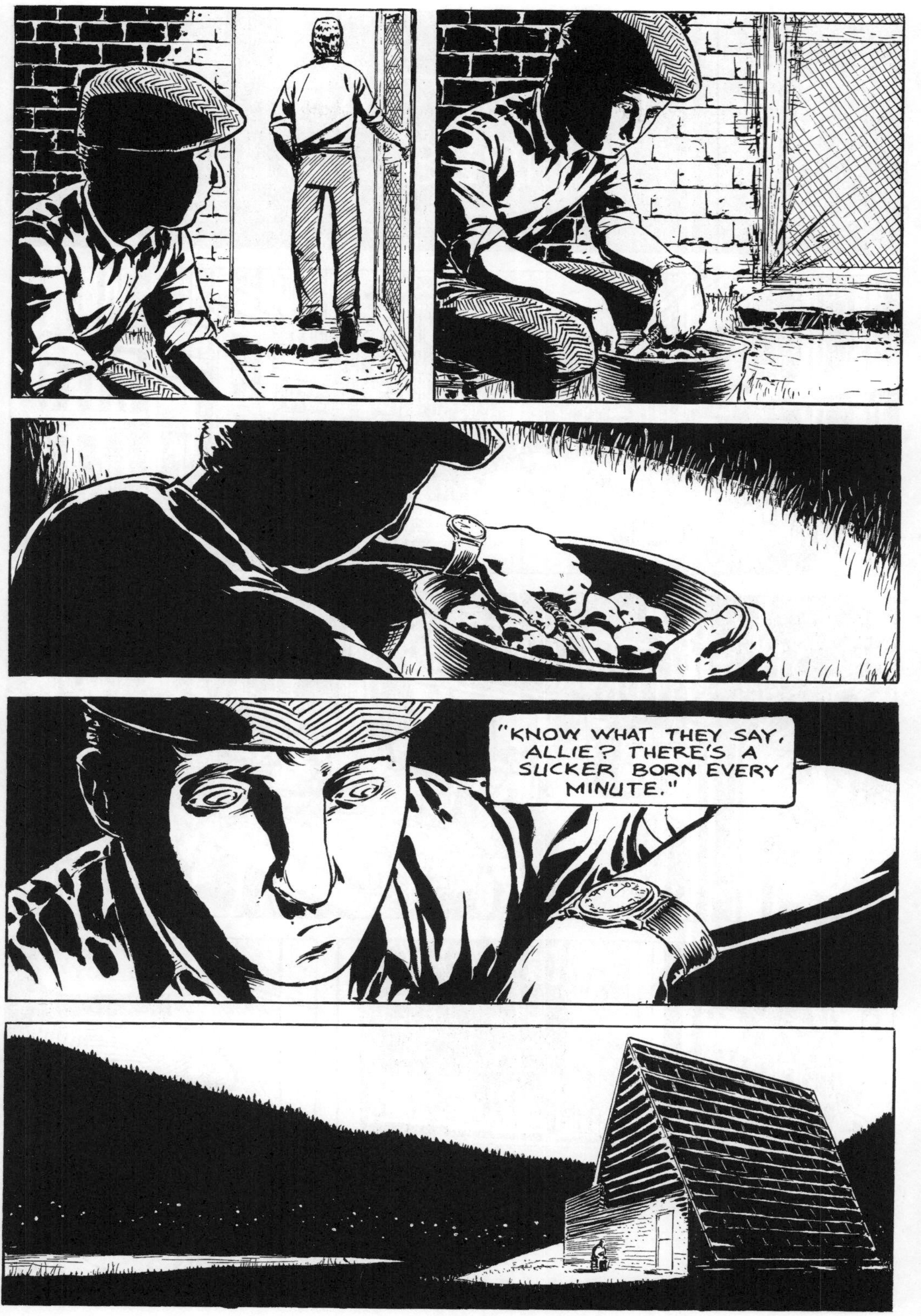
"KNOW WHAT THEY SAY, ALLIE? THERE'S A SUCKER BORN EVERY MINUTE."

MANHATTAN 1928

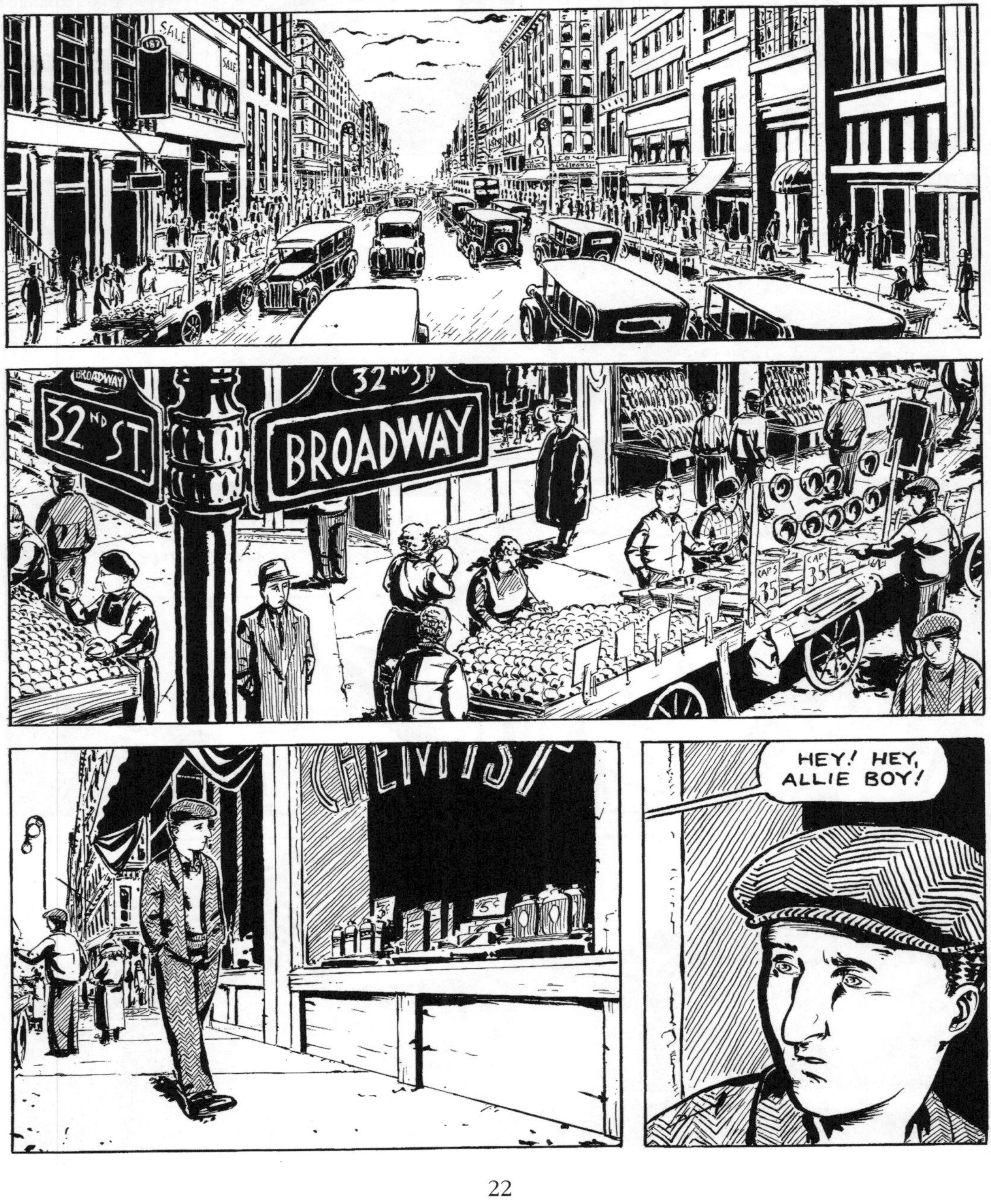
SALE
SALE
BROADWAY
32ND ST.
32ND ST.
BROADWAY
CAPS 35
CAPS 35
HEY! HEY, ALLIE BOY!

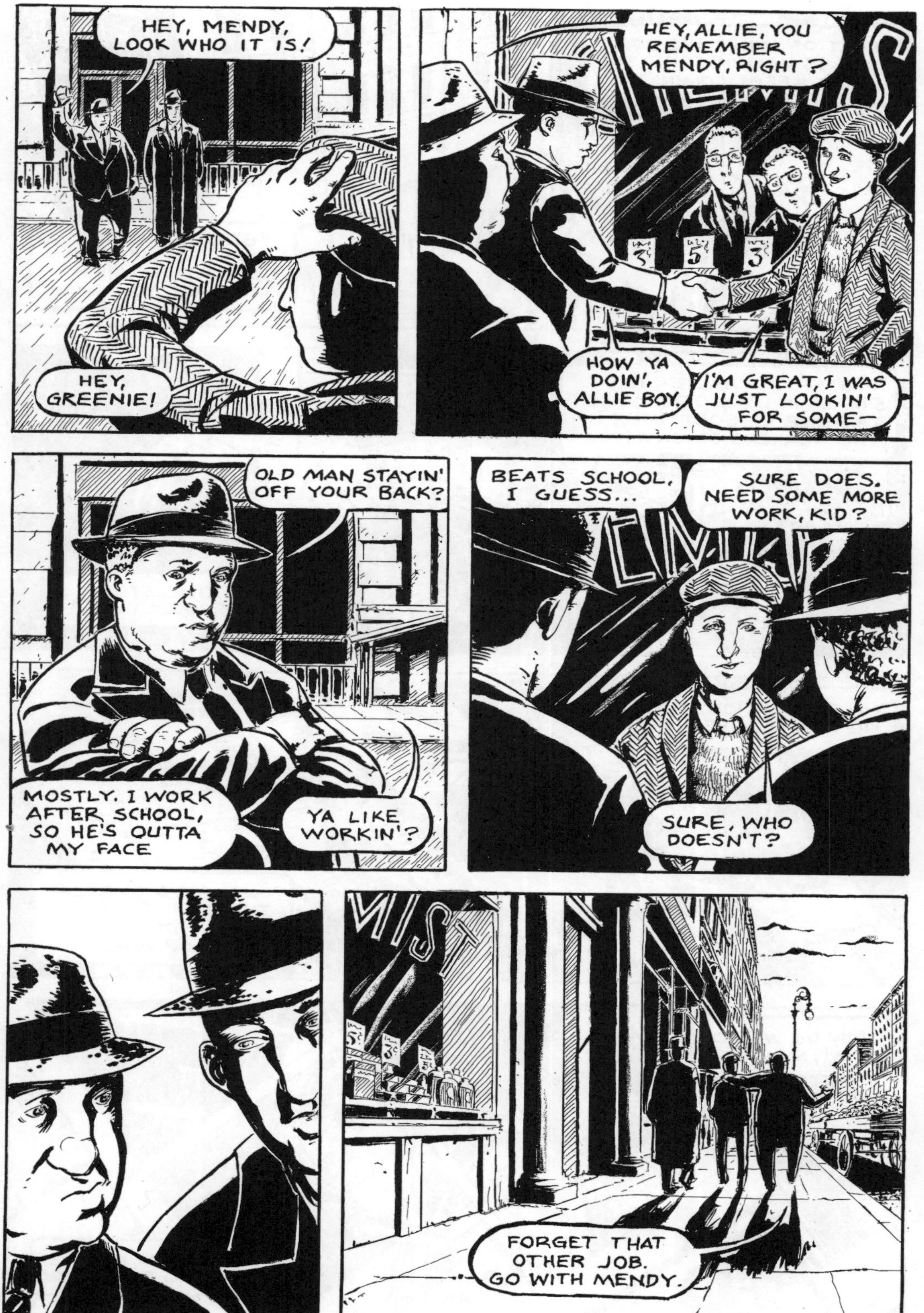
HEY, MENDY, LOOK WHO IT IS!
HEY, GREENIE!
HEY, ALLIE, YOU REMEMBER MENDY, RIGHT?
HOW YA DOIN', ALLIE BOY.
I'M GREAT, I WAS JUST LOOKIN' FOR SOME—
OLD MAN STAYIN' OFF YOUR BACK?
MOSTLY. I WORK AFTER SCHOOL, SO HE'S OUTTA MY FACE
YA LIKE WORKIN'?
BEATS SCHOOL, I GUESS...
SURE DOES. NEED SOME MORE WORK, KID?
SURE, WHO DOESN'T?
FORGET THAT OTHER JOB. GO WITH MENDY.

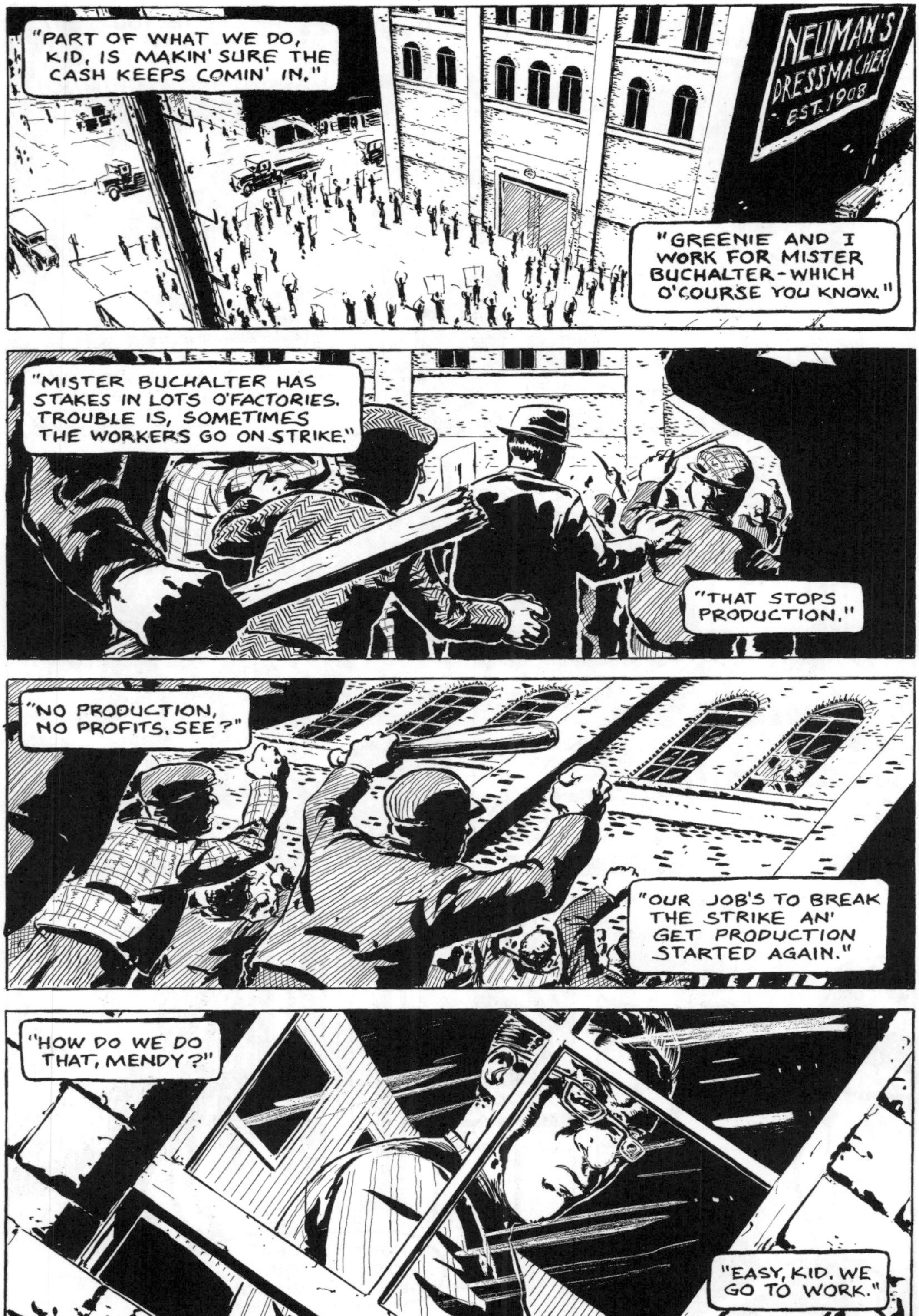
"PART OF WHAT WE DO, KID, IS MAKIN' SURE THE CASH KEEPS COMIN' IN."
NEUMAN'S DRESSMACHER EST. 1908
"GREENIE AND I WORK FOR MISTER BUCHALTER - WHICH O'COURSE YOU KNOW."
"MISTER BUCHALTER HAS STAKES IN LOTS O'FACTORIES. TROUBLE IS, SOMETIMES THE WORKERS GO ON STRIKE."
"THAT STOPS PRODUCTION."
"NO PRODUCTION, NO PROFITS, SEE?"
"OUR JOB'S TO BREAK THE STRIKE AN' GET PRODUCTION STARTED AGAIN."
"HOW DO WE DO THAT, MENDY?"
"EASY, KID. WE GO TO WORK."

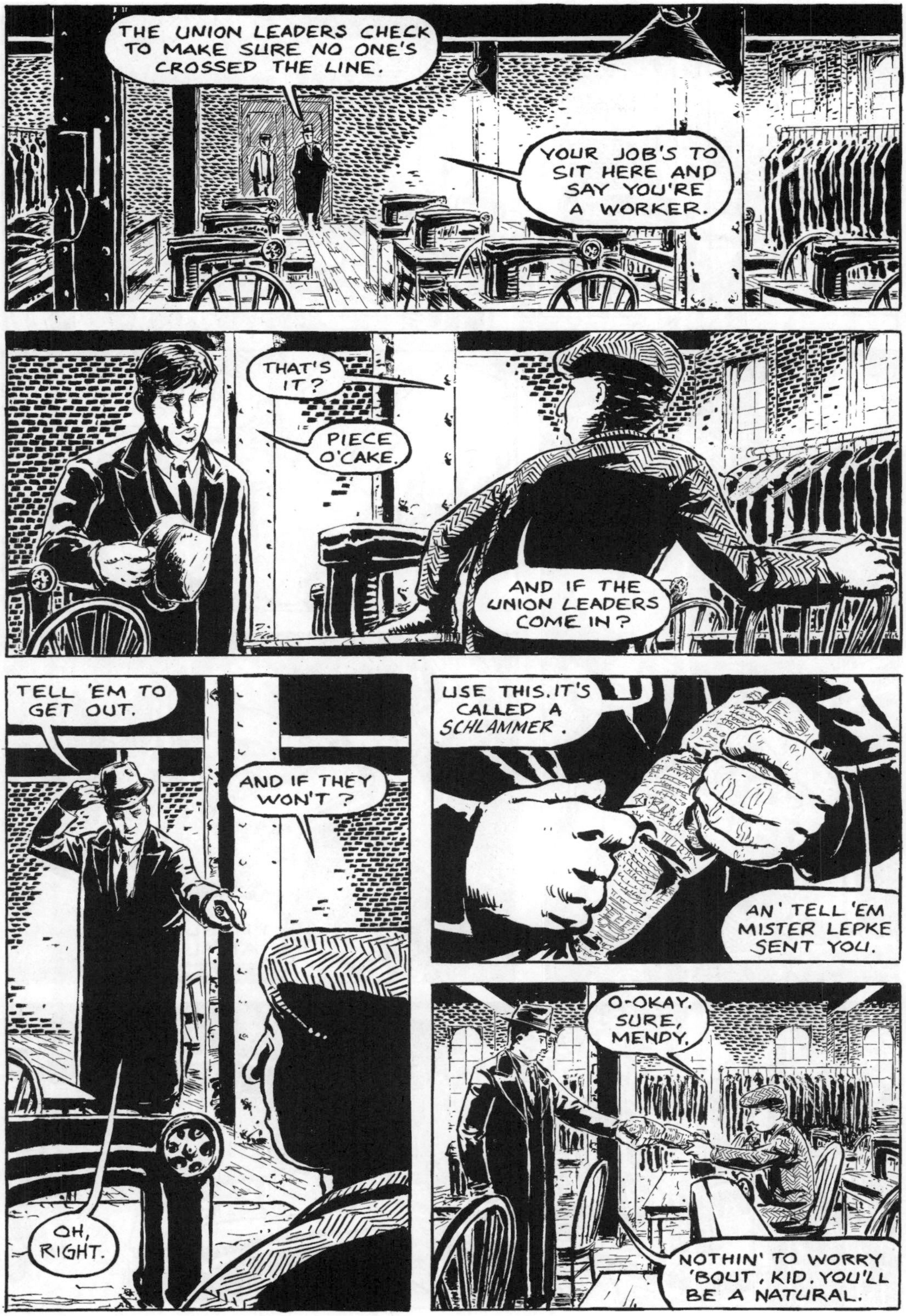
THE UNION LEADERS CHECK TO MAKE SURE NO ONE'S CROSSED THE LINE.
YOUR JOB'S TO SIT HERE AND SAY YOU'RE A WORKER.
THAT'S IT?
PIECE O'CAKE.
AND IF THE UNION LEADERS COME IN?
TELL 'EM TO GET OUT.
AND IF THEY WON'T?
OH, RIGHT.
USE THIS. IT'S CALLED A *SCHLAMMER*.
AN' TELL 'EM MISTER LEPKE SENT YOU.
O-OKAY. SURE, MENDY.
NOTHIN' TO WORRY 'BOUT, KID. YOU'LL BE A NATURAL.

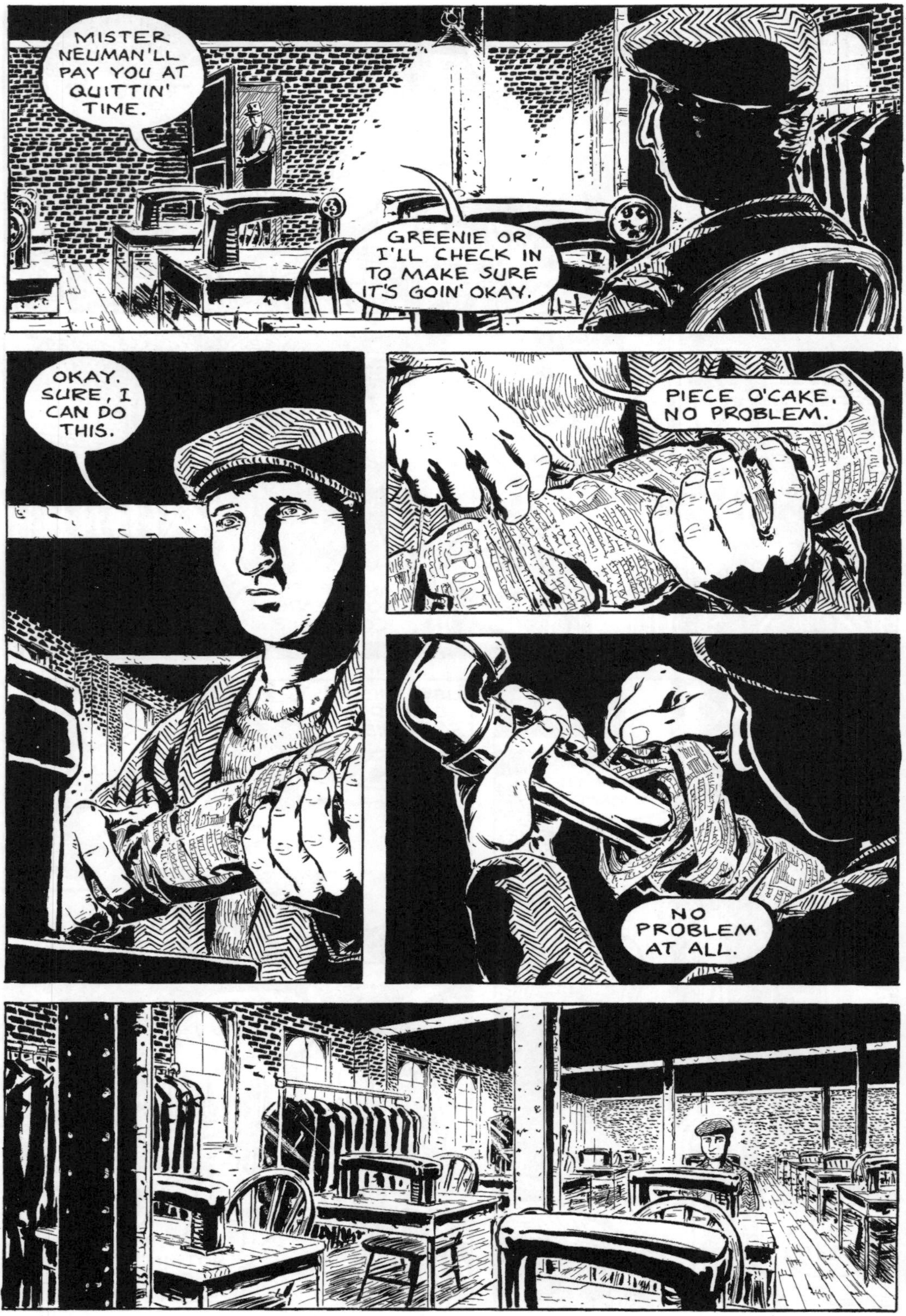
MISTER NEUMAN'LL PAY YOU AT QUITTIN' TIME.
GREENIE OR I'LL CHECK IN TO MAKE SURE IT'S GOIN' OKAY.
OKAY. SURE, I CAN DO THIS.
PIECE O'CAKE. NO PROBLEM.
NO PROBLEM AT ALL.

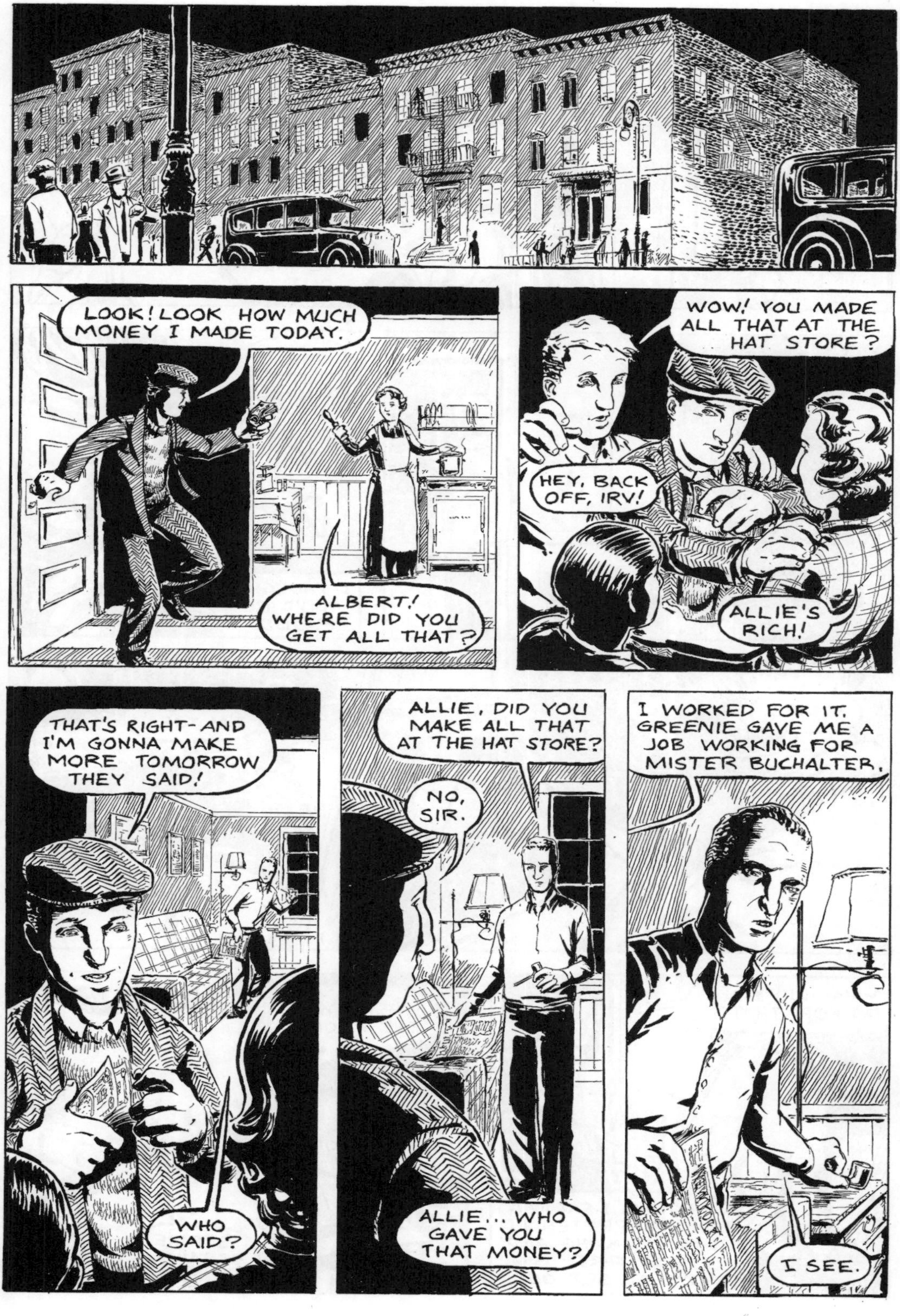
LOOK! LOOK HOW MUCH MONEY I MADE TODAY.
ALBERT! WHERE DID YOU GET ALL THAT?
WOW! YOU MADE ALL THAT AT THE HAT STORE?
HEY, BACK OFF, IRV!
ALLIE'S RICH!
THAT'S RIGHT- AND I'M GONNA MAKE MORE TOMORROW THEY SAID!
WHO SAID?
ALLIE, DID YOU MAKE ALL THAT AT THE HAT STORE?
NO, SIR.
ALLIE... WHO GAVE YOU THAT MONEY?
I WORKED FOR IT. GREENIE GAVE ME A JOB WORKING FOR MISTER BUCHALTER.
I SEE.

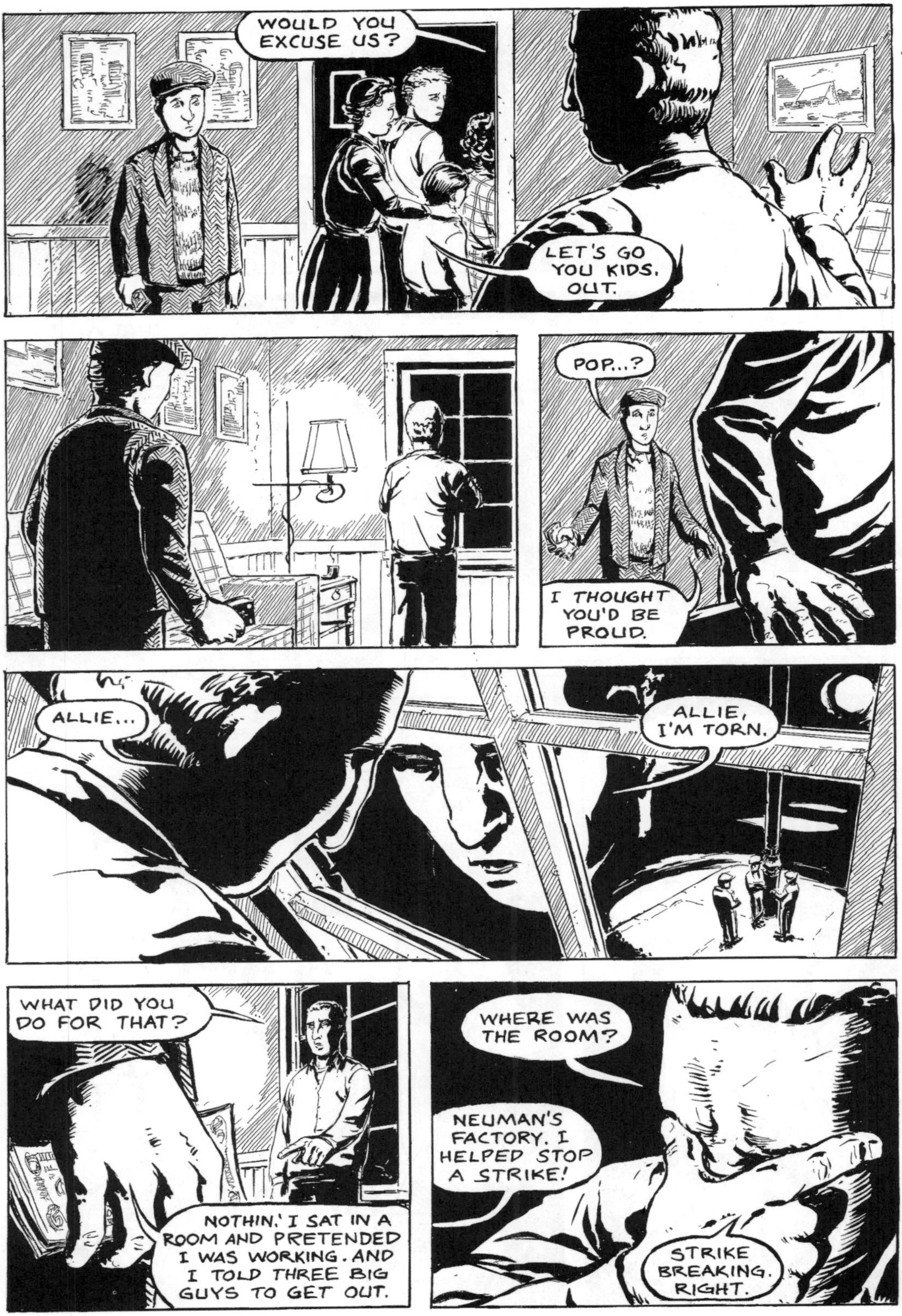
WOULD YOU EXCUSE US?
LET'S GO YOU KIDS. OUT.
POP...?
I THOUGHT YOU'D BE PROUD.
ALLIE...
ALLIE, I'M TORN.
WHAT DID YOU DO FOR THAT?
NOTHIN.' I SAT IN A ROOM AND PRETENDED I WAS WORKING. AND I TOLD THREE BIG GUYS TO GET OUT.
WHERE WAS THE ROOM?
NEUMAN'S FACTORY. I HELPED STOP A STRIKE!
STRIKE BREAKING. RIGHT.

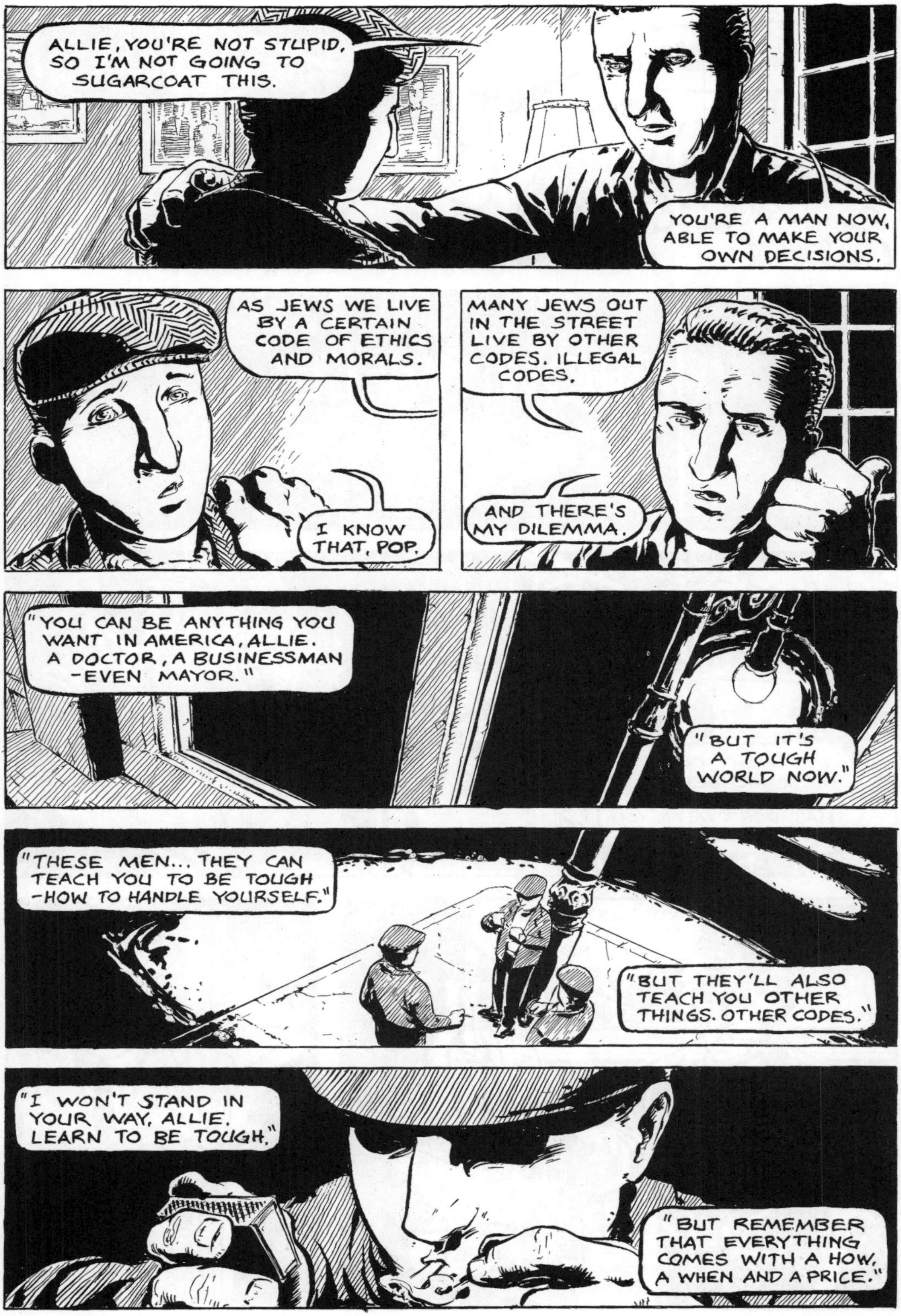
ALLIE, YOU'RE NOT STUPID, SO I'M NOT GOING TO SUGARCOAT THIS.
YOU'RE A MAN NOW, ABLE TO MAKE YOUR OWN DECISIONS.
AS JEWS WE LIVE BY A CERTAIN CODE OF ETHICS AND MORALS.
I KNOW THAT, POP.
MANY JEWS OUT IN THE STREET LIVE BY OTHER CODES. ILLEGAL CODES.
AND THERE'S MY DILEMMA.
"YOU CAN BE ANYTHING YOU WANT IN AMERICA, ALLIE. A DOCTOR, A BUSINESSMAN -EVEN MAYOR."
"BUT IT'S A TOUGH WORLD NOW."
"THESE MEN... THEY CAN TEACH YOU TO BE TOUGH -HOW TO HANDLE YOURSELF."
"BUT THEY'LL ALSO TEACH YOU OTHER THINGS. OTHER CODES."
"I WON'T STAND IN YOUR WAY, ALLIE. LEARN TO BE TOUGH."
"BUT REMEMBER THAT EVERYTHING COMES WITH A HOW, A WHEN AND A PRICE."

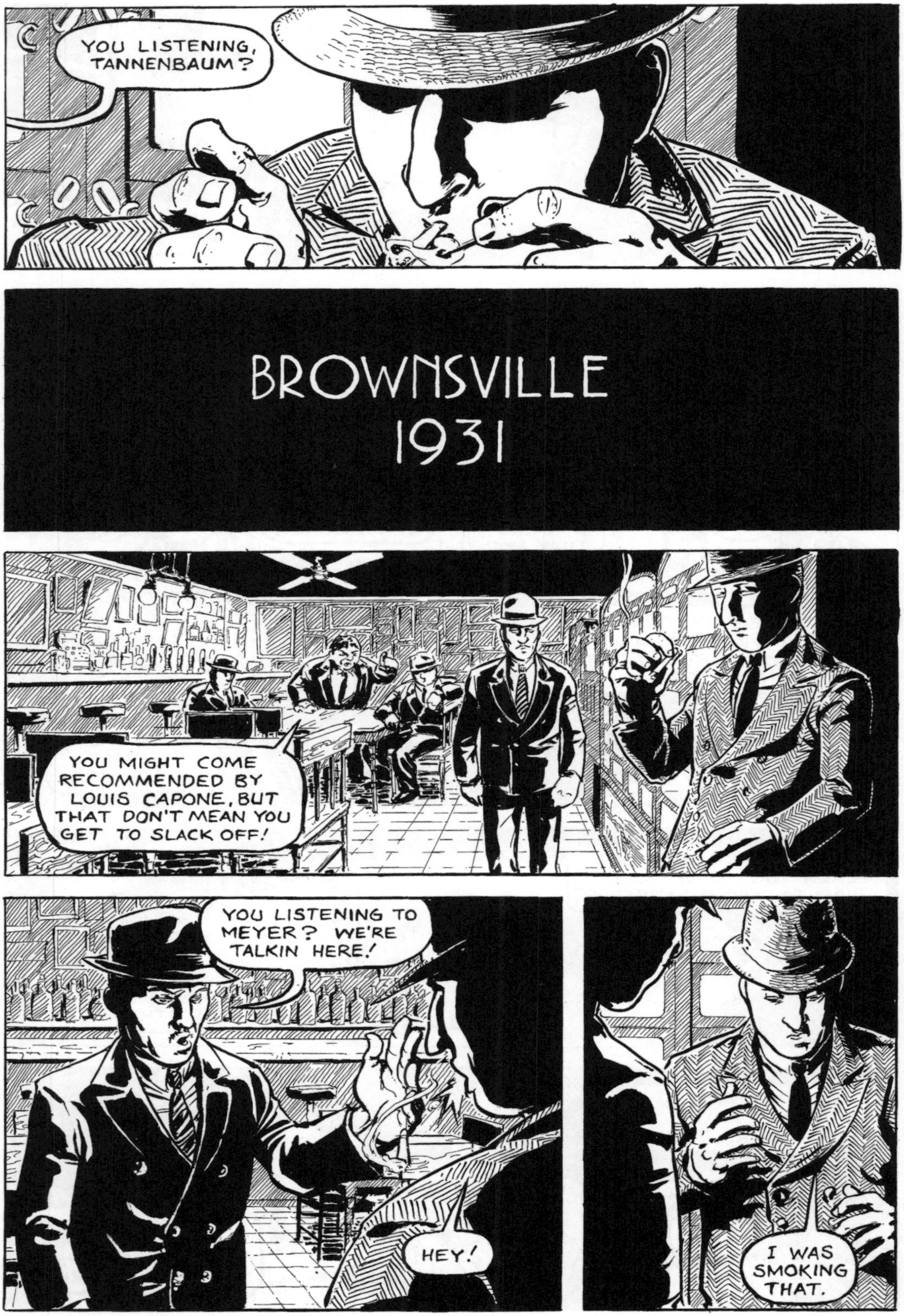
YOU LISTENING, TANNENBAUM?
BROWNSVILLE 1931
YOU MIGHT COME RECOMMENDED BY LOUIS CAPONE, BUT THAT DON'T MEAN YOU GET TO SLACK OFF!
YOU LISTENING TO MEYER? WE'RE TALKIN HERE!
HEY!
I WAS SMOKING THAT.

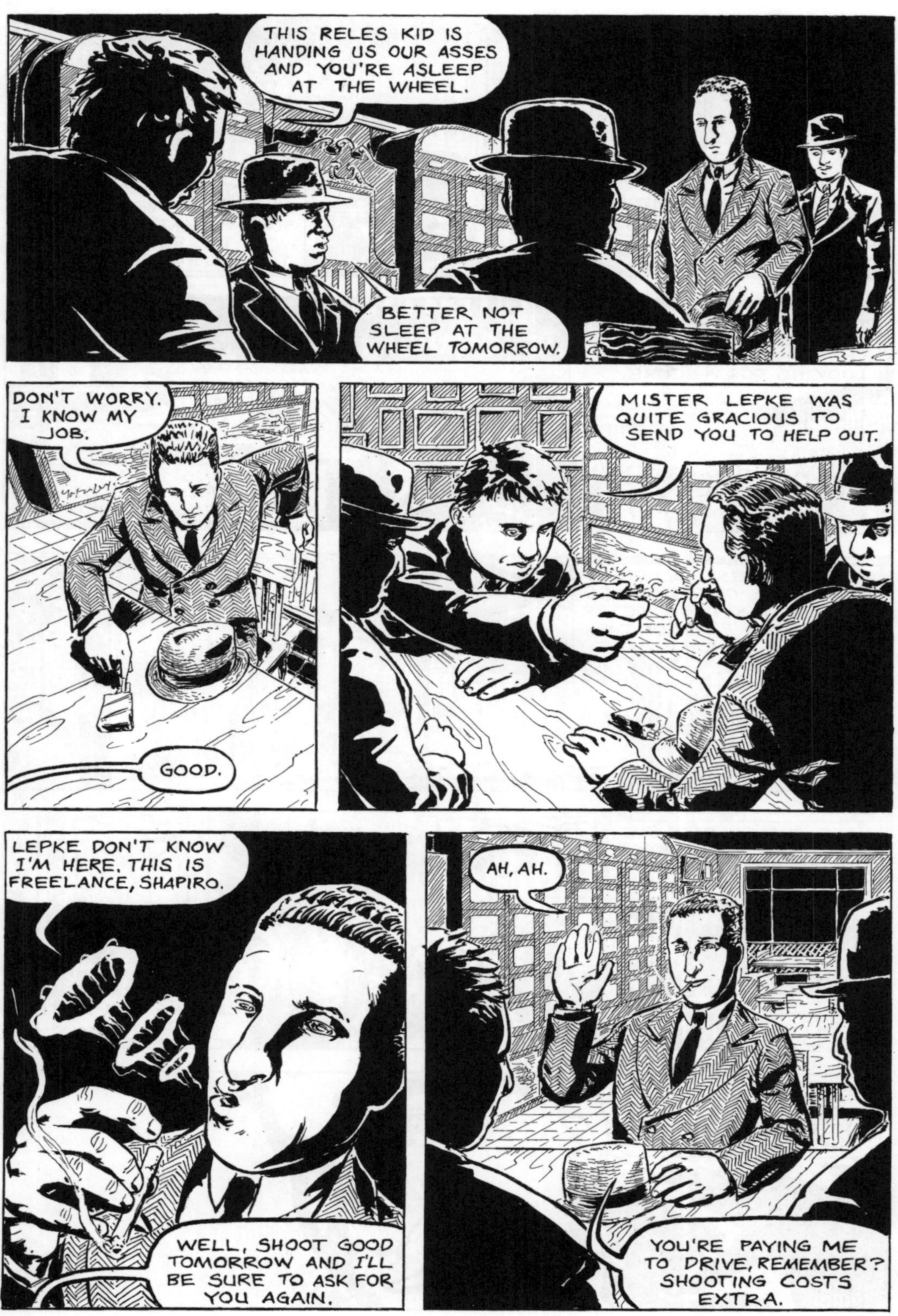
THIS RELES KID IS HANDING US OUR ASSES AND YOU'RE ASLEEP AT THE WHEEL.
BETTER NOT SLEEP AT THE WHEEL TOMORROW.
DON'T WORRY. I KNOW MY JOB.
GOOD.
MISTER LEPKE WAS QUITE GRACIOUS TO SEND YOU TO HELP OUT.
LEPKE DON'T KNOW I'M HERE. THIS IS FREELANCE, SHAPIRO.
WELL, SHOOT GOOD TOMORROW AND I'LL BE SURE TO ASK FOR YOU AGAIN.
AH, AH.
YOU'RE PAYING ME TO DRIVE, REMEMBER? SHOOTING COSTS EXTRA.

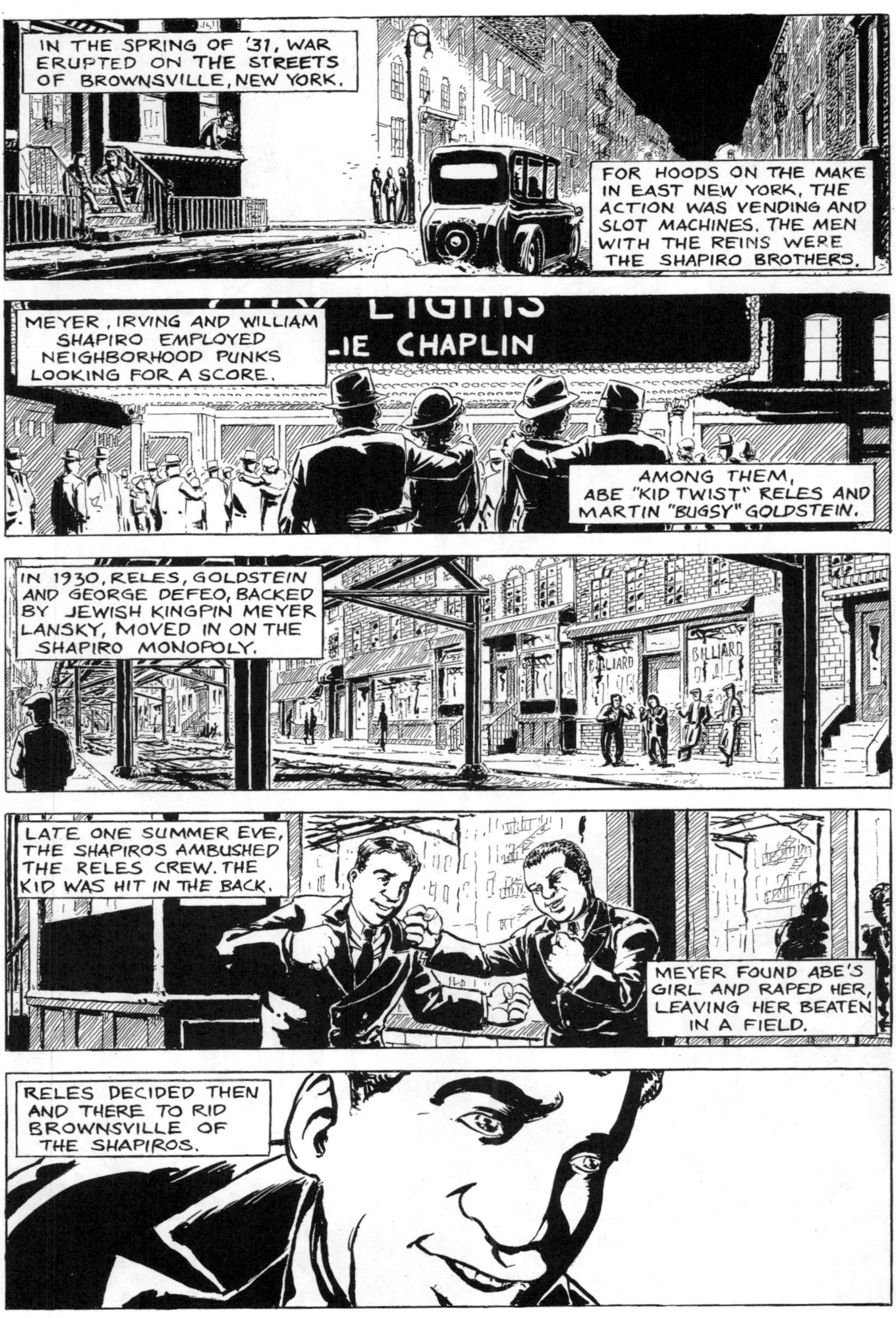
IN THE SPRING OF '31, WAR ERUPTED ON THE STREETS OF BROWNSVILLE, NEW YORK.
FOR HOODS ON THE MAKE IN EAST NEW YORK, THE ACTION WAS VENDING AND SLOT MACHINES. THE MEN WITH THE REINS WERE THE SHAPIRO BROTHERS.
MEYER, IRVING AND WILLIAM SHAPIRO EMPLOYED NEIGHBORHOOD PUNKS LOOKING FOR A SCORE.
CHAPLIN
AMONG THEM, ABE "KID TWIST" RELES AND MARTIN "BUGSY" GOLDSTEIN.
IN 1930, RELES, GOLDSTEIN AND GEORGE DEFEO, BACKED BY JEWISH KINGPIN MEYER LANSKY, MOVED IN ON THE SHAPIRO MONOPOLY.
BILLIARD
BILLIARD
LATE ONE SUMMER EVE, THE SHAPIROS AMBUSHED THE RELES CREW. THE KID WAS HIT IN THE BACK.
MEYER FOUND ABE'S GIRL AND RAPED HER, LEAVING HER BEATEN IN A FIELD.
RELES DECIDED THEN AND THERE TO RID BROWNSVILLE OF THE SHAPIROS.

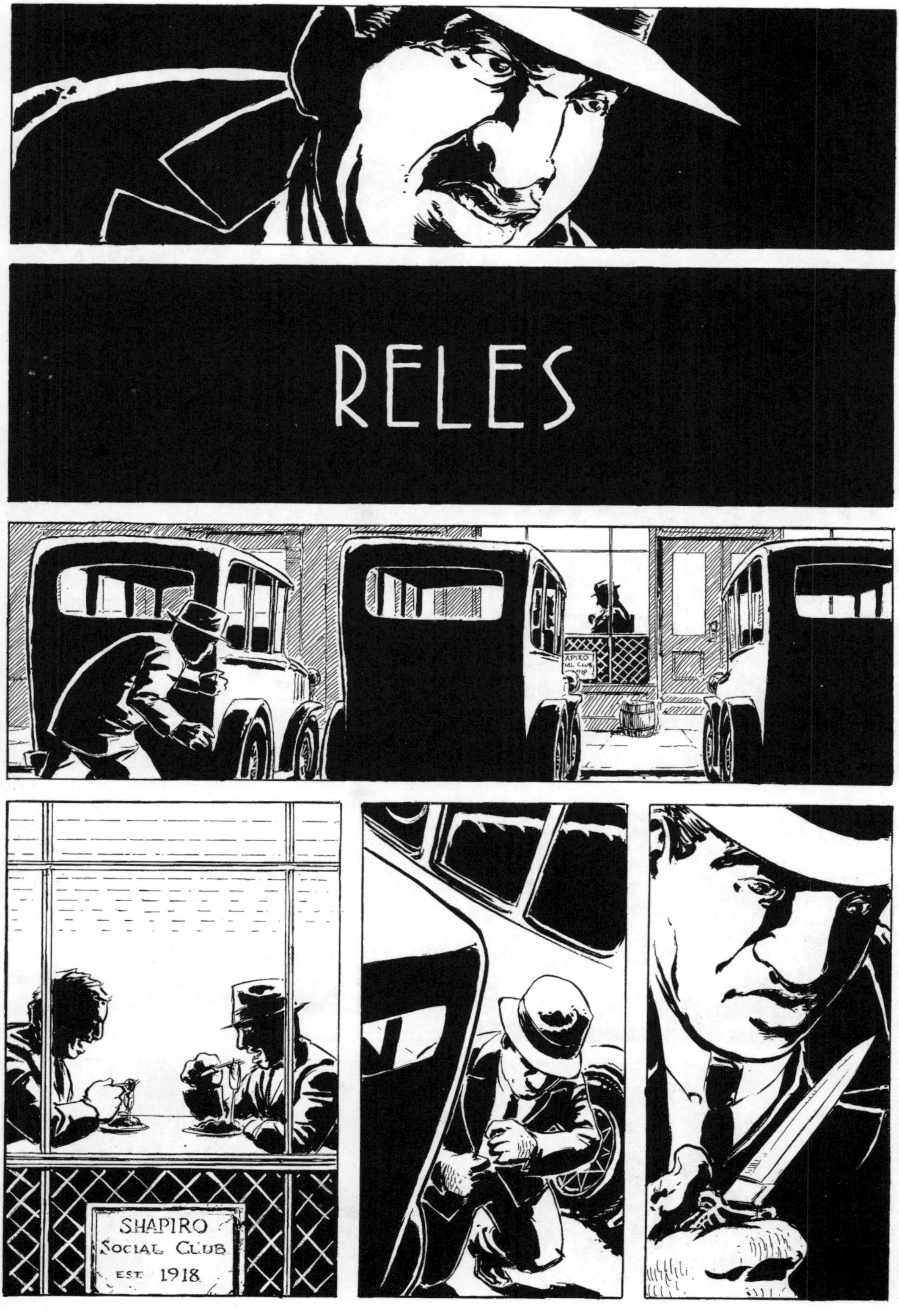
RELES
SHAPIRO
SOCIAL CLUB
EST. 1918

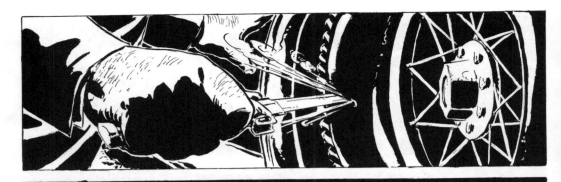

BROWNSVILLE,
THE DINER
1931

THEY'RE NOT HERE, ABE.

THEY WILL BE.

WHY DO WE NEED THESE WOPS?

DASHER AND HAPPY RUN OCEAN HILL, THE TOUGHEST GANG IN BROOKLYN. GET 'EM WITH US, AND MEYER'S TOAST.

AND IF WE DON'T?

SOMETHING'LL COME UP, HARRY IT ALWAYS DOES.

HERE COMES BUGSY.

THEY HERE YET?

NOT YET. SEEN DEFEO?

THOUGHT HE WAS WITH YOU.

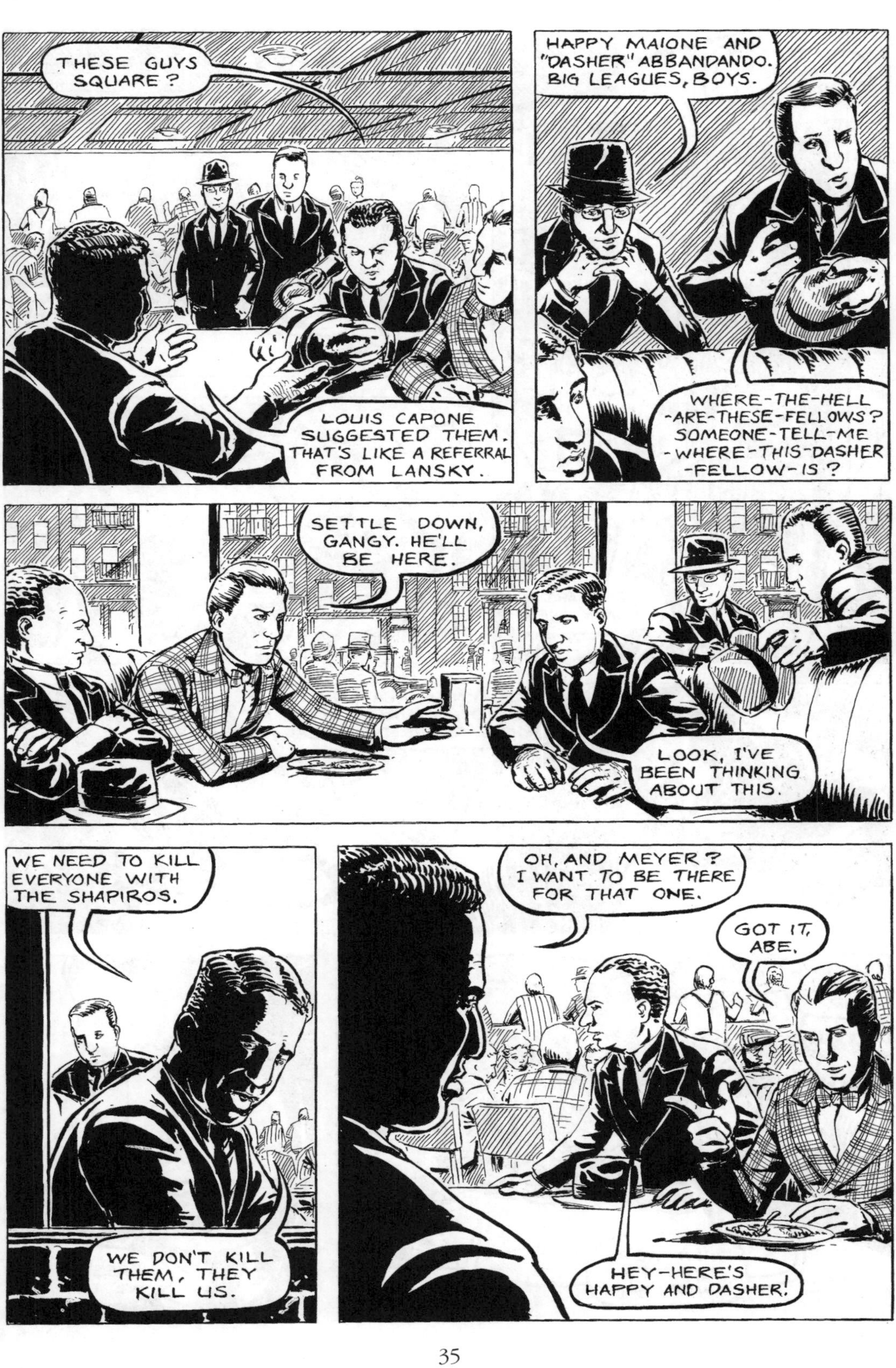
THESE GUYS SQUARE?
LOUIS CAPONE SUGGESTED THEM. THAT'S LIKE A REFERRAL FROM LANSKY.
HAPPY MAIONE AND "DASHER" ABBANDANDO. BIG LEAGUES, BOYS.
WHERE-THE-HELL-ARE-THESE-FELLOWS? SOMEONE-TELL-ME-WHERE-THIS-DASHER-FELLOW-IS?
SETTLE DOWN, GANGY. HE'LL BE HERE.
LOOK, I'VE BEEN THINKING ABOUT THIS.
WE NEED TO KILL EVERYONE WITH THE SHAPIROS.
WE DON'T KILL THEM, THEY KILL US.
OH, AND MEYER? I WANT TO BE THERE FOR THAT ONE.
GOT IT, ABE.
HEY-HERE'S HAPPY AND DASHER!

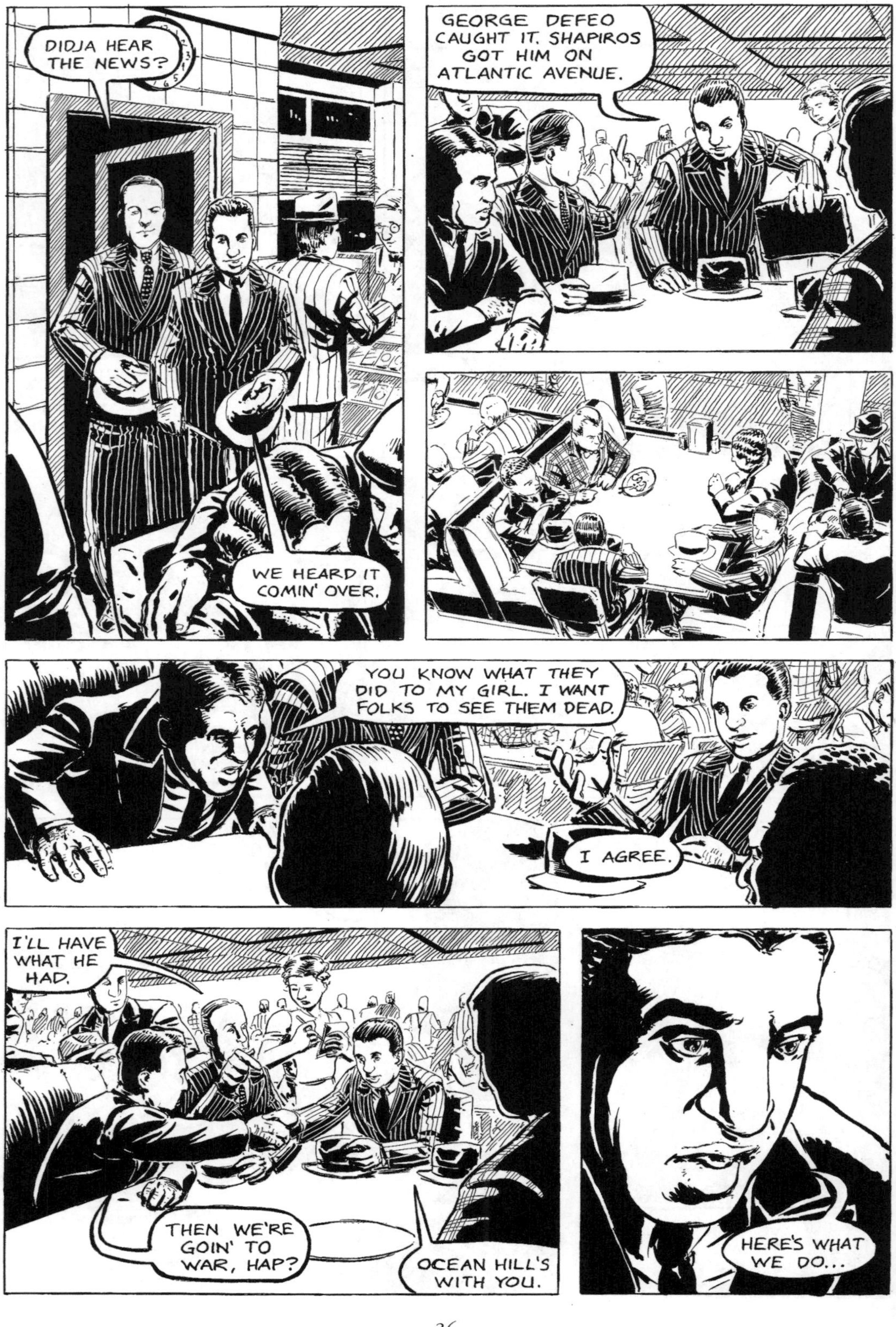
DIDJA HEAR THE NEWS?
WE HEARD IT COMIN' OVER.
GEORGE DEFEO CAUGHT IT. SHAPIROS GOT HIM ON ATLANTIC AVENUE.
YOU KNOW WHAT THEY DID TO MY GIRL. I WANT FOLKS TO SEE THEM DEAD.
I AGREE.
I'LL HAVE WHAT HE HAD.
THEN WE'RE GOIN' TO WAR, HAP?
OCEAN HILL'S WITH YOU.
HERE'S WHAT WE DO...

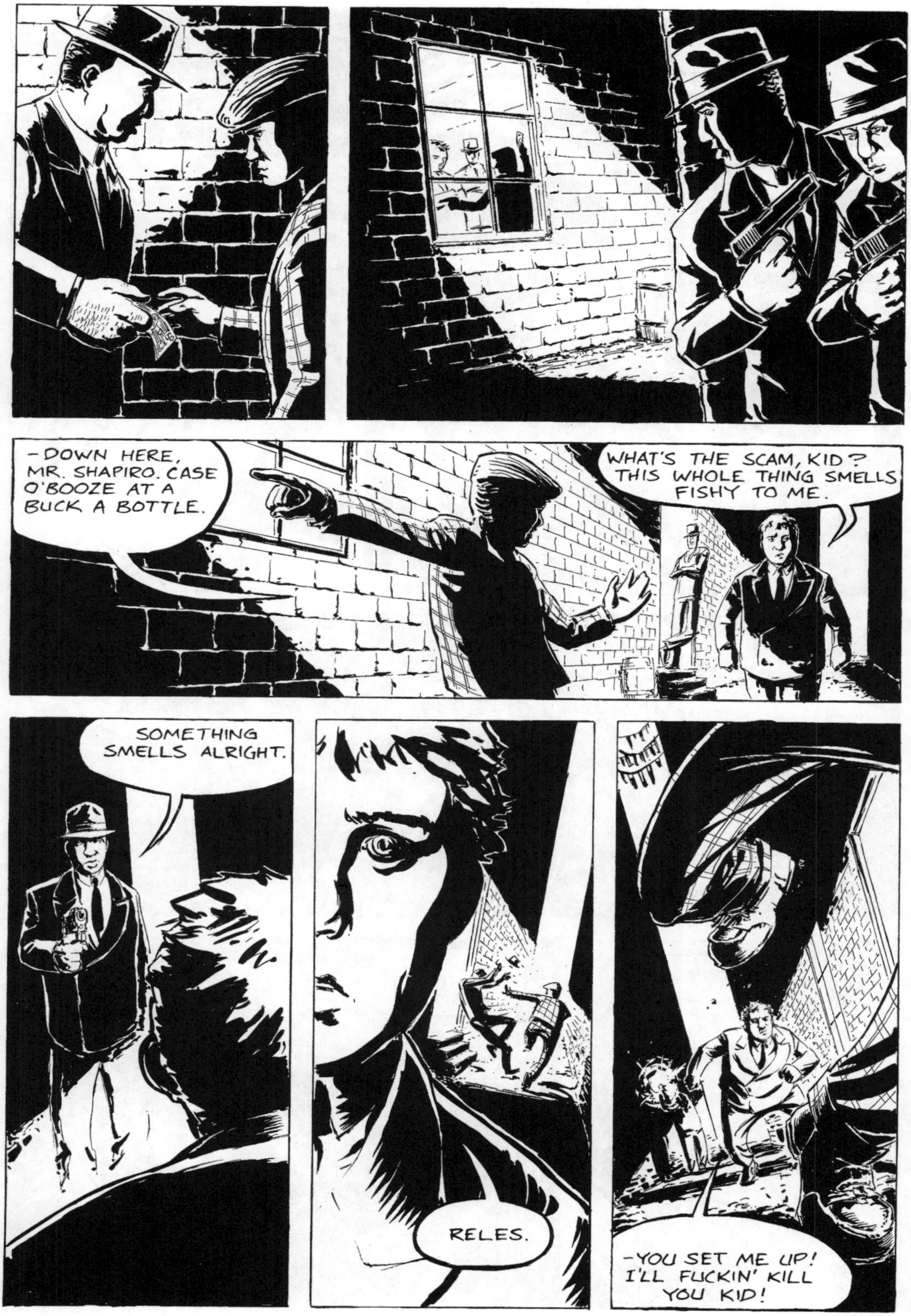

-DOWN HERE, MR. SHAPIRO. CASE O'BOOZE AT A BUCK A BOTTLE.
WHAT'S THE SCAM, KID? THIS WHOLE THING SMELLS FISHY TO ME.
SOMETHING SMELLS ALRIGHT.
RELES.
-YOU SET ME UP! I'LL FUCKIN' KILL YOU KID!

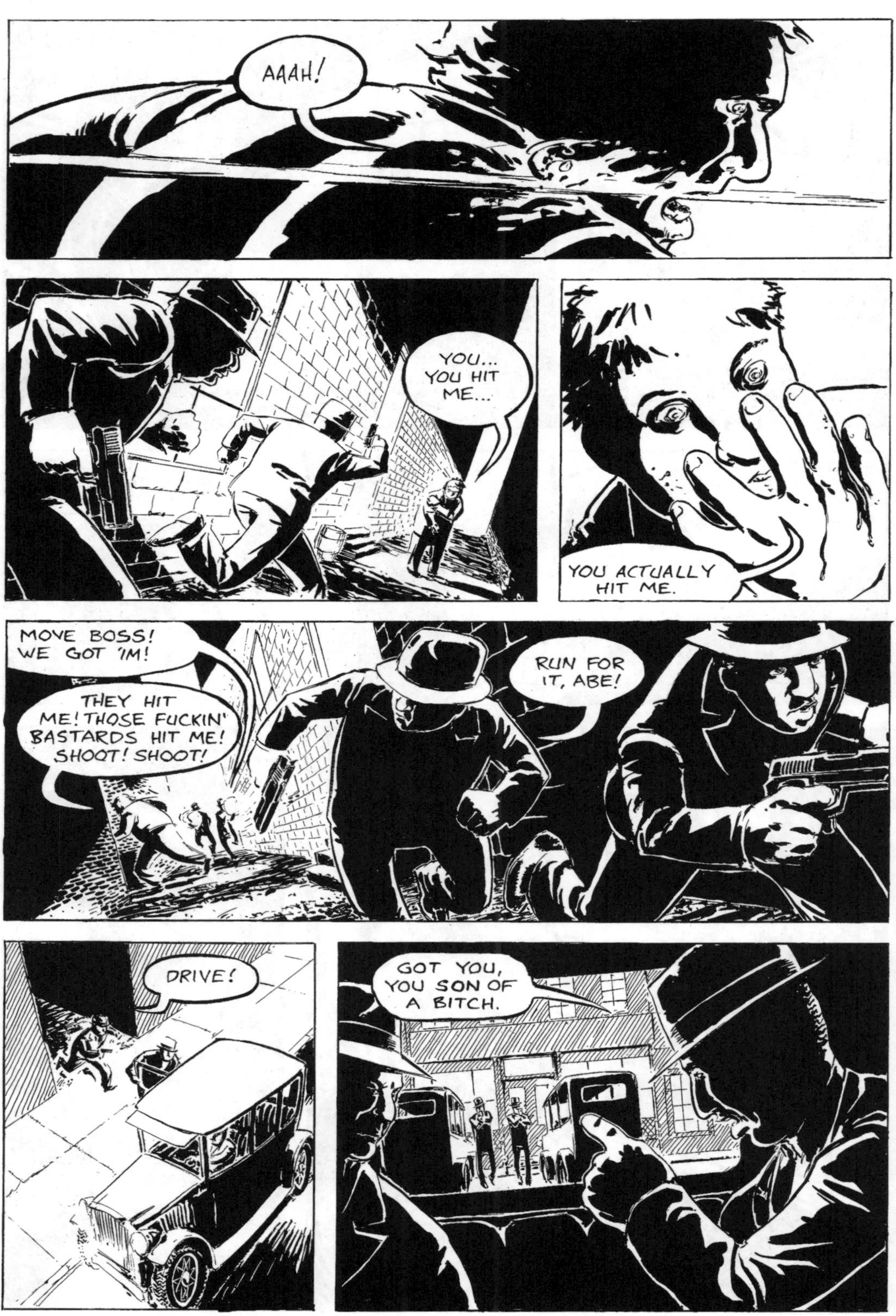
AAAH!
YOU... YOU HIT ME...
YOU ACTUALLY HIT ME.
MOVE BOSS! WE GOT 'IM!
THEY HIT ME! THOSE FUCKIN' BASTARDS HIT ME! SHOOT! SHOOT!
RUN FOR IT, ABE!
DRIVE!
GOT YOU, YOU SON OF A BITCH.

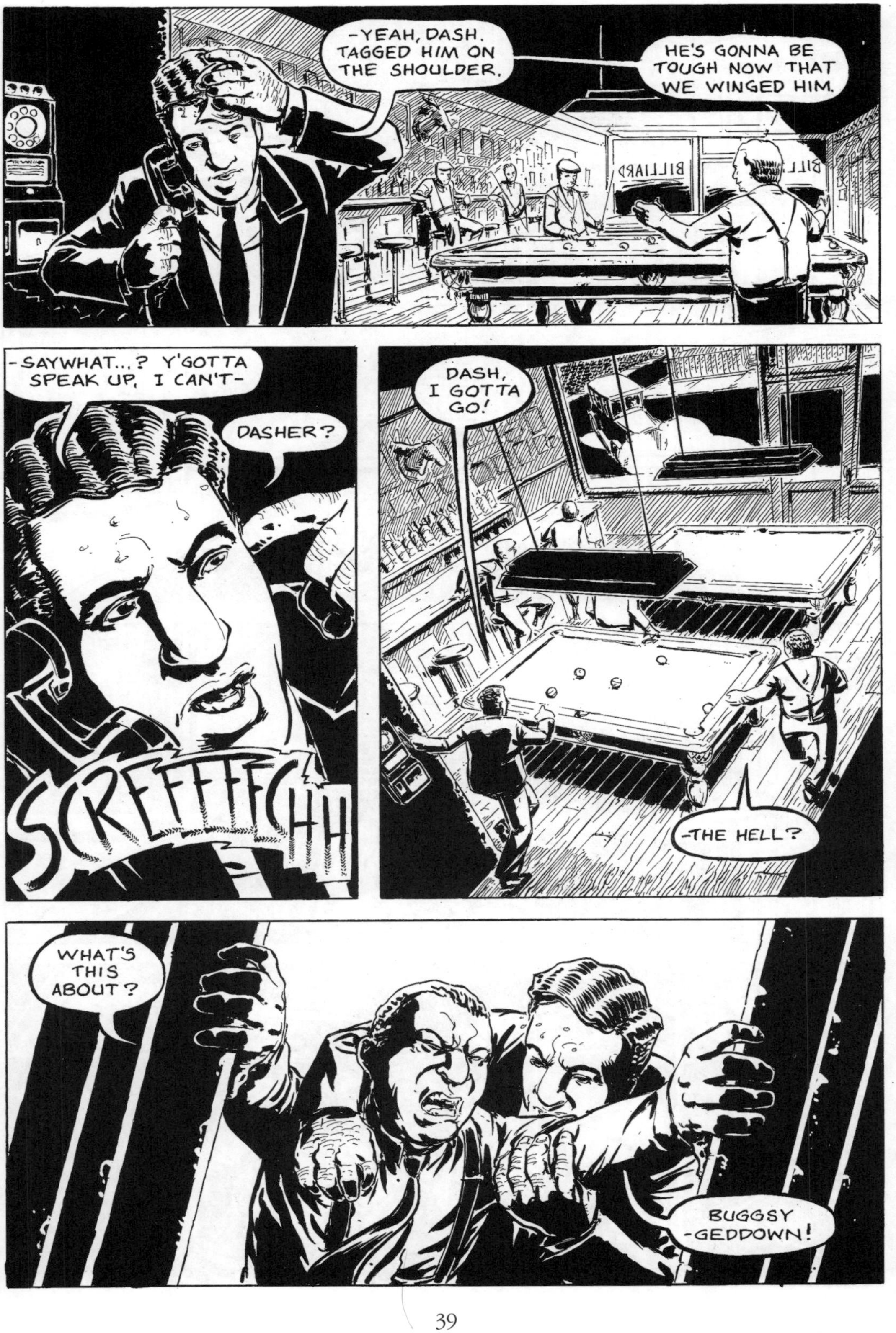
-YEAH, DASH. TAGGED HIM ON THE SHOULDER.
HE'S GONNA BE TOUGH NOW THAT WE WINGED HIM.
BILLIARD
-SAYWHAT...? Y'GOTTA SPEAK UP, I CAN'T-
DASHER?
SCREEEECHH
DASH, I GOTTA GO!
-THE HELL?
WHAT'S THIS ABOUT?
BUGGSY -GEDDOWN!

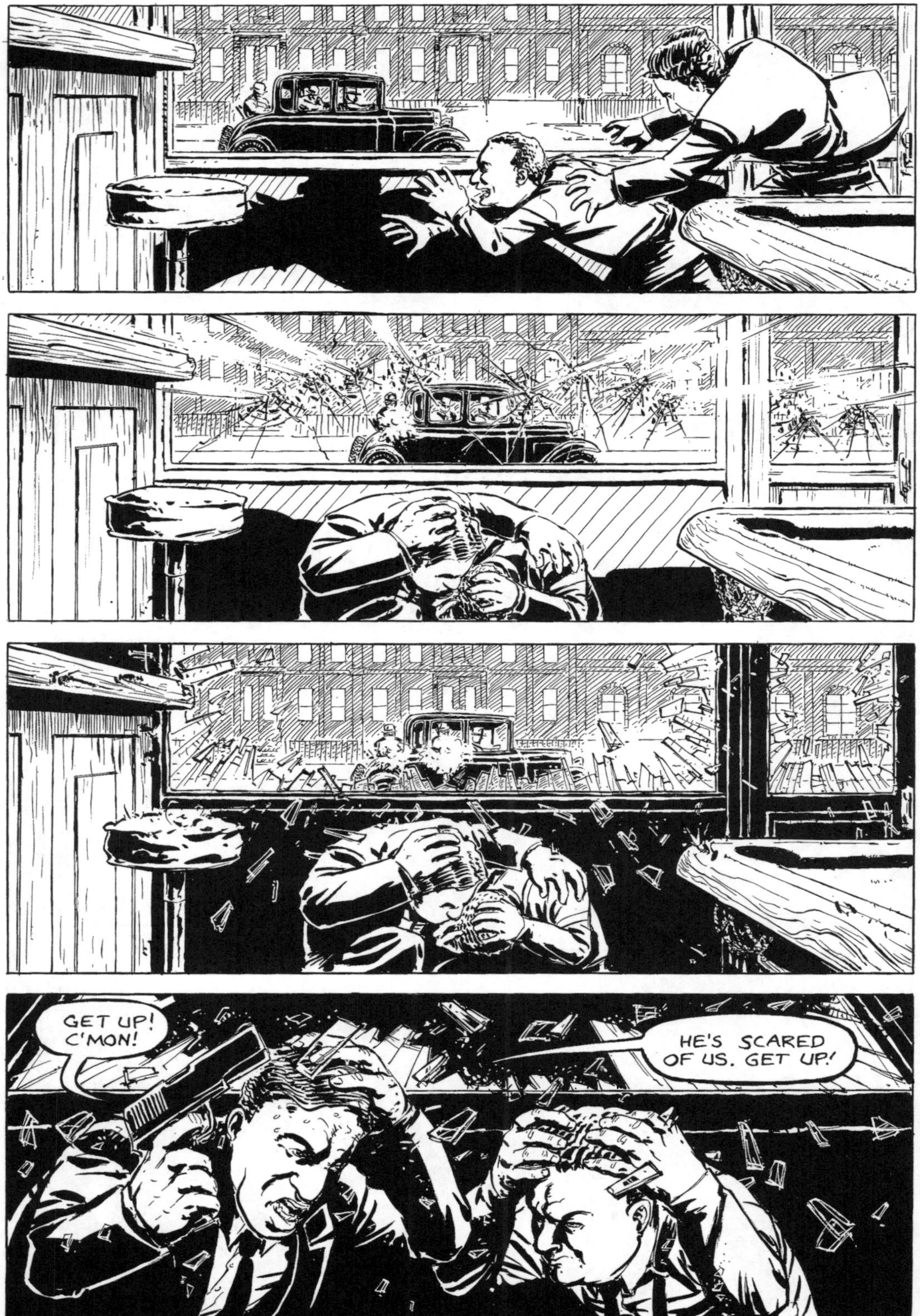
GET UP! C'MON!
HE'S SCARED OF US. GET UP!

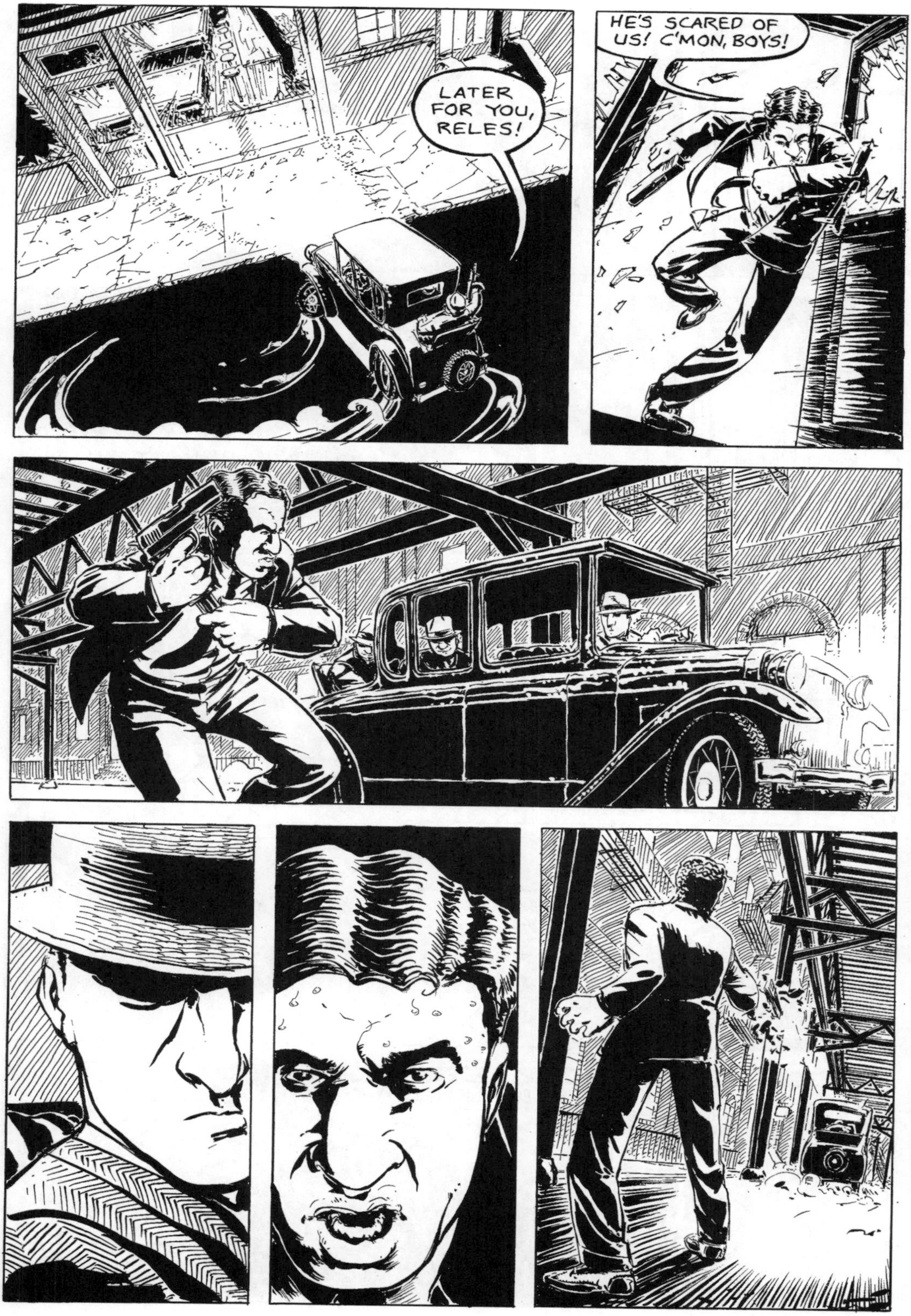
LATER FOR YOU, RELES!
HE'S SCARED OF US! C'MON, BOYS!

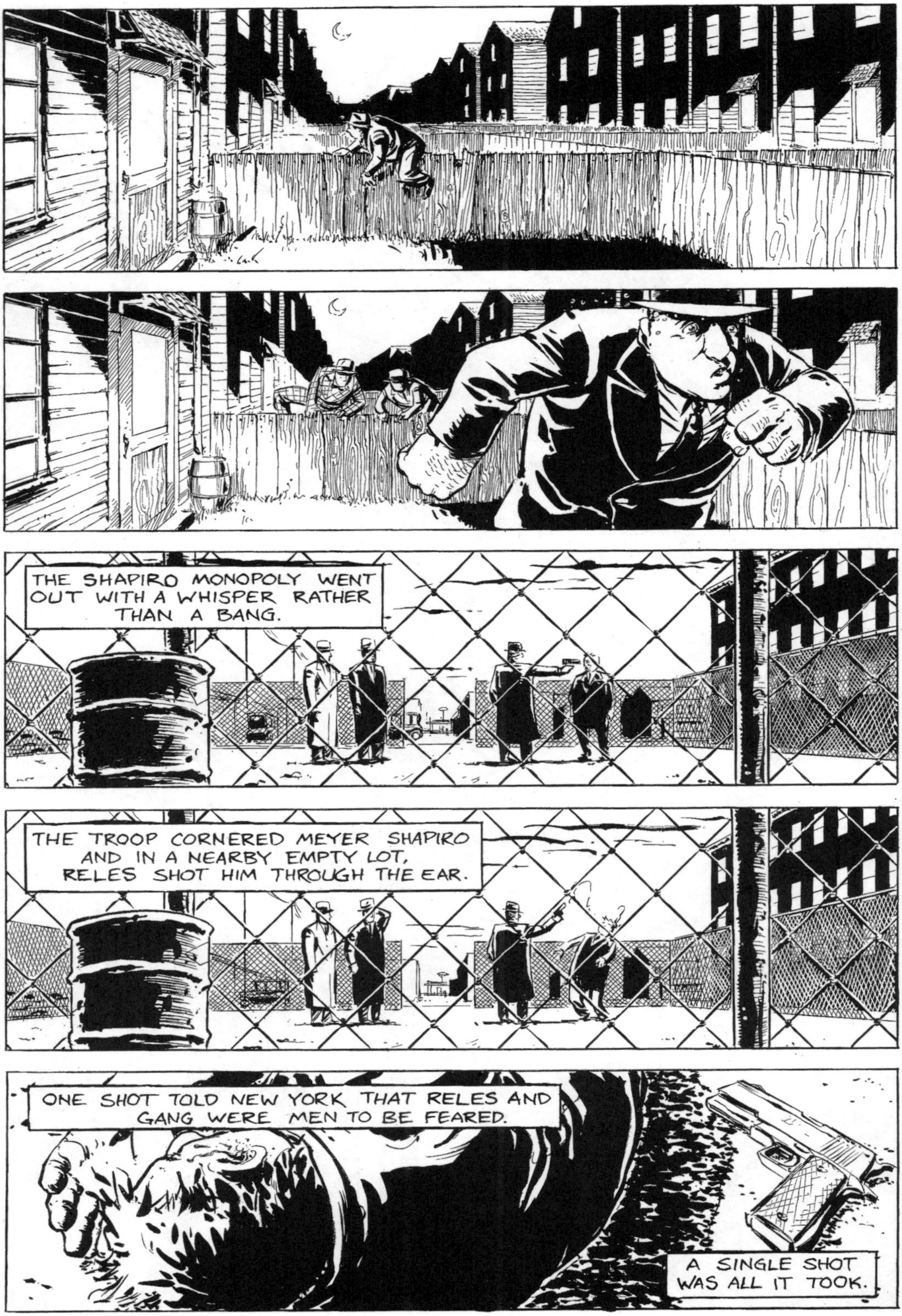
THE SHAPIRO MONOPOLY WENT OUT WITH A WHISPER RATHER THAN A BANG.
THE TROOP CORNERED MEYER SHAPIRO AND IN A NEARBY EMPTY LOT, RELES SHOT HIM THROUGH THE EAR.
ONE SHOT TOLD NEW YORK THAT RELES AND GANG WERE MEN TO BE FEARED.
A SINGLE SHOT WAS ALL IT TOOK.

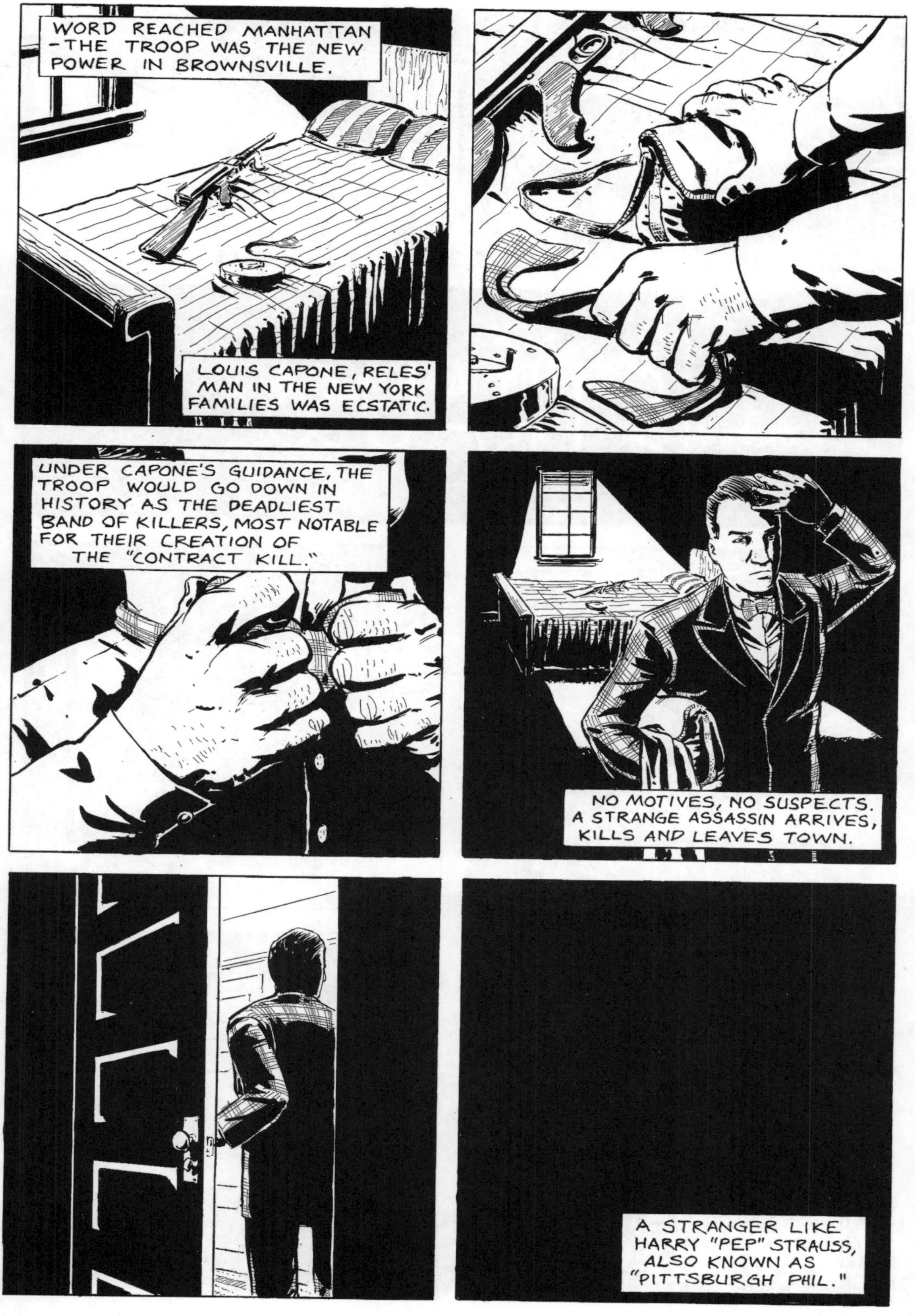
WORD REACHED MANHATTAN -THE TROOP WAS THE NEW POWER IN BROWNSVILLE.
LOUIS CAPONE, RELES' MAN IN THE NEW YORK FAMILIES WAS ECSTATIC.
UNDER CAPONE'S GUIDANCE, THE TROOP WOULD GO DOWN IN HISTORY AS THE DEADLIEST BAND OF KILLERS, MOST NOTABLE FOR THEIR CREATION OF THE "CONTRACT KILL."
NO MOTIVES, NO SUSPECTS. A STRANGE ASSASSIN ARRIVES, KILLS AND LEAVES TOWN.
A STRANGER LIKE HARRY "PEP" STRAUSS, ALSO KNOWN AS "PITTSBURGH PHIL."

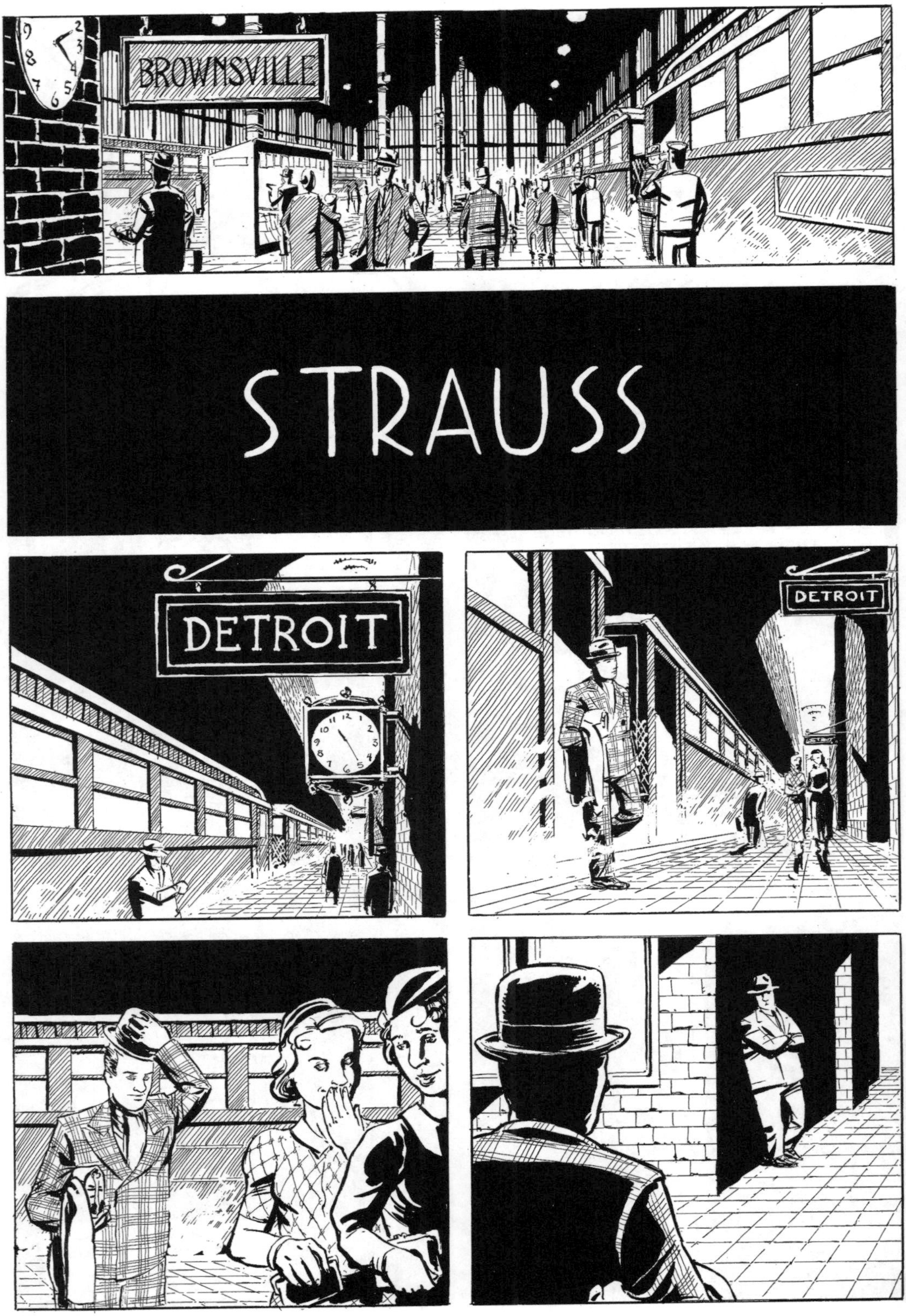
BROWNSVILLE
STRAUSS
DETROIT
DETROIT

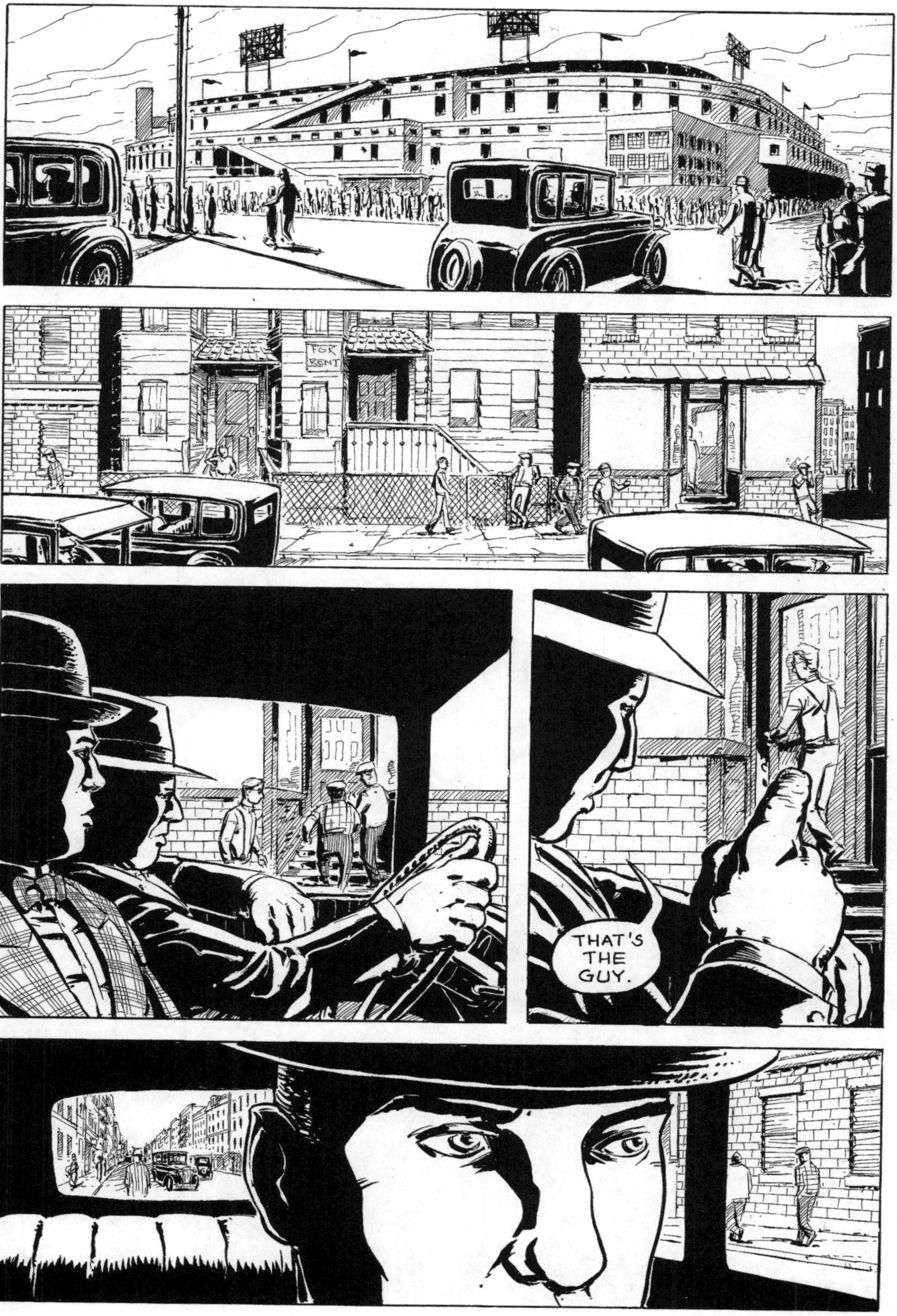
FOR RENT
THAT'S THE GUY.

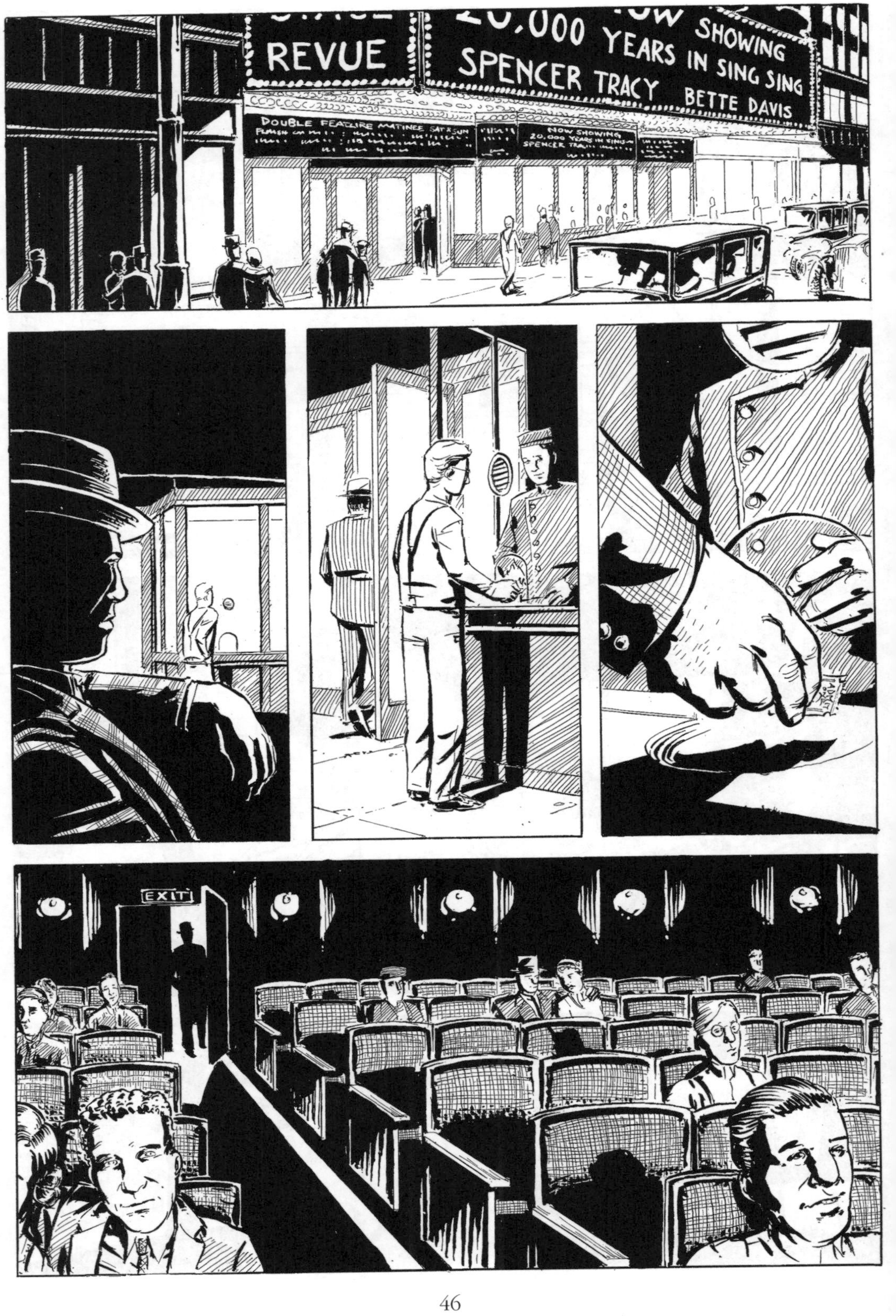
REVUE
SHOWING
20,000 YEARS IN SING SING
SPENCER TRACY
BETTE DAVIS
DOUBLE FEATURE MATINEE SAT & SUN
NOW SHOWING
20,000 YEARS IN SING SING
EXIT

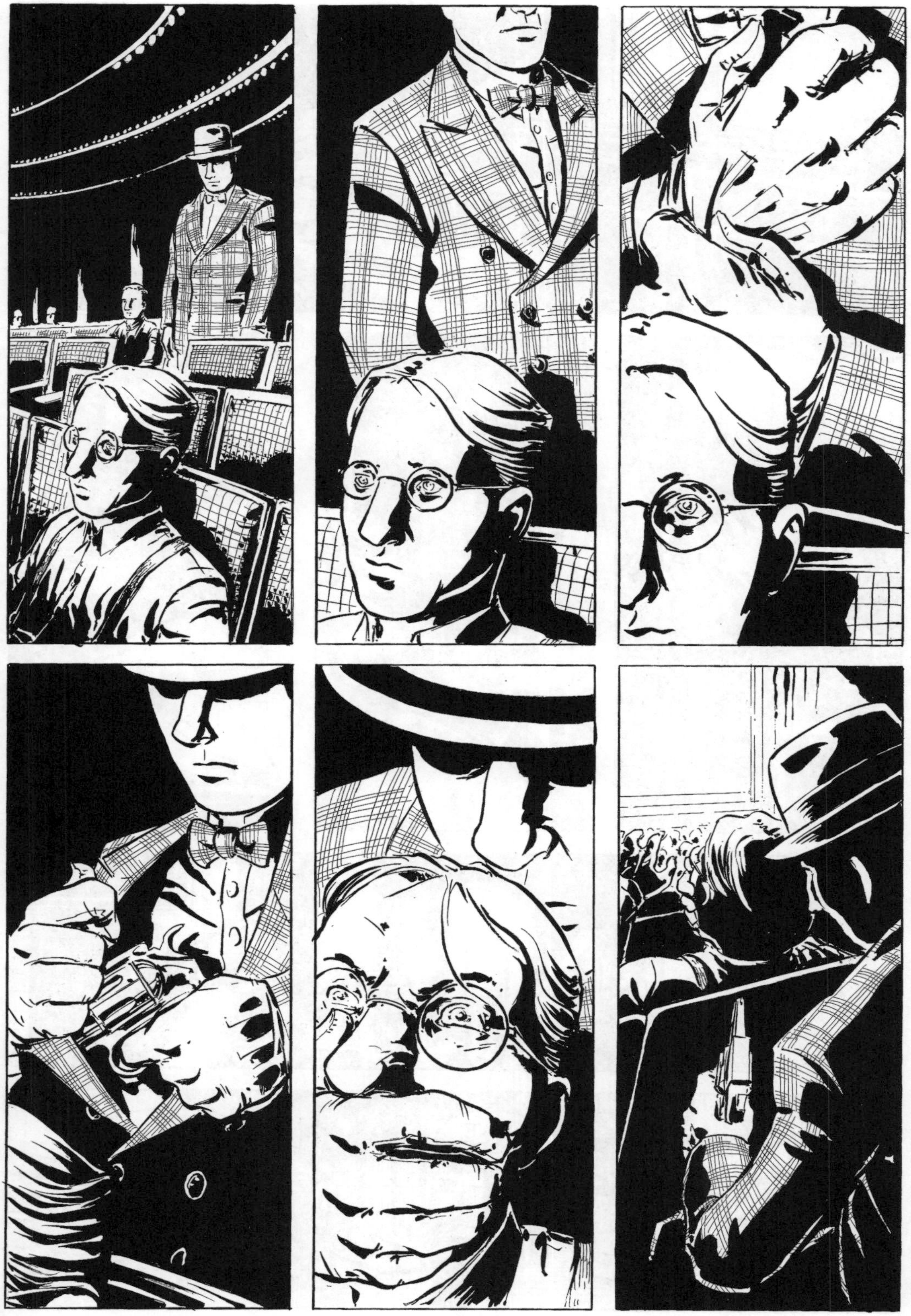

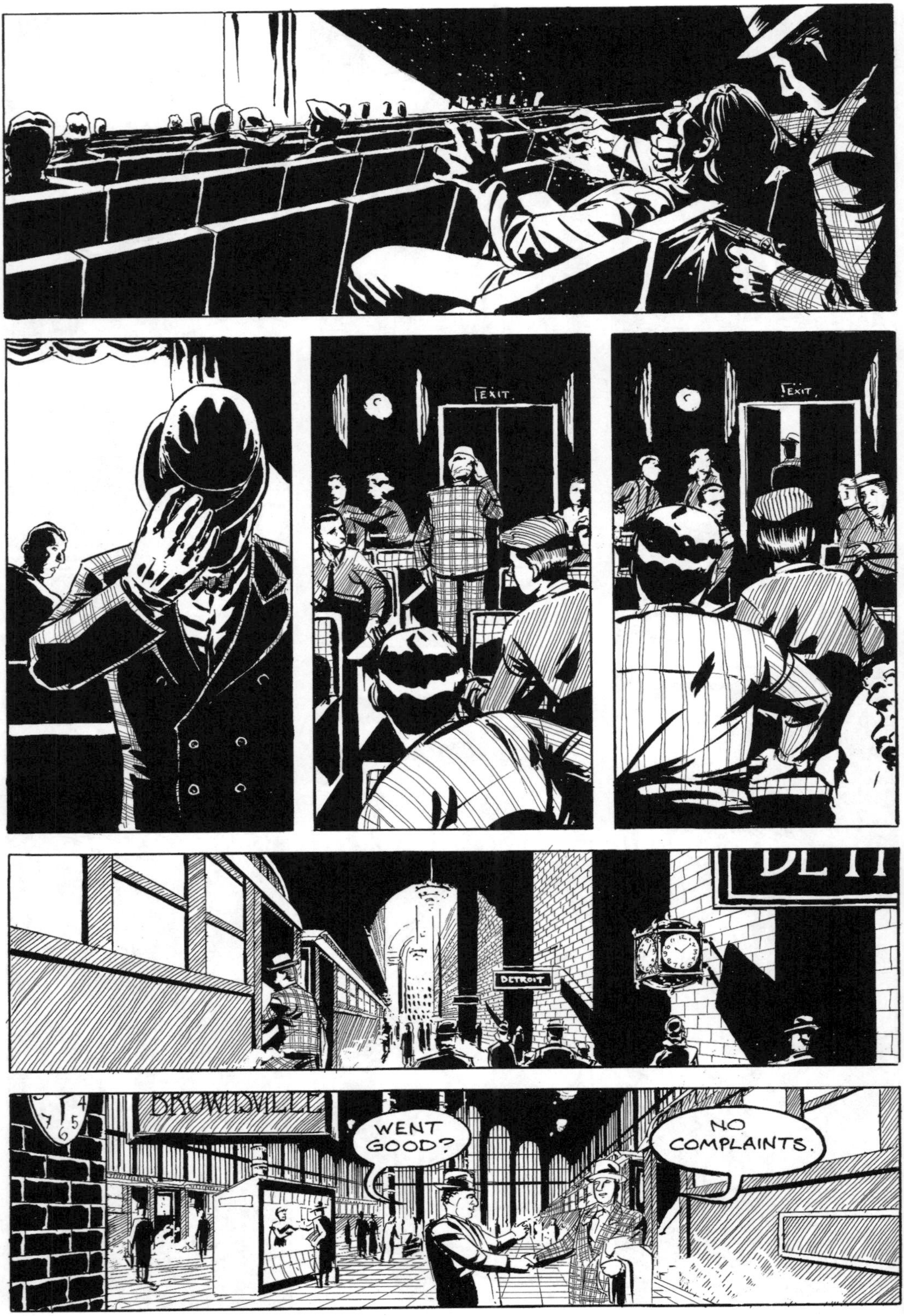
EXIT
EXIT
DETROIT
BROWNSVILLE
WENT GOOD?
NO COMPLAINTS.

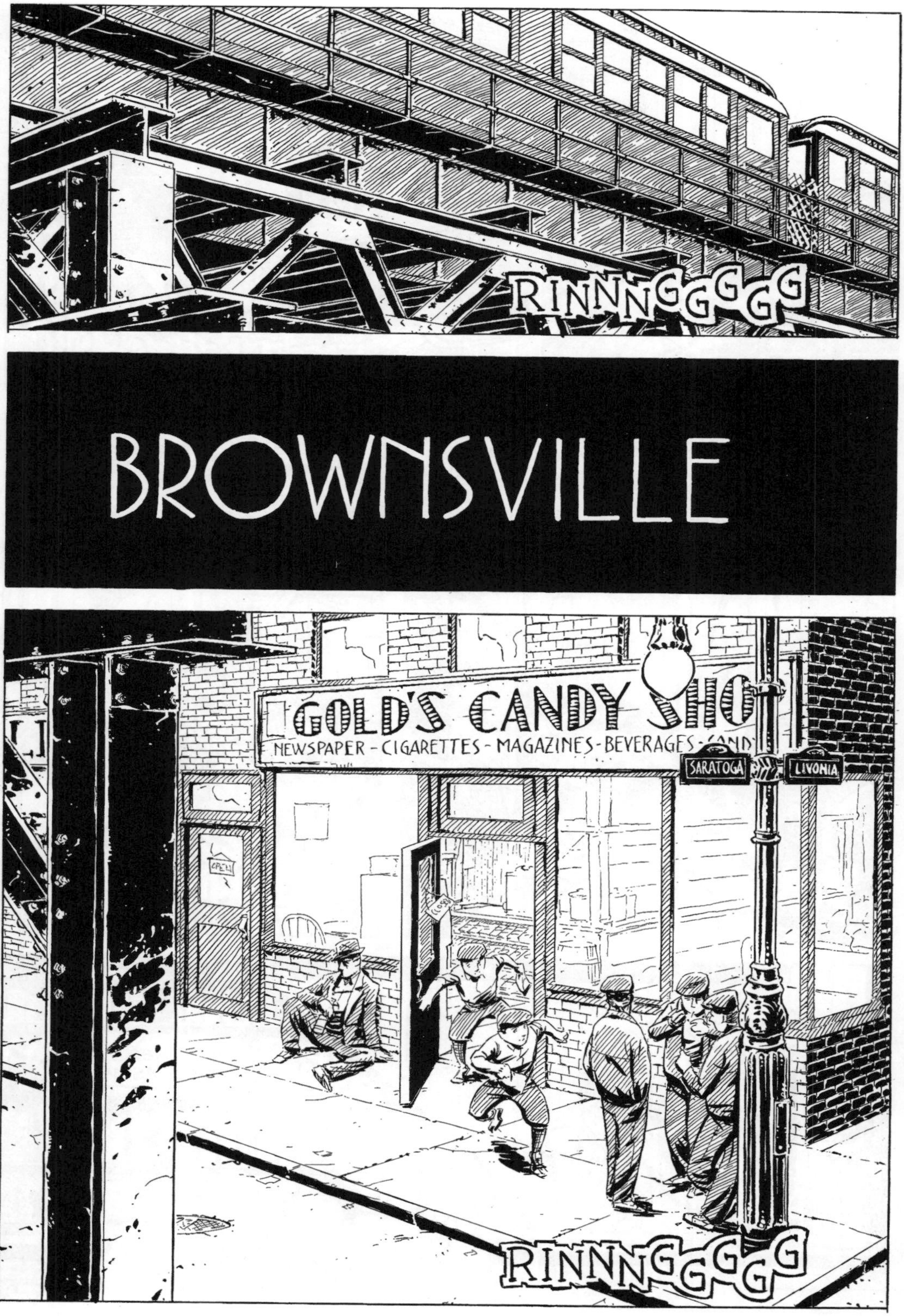
RINNNGGGGG
BROWNSVILLE
GOLD'S CANDY SHO
NEWSPAPER - CIGARETTES - MAGAZINES - BEVERAGES - CAND
SARATOGA
LIVONIA
OPEN
RINNNGGGGG

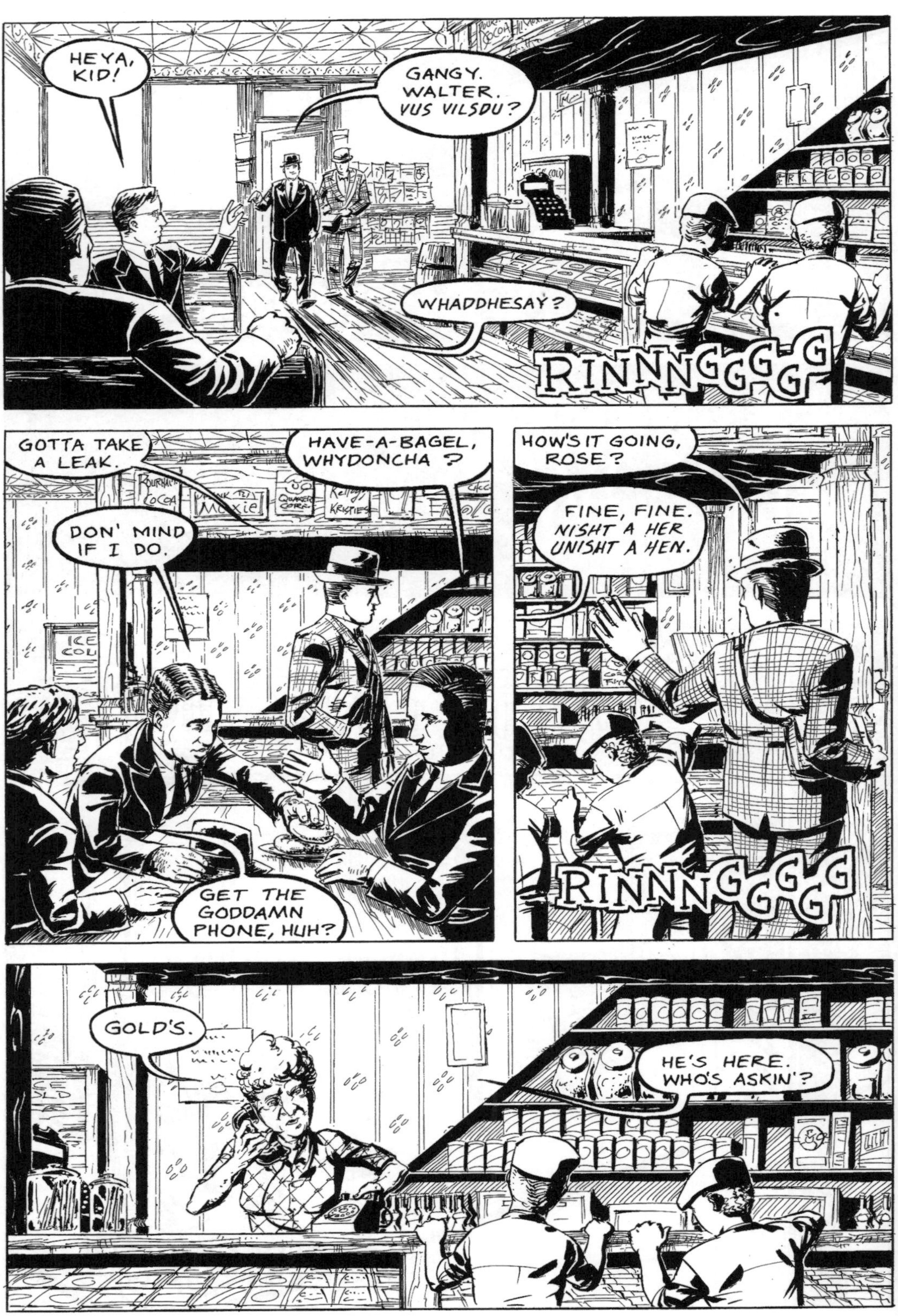
HEYA, KID!
GANGY. WALTER. VUS VILSDU?
WHADDHESAY?
RINNNGGGG
GOTTA TAKE A LEAK.
HAVE-A-BAGEL, WHYDONCHA?
DON' MIND IF I DO.
GET THE GODDAMN PHONE, HUH?
HOW'S IT GOING, ROSE?
FINE, FINE. NISHT A HER UNISHT A HEN.
RINNNGGGG
GOLD'S.
HE'S HERE. WHO'S ASKIN'?

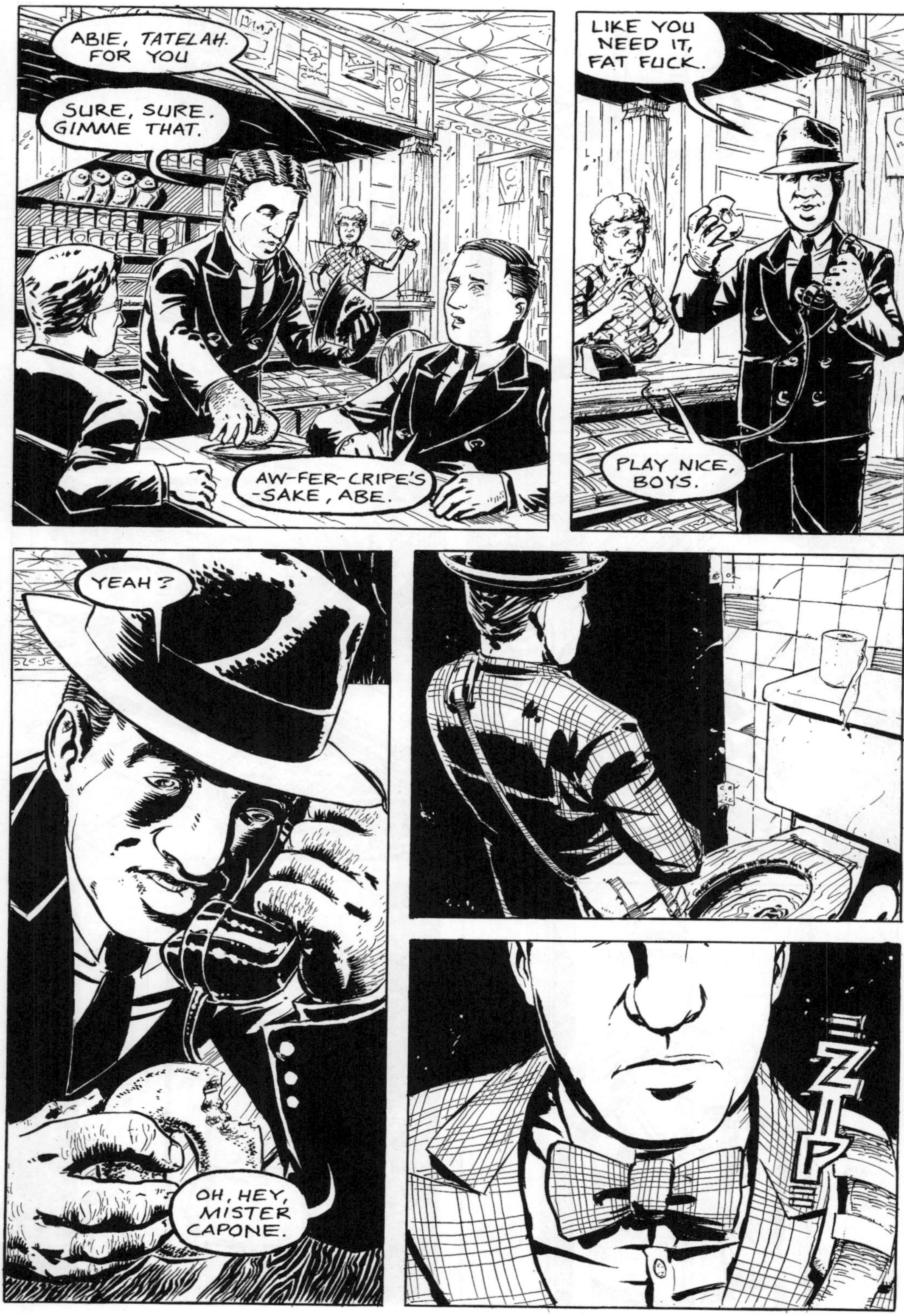
ABIE, TATELAH. FOR YOU
SURE, SURE. GIMME THAT.
AW-FER-CRIPE'S -SAKE, ABE.
LIKE YOU NEED IT, FAT FUCK.
PLAY NICE, BOYS.
YEAH?
OH, HEY, MISTER CAPONE.
ZZIP

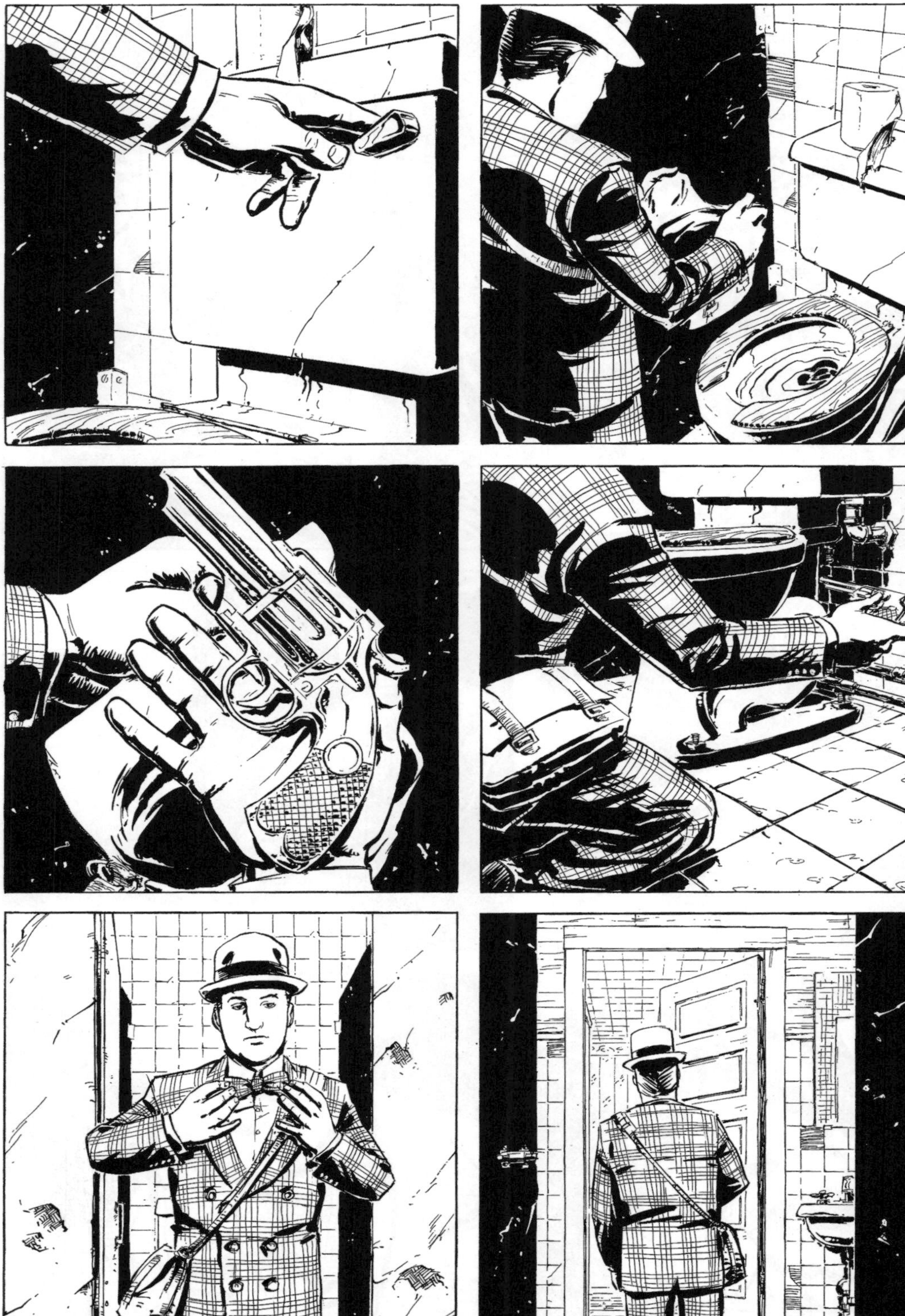

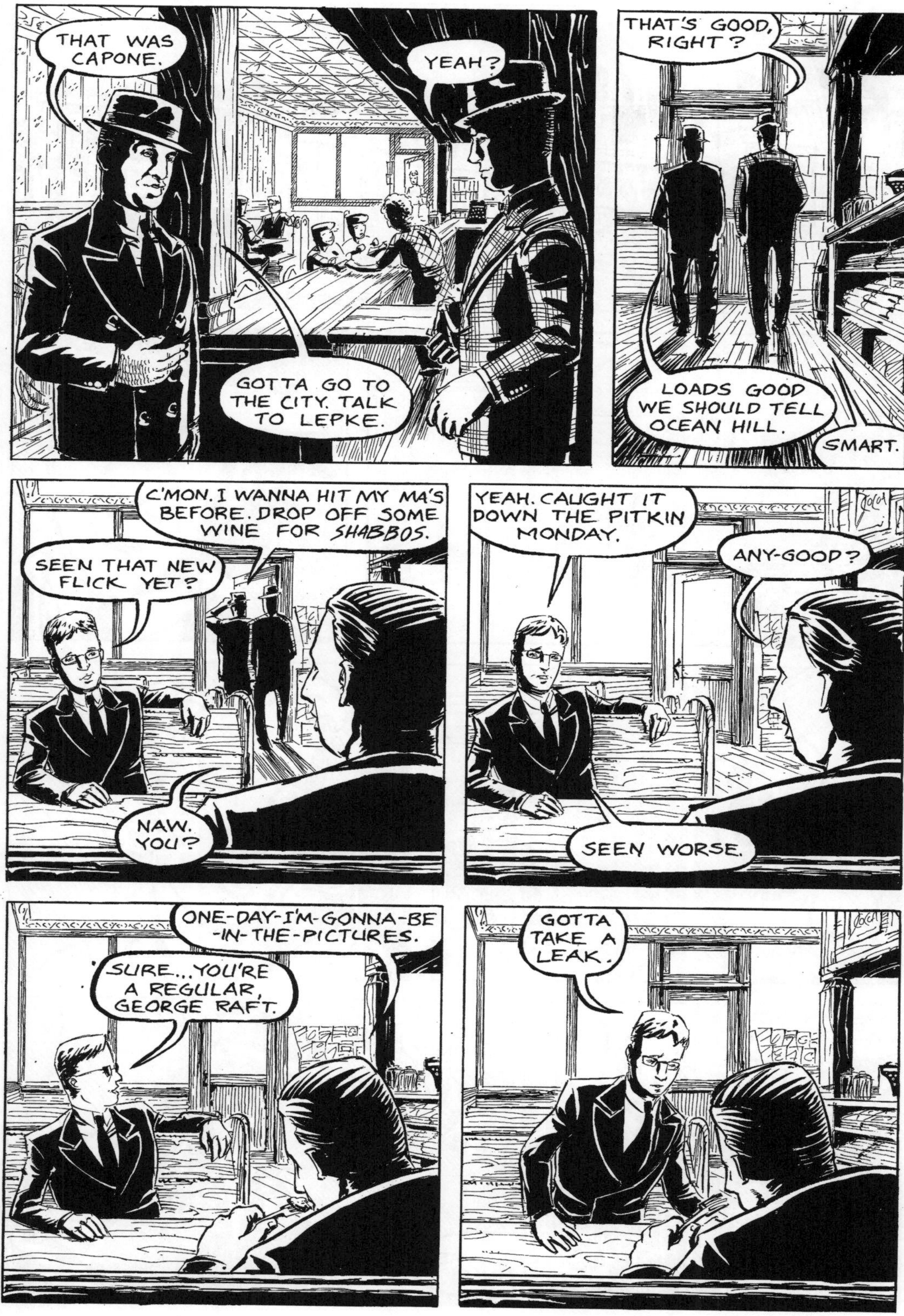
THAT WAS CAPONE.
YEAH?
GOTTA GO TO THE CITY. TALK TO LEPKE.
THAT'S GOOD, RIGHT?
LOADS GOOD WE SHOULD TELL OCEAN HILL.
SMART.
SEEN THAT NEW FLICK YET?
C'MON. I WANNA HIT MY MA'S BEFORE. DROP OFF SOME WINE FOR *SHABBOS*.
NAW. YOU?
YEAH. CAUGHT IT DOWN THE PITKIN MONDAY.
ANY-GOOD?
SEEN WORSE.
ONE-DAY-I'M-GONNA-BE-IN-THE-PICTURES.
SURE... YOU'RE A REGULAR, GEORGE RAFT.
GOTTA TAKE A LEAK.

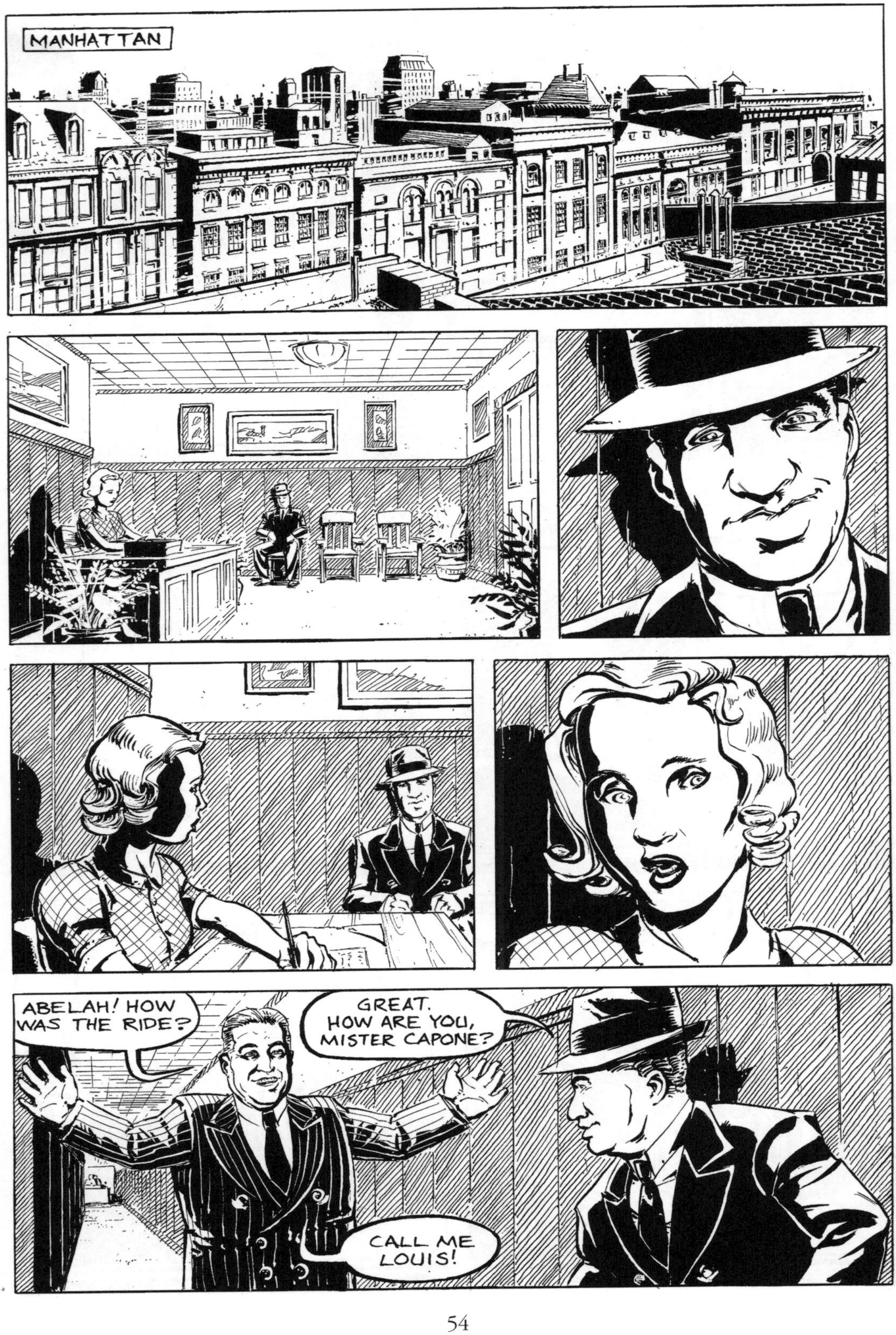
MANHATTAN
ABELAH! HOW WAS THE RIDE?
GREAT. HOW ARE YOU, MISTER CAPONE?
CALL ME LOUIS!

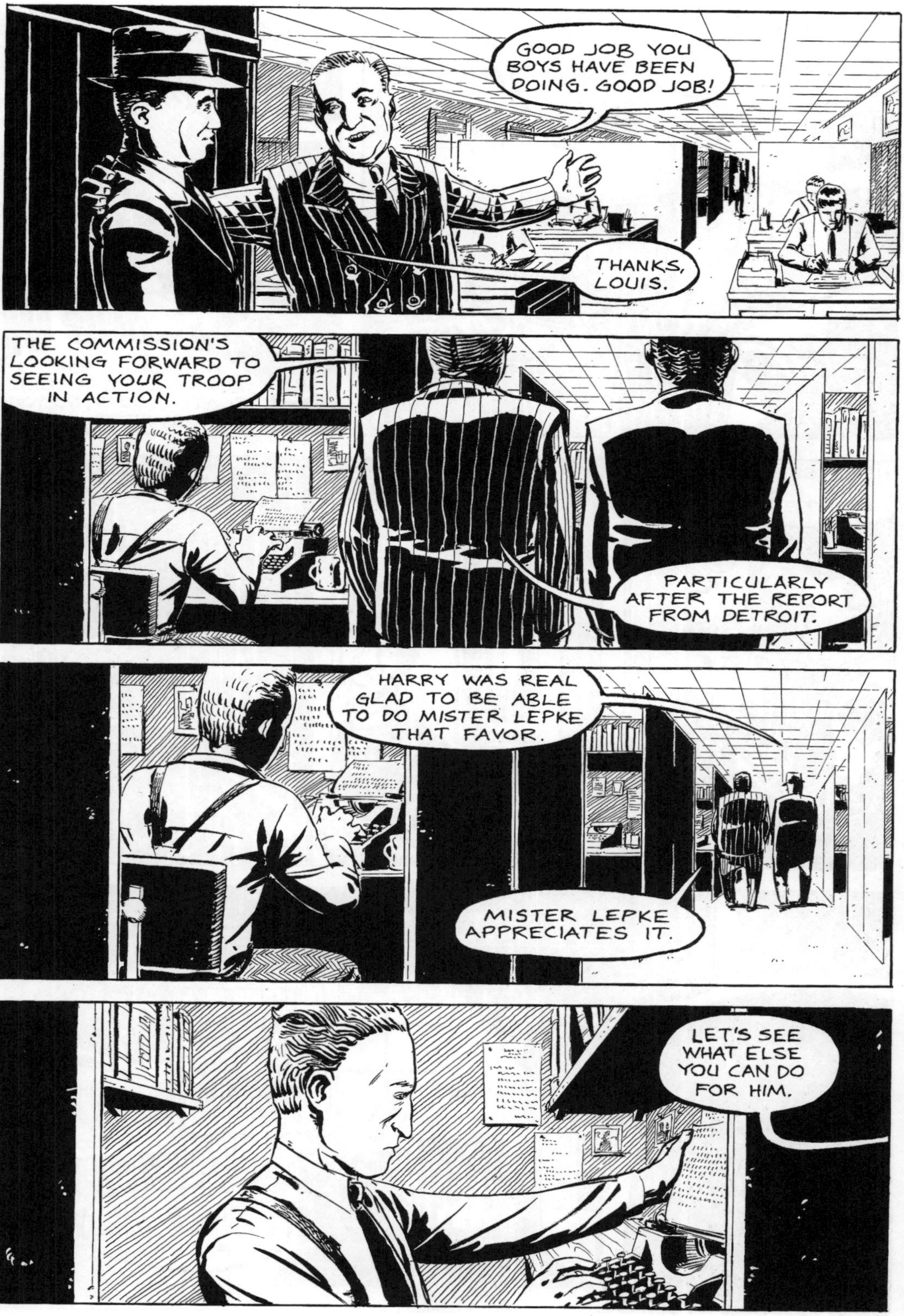
GOOD JOB YOU BOYS HAVE BEEN DOING. GOOD JOB!
THANKS, LOUIS.
THE COMMISSION'S LOOKING FORWARD TO SEEING YOUR TROOP IN ACTION.
PARTICULARLY AFTER THE REPORT FROM DETROIT.
HARRY WAS REAL GLAD TO BE ABLE TO DO MISTER LEPKE THAT FAVOR.
MISTER LEPKE APPRECIATES IT.
LET'S SEE WHAT ELSE YOU CAN DO FOR HIM.

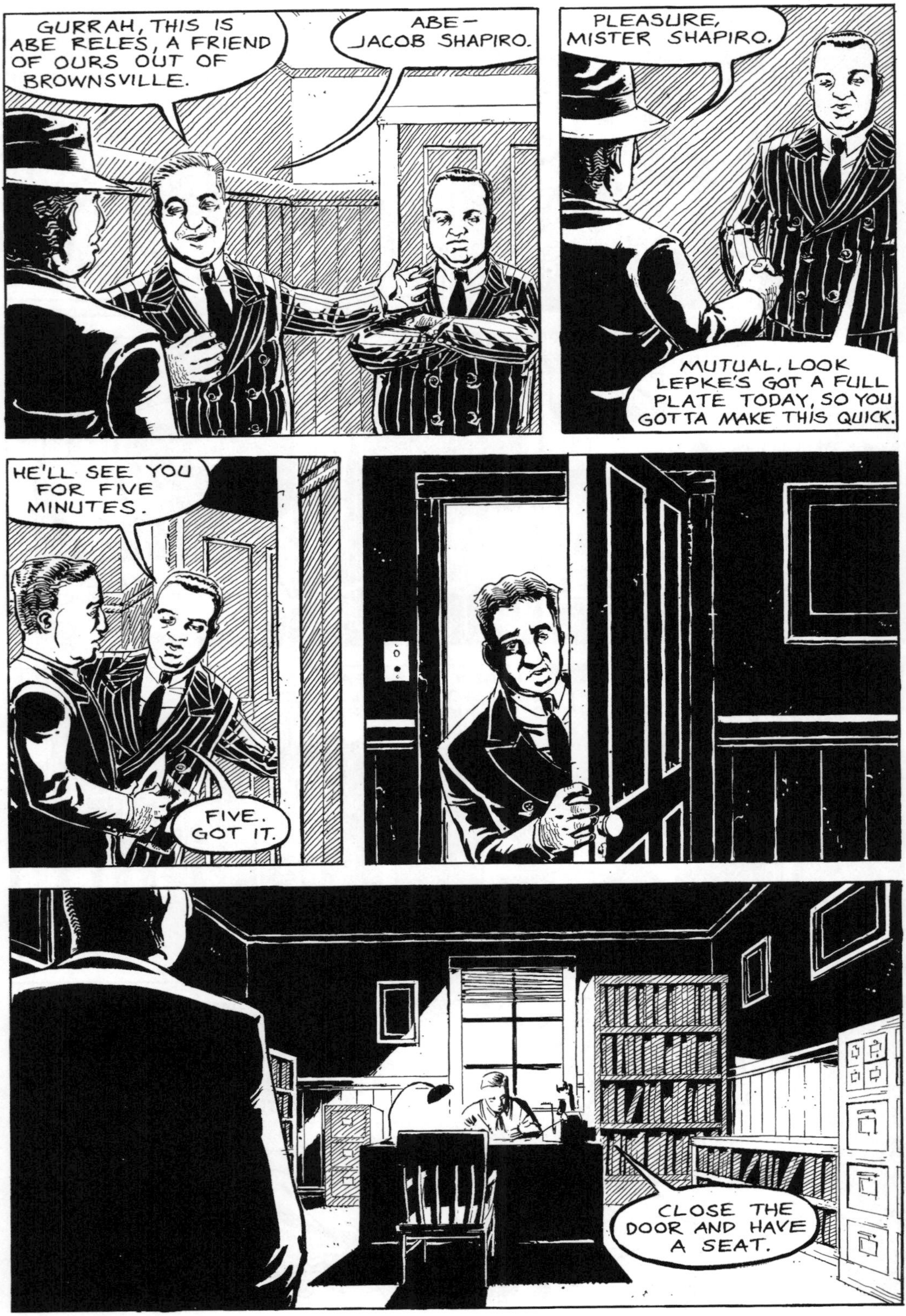
GURRAH, THIS IS ABE RELES, A FRIEND OF OURS OUT OF BROWNSVILLE.
ABE— JACOB SHAPIRO.
PLEASURE, MISTER SHAPIRO.
MUTUAL. LOOK LEPKE'S GOT A FULL PLATE TODAY, SO YOU GOTTA MAKE THIS QUICK.
HE'LL SEE YOU FOR FIVE MINUTES.
FIVE. GOT IT.
CLOSE THE DOOR AND HAVE A SEAT.

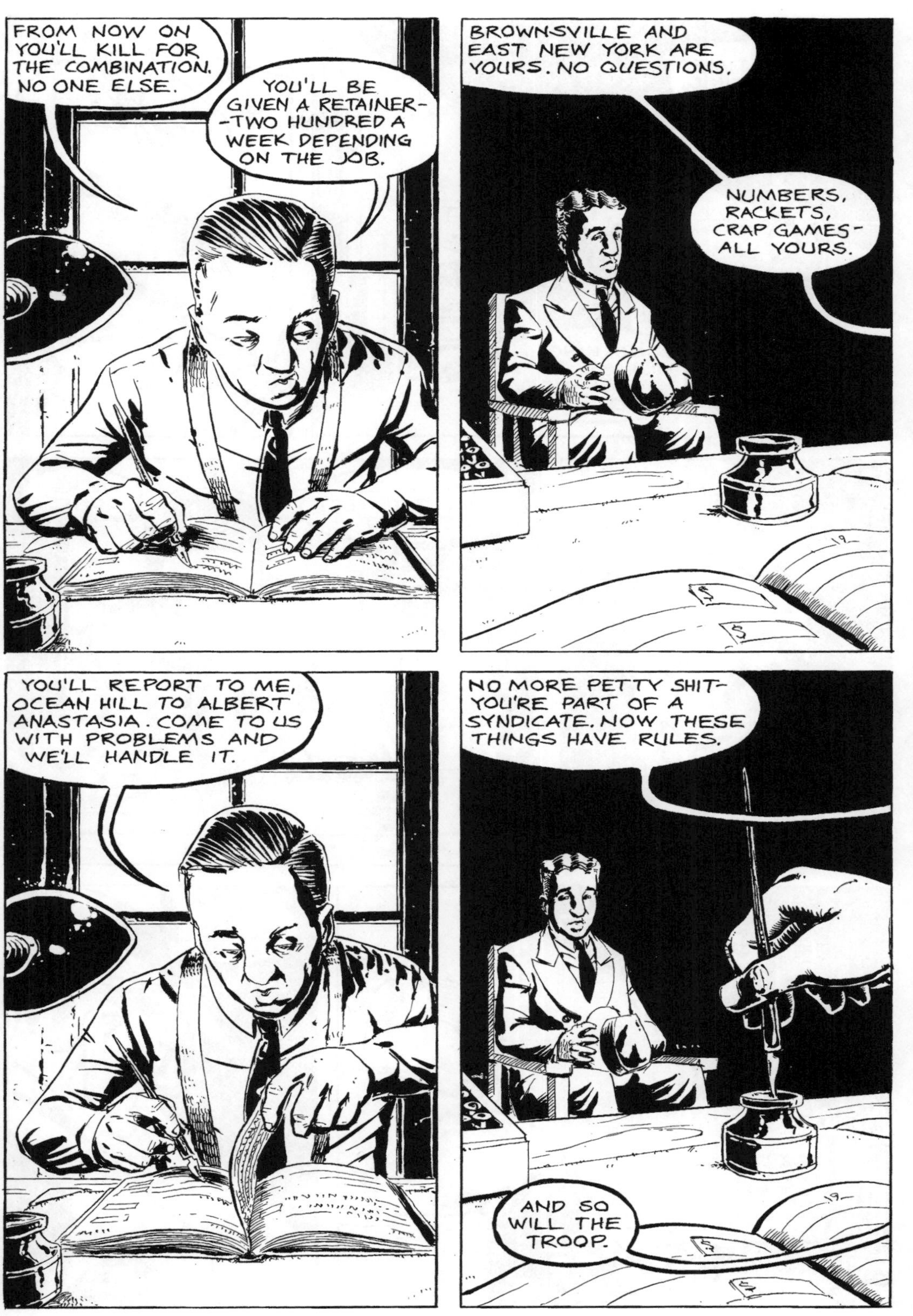
FROM NOW ON YOU'LL KILL FOR THE COMBINATION. NO ONE ELSE.
YOU'LL BE GIVEN A RETAINER--TWO HUNDRED A WEEK DEPENDING ON THE JOB.
BROWNSVILLE AND EAST NEW YORK ARE YOURS. NO QUESTIONS.
NUMBERS, RACKETS, CRAP GAMES-ALL YOURS.
YOU'LL REPORT TO ME, OCEAN HILL TO ALBERT ANASTASIA. COME TO US WITH PROBLEMS AND WE'LL HANDLE IT.
NO MORE PETTY SHIT-YOU'RE PART OF A SYNDICATE. NOW THESE THINGS HAVE RULES.
AND SO WILL THE TROOP.

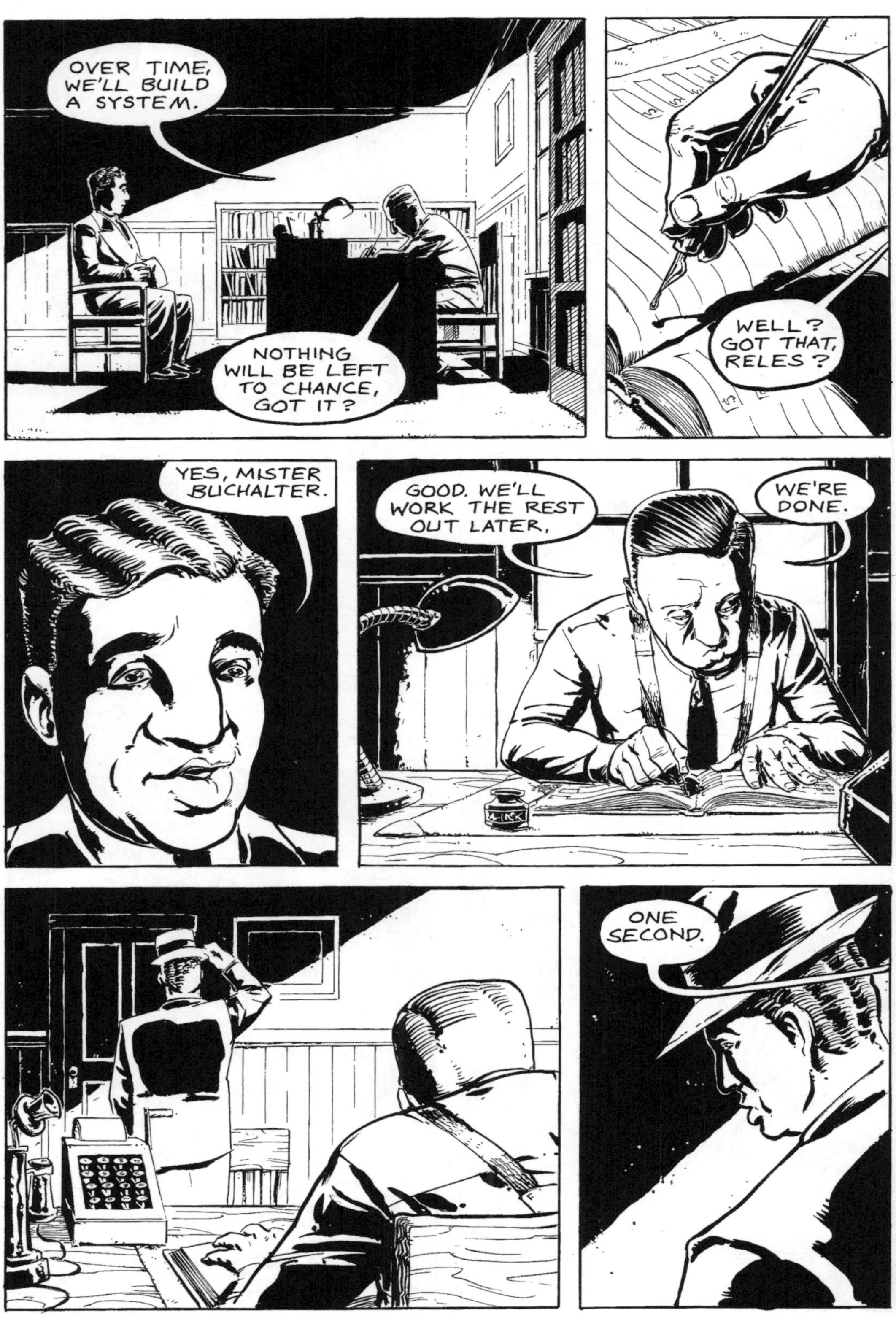
OVER TIME, WE'LL BUILD A SYSTEM.
NOTHING WILL BE LEFT TO CHANCE, GOT IT?
WELL? GOT THAT, RELES?
YES, MISTER BUCHALTER.
GOOD. WE'LL WORK THE REST OUT LATER.
WE'RE DONE.
ONE SECOND.

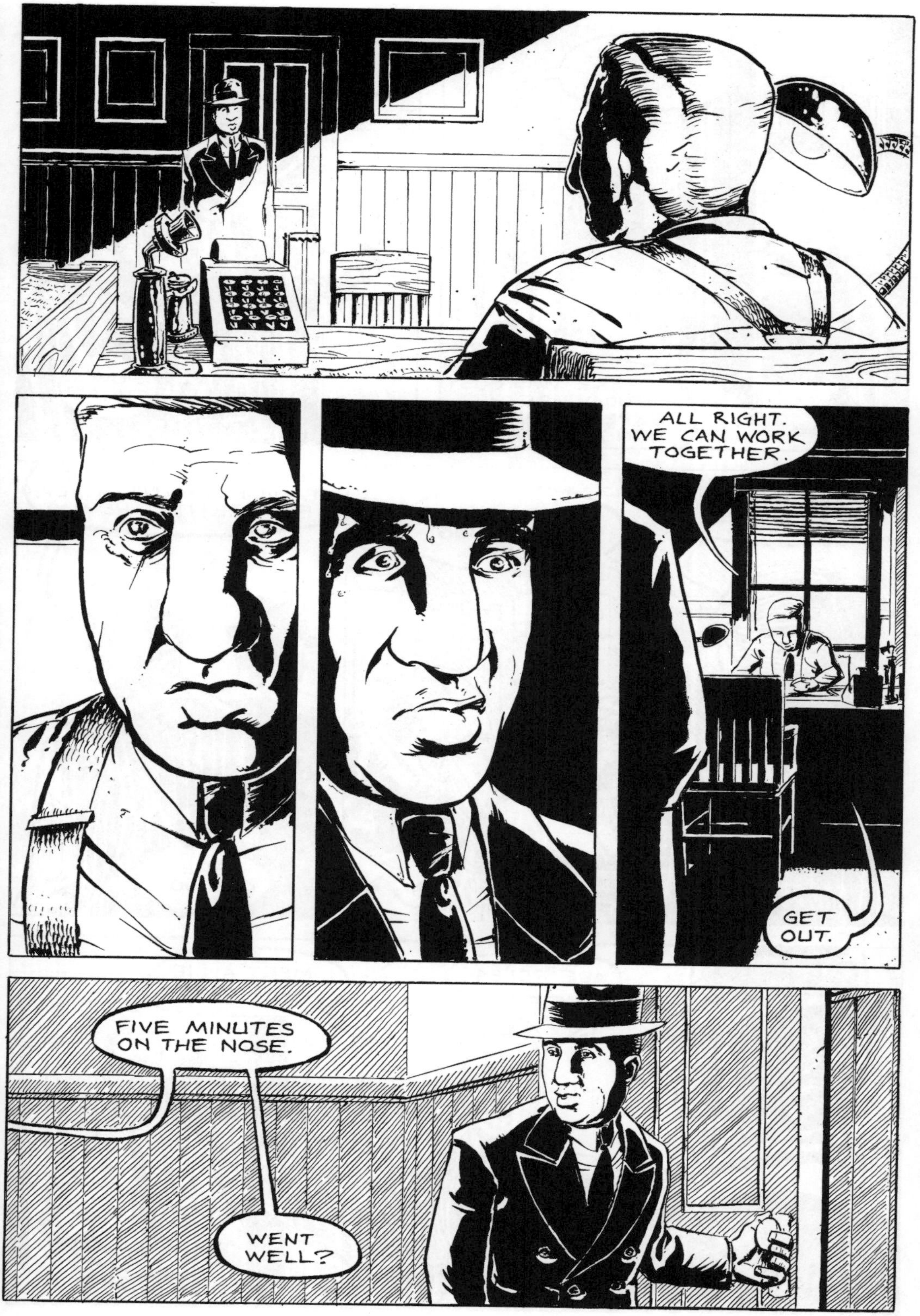
ALL RIGHT. WE CAN WORK TOGETHER.
GET OUT.
FIVE MINUTES ON THE NOSE.
WENT WELL?

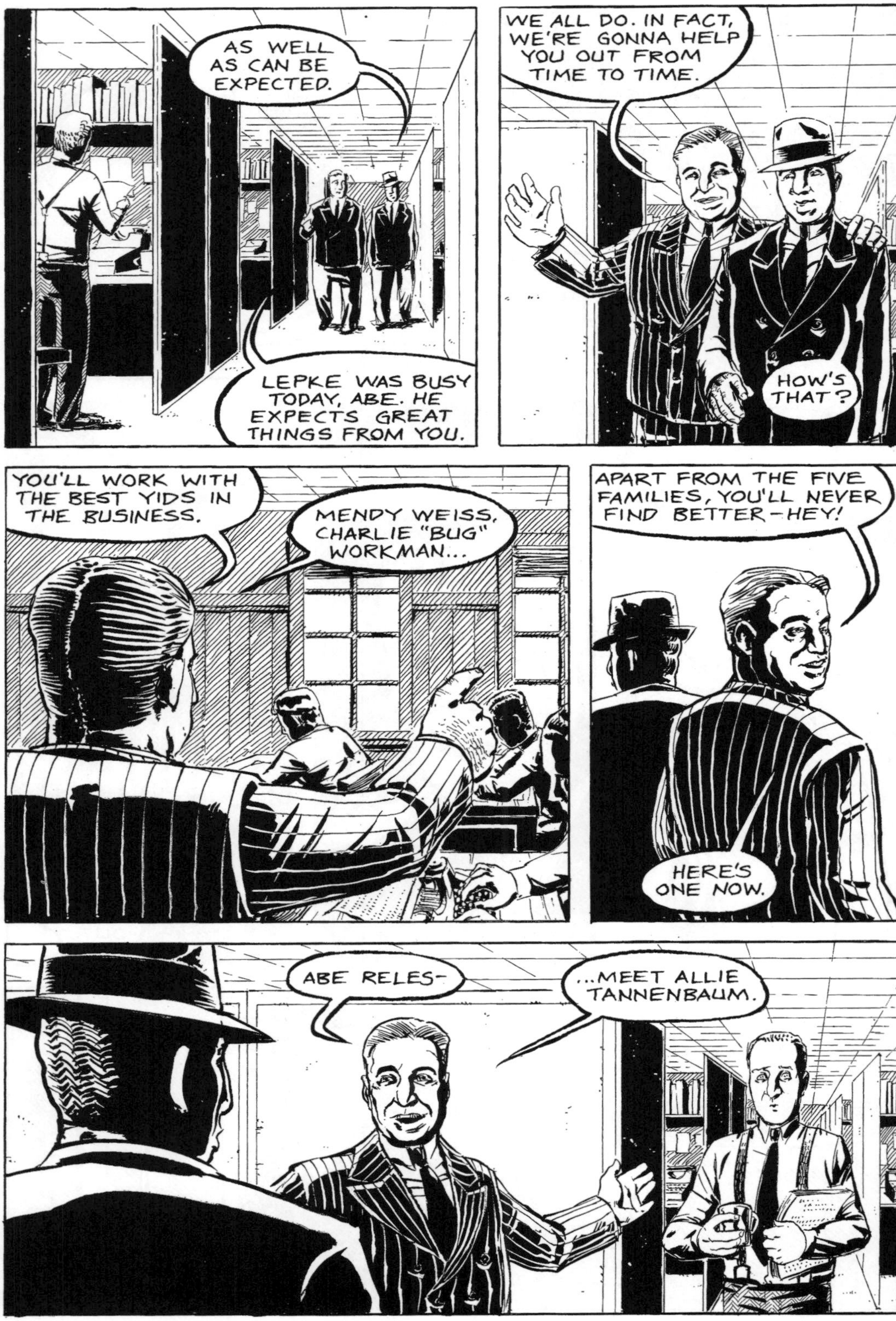
AS WELL AS CAN BE EXPECTED.
LEPKE WAS BUSY TODAY, ABE. HE EXPECTS GREAT THINGS FROM YOU.
WE ALL DO. IN FACT, WE'RE GONNA HELP YOU OUT FROM TIME TO TIME.
HOW'S THAT?
YOU'LL WORK WITH THE BEST YIDS IN THE BUSINESS.
MENDY WEISS, CHARLIE "BUG" WORKMAN...
APART FROM THE FIVE FAMILIES, YOU'LL NEVER FIND BETTER-HEY!
HERE'S ONE NOW.
ABE RELES-
...MEET ALLIE TANNENBAUM.

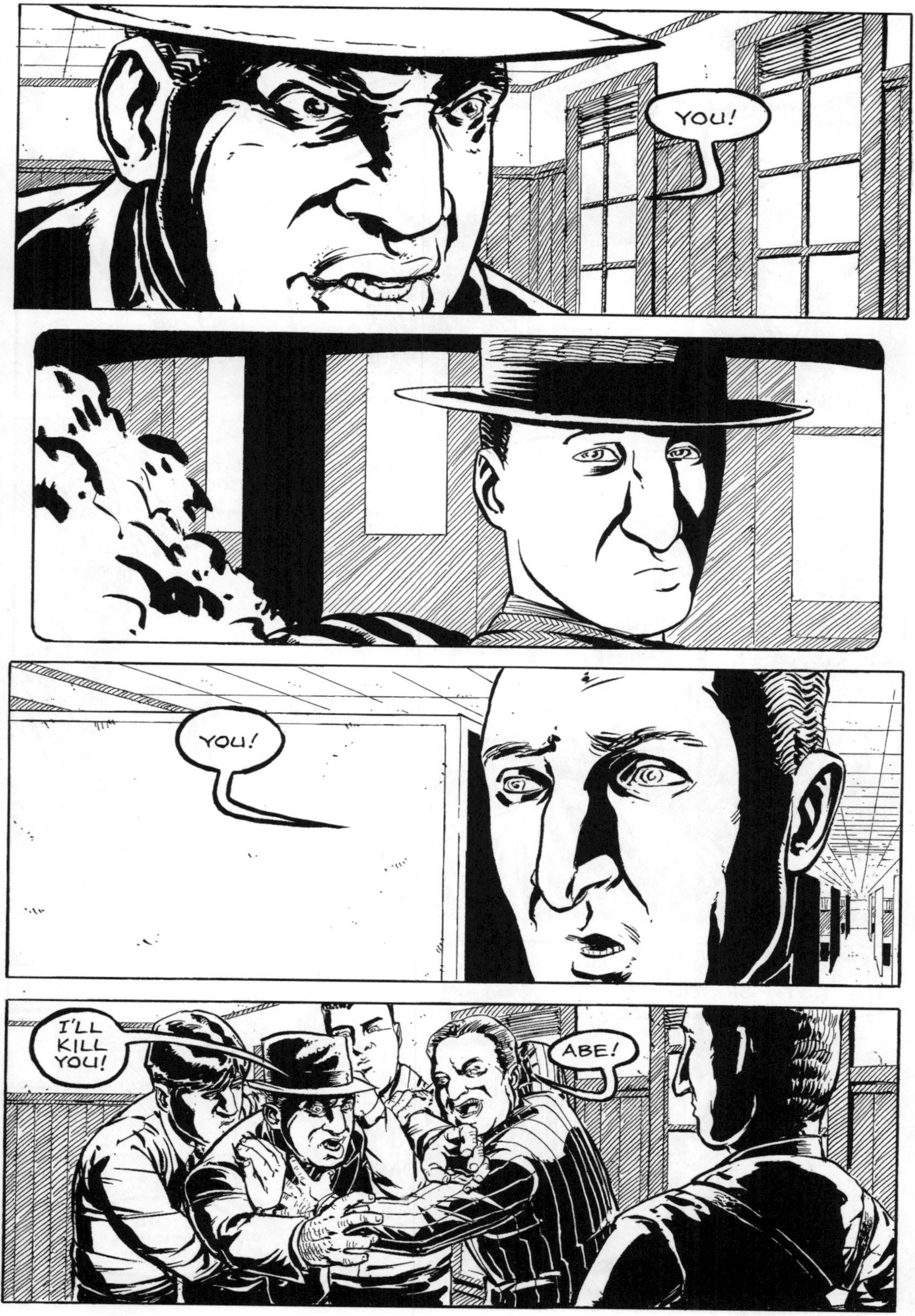
YOU!
YOU!
I'LL KILL YOU!
ABE!

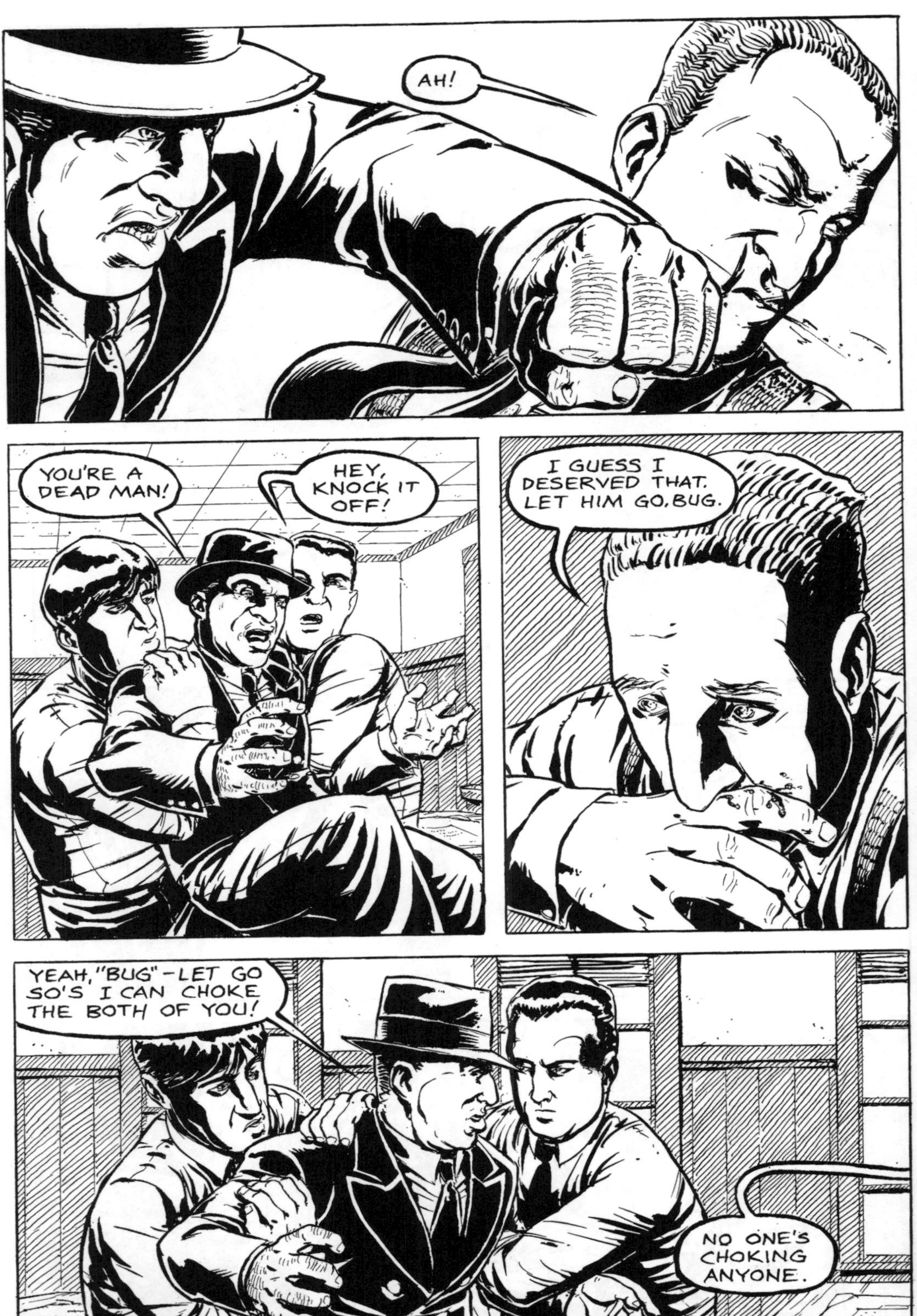
AH!
YOU'RE A DEAD MAN!
HEY, KNOCK IT OFF!
I GUESS I DESERVED THAT. LET HIM GO, BUG.
YEAH, "BUG"-LET GO SO'S I CAN CHOKE THE BOTH OF YOU!
NO ONE'S CHOKING ANYONE.

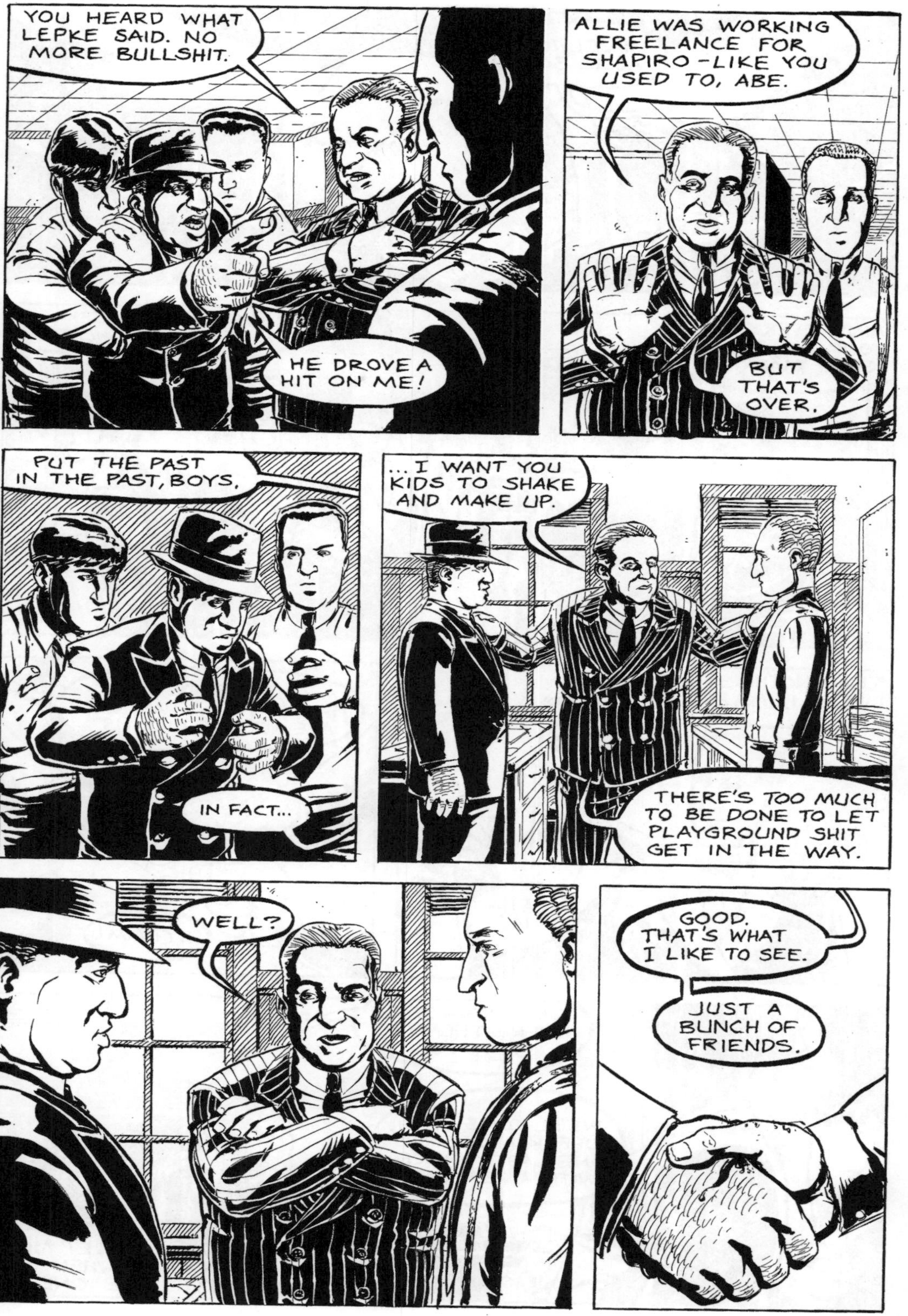
YOU HEARD WHAT LEPKE SAID. NO MORE BULLSHIT.
HE DROVE A HIT ON ME!
ALLIE WAS WORKING FREELANCE FOR SHAPIRO - LIKE YOU USED TO, ABE.
BUT THAT'S OVER.
PUT THE PAST IN THE PAST, BOYS.
IN FACT...
... I WANT YOU KIDS TO SHAKE AND MAKE UP.
THERE'S TOO MUCH TO BE DONE TO LET PLAYGROUND SHIT GET IN THE WAY.
WELL?
GOOD. THAT'S WHAT I LIKE TO SEE.
JUST A BUNCH OF FRIENDS.

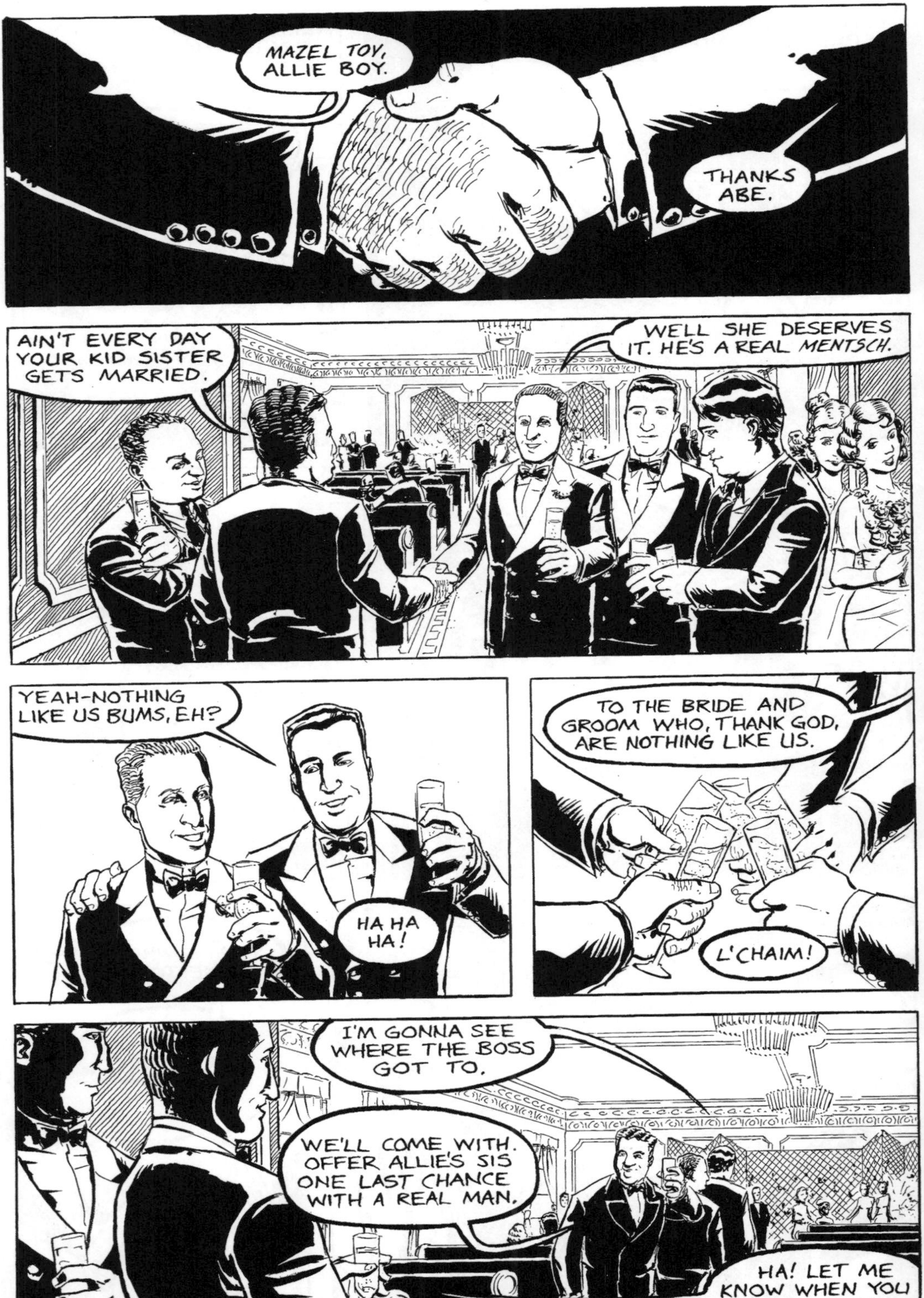
MAZEL TOV, ALLIE BOY.
THANKS ABE.
AIN'T EVERY DAY YOUR KID SISTER GETS MARRIED.
WE'LL SHE DESERVES IT. HE'S A REAL MENTSCH.
YEAH-NOTHING LIKE US BUMS, EH?
HA HA HA!
TO THE BRIDE AND GROOM WHO, THANK GOD, ARE NOTHING LIKE US.
L'CHAIM!
I'M GONNA SEE WHERE THE BOSS GOT TO.
WE'LL COME WITH. OFFER ALLIE'S SIS ONE LAST CHANCE WITH A REAL MAN.
HA! LET ME KNOW WHEN YOU SEE ONE.

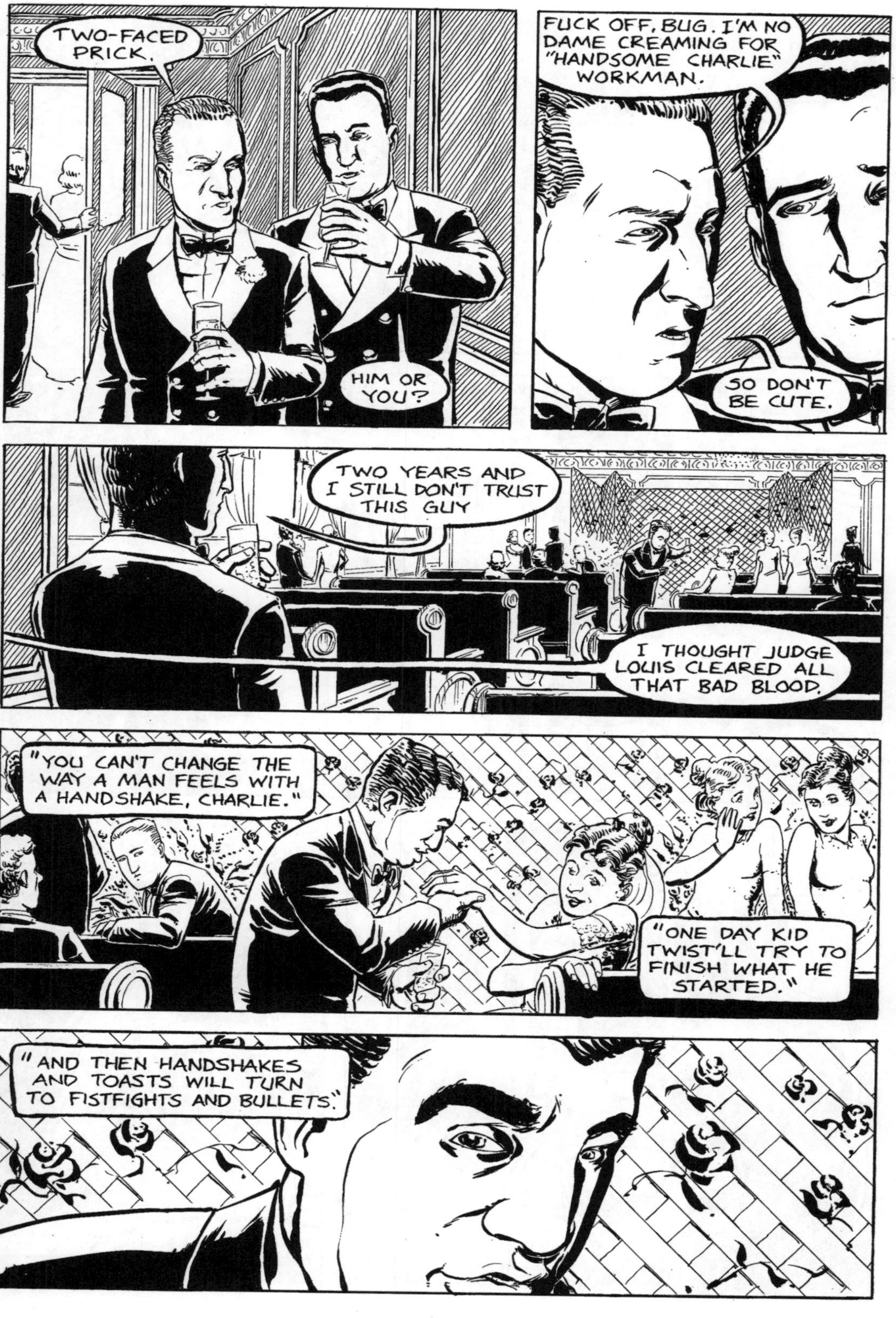
TWO-FACED PRICK.
HIM OR YOU?
FUCK OFF, BUG. I'M NO DAME CREAMING FOR "HANDSOME CHARLIE" WORKMAN.
SO DON'T BE CUTE.
TWO YEARS AND I STILL DON'T TRUST THIS GUY
I THOUGHT JUDGE LOUIS CLEARED ALL THAT BAD BLOOD.
"YOU CAN'T CHANGE THE WAY A MAN FEELS WITH A HANDSHAKE, CHARLIE."
"ONE DAY KID TWIST'LL TRY TO FINISH WHAT HE STARTED."
"AND THEN HANDSHAKES AND TOASTS WILL TURN TO FISTFIGHTS AND BULLETS."

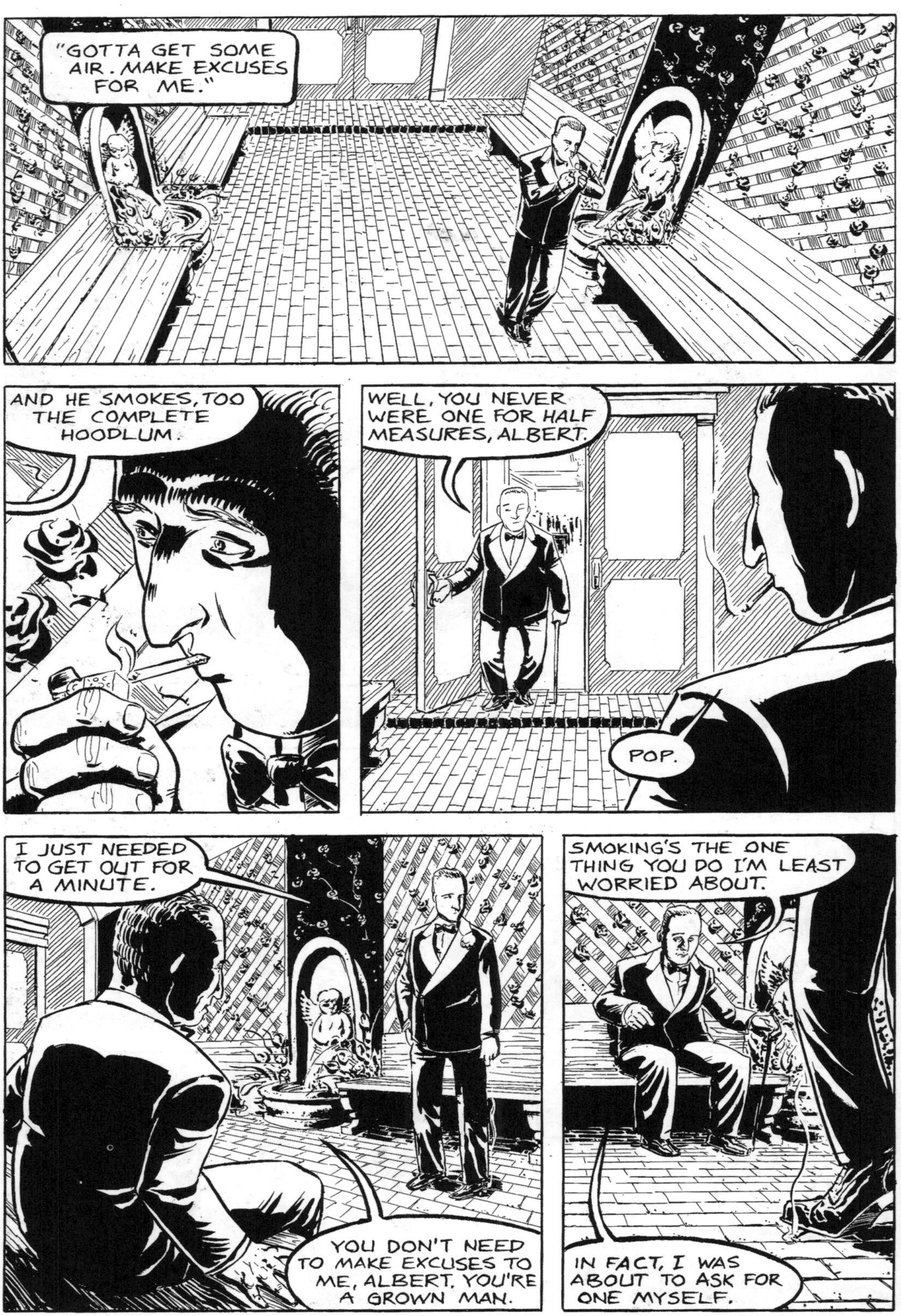
"GOTTA GET SOME AIR. MAKE EXCUSES FOR ME."
AND HE SMOKES, TOO THE COMPLETE HOODLUM.
WELL, YOU NEVER WERE ONE FOR HALF MEASURES, ALBERT.
POP.
I JUST NEEDED TO GET OUT FOR A MINUTE.
YOU DON'T NEED TO MAKE EXCUSES TO ME, ALBERT. YOU'RE A GROWN MAN.
SMOKING'S THE ONE THING YOU DO I'M LEAST WORRIED ABOUT.
IN FACT, I WAS ABOUT TO ASK FOR ONE MYSELF.

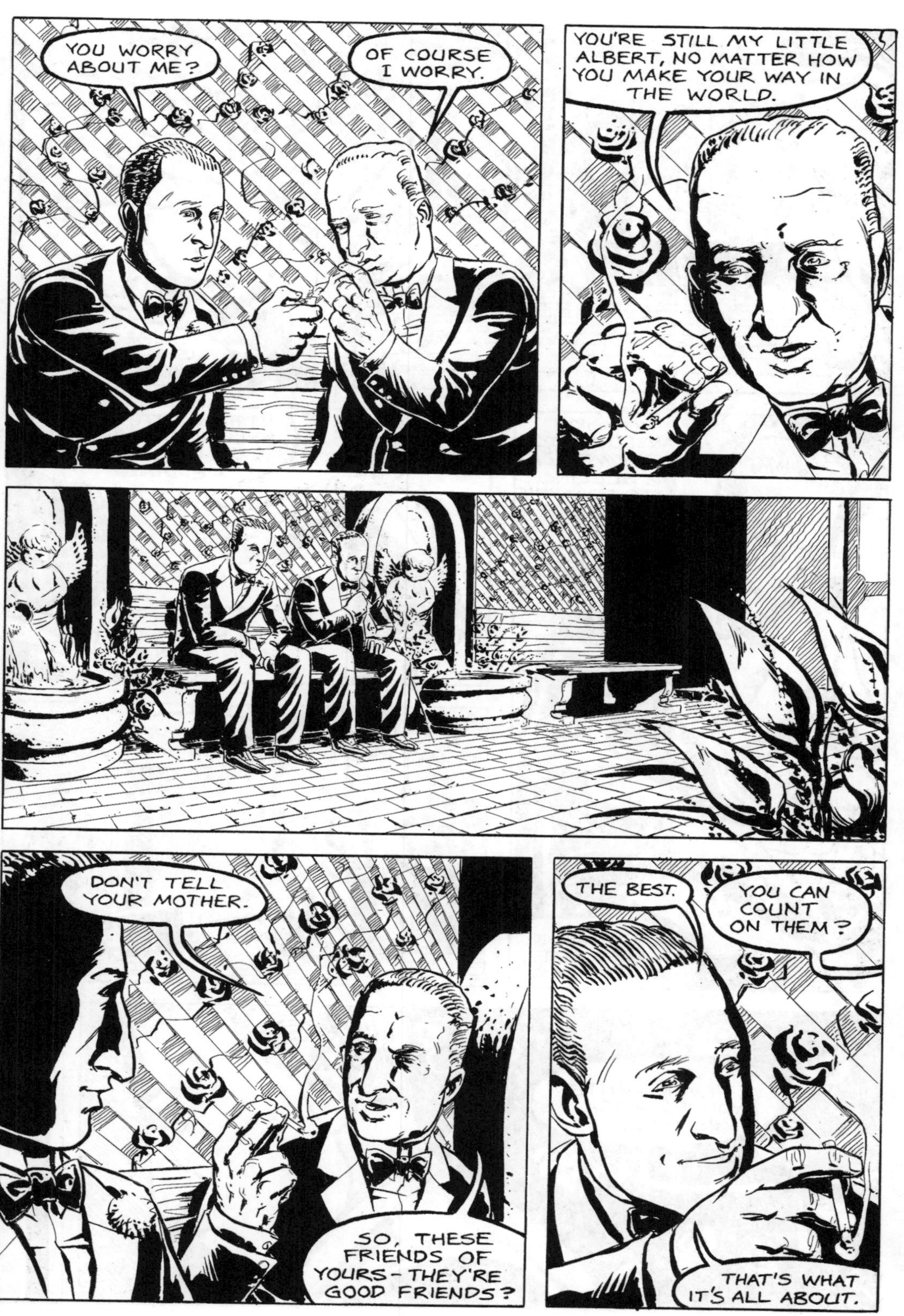
YOU WORRY ABOUT ME?
OF COURSE I WORRY.
YOU'RE STILL MY LITTLE ALBERT, NO MATTER HOW YOU MAKE YOUR WAY IN THE WORLD.
DON'T TELL YOUR MOTHER.
SO, THESE FRIENDS OF YOURS- THEY'RE GOOD FRIENDS?
THE BEST.
YOU CAN COUNT ON THEM?
THAT'S WHAT IT'S ALL ABOUT.

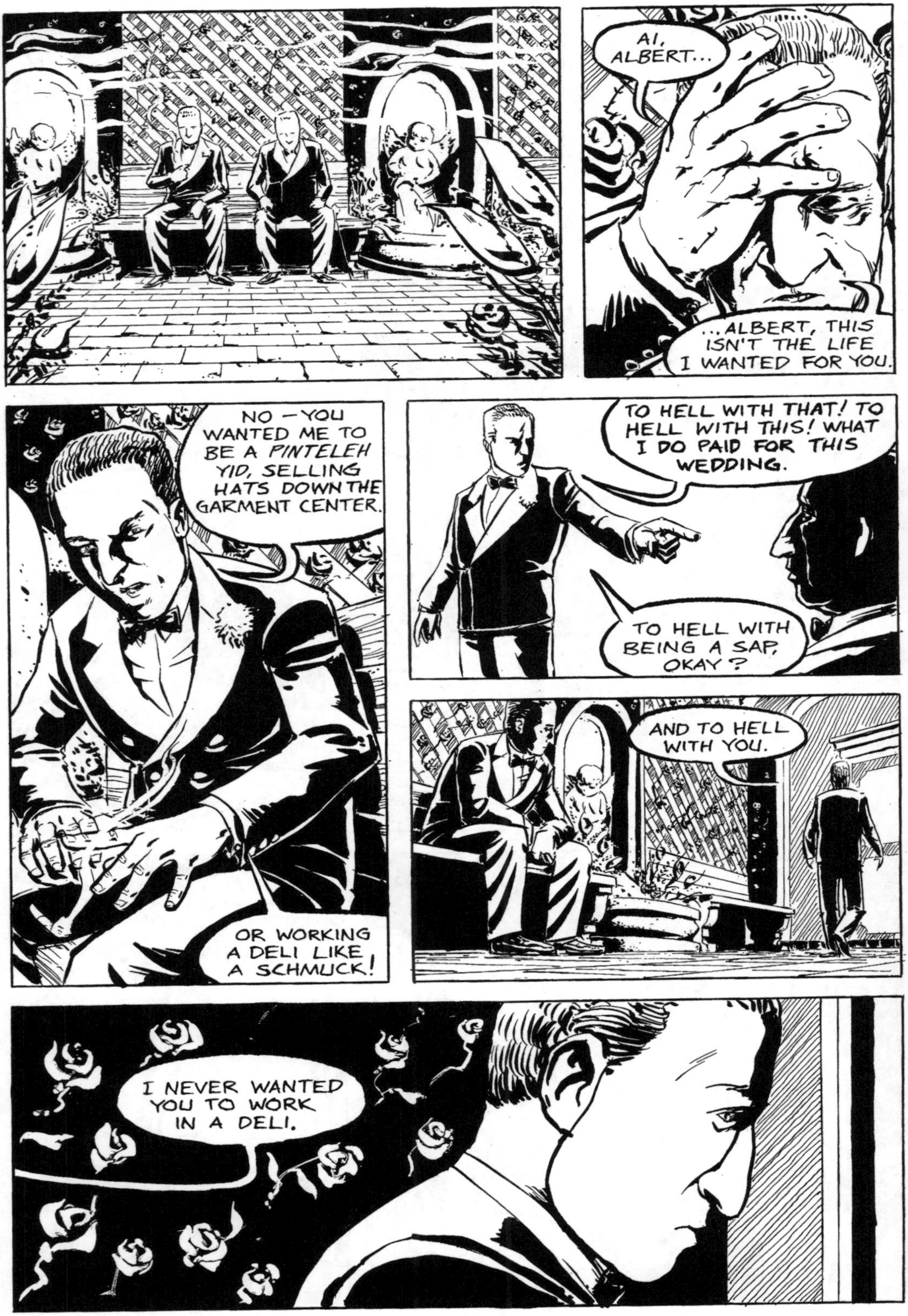
AI, ALBERT...
...ALBERT, THIS ISN'T THE LIFE I WANTED FOR YOU.
NO —YOU WANTED ME TO BE A *PINTELEH YID*, SELLING HATS DOWN THE GARMENT CENTER.
OR WORKING A DELI LIKE A SCHMUCK!
TO HELL WITH THAT! TO HELL WITH THIS! WHAT I DO PAID FOR THIS WEDDING.
TO HELL WITH BEING A SAP, OKAY?
AND TO HELL WITH YOU.
I NEVER WANTED YOU TO WORK IN A DELI.

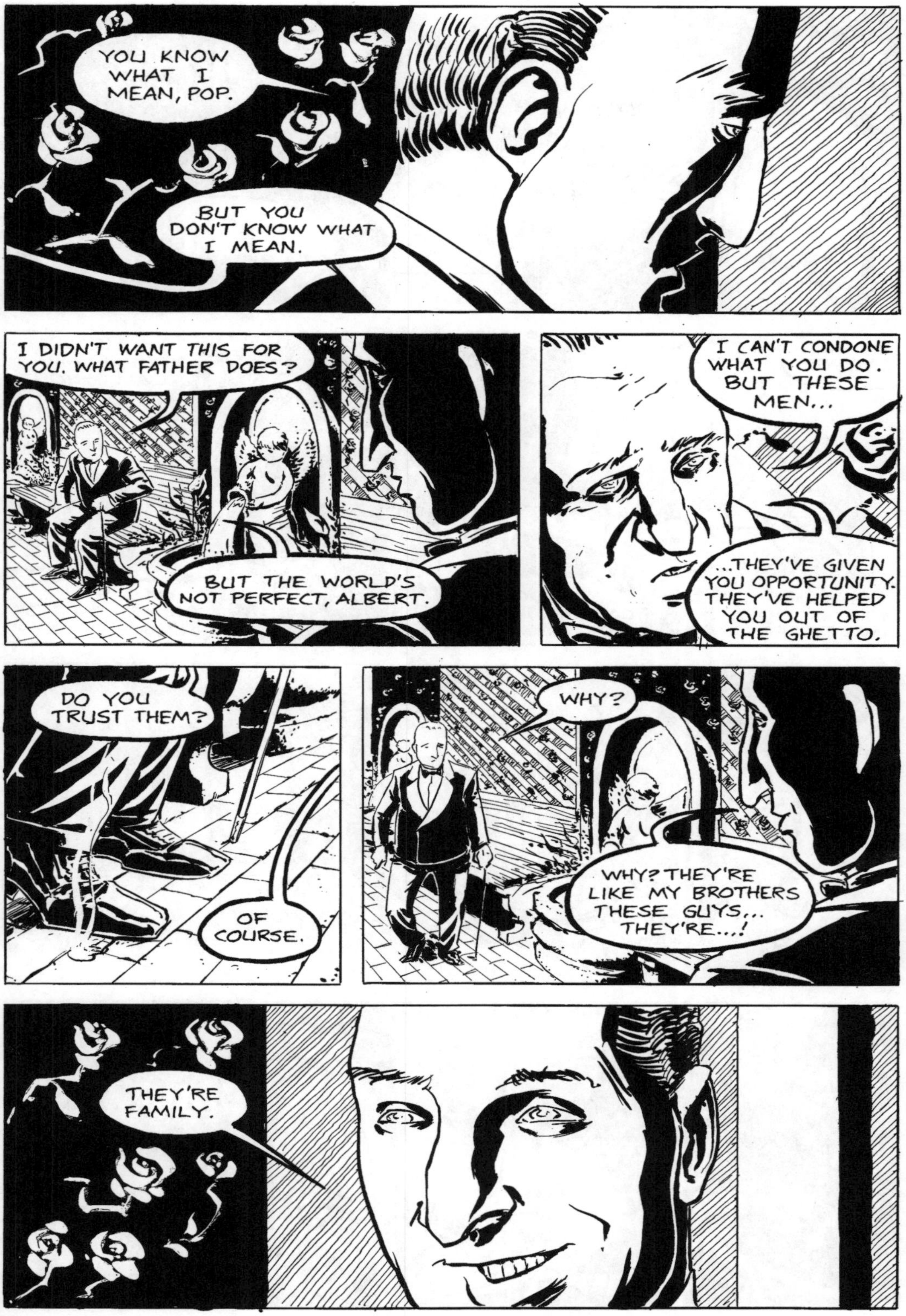
YOU KNOW WHAT I MEAN, POP.
BUT YOU DON'T KNOW WHAT I MEAN.
I DIDN'T WANT THIS FOR YOU. WHAT FATHER DOES?
BUT THE WORLD'S NOT PERFECT, ALBERT.
I CAN'T CONDONE WHAT YOU DO. BUT THESE MEN...
...THEY'VE GIVEN YOU OPPORTUNITY. THEY'VE HELPED YOU OUT OF THE GHETTO.
DO YOU TRUST THEM?
OF COURSE.
WHY?
WHY? THEY'RE LIKE MY BROTHERS THESE GUYS... THEY'RE...!
THEY'RE FAMILY.

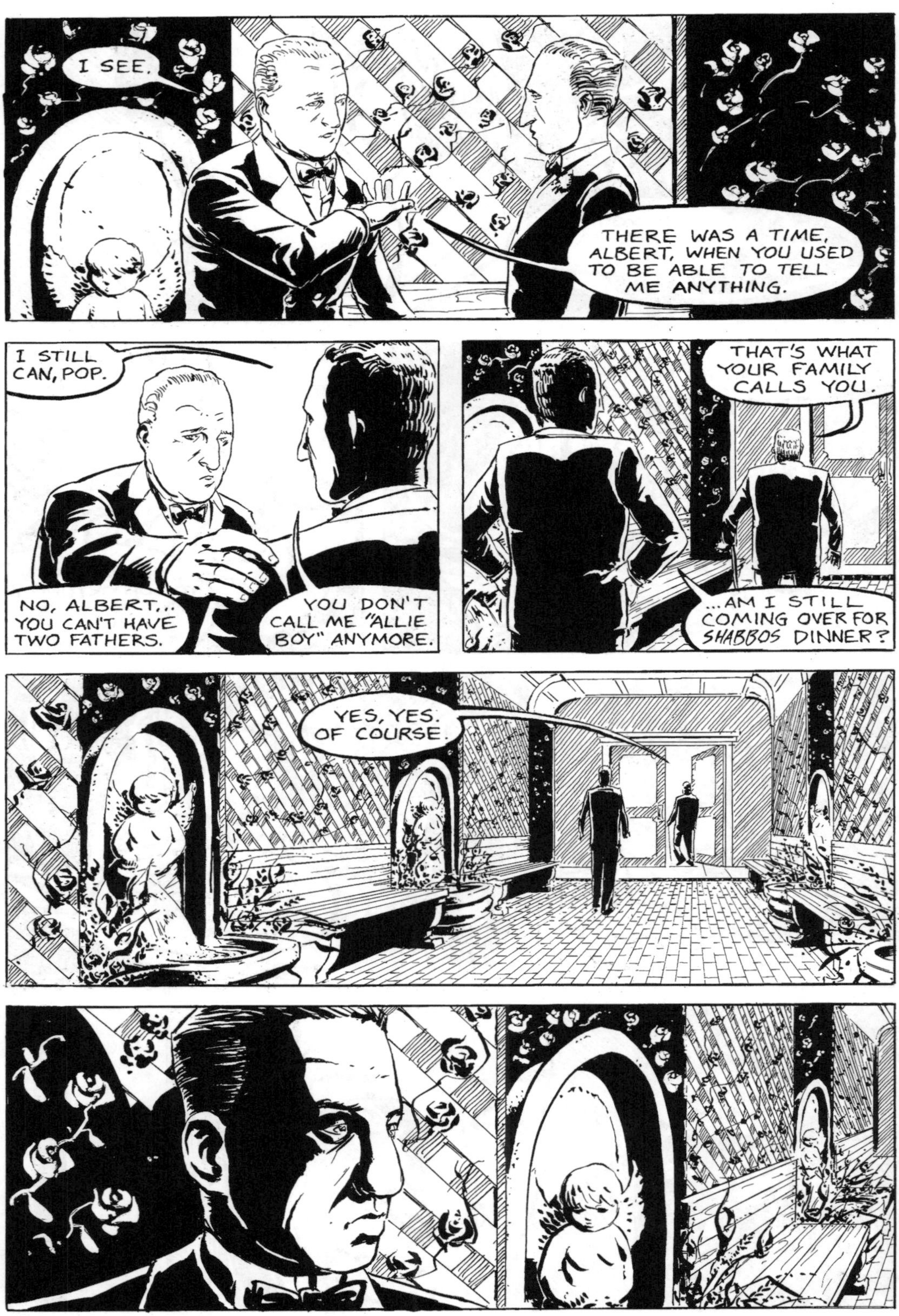
I SEE.
THERE WAS A TIME, ALBERT, WHEN YOU USED TO BE ABLE TO TELL ME ANYTHING.
I STILL CAN, POP.
NO, ALBERT... YOU CAN'T HAVE TWO FATHERS.
YOU DON'T CALL ME "ALLIE BOY" ANYMORE.
THAT'S WHAT YOUR FAMILY CALLS YOU.
...AM I STILL COMING OVER FOR SHABBOS DINNER?
YES, YES. OF COURSE.

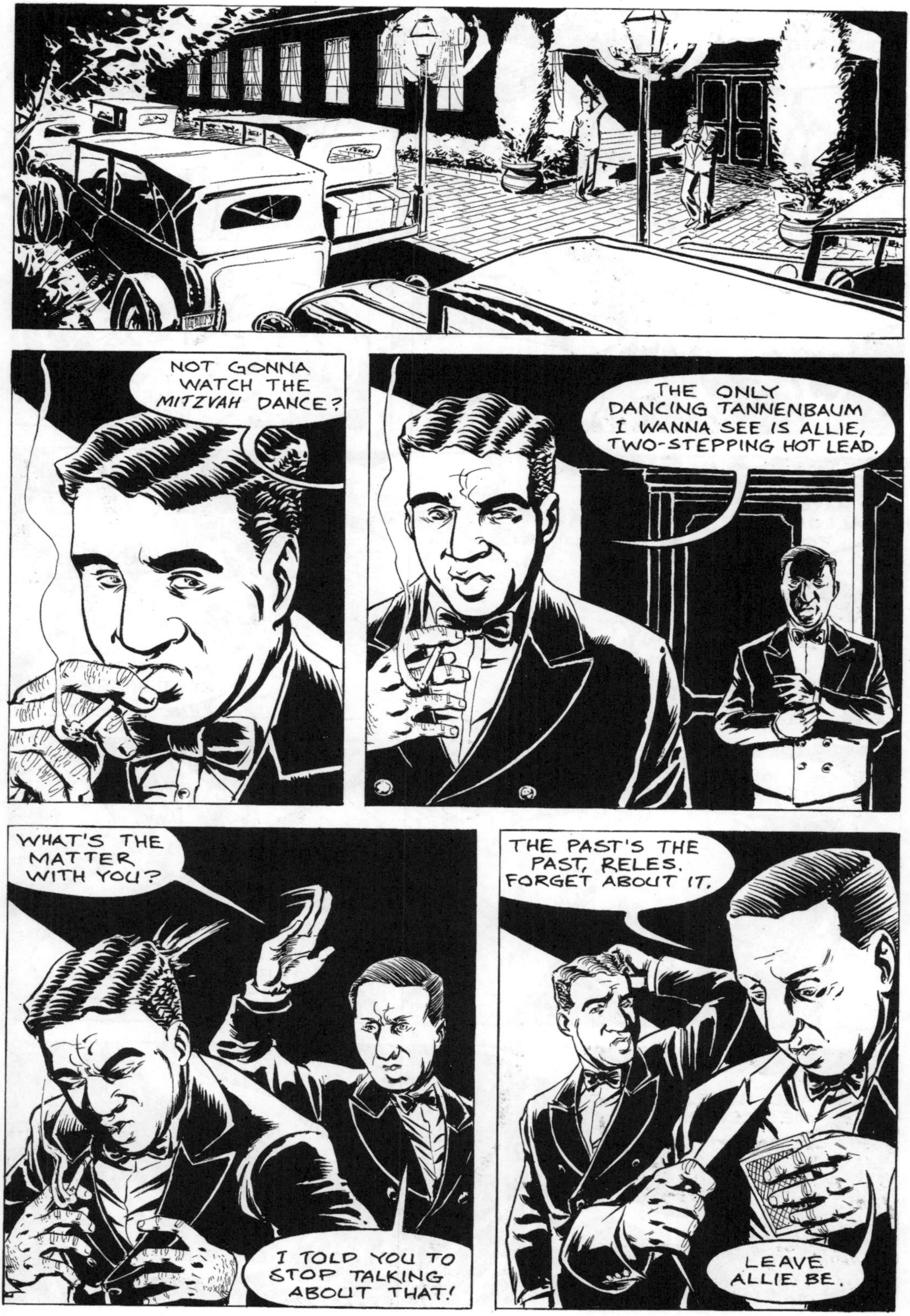
NOT GONNA WATCH THE *MITZVAH* DANCE?
THE ONLY DANCING TANNENBAUM I WANNA SEE IS ALLIE, TWO-STEPPING HOT LEAD.
WHAT'S THE MATTER WITH YOU?
I TOLD YOU TO STOP TALKING ABOUT THAT!
THE PAST'S THE PAST, RELES. FORGET ABOUT IT.
LEAVE ALLIE BE.

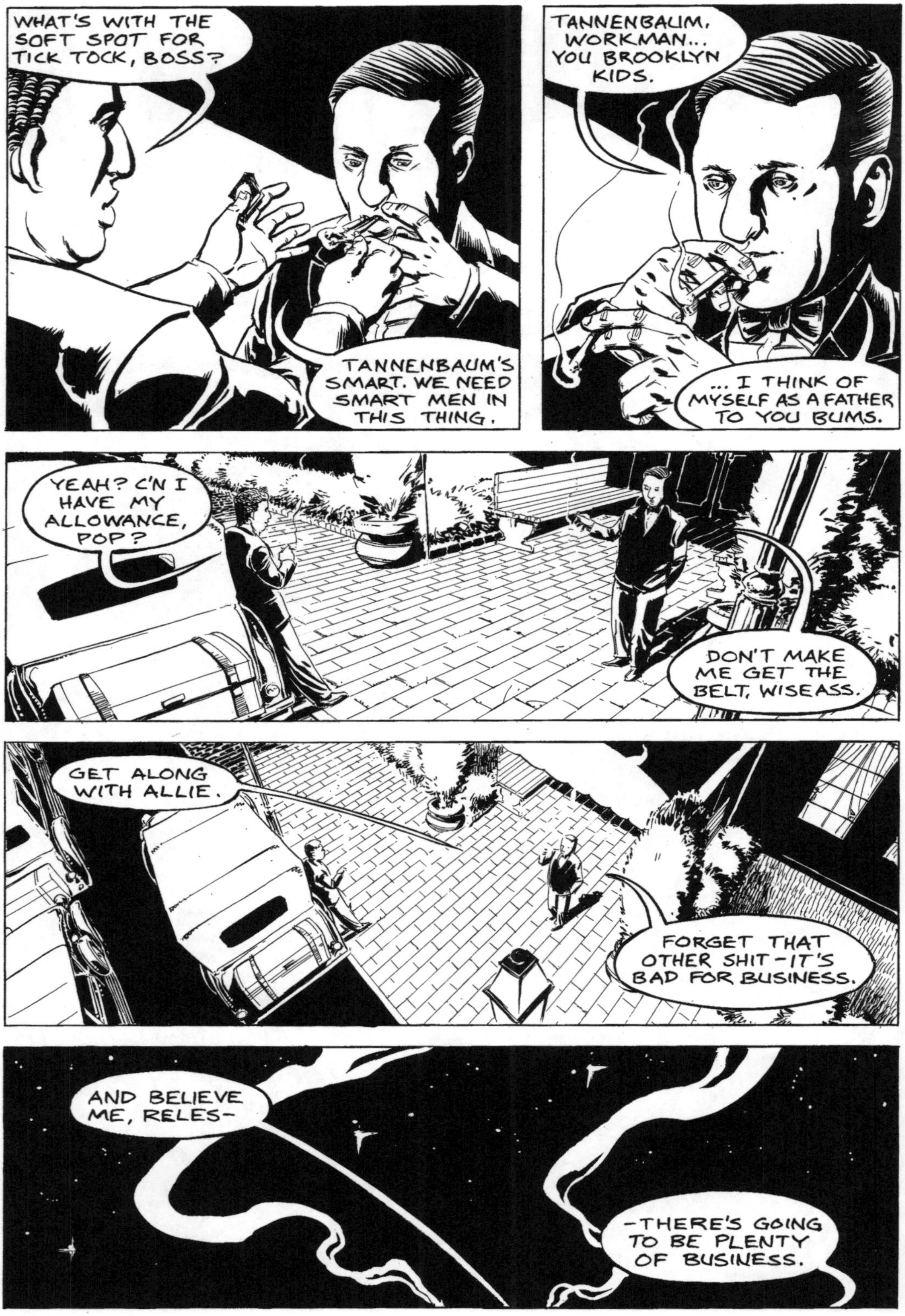
WHAT'S WITH THE SOFT SPOT FOR TICK TOCK, BOSS?
TANNENBAUM'S SMART. WE NEED SMART MEN IN THIS THING.
TANNENBAUM, WORKMAN... YOU BROOKLYN KIDS.
... I THINK OF MYSELF AS A FATHER TO YOU BUMS.
YEAH? C'N I HAVE MY ALLOWANCE, POP?
DON'T MAKE ME GET THE BELT, WISEASS.
GET ALONG WITH ALLIE.
FORGET THAT OTHER SHIT - IT'S BAD FOR BUSINESS.
AND BELIEVE ME, RELES-
-THERE'S GOING TO BE PLENTY OF BUSINESS.

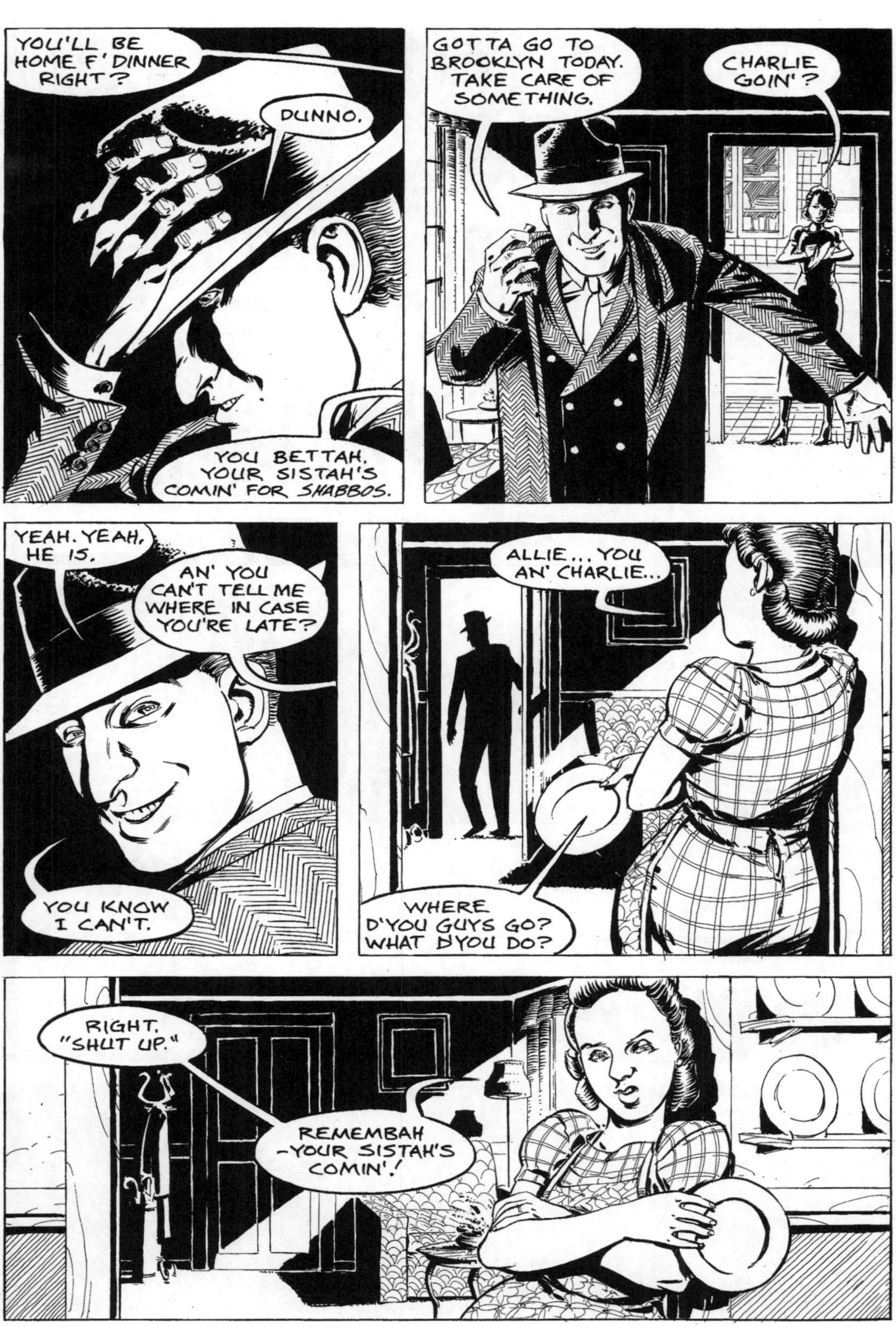
YOU'LL BE HOME F' DINNER RIGHT?
DUNNO.
YOU BETTAH. YOUR SISTAH'S COMIN' FOR SHABBOS.
GOTTA GO TO BROOKLYN TODAY. TAKE CARE OF SOMETHING.
CHARLIE GOIN'?
YEAH. YEAH, HE IS.
AN' YOU CAN'T TELL ME WHERE IN CASE YOU'RE LATE?
YOU KNOW I CAN'T.
ALLIE... YOU AN' CHARLIE...
WHERE D'YOU GUYS GO? WHAT D'YOU DO?
RIGHT. "SHUT UP."
REMEMBAH -YOUR SISTAH'S COMIN'!

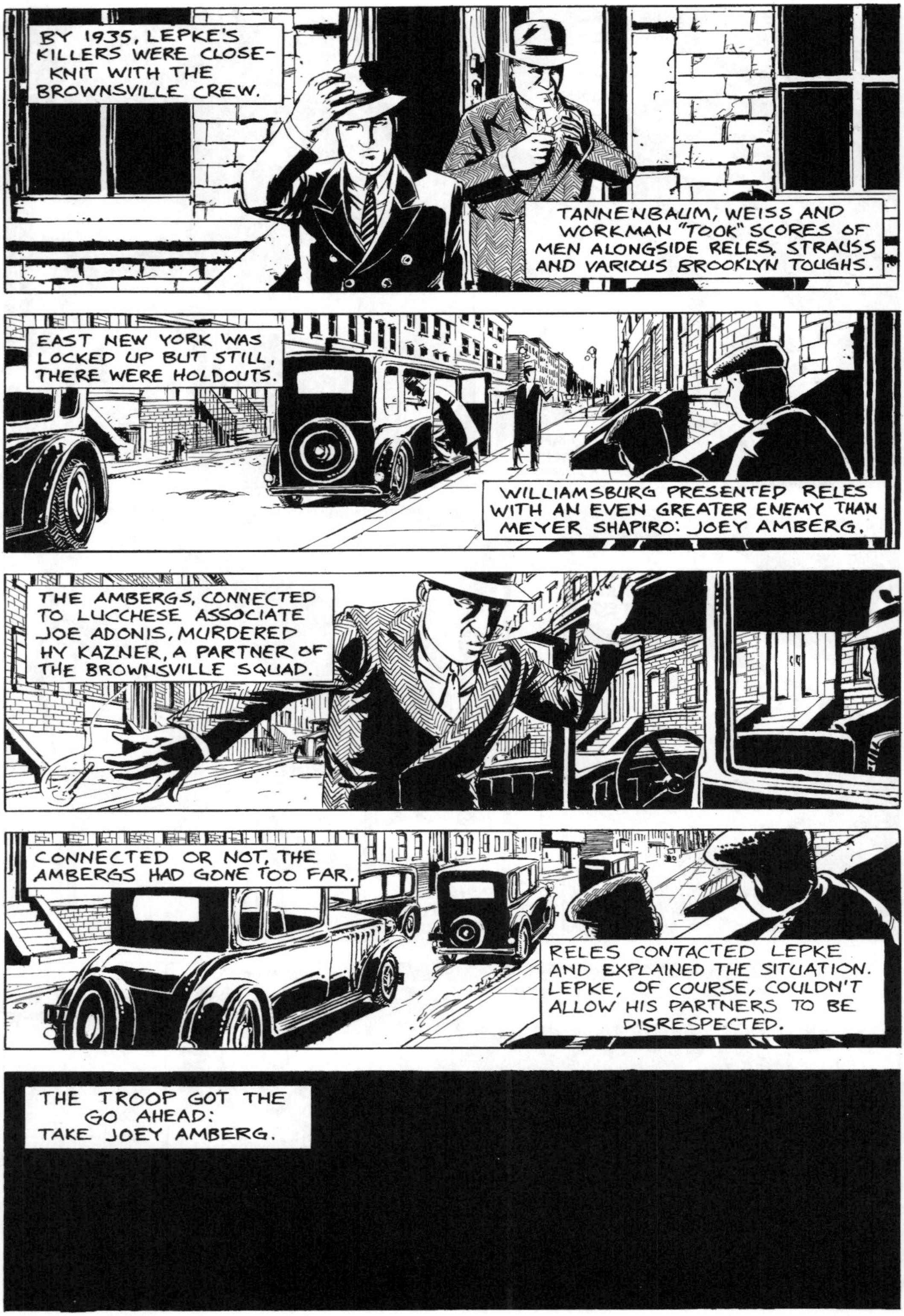
BY 1935, LEPKE'S KILLERS WERE CLOSE-KNIT WITH THE BROWNSVILLE CREW.
TANNENBAUM, WEISS AND WORKMAN "TOOK" SCORES OF MEN ALONGSIDE RELES, STRAUSS AND VARIOUS BROOKLYN TOUGHS.
EAST NEW YORK WAS LOCKED UP BUT STILL, THERE WERE HOLDOUTS.
WILLIAMSBURG PRESENTED RELES WITH AN EVEN GREATER ENEMY THAN MEYER SHAPIRO: JOEY AMBERG.
THE AMBERGS, CONNECTED TO LUCCHESE ASSOCIATE JOE ADONIS, MURDERED HY KAZNER, A PARTNER OF THE BROWNSVILLE SQUAD.
CONNECTED OR NOT, THE AMBERGS HAD GONE TOO FAR.
RELES CONTACTED LEPKE AND EXPLAINED THE SITUATION. LEPKE, OF COURSE, COULDN'T ALLOW HIS PARTNERS TO BE DISRESPECTED.
THE TROOP GOT THE GO AHEAD: TAKE JOEY AMBERG.

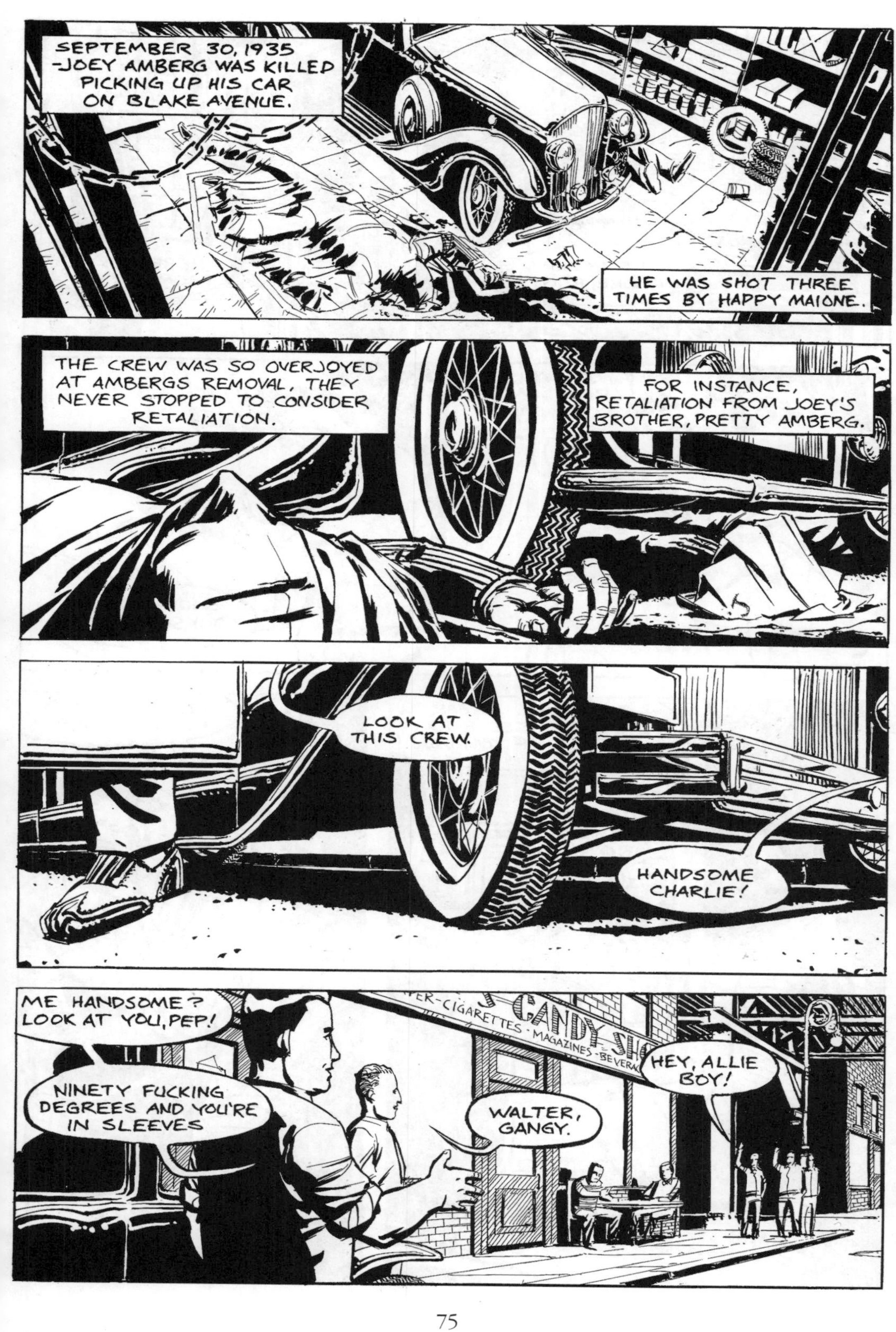
SEPTEMBER 30, 1935 -JOEY AMBERG WAS KILLED PICKING UP HIS CAR ON BLAKE AVENUE.
HE WAS SHOT THREE TIMES BY HAPPY MAIONE.
THE CREW WAS SO OVERJOYED AT AMBERGS REMOVAL, THEY NEVER STOPPED TO CONSIDER RETALIATION.
FOR INSTANCE, RETALIATION FROM JOEY'S BROTHER, PRETTY AMBERG.
LOOK AT THIS CREW.
HANDSOME CHARLIE!
ME HANDSOME? LOOK AT YOU, PEP!
NINETY FUCKING DEGREES AND YOU'RE IN SLEEVES
WALTER, GANGY.
HEY, ALLIE BOY!

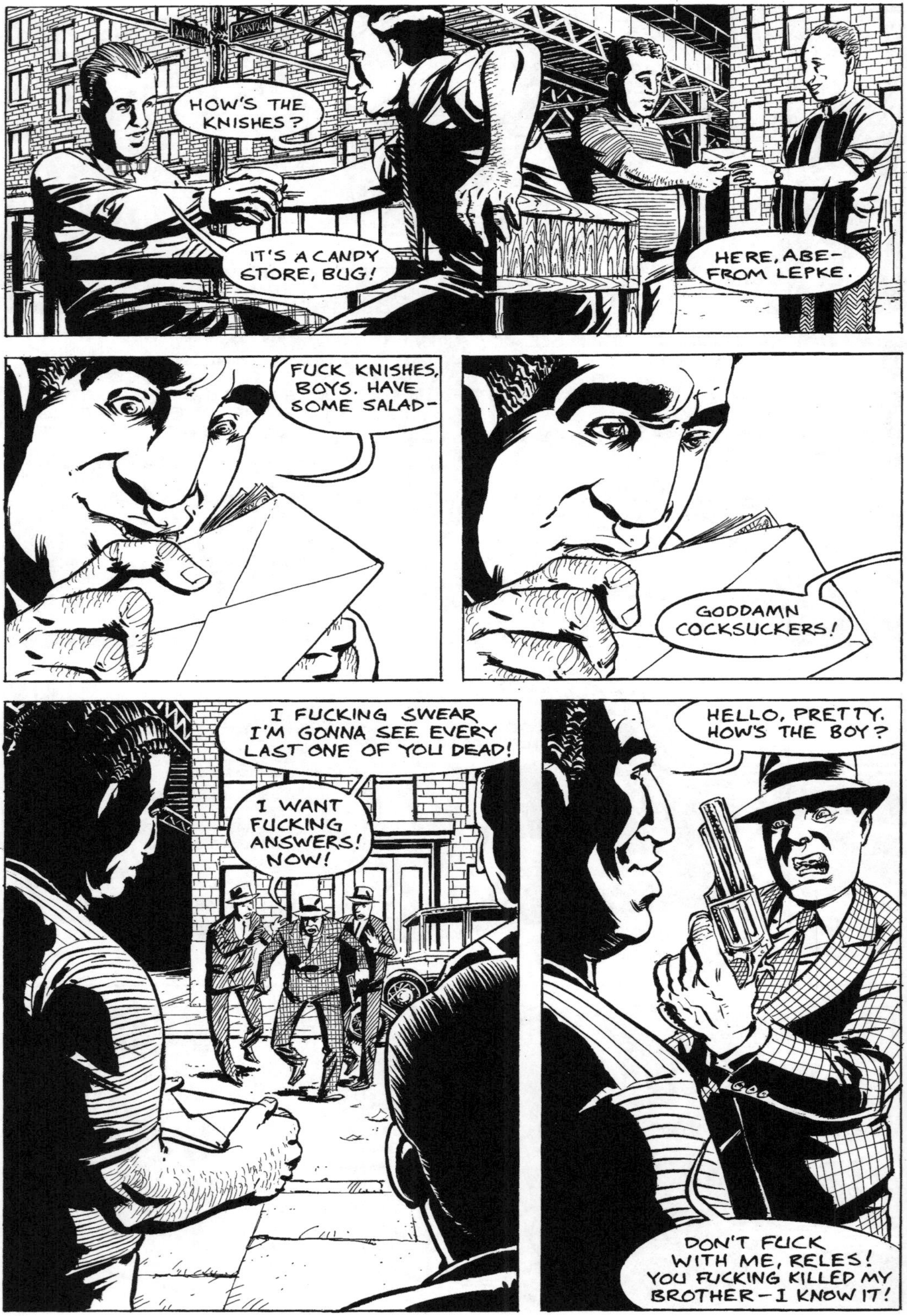
HOW'S THE KNISHES?
IT'S A CANDY STORE, BUG!
HERE, ABE- FROM LEPKE.
FUCK KNISHES, BOYS. HAVE SOME SALAD-
GODDAMN COCKSUCKERS!
I FUCKING SWEAR I'M GONNA SEE EVERY LAST ONE OF YOU DEAD!
I WANT FUCKING ANSWERS! NOW!
HELLO, PRETTY. HOW'S THE BOY?
DON'T FUCK WITH ME, RELES! YOU FUCKING KILLED MY BROTHER - I KNOW IT!

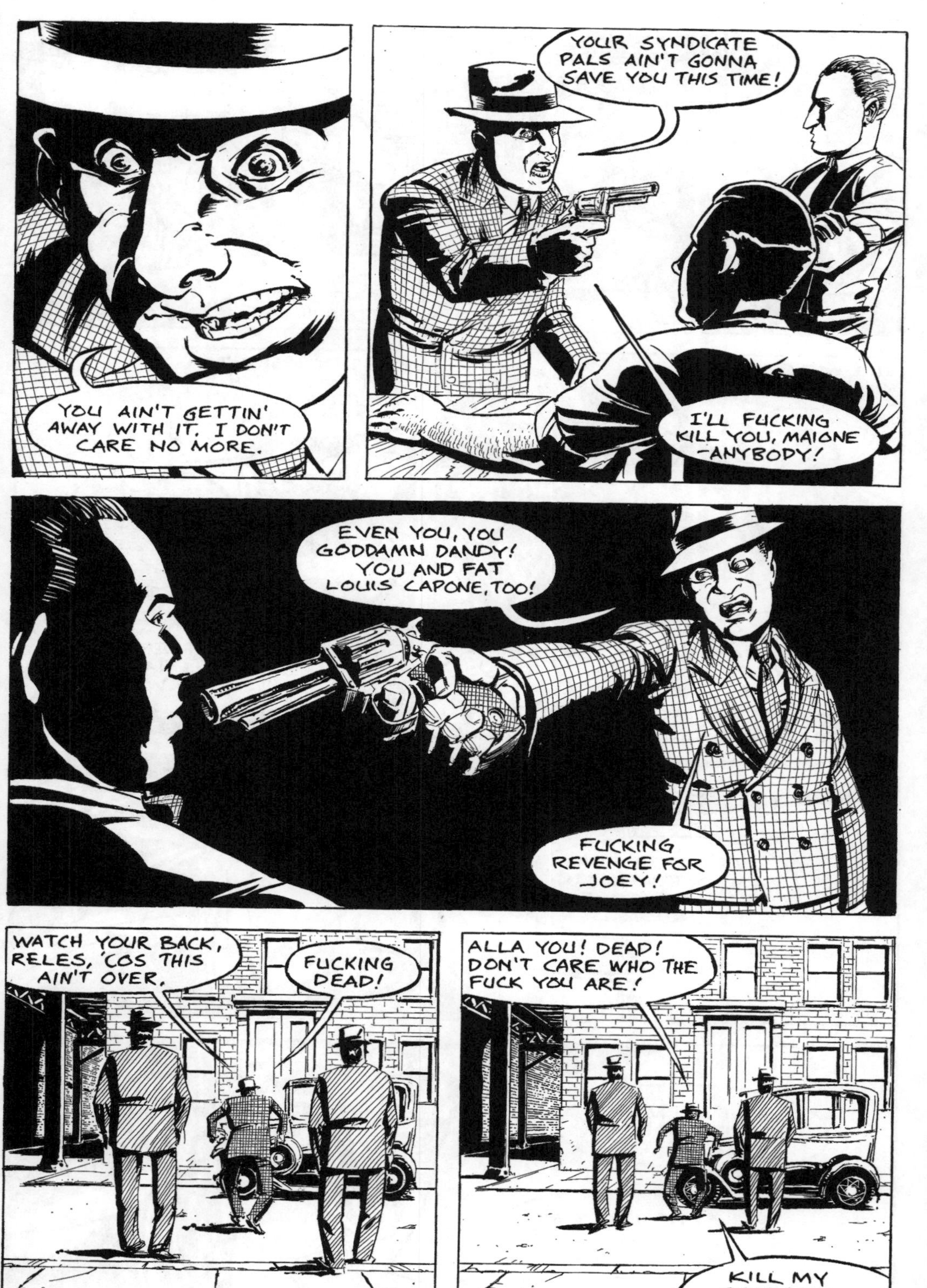
YOU AIN'T GETTIN' AWAY WITH IT. I DON'T CARE NO MORE.
YOUR SYNDICATE PALS AIN'T GONNA SAVE YOU THIS TIME!
I'LL FUCKING KILL YOU, MAIONE -ANYBODY!
EVEN YOU, YOU GODDAMN DANDY! YOU AND FAT LOUIS CAPONE, TOO!
FUCKING REVENGE FOR JOEY!
WATCH YOUR BACK, RELES, 'COS THIS AIN'T OVER.
FUCKING DEAD!
ALLA YOU! DEAD! DON'T CARE WHO THE FUCK YOU ARE!
KILL MY GODDAMN BROTHER?! DEAD!

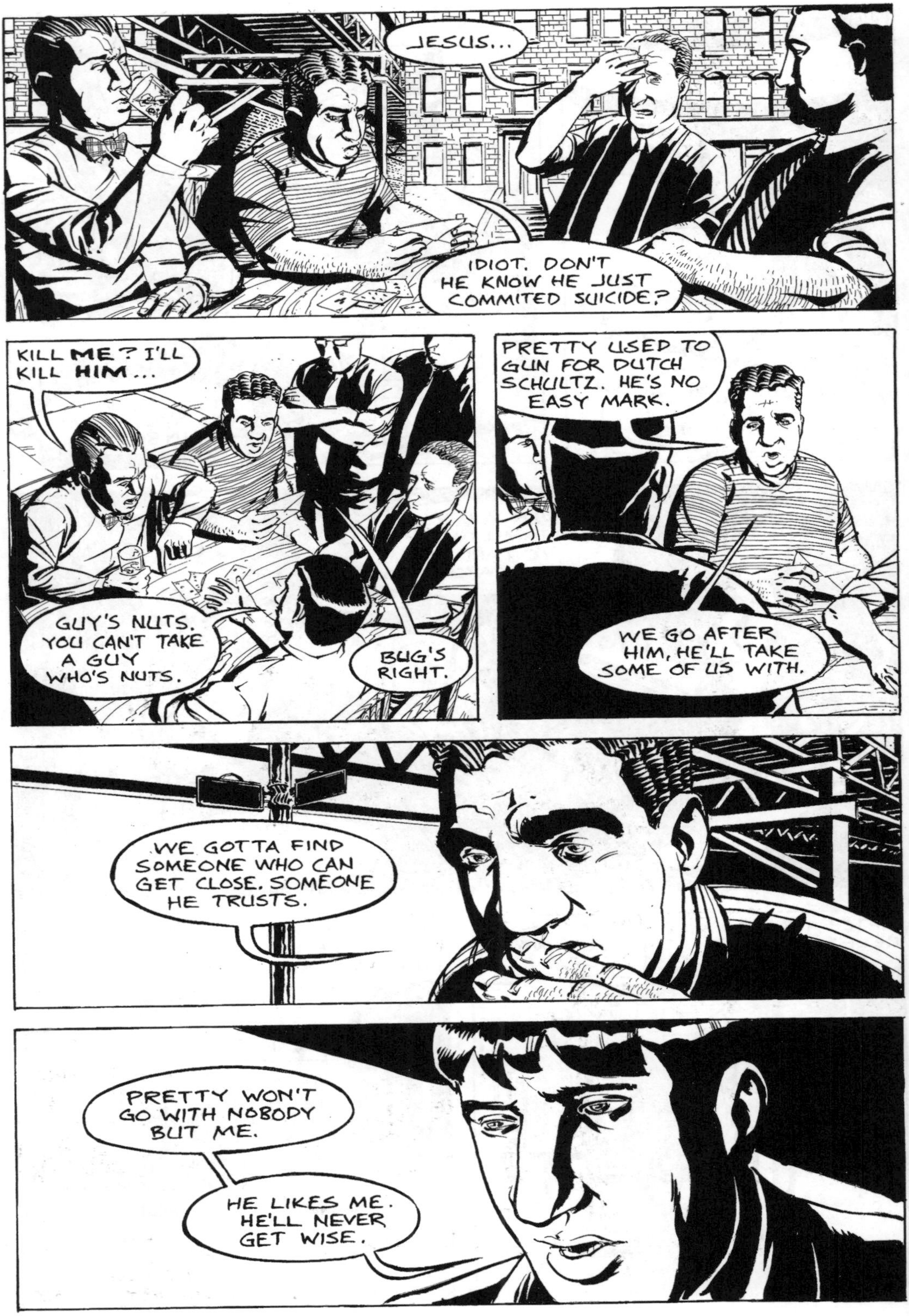
JESUS...
IDIOT. DON'T HE KNOW HE JUST COMMITED SUICIDE?
KILL ME? I'LL KILL HIM...
GUY'S NUTS. YOU CAN'T TAKE A GUY WHO'S NUTS.
BUG'S RIGHT.
PRETTY USED TO GUN FOR DUTCH SCHULTZ. HE'S NO EASY MARK.
WE GO AFTER HIM, HE'LL TAKE SOME OF US WITH.
WE GOTTA FIND SOMEONE WHO CAN GET CLOSE. SOMEONE HE TRUSTS.
PRETTY WON'T GO WITH NOBODY BUT ME.
HE LIKES ME. HE'LL NEVER GET WISE.

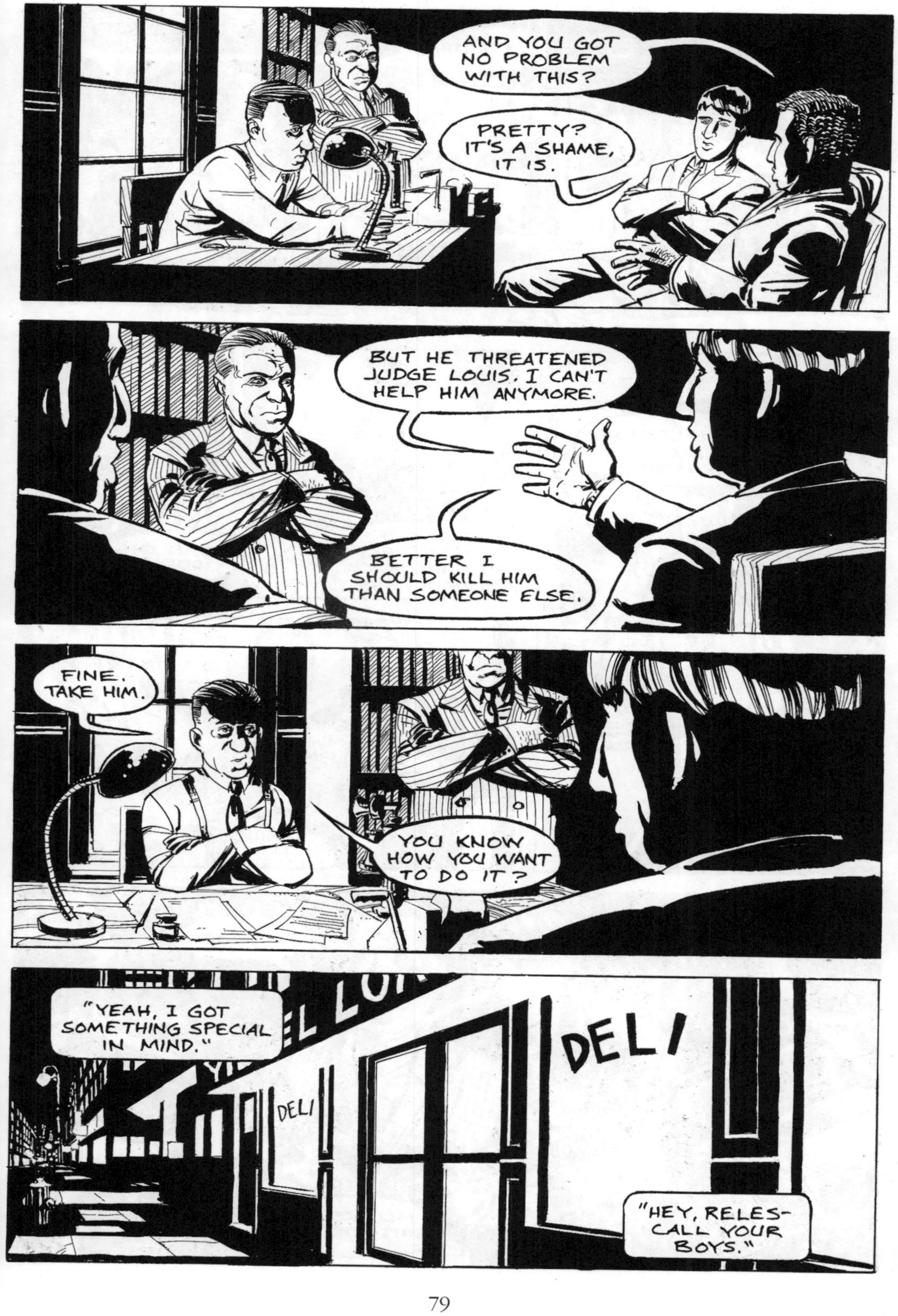
AND YOU GOT NO PROBLEM WITH THIS?
PRETTY? IT'S A SHAME, IT IS.
BUT HE THREATENED JUDGE LOUIS. I CAN'T HELP HIM ANYMORE.
BETTER I SHOULD KILL HIM THAN SOMEONE ELSE.
FINE. TAKE HIM.
YOU KNOW HOW YOU WANT TO DO IT?
"YEAH, I GOT SOMETHING SPECIAL IN MIND."
DELI
DELI
"HEY, RELES-CALL YOUR BOYS."

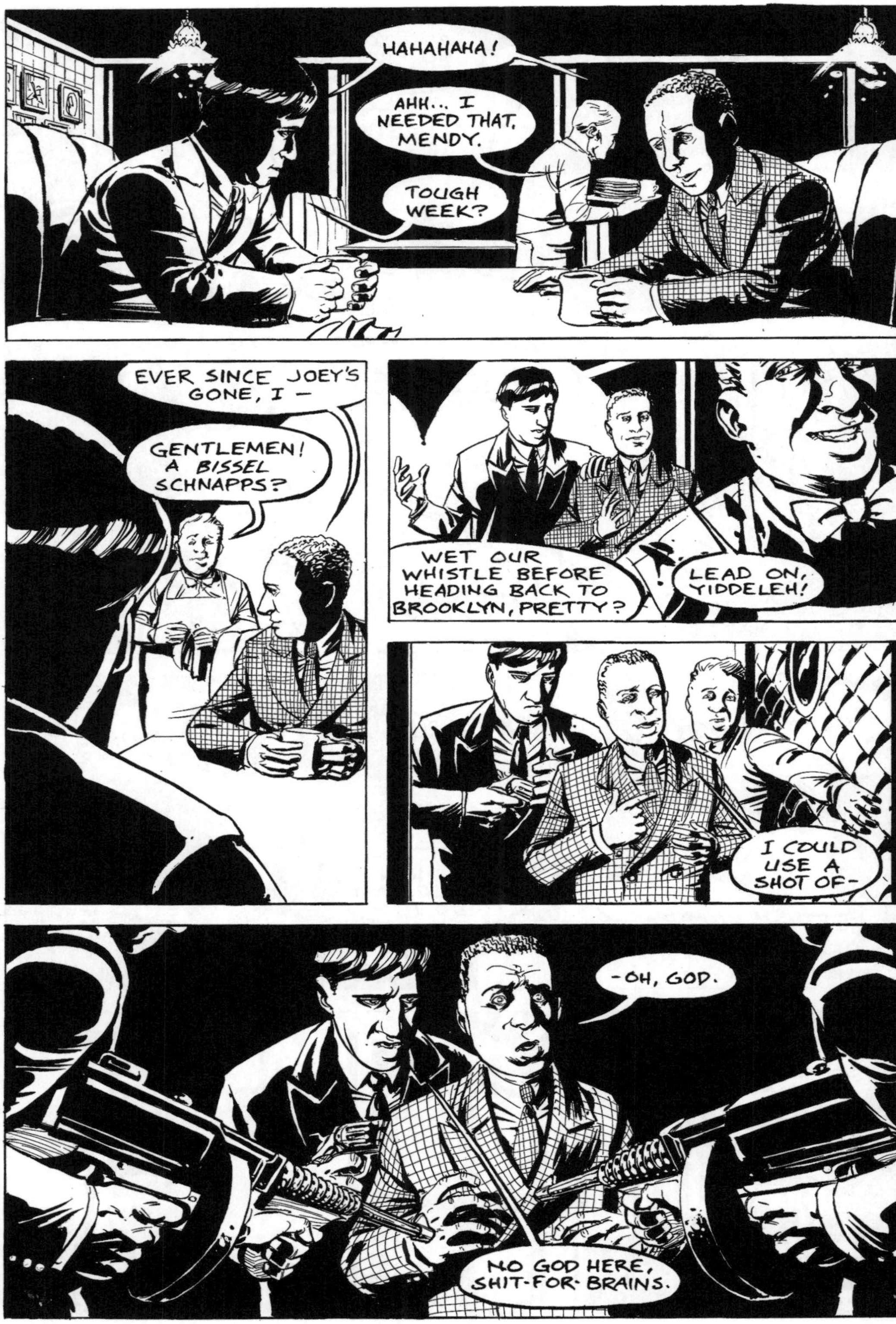
HAHAHAHA!
AHH... I NEEDED THAT, MENDY.
TOUGH WEEK?
EVER SINCE JOEY'S GONE, I —
GENTLEMEN! A BISSEL SCHNAPPS?
WET OUR WHISTLE BEFORE HEADING BACK TO BROOKLYN, PRETTY?
LEAD ON, YIDDELEH!
I COULD USE A SHOT OF-
-OH, GOD.
NO GOD HERE, SHIT-FOR-BRAINS.

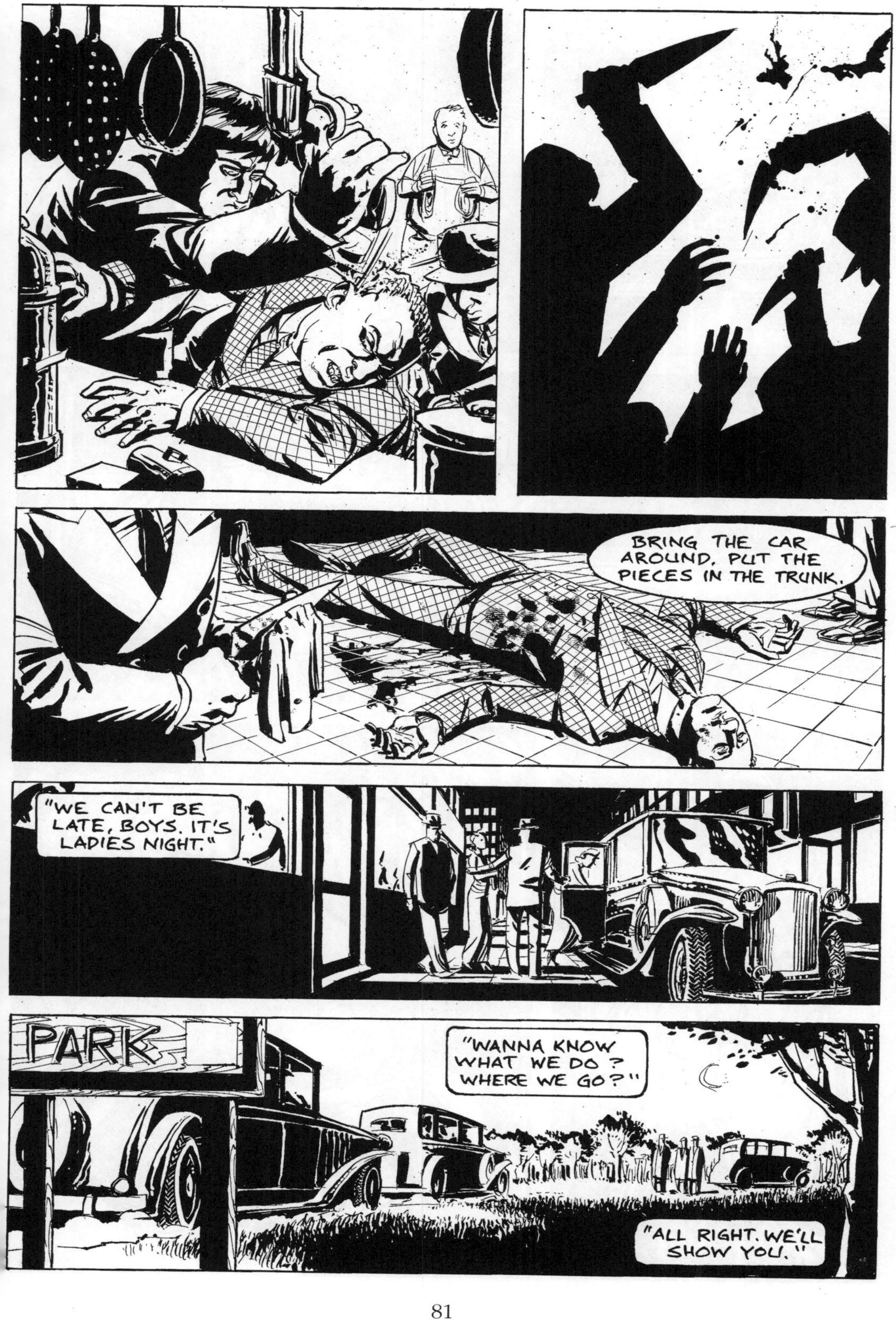
BRING THE CAR AROUND. PUT THE PIECES IN THE TRUNK.
"WE CAN'T BE LATE, BOYS. IT'S LADIES NIGHT."
PARK
"WANNA KNOW WHAT WE DO? WHERE WE GO?"
"ALL RIGHT. WE'LL SHOW YOU."

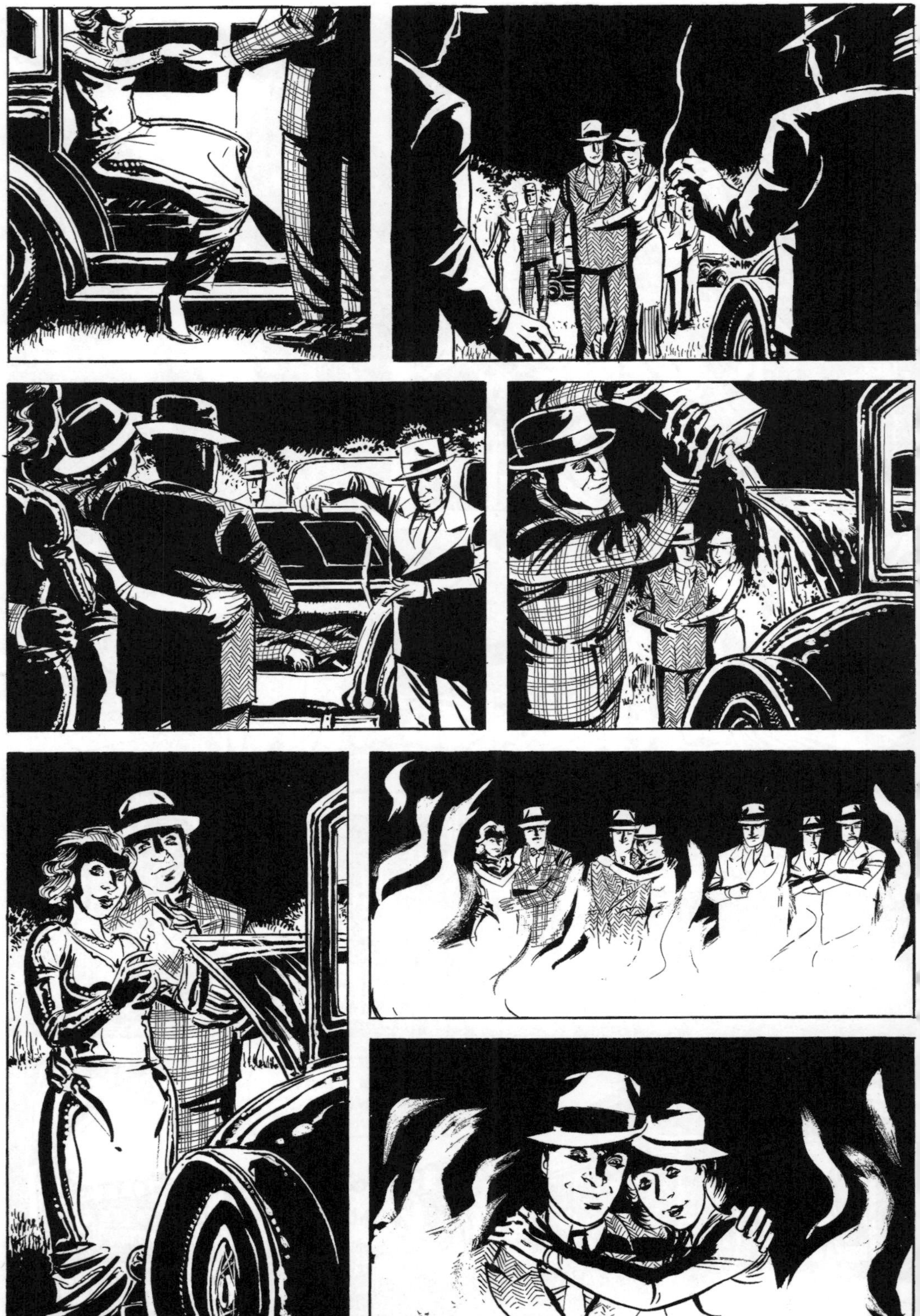

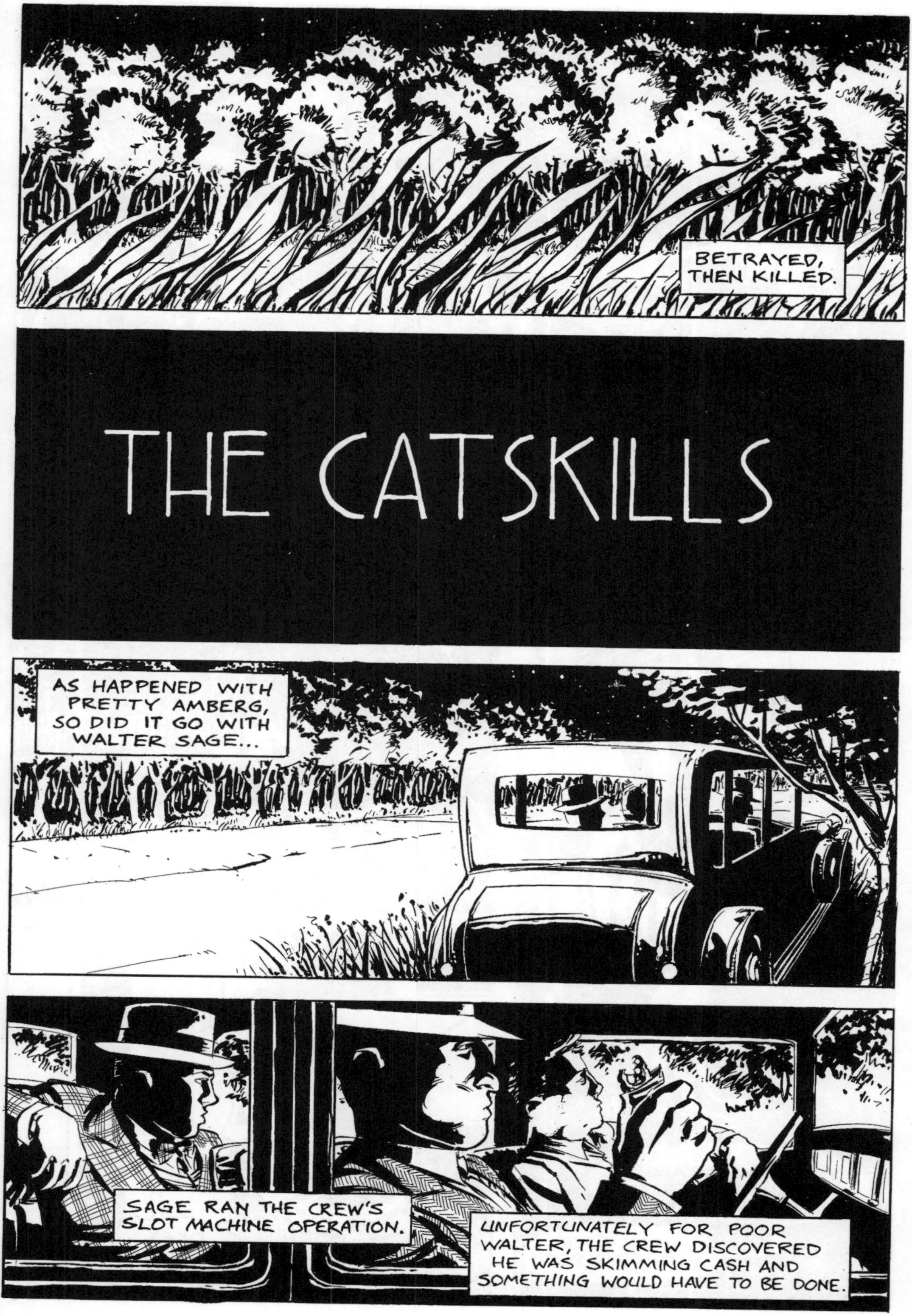
BETRAYED, THEN KILLED.
THE CATSKILLS
AS HAPPENED WITH PRETTY AMBERG, SO DID IT GO WITH WALTER SAGE...
SAGE RAN THE CREW'S SLOT MACHINE OPERATION.
UNFORTUNATELY FOR POOR WALTER, THE CREW DISCOVERED HE WAS SKIMMING CASH AND SOMETHING WOULD HAVE TO BE DONE.

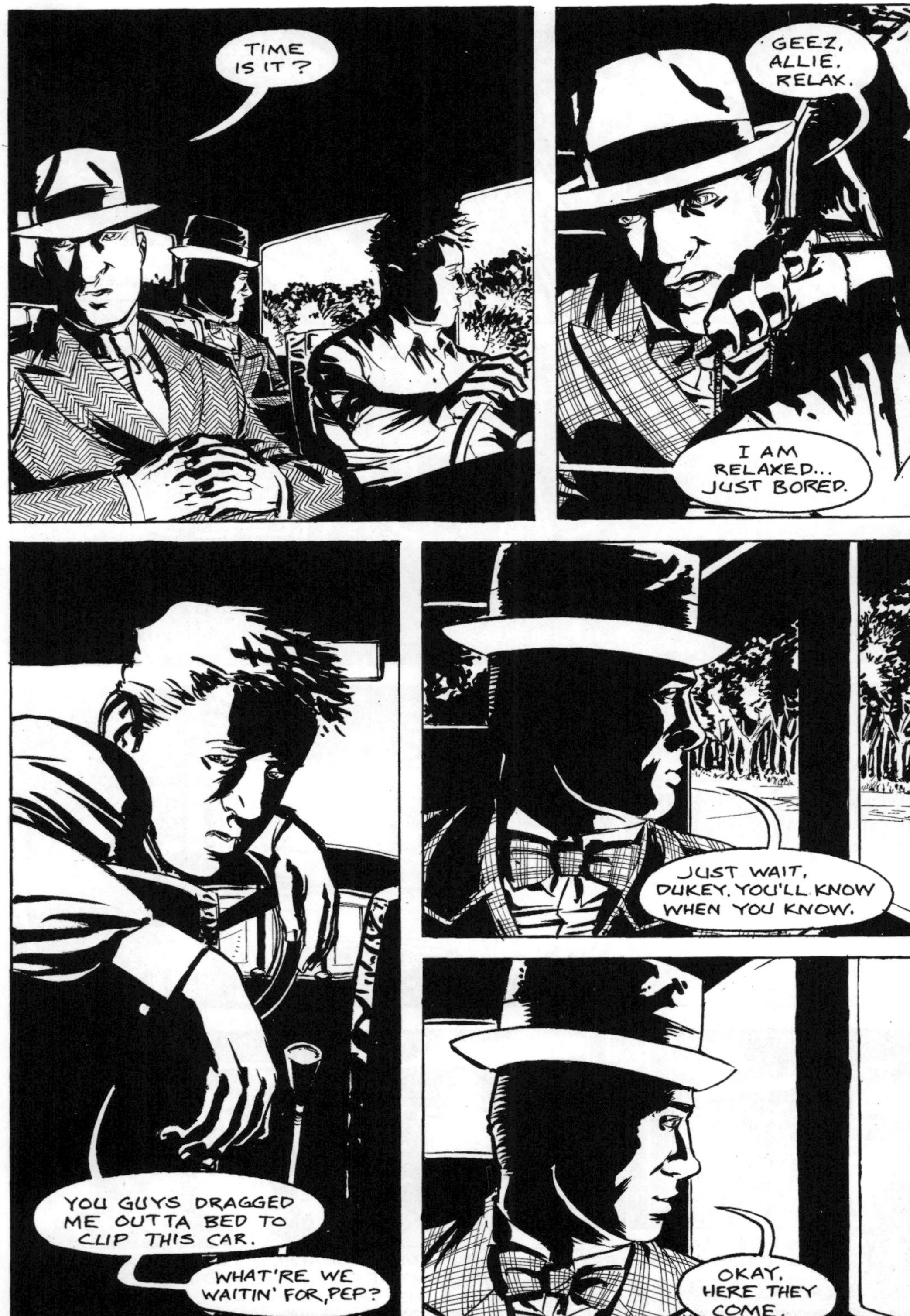
TIME IS IT?
GEEZ, ALLIE. RELAX.
I AM RELAXED... JUST BORED.
YOU GUYS DRAGGED ME OUTTA BED TO CLIP THIS CAR.
WHAT'RE WE WAITIN' FOR, PEP?
JUST WAIT, DUKEY. YOU'LL KNOW WHEN YOU KNOW.
OKAY. HERE THEY COME.

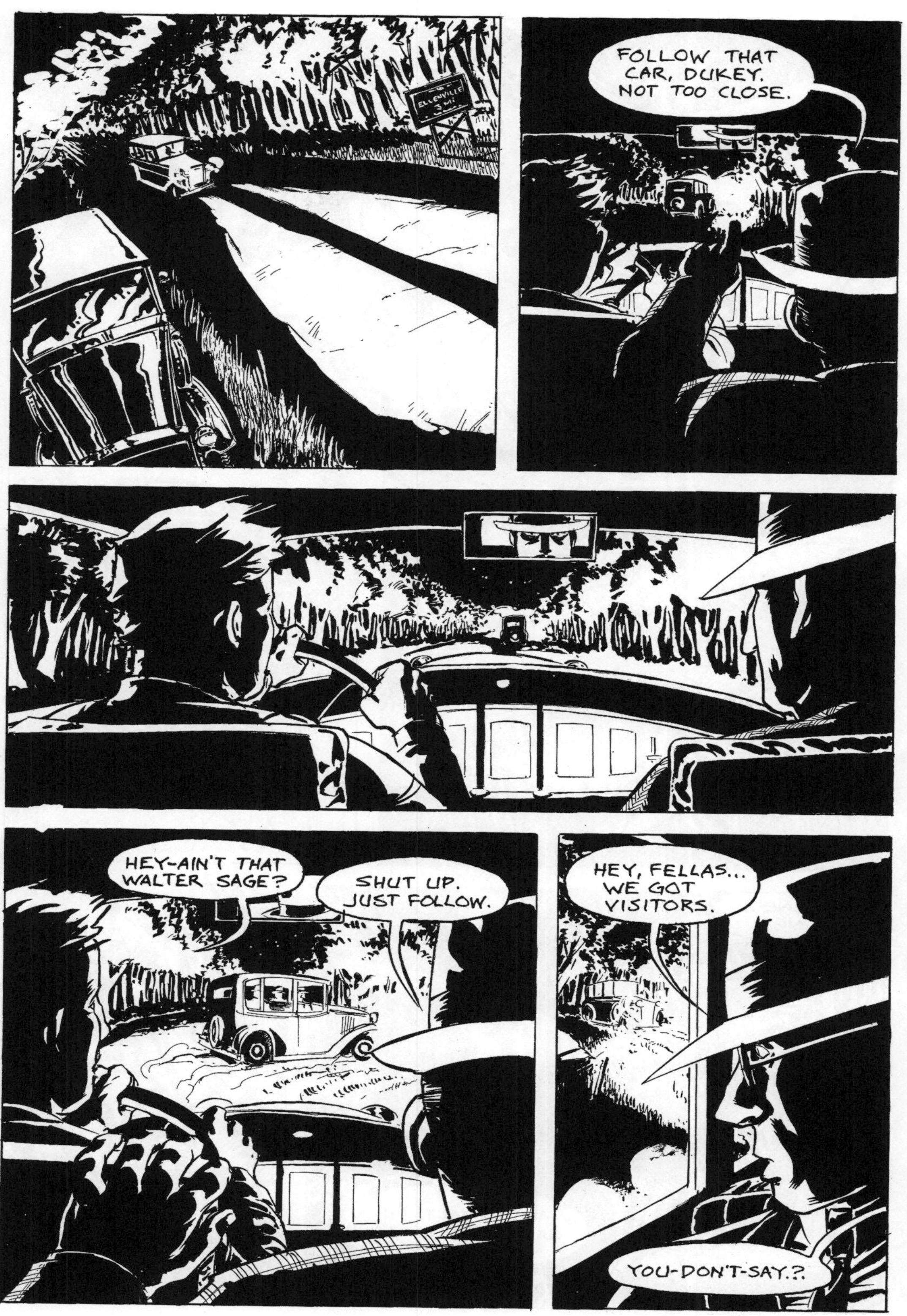
ELLENVILLE 3 MI
FOLLOW THAT CAR, DUKEY. NOT TOO CLOSE.
HEY-AIN'T THAT WALTER SAGE?
SHUT UP. JUST FOLLOW.
HEY, FELLAS... WE GOT VISITORS.
YOU-DON'T-SAY.?

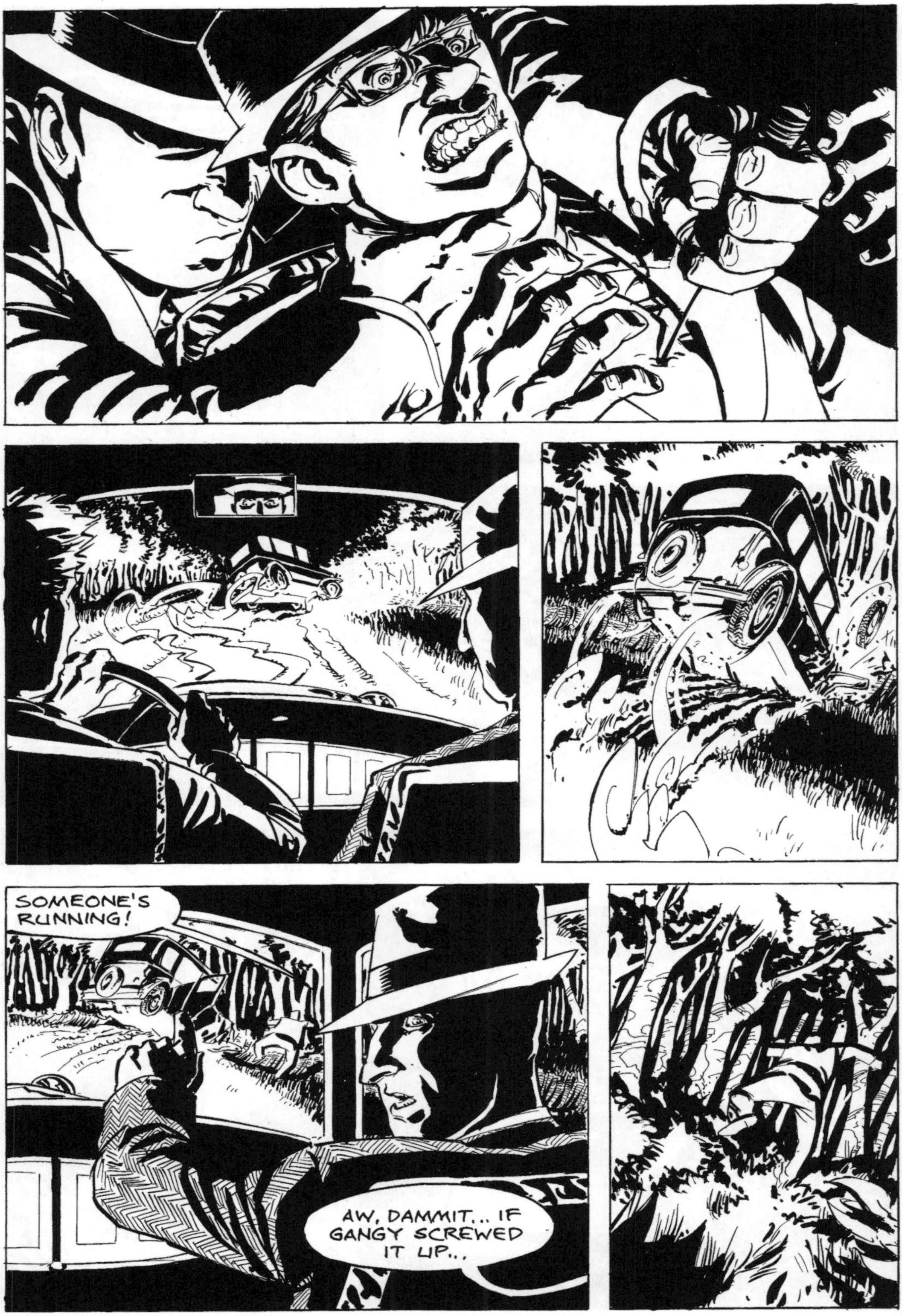
SOMEONE'S RUNNING!
AW, DAMMIT... IF GANGY SCREWED IT UP...

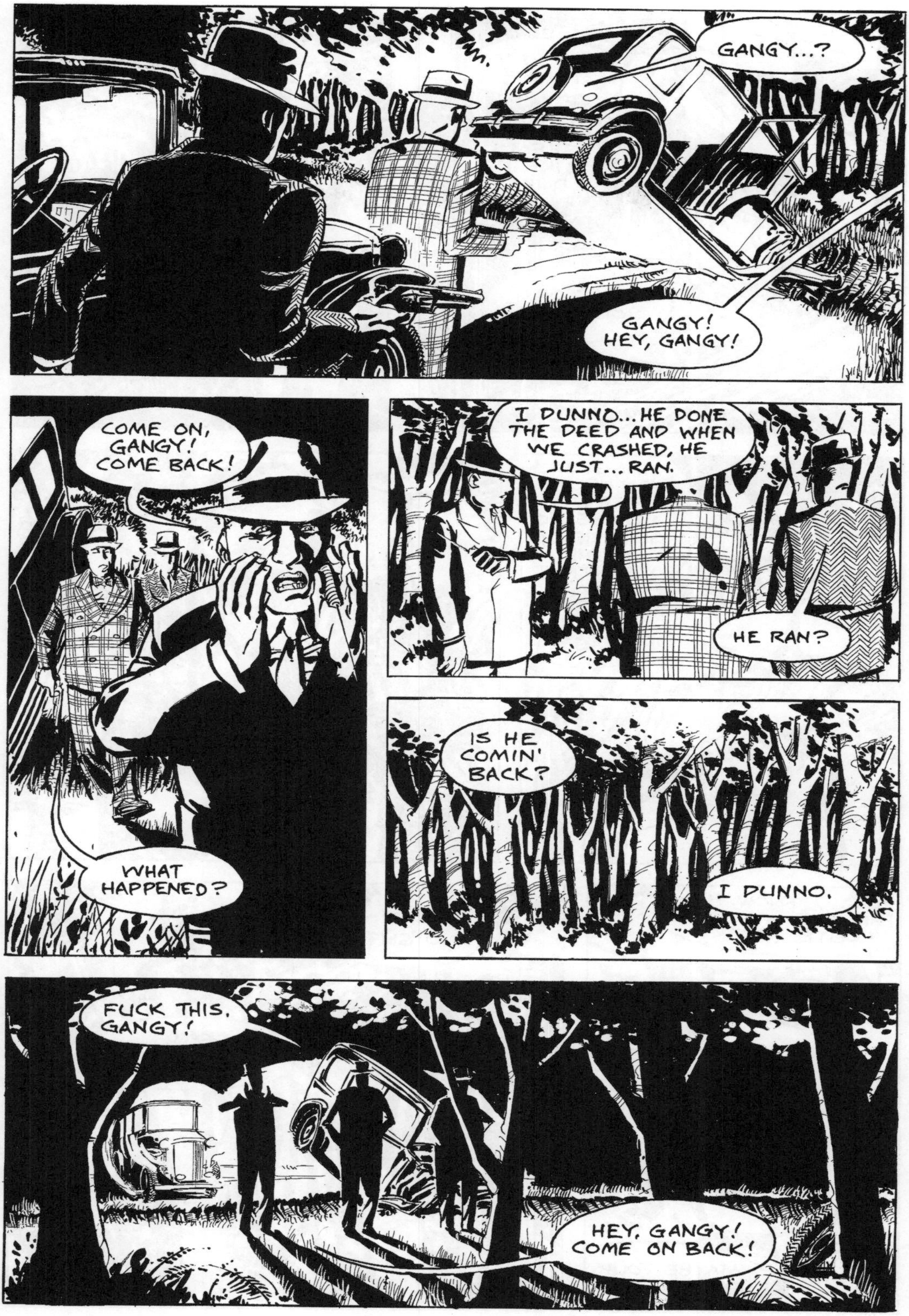
GANGY...?
GANGY! HEY, GANGY!
COME ON, GANGY! COME BACK!
WHAT HAPPENED?
I DUNNO... HE DONE THE DEED AND WHEN WE CRASHED, HE JUST... RAN.
HE RAN?
IS HE COMIN' BACK?
I DUNNO.
FUCK THIS, GANGY!
HEY, GANGY! COME ON BACK!

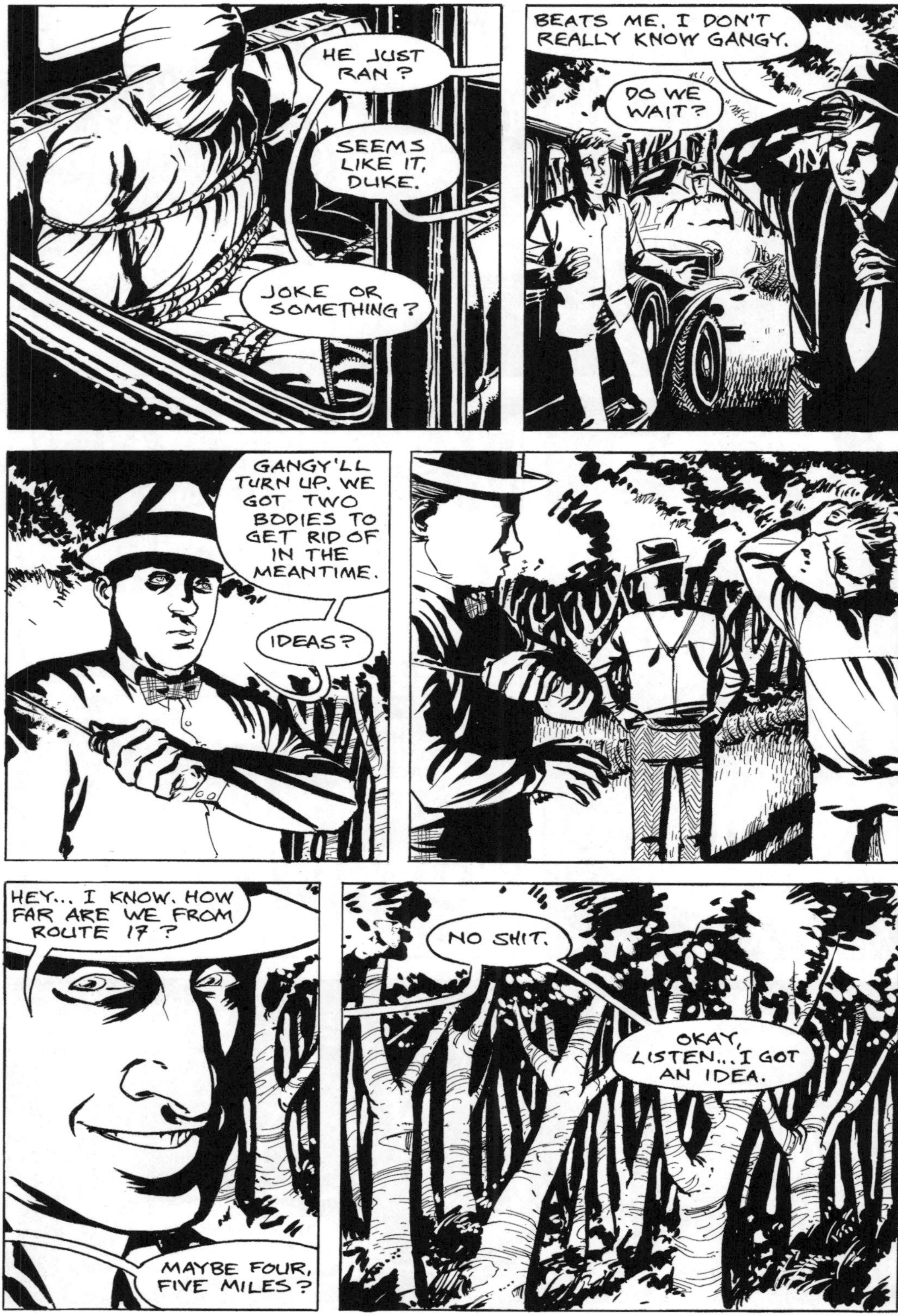
HE JUST RAN?
SEEMS LIKE IT, DUKE.
JOKE OR SOMETHING?
BEATS ME, I DON'T REALLY KNOW GANGY.
DO WE WAIT?
GANGY'LL TURN UP. WE GOT TWO BODIES TO GET RID OF IN THE MEANTIME.
IDEAS?
HEY... I KNOW. HOW FAR ARE WE FROM ROUTE 17?
MAYBE FOUR, FIVE MILES?
NO SHIT.
OKAY, LISTEN... I GOT AN IDEA.

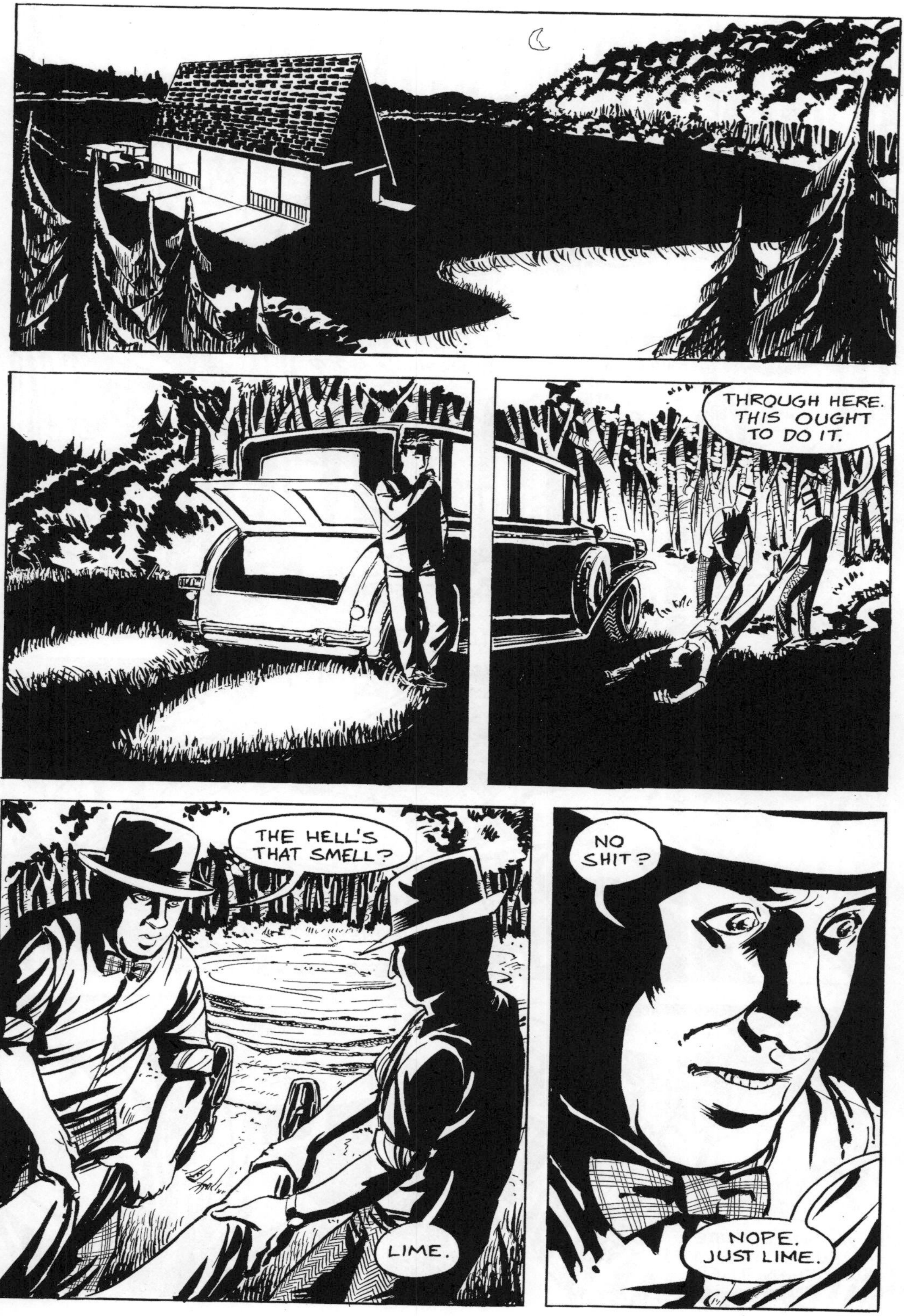
THROUGH HERE. THIS OUGHT TO DO IT.
THE HELL'S THAT SMELL?
LIME.
NO SHIT?
NOPE. JUST LIME.

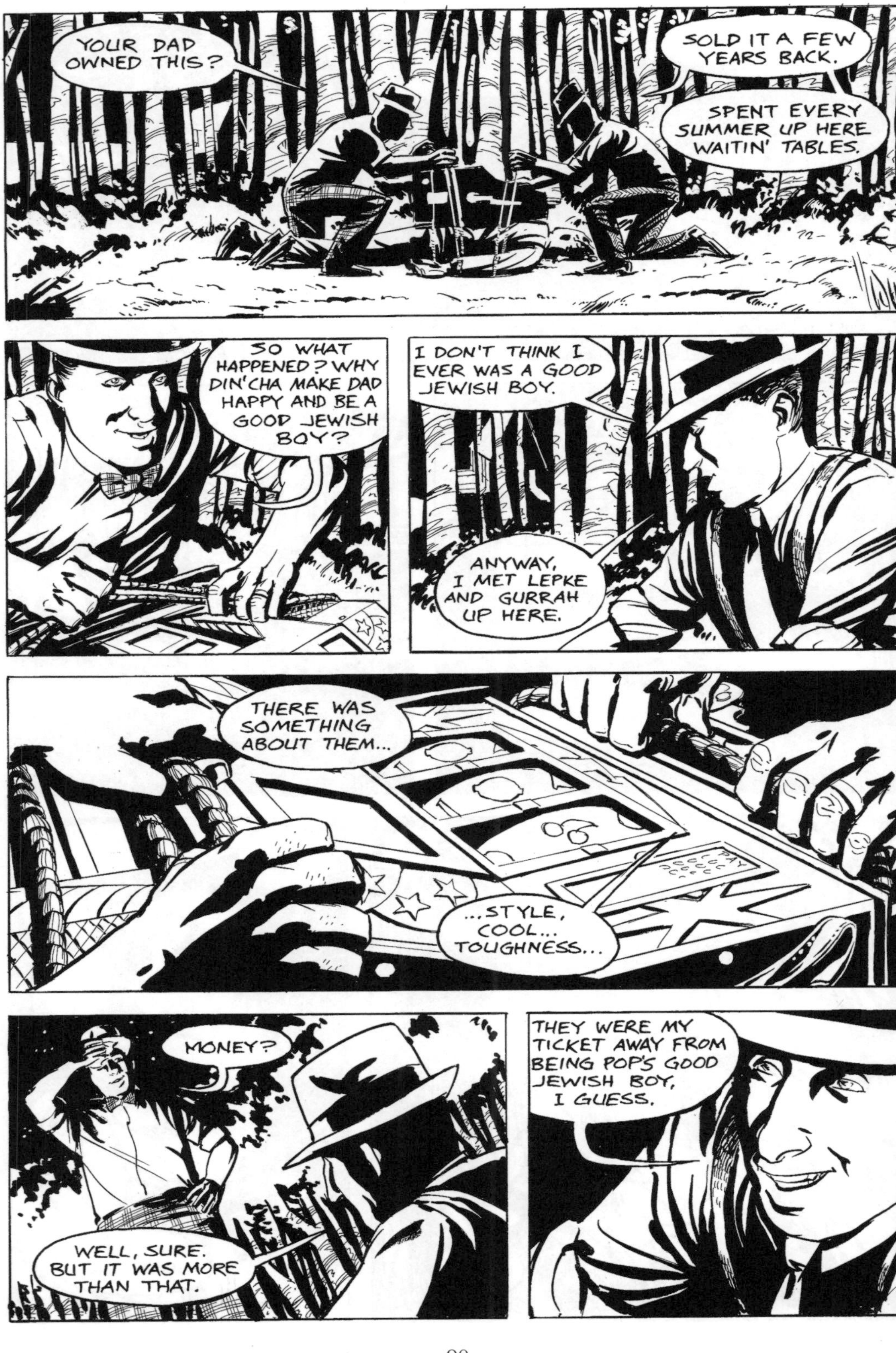
YOUR DAD OWNED THIS?
SOLD IT A FEW YEARS BACK.
SPENT EVERY SUMMER UP HERE WAITIN' TABLES.
SO WHAT HAPPENED? WHY DIN'CHA MAKE DAD HAPPY AND BE A GOOD JEWISH BOY?
I DON'T THINK I EVER WAS A GOOD JEWISH BOY.
ANYWAY, I MET LEPKE AND GURRAH UP HERE.
THERE WAS SOMETHING ABOUT THEM...
PAY
...STYLE, COOL... TOUGHNESS...
MONEY?
WELL, SURE. BUT IT WAS MORE THAN THAT.
THEY WERE MY TICKET AWAY FROM BEING POP'S GOOD JEWISH BOY, I GUESS.

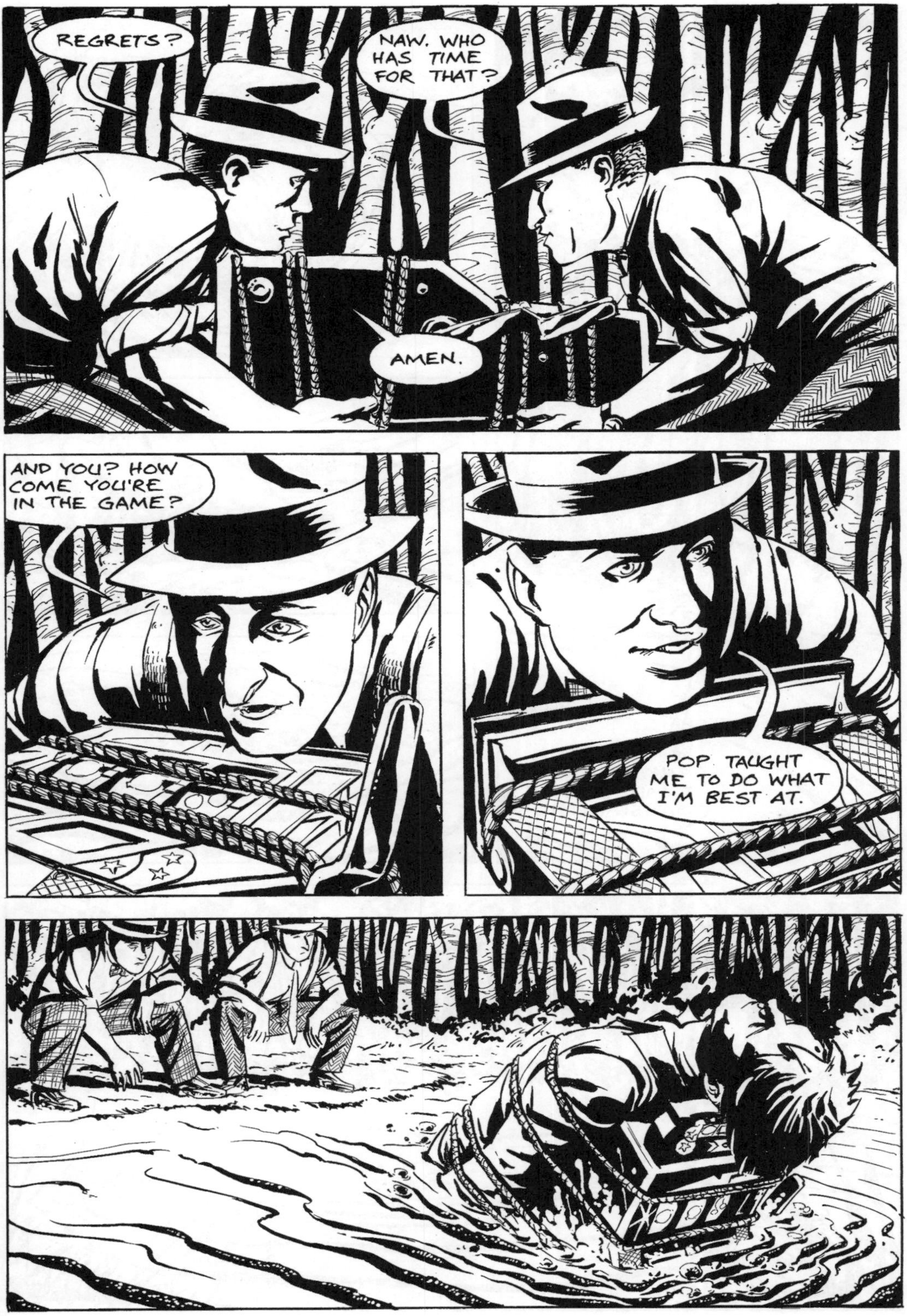
REGRETS?
NAW. WHO HAS TIME FOR THAT?
AMEN.
AND YOU? HOW COME YOU'RE IN THE GAME?
POP TAUGHT ME TO DO WHAT I'M BEST AT.

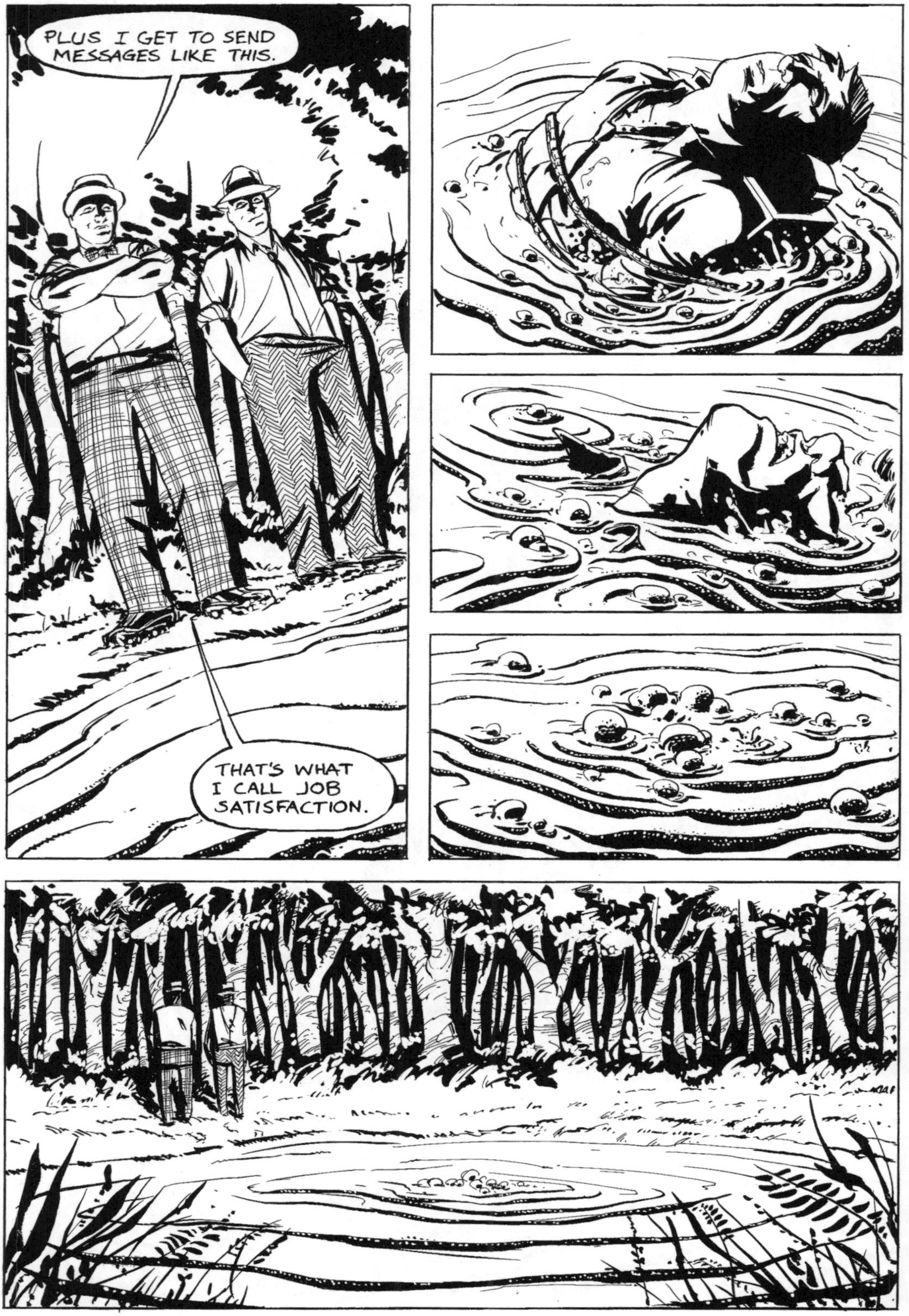
PLUS I GET TO SEND MESSAGES LIKE THIS.
THAT'S WHAT I CALL JOB SATISFACTION.

THE MOST DANGEROUS MEN IN AMERICA

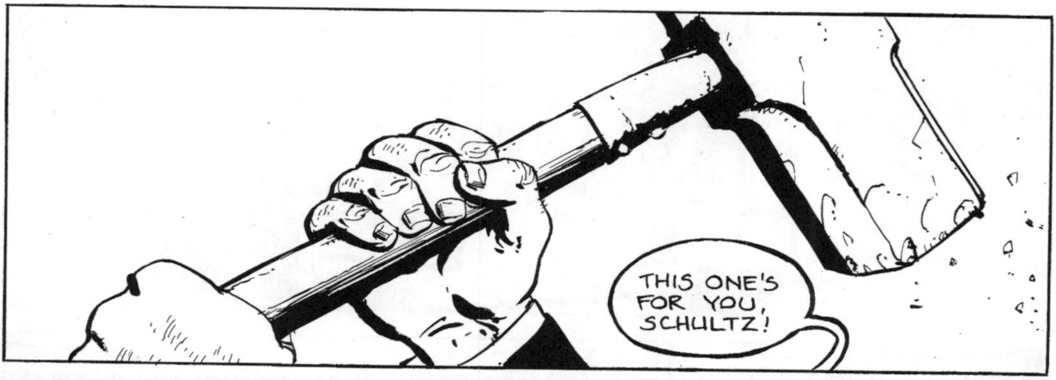
THIS ONE'S FOR YOU, SCHULTZ!

THOMAS DEWEY AND THE FALL OF DUTCH SCHULTZ

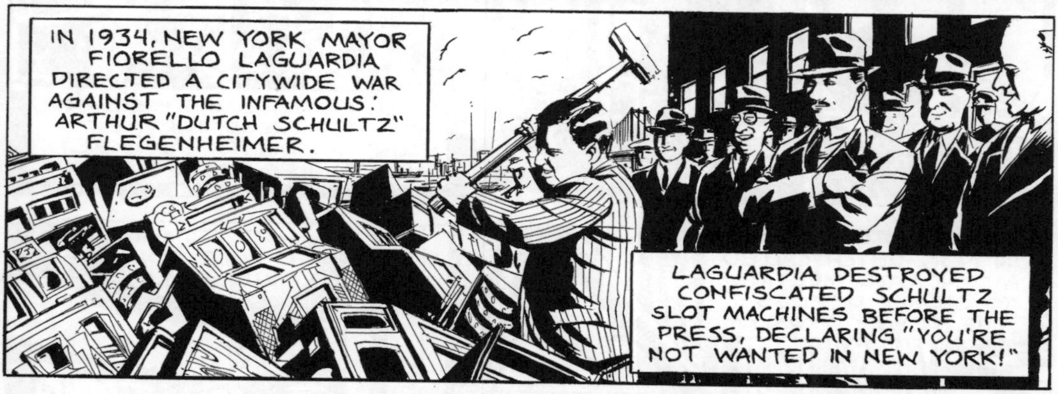
IN 1934, NEW YORK MAYOR FIORELLO LAGUARDIA DIRECTED A CITYWIDE WAR AGAINST THE INFAMOUS: ARTHUR "DUTCH SCHULTZ" FLEGENHEIMER.
LAGUARDIA DESTROYED CONFISCATED SCHULTZ SLOT MACHINES BEFORE THE PRESS, DECLARING "YOU'RE NOT WANTED IN NEW YORK!"

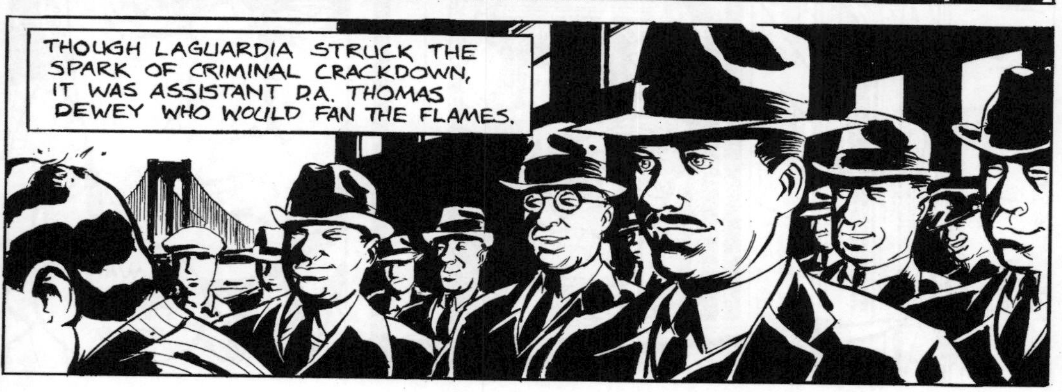
THOUGH LAGUARDIA STRUCK THE SPARK OF CRIMINAL CRACKDOWN, IT WAS ASSISTANT D.A. THOMAS DEWEY WHO WOULD FAN THE FLAMES.

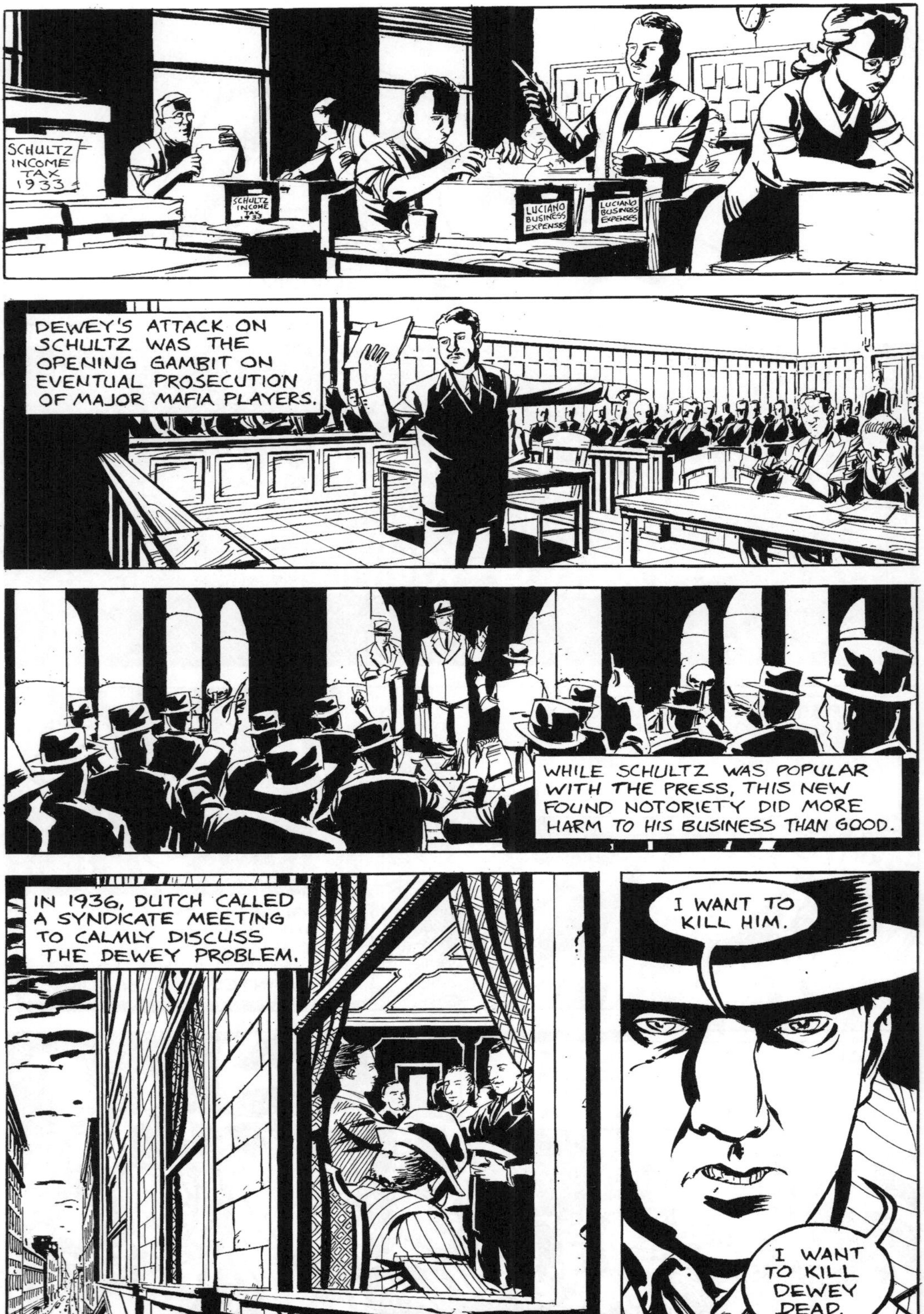
SCHULTZ INCOME TAX 1933
LUCIANO BUSINESS EXPENSES
DEWEY'S ATTACK ON SCHULTZ WAS THE OPENING GAMBIT ON EVENTUAL PROSECUTION OF MAJOR MAFIA PLAYERS.
WHILE SCHULTZ WAS POPULAR WITH THE PRESS, THIS NEW FOUND NOTORIETY DID MORE HARM TO HIS BUSINESS THAN GOOD.
IN 1936, DUTCH CALLED A SYNDICATE MEETING TO CALMLY DISCUSS THE DEWEY PROBLEM.
I WANT TO KILL HIM.
I WANT TO KILL DEWEY DEAD.

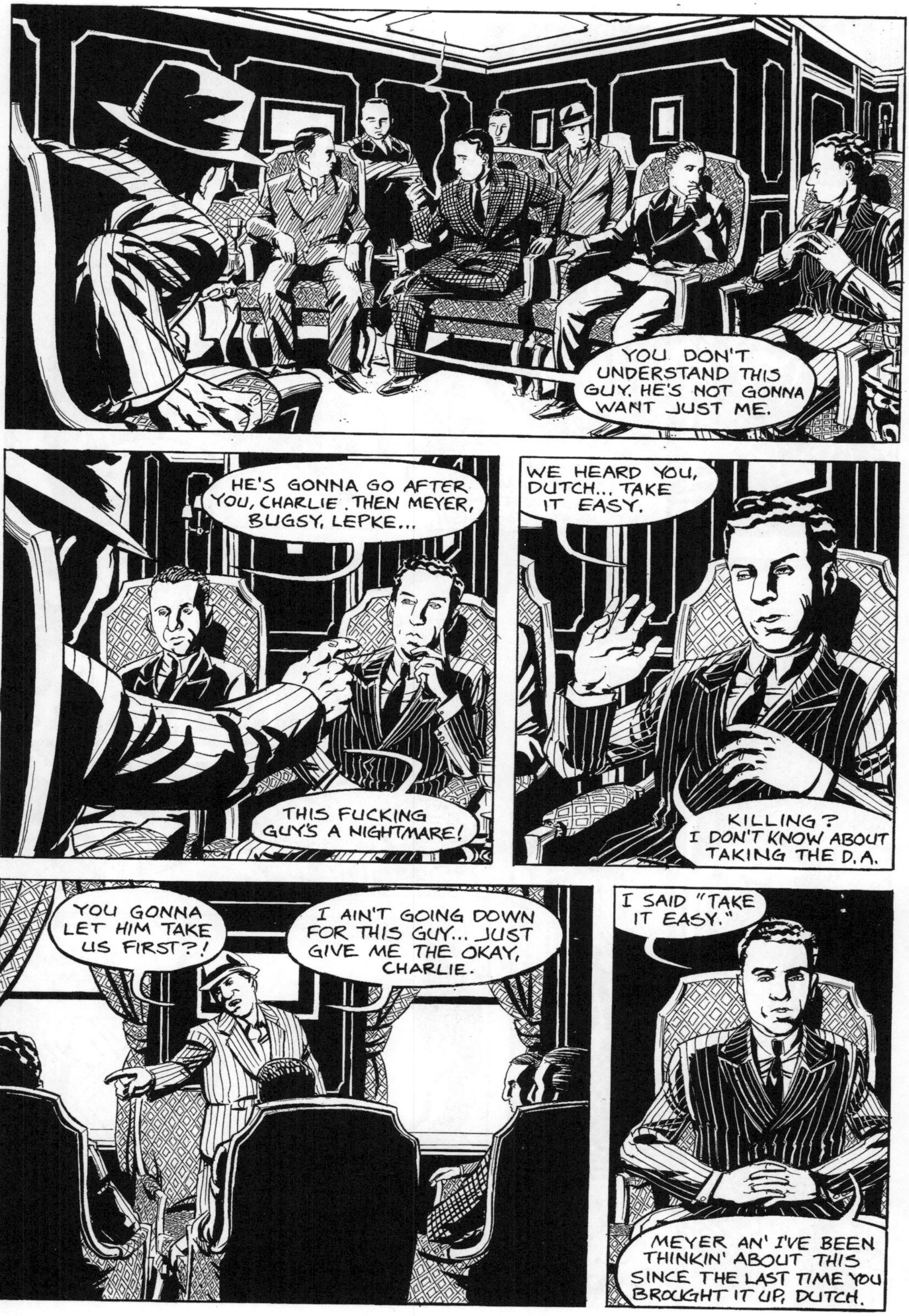
YOU DON'T UNDERSTAND THIS GUY. HE'S NOT GONNA WANT JUST ME.
HE'S GONNA GO AFTER YOU, CHARLIE. THEN MEYER, BUGSY, LEPKE...
THIS FUCKING GUY'S A NIGHTMARE!
WE HEARD YOU, DUTCH..., TAKE IT EASY.
KILLING? I DON'T KNOW ABOUT TAKING THE D.A.
YOU GONNA LET HIM TAKE US FIRST?!
I AIN'T GOING DOWN FOR THIS GUY... JUST GIVE ME THE OKAY, CHARLIE.
I SAID "TAKE IT EASY."
MEYER AN' I'VE BEEN THINKIN' ABOUT THIS SINCE THE LAST TIME YOU BROUGHT IT UP, DUTCH.

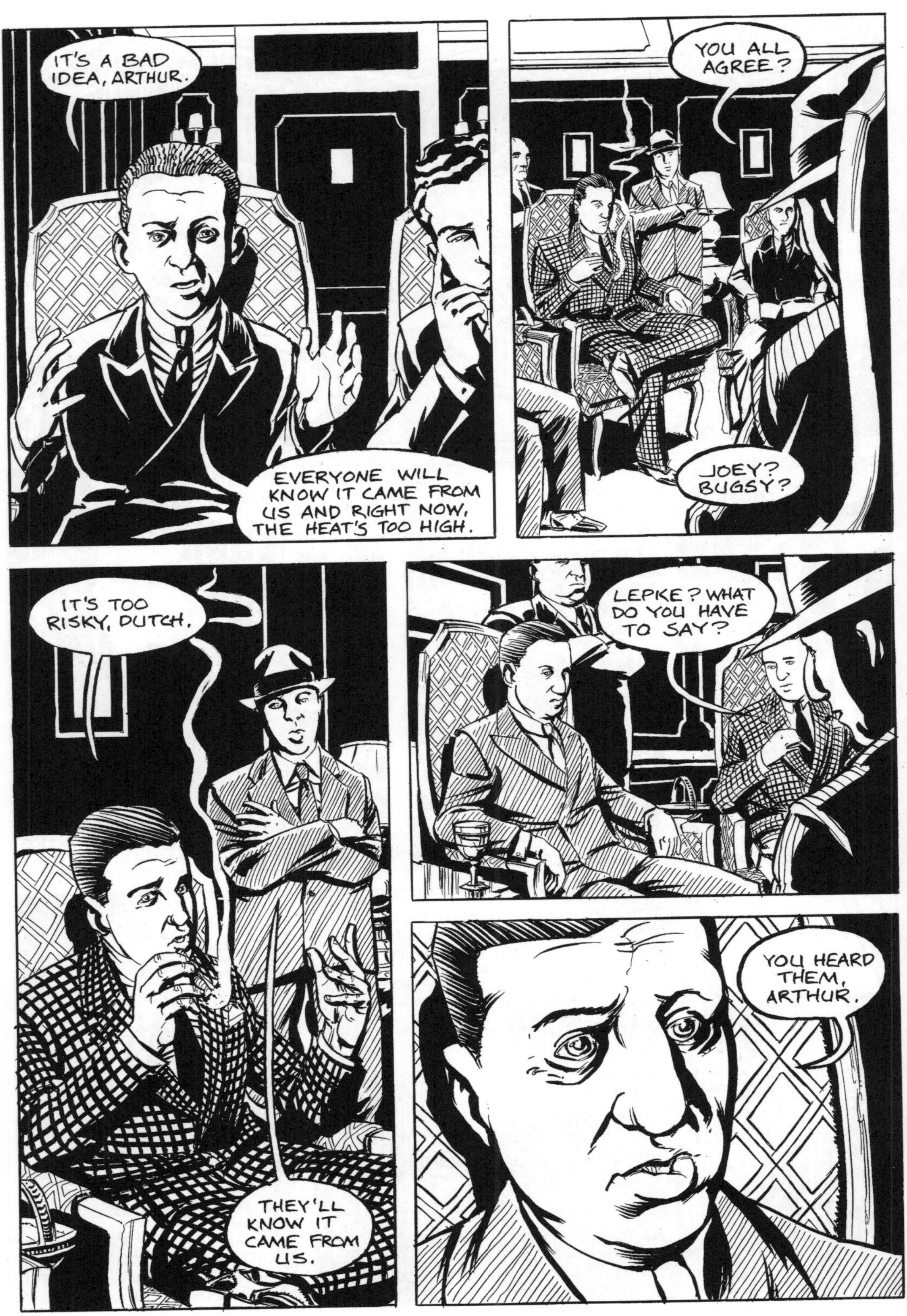
IT'S A BAD IDEA, ARTHUR.
EVERYONE WILL KNOW IT CAME FROM US AND RIGHT NOW, THE HEAT'S TOO HIGH.
YOU ALL AGREE?
JOEY? BUGSY?
IT'S TOO RISKY, DUTCH.
THEY'LL KNOW IT CAME FROM US.
LEPKE? WHAT DO YOU HAVE TO SAY?
YOU HEARD THEM, ARTHUR.

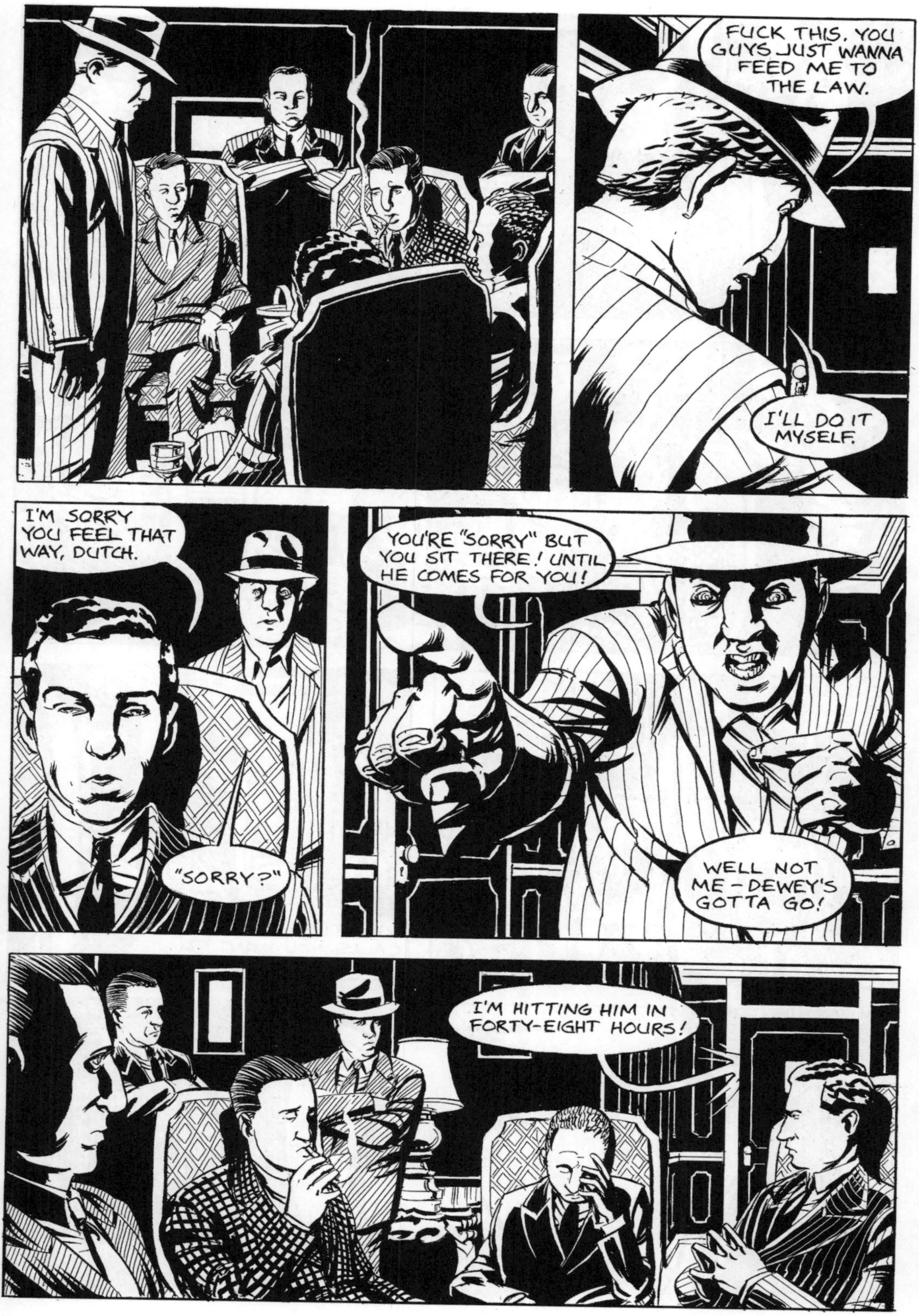
FUCK THIS. YOU GUYS JUST WANNA FEED ME TO THE LAW.
I'LL DO IT MYSELF.
I'M SORRY YOU FEEL THAT WAY, DUTCH.
"SORRY?"
YOU'RE "SORRY" BUT YOU SIT THERE! UNTIL HE COMES FOR YOU!
WELL NOT ME - DEWEY'S GOTTA GO!
I'M HITTING HIM IN FORTY-EIGHT HOURS!

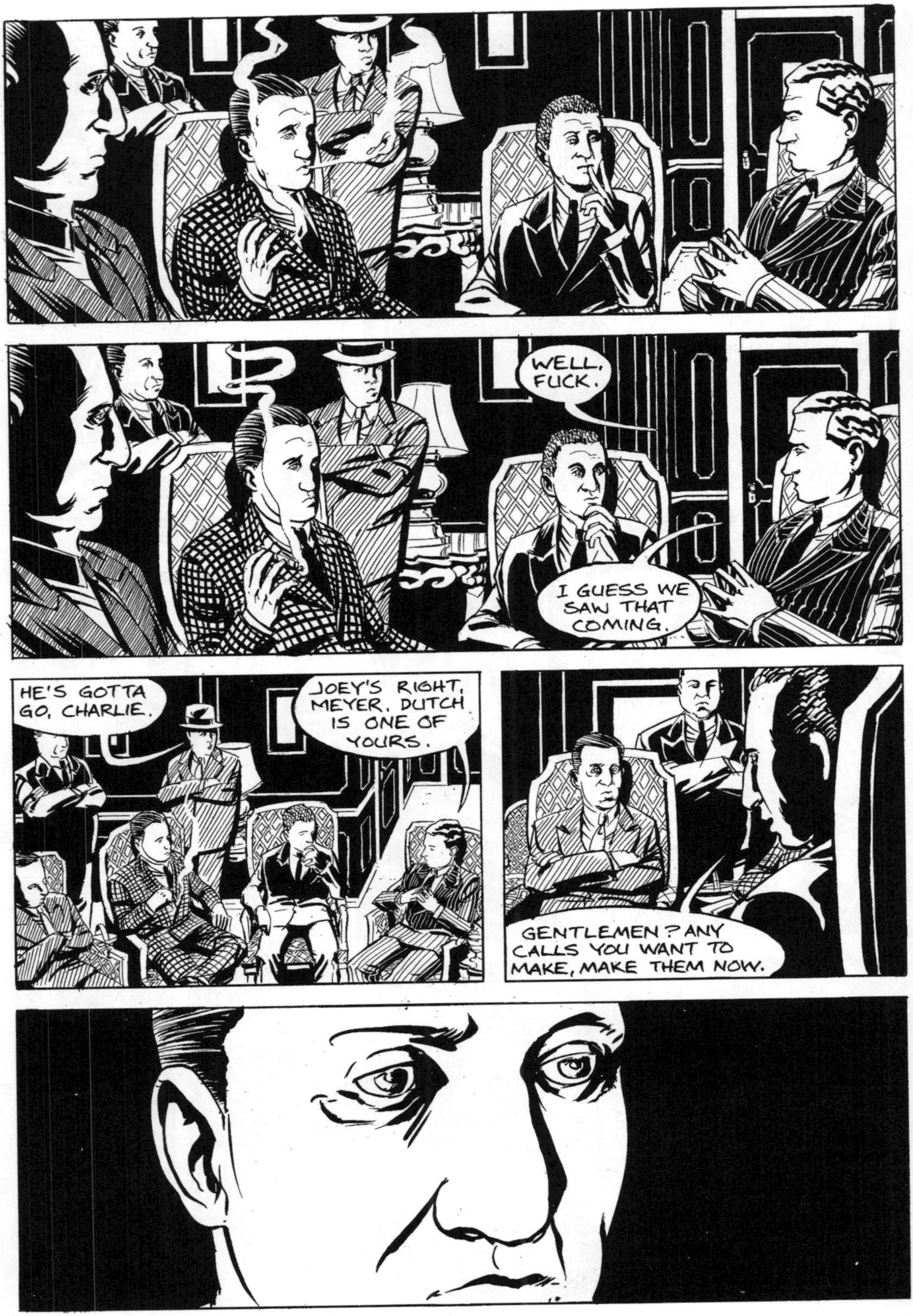
WELL, FUCK.
I GUESS WE SAW THAT COMING.
HE'S GOTTA GO, CHARLIE.
JOEY'S RIGHT, MEYER. DUTCH IS ONE OF YOURS.
GENTLEMEN? ANY CALLS YOU WANT TO MAKE, MAKE THEM NOW.

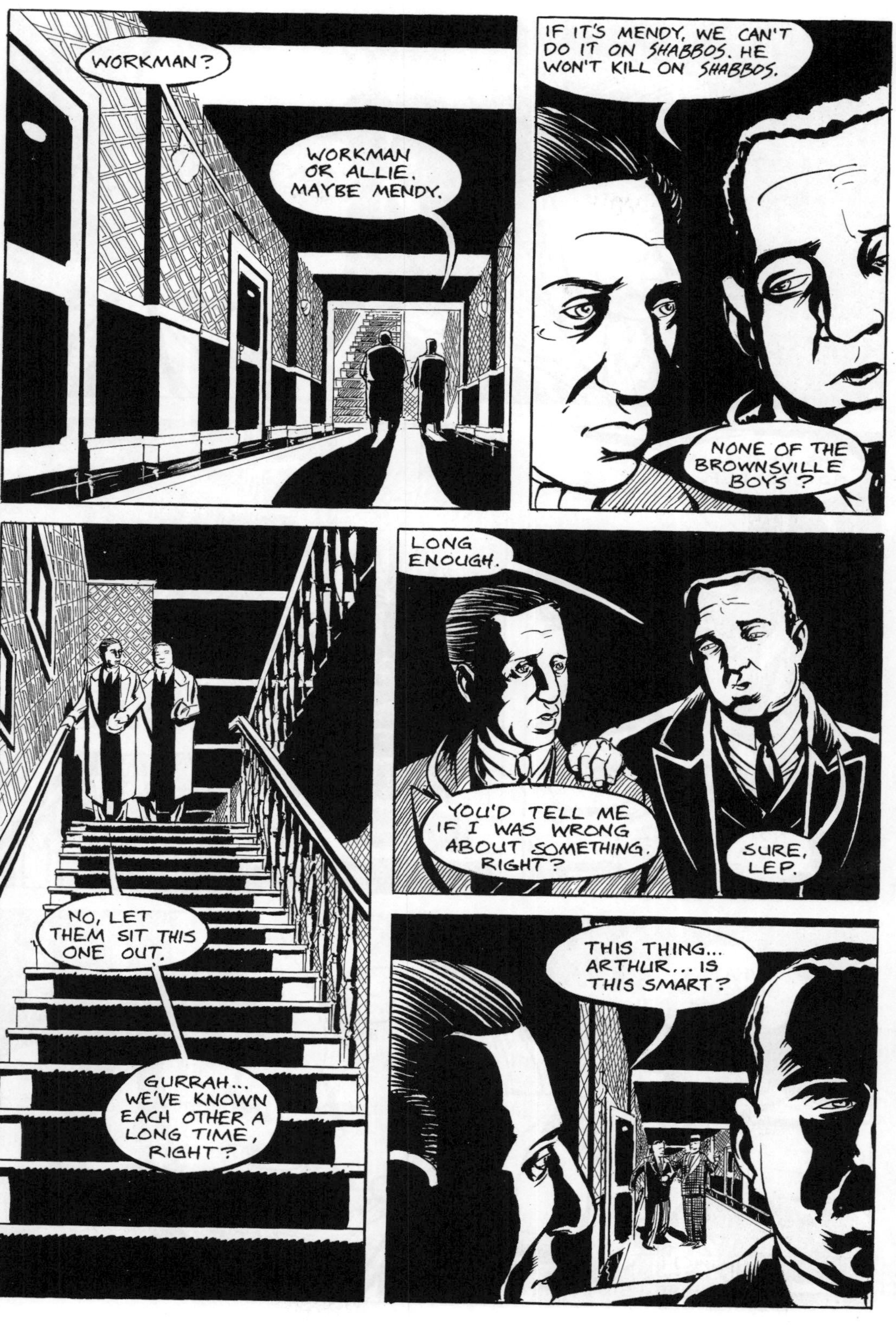
WORKMAN?
WORKMAN OR ALLIE. MAYBE MENDY.
IF IT'S MENDY, WE CAN'T DO IT ON SHABBOS. HE WON'T KILL ON SHABBOS.
NONE OF THE BROWNSVILLE BOYS?
NO, LET THEM SIT THIS ONE OUT.
GURRAH... WE'VE KNOWN EACH OTHER A LONG TIME, RIGHT?
LONG ENOUGH.
YOU'D TELL ME IF I WAS WRONG ABOUT SOMETHING. RIGHT?
SURE, LEP.
THIS THING... ARTHUR... IS THIS SMART?

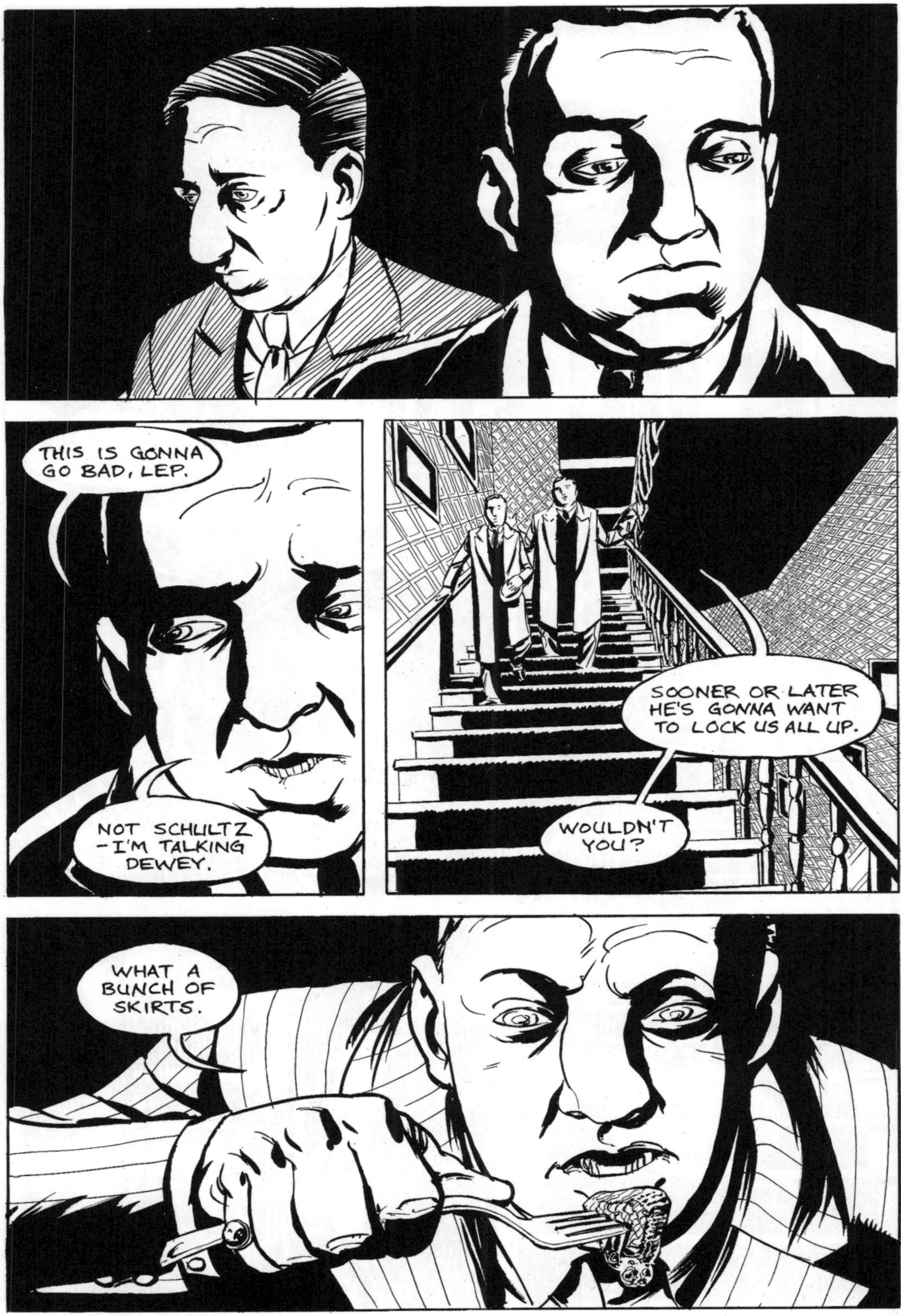
THIS IS GONNA GO BAD, LEP.
NOT SCHULTZ -I'M TALKING DEWEY.
SOONER OR LATER HE'S GONNA WANT TO LOCK US ALL UP.
WOULDN'T YOU?
WHAT A BUNCH OF SKIRTS.

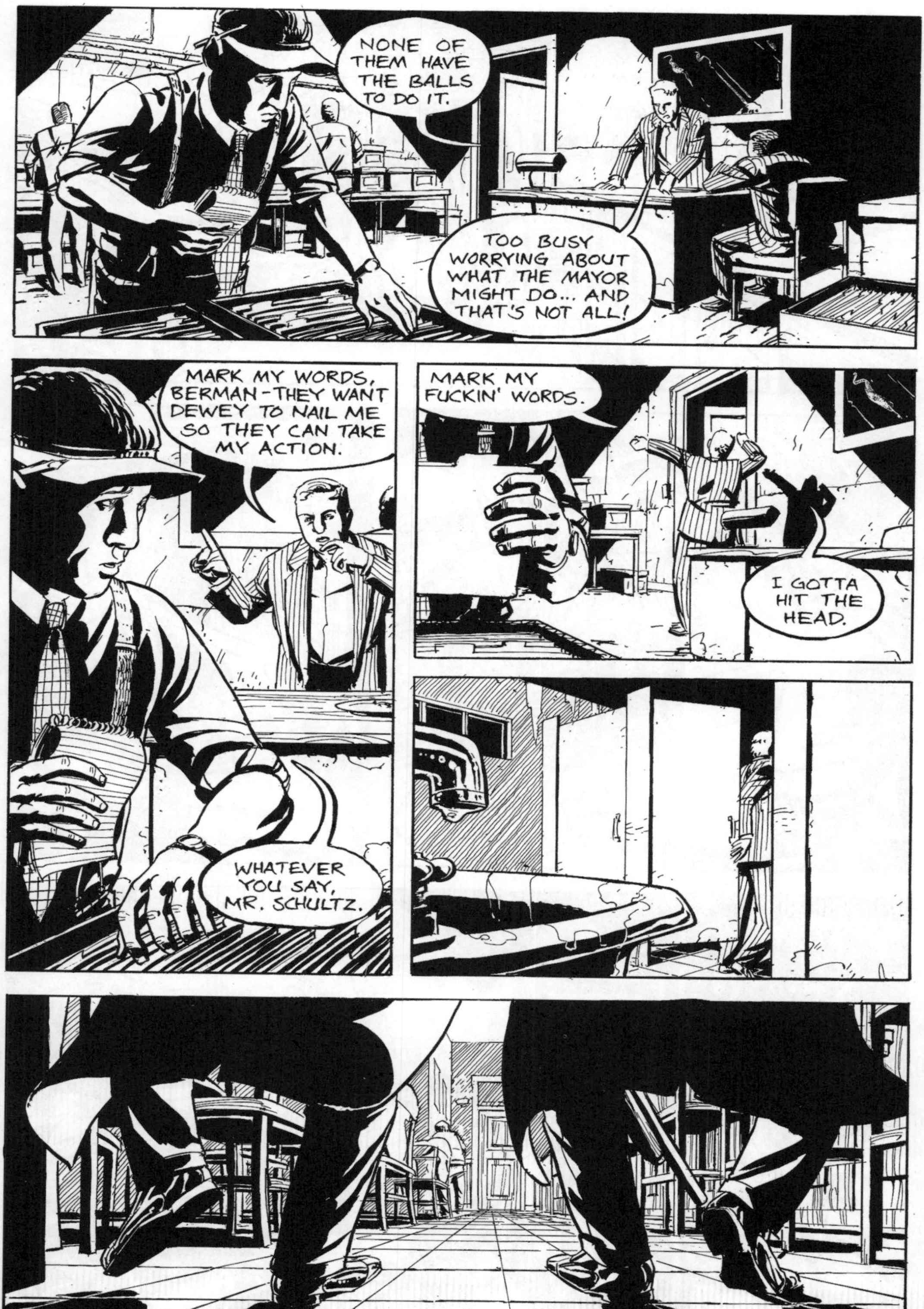
NONE OF THEM HAVE THE BALLS TO DO IT.
TOO BUSY WORRYING ABOUT WHAT THE MAYOR MIGHT DO... AND THAT'S NOT ALL!
MARK MY WORDS, BERMAN-THEY WANT DEWEY TO NAIL ME SO THEY CAN TAKE MY ACTION.
WHATEVER YOU SAY, MR. SCHULTZ.
MARK MY FUCKIN' WORDS.
I GOTTA HIT THE HEAD.

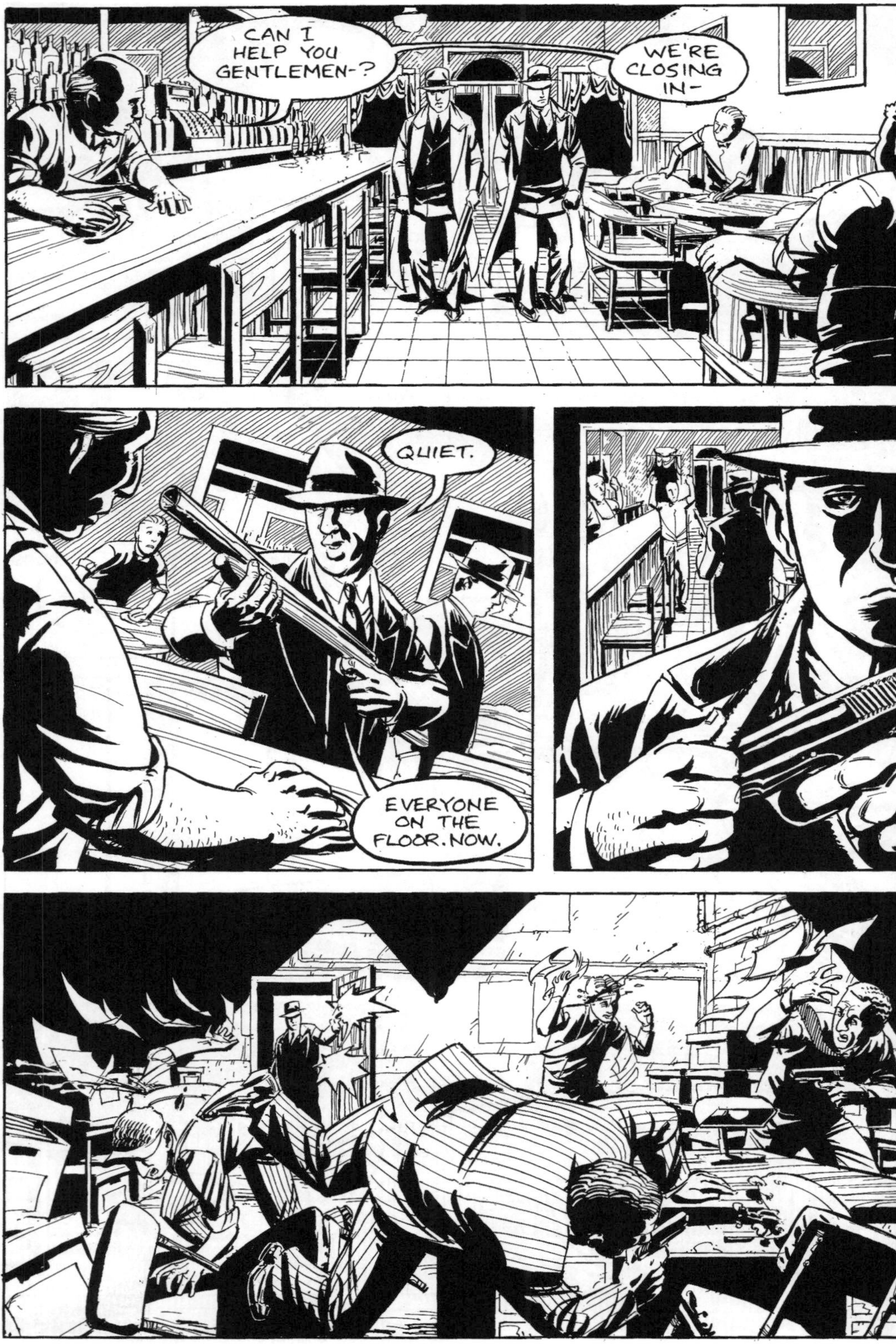
CAN I HELP YOU GENTLEMEN-?
WE'RE CLOSING IN-
QUIET.
EVERYONE ON THE FLOOR. NOW.

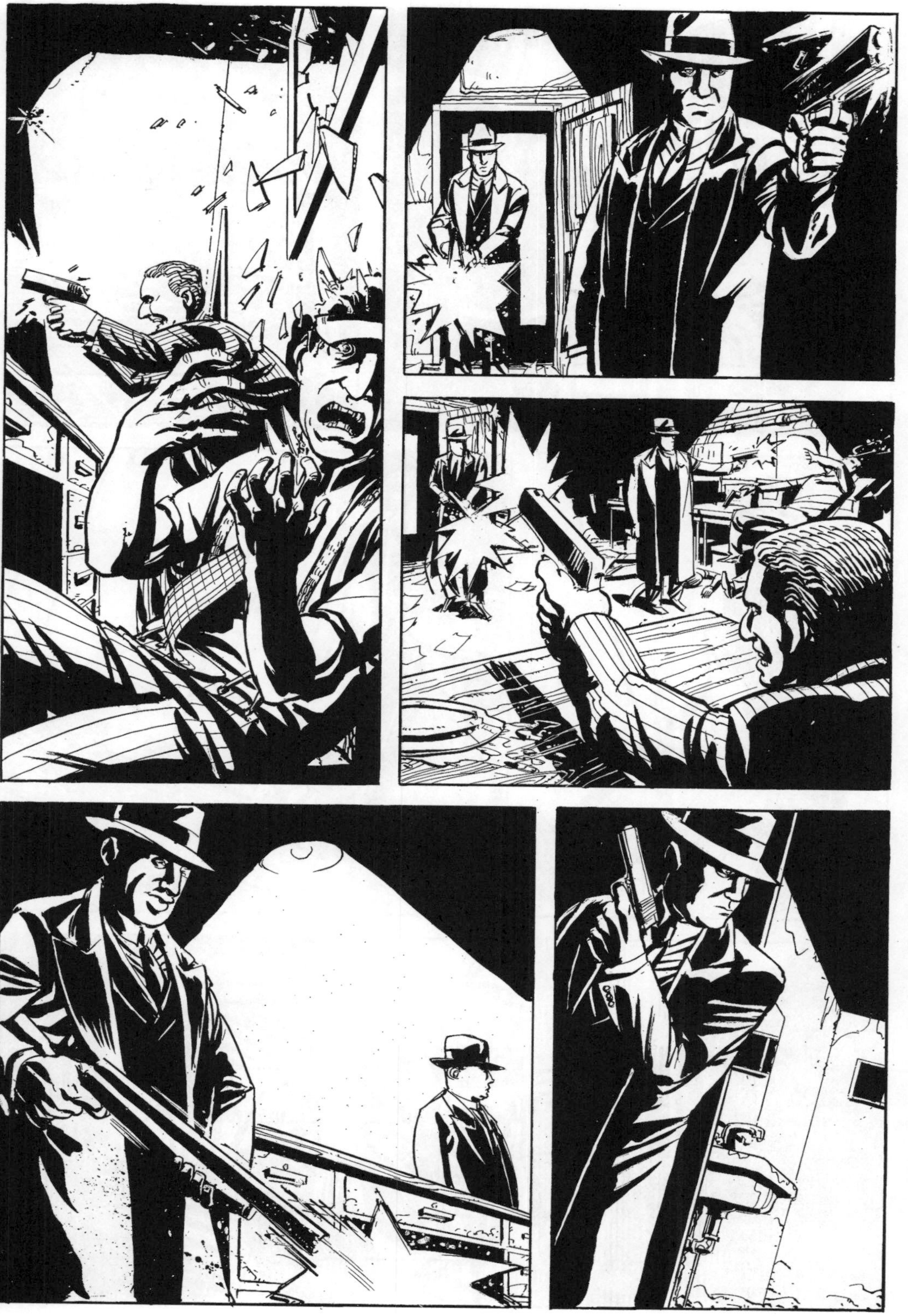

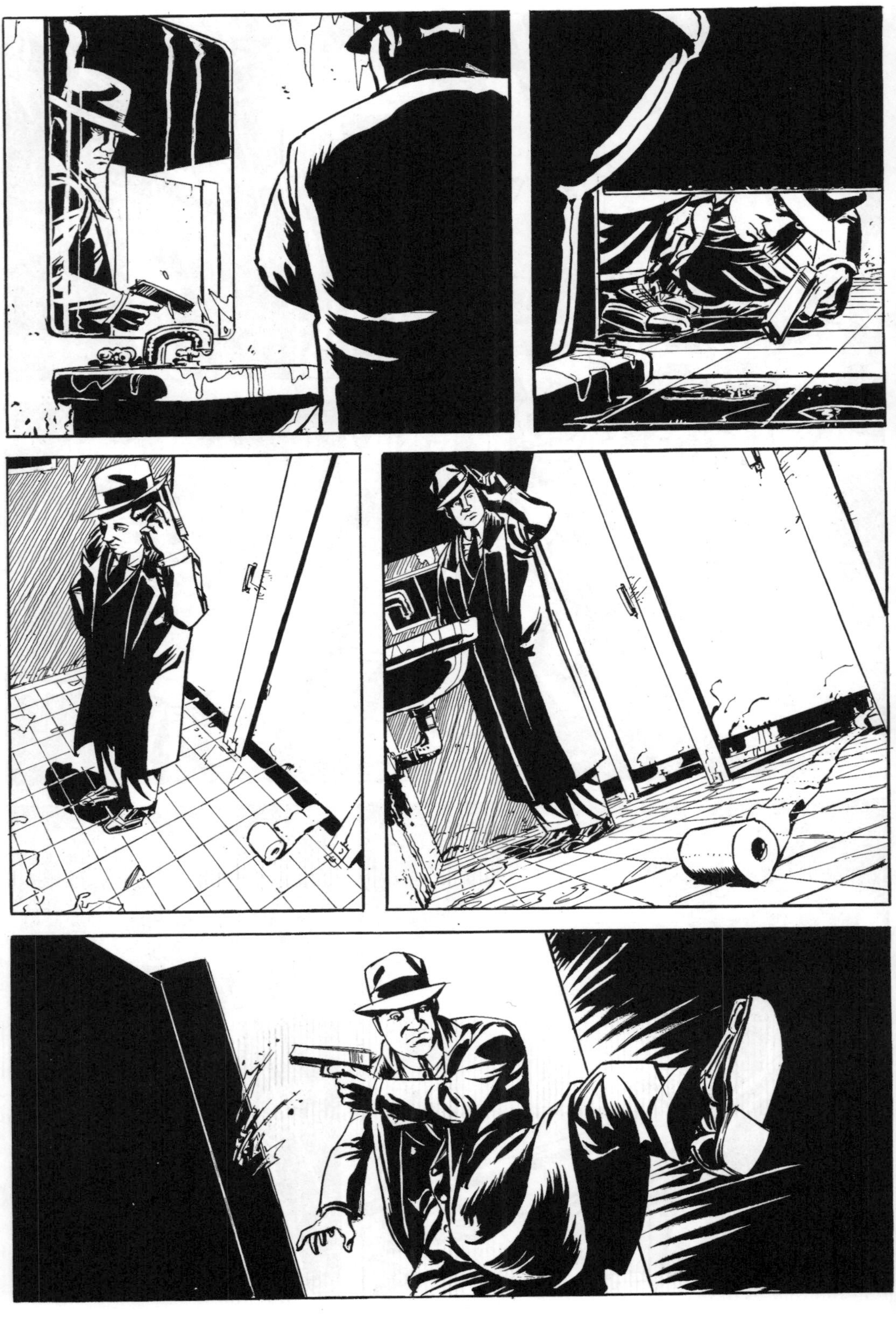

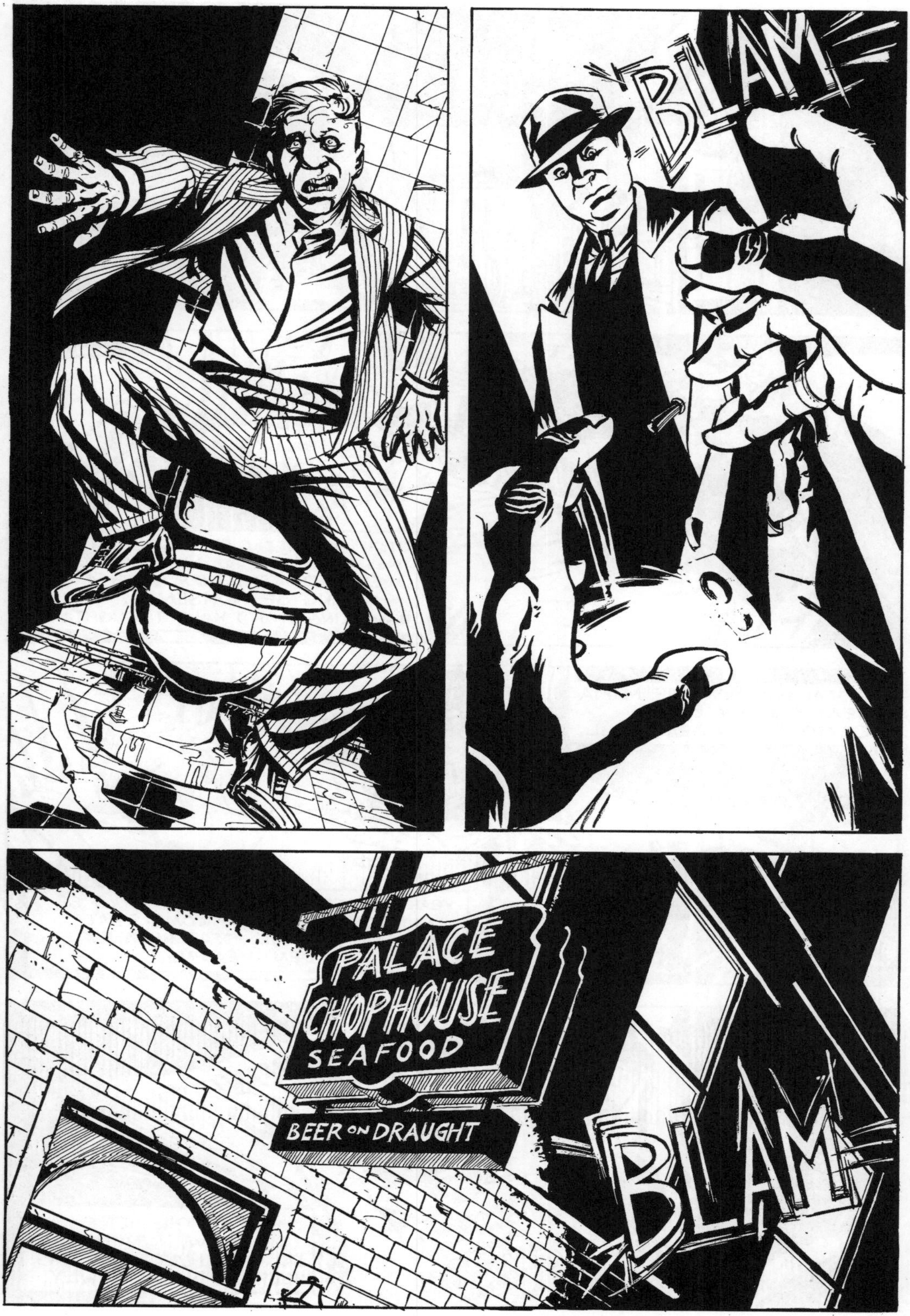
BLAM
PALACE
CHOPHOUSE
SEAFOOD
BEER ON DRAUGHT
BLAM

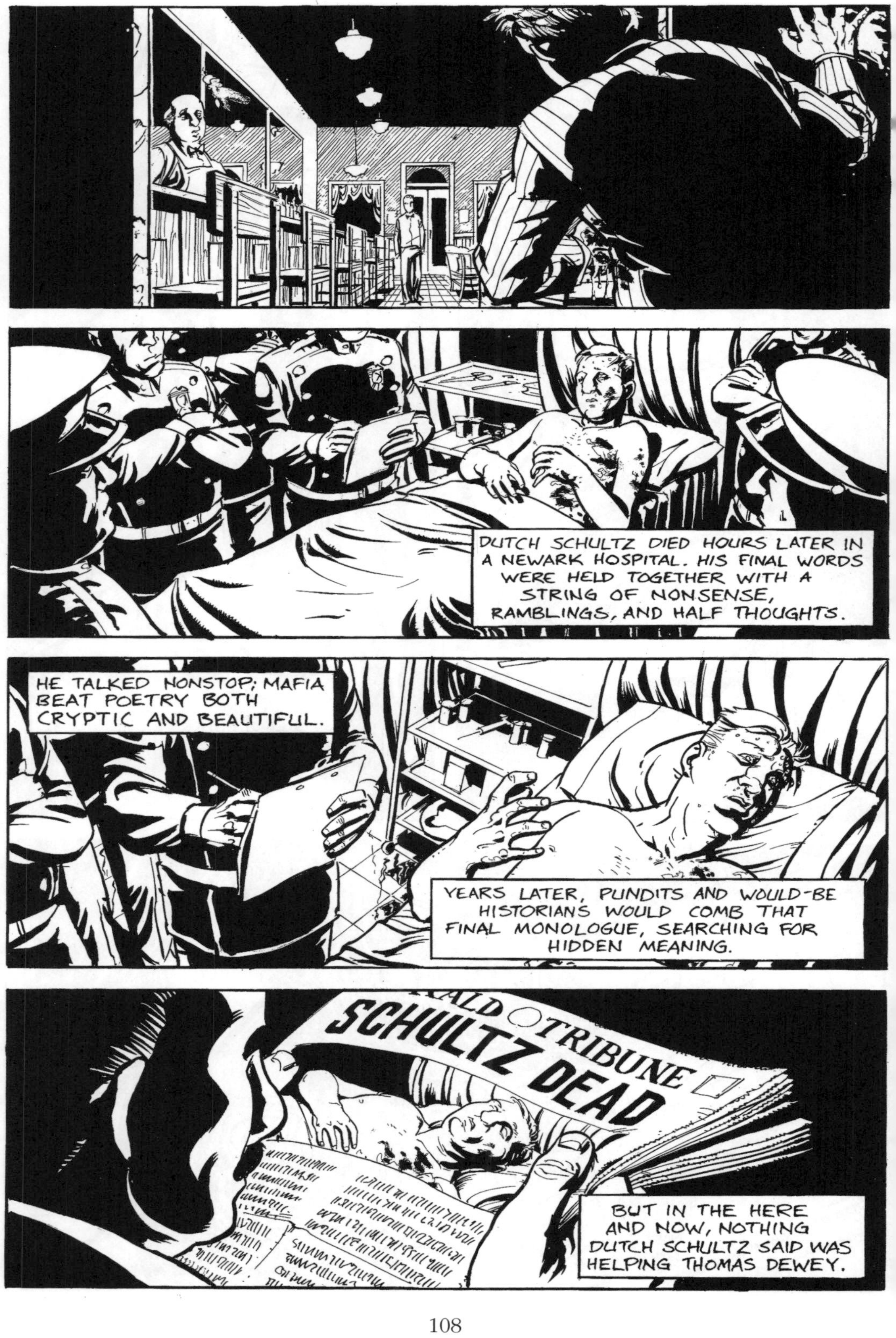
DUTCH SCHULTZ DIED HOURS LATER IN A NEWARK HOSPITAL. HIS FINAL WORDS WERE HELD TOGETHER WITH A STRING OF NONSENSE, RAMBLINGS, AND HALF THOUGHTS.
HE TALKED NONSTOP; MAFIA BEAT POETRY BOTH CRYPTIC AND BEAUTIFUL.
YEARS LATER, PUNDITS AND WOULD-BE HISTORIANS WOULD COMB THAT FINAL MONOLOGUE, SEARCHING FOR HIDDEN MEANING.
TRIBUNE
SCHULTZ DEAD
BUT IN THE HERE AND NOW, NOTHING DUTCH SCHULTZ SAID WAS HELPING THOMAS DEWEY.

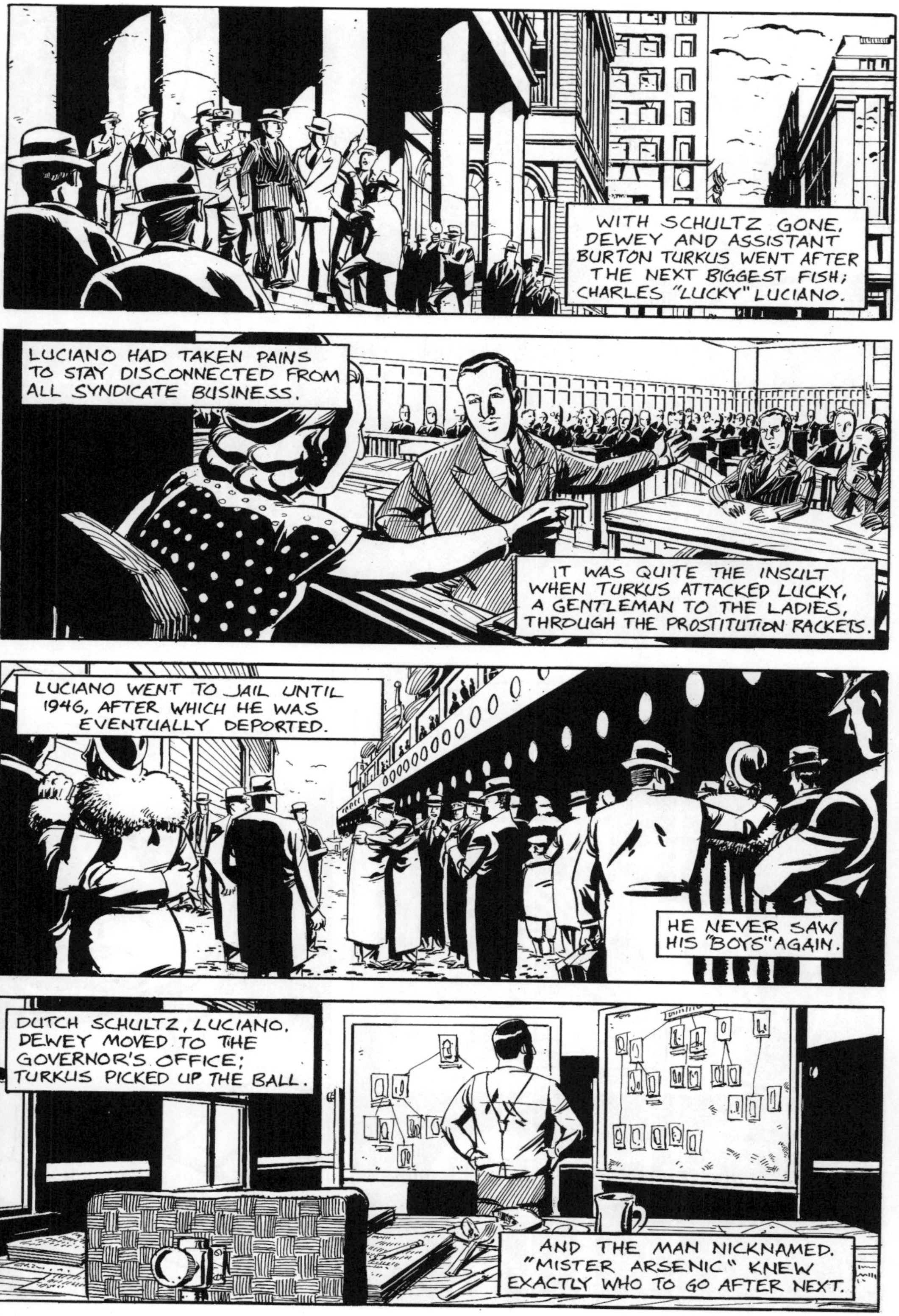
WITH SCHULTZ GONE, DEWEY AND ASSISTANT BURTON TURKUS WENT AFTER THE NEXT BIGGEST FISH; CHARLES "LUCKY" LUCIANO.
LUCIANO HAD TAKEN PAINS TO STAY DISCONNECTED FROM ALL SYNDICATE BUSINESS.
IT WAS QUITE THE INSULT WHEN TURKUS ATTACKED LUCKY, A GENTLEMAN TO THE LADIES, THROUGH THE PROSTITUTION RACKETS.
LUCIANO WENT TO JAIL UNTIL 1946, AFTER WHICH HE WAS EVENTUALLY DEPORTED.
HE NEVER SAW HIS "BOYS" AGAIN.
DUTCH SCHULTZ, LUCIANO. DEWEY MOVED TO THE GOVERNOR'S OFFICE; TURKUS PICKED UP THE BALL.
AND THE MAN NICKNAMED. "MISTER ARSENIC" KNEW EXACTLY WHO TO GO AFTER NEXT.

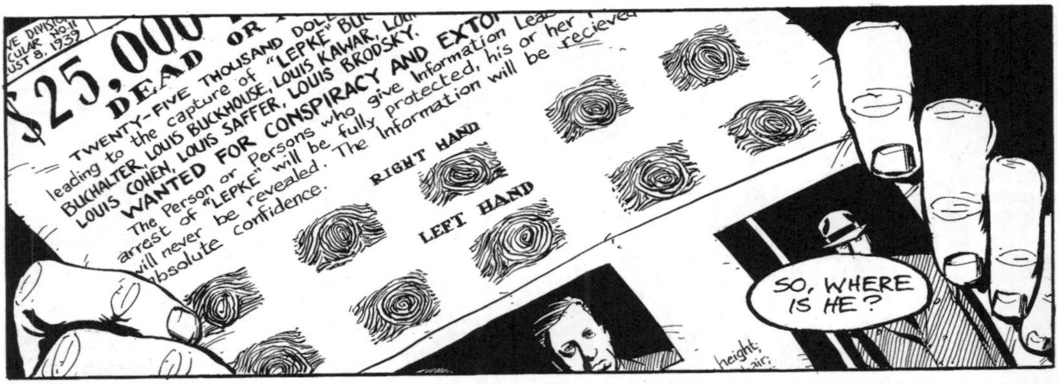
$25,000
DEAD OR
TWENTY-FIVE THOUSAND DOLL
leading to the capture of "LEPKE" BU
BUCHALTER, LOUIS BUCKHOUSE, LOUIS KAWAR, LOU
LOUIS COHEN, LOUIS SAFFER, LOUIS BRODSKY.
WANTED FOR CONSPIRACY AND EXTO
The Person or Persons who give Information Lea
arrest of "LEPKE" will be fully protected, his or her
will never be revealed. The Information will be recieved
absolute confidence.
RIGHT HAND
LEFT HAND
SO, WHERE IS HE?

THE NORMAL LIFE

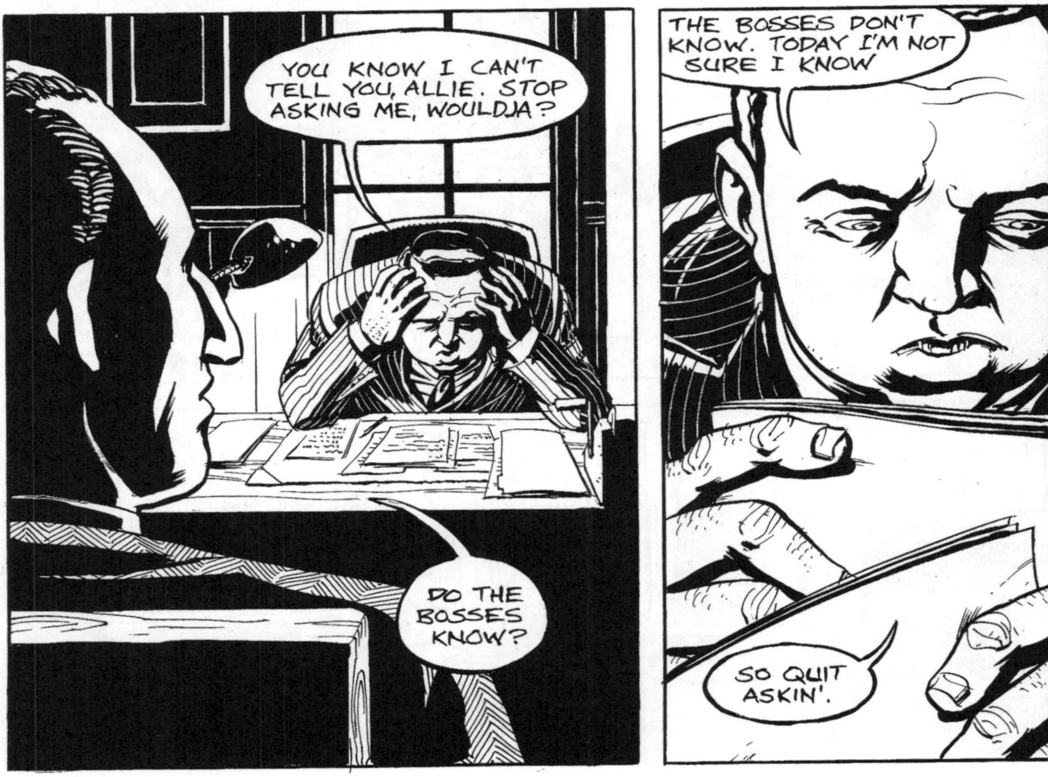
YOU KNOW I CAN'T TELL YOU, ALLIE. STOP ASKING ME, WOULDJA?
DO THE BOSSES KNOW?
THE BOSSES DON'T KNOW. TODAY I'M NOT SURE I KNOW
SO QUIT ASKIN'.

HOW ARE WE GONNA WORK?

BUSINESS AIN'T GONNA STOP JUST 'CAUSE LEPKE'S ON THE LAM, GURRAH.

I KNOW.

AND THIS AIN'T GONNA HELP MATTERS!

$25,000 DEAD OR ALIVE

D'YOU KNOW WHAT THE HEAT'S LIKE OUT THERE RIGHT NOW?

HOW D'YOU RUN A RACKET WHEN ANY SECOND A FED'S GONNA GO-VOOT!

"WHERE'S LEPKE?!"

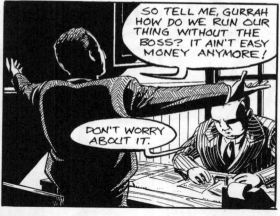

SO TELL ME, GURRAH HOW DO WE RUN OUR THING WITHOUT THE BOSS? IT AIN'T EASY MONEY ANYMORE!

DON'T WORRY ABOUT IT.

IT'S NOT YOUR PROBLEM.

THINGS ARE BEING TAKEN CARE OF.

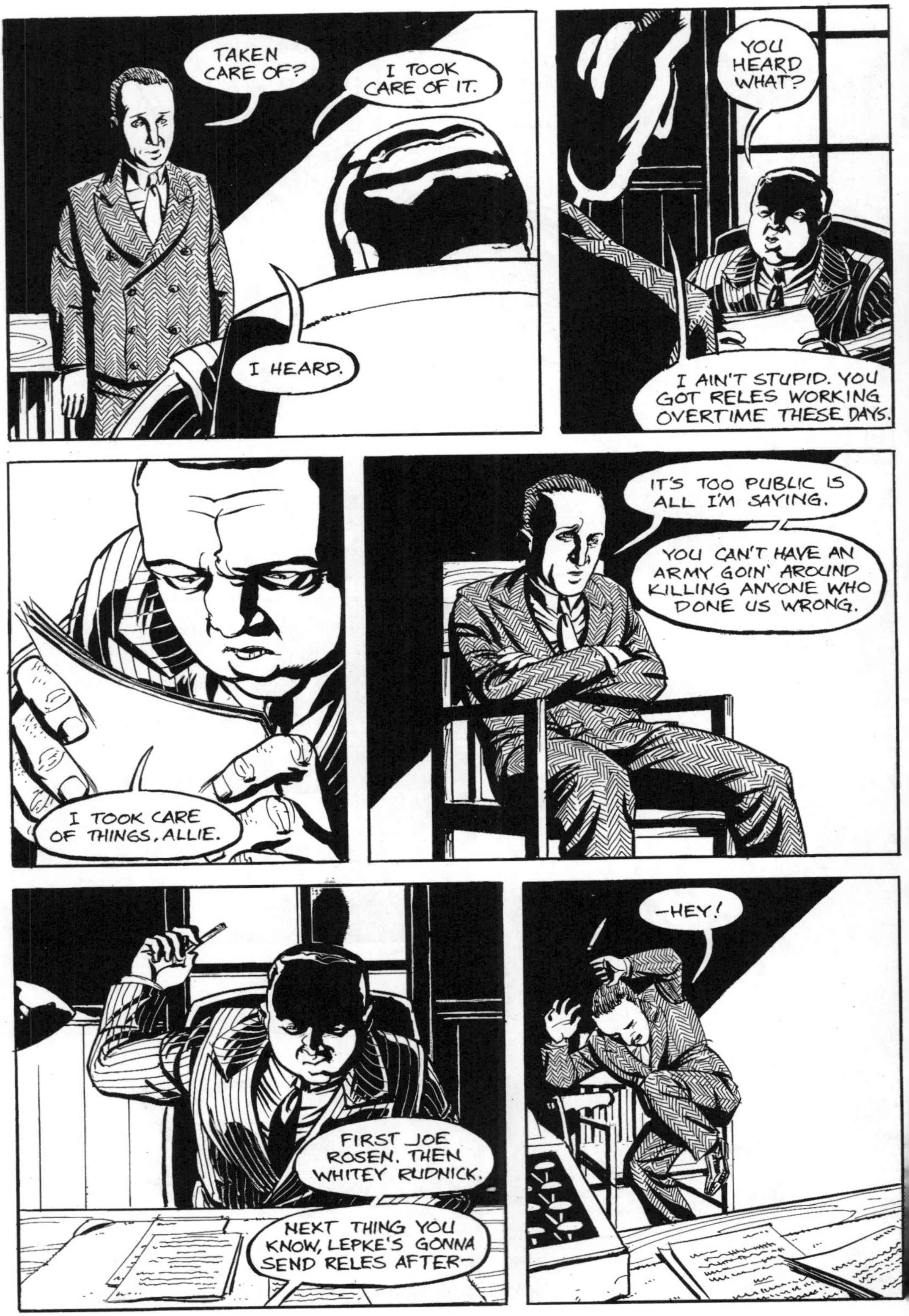
TAKEN CARE OF?
I TOOK CARE OF IT.
I HEARD.
YOU HEARD WHAT?
I AIN'T STUPID. YOU GOT RELES WORKING OVERTIME THESE DAYS.
I TOOK CARE OF THINGS, ALLIE.
IT'S TOO PUBLIC IS ALL I'M SAYING.
YOU CAN'T HAVE AN ARMY GOIN' AROUND KILLING ANYONE WHO DONE US WRONG.
FIRST JOE ROSEN. THEN WHITEY RUDNICK.
NEXT THING YOU KNOW, LEPKE'S GONNA SEND RELES AFTER-
-HEY!

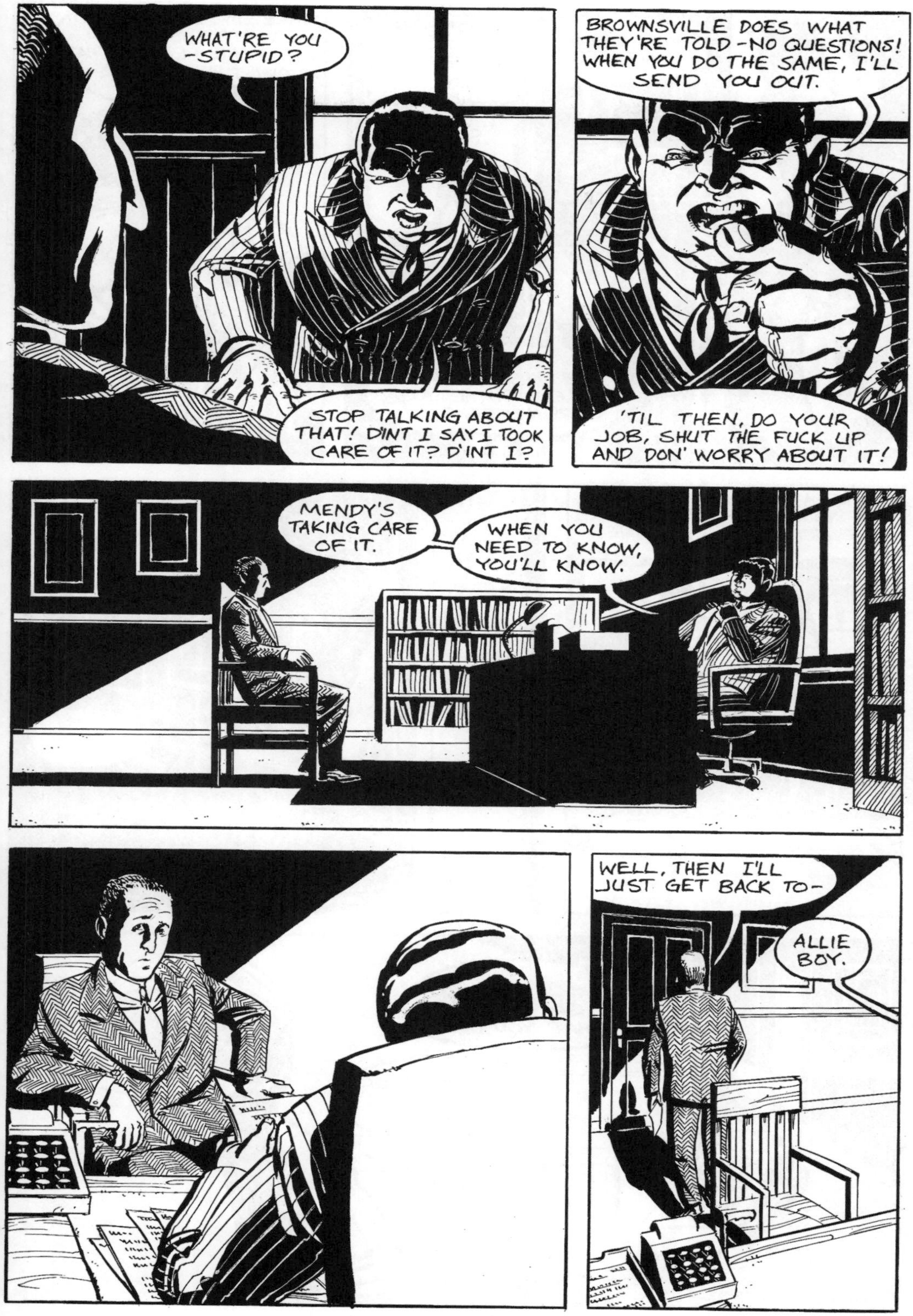
WHAT'RE YOU -STUPID?
STOP TALKING ABOUT THAT! D'INT I SAY I TOOK CARE OF IT? D'INT I?
BROWNSVILLE DOES WHAT THEY'RE TOLD - NO QUESTIONS! WHEN YOU DO THE SAME, I'LL SEND YOU OUT.
'TIL THEN, DO YOUR JOB, SHUT THE FUCK UP AND DON' WORRY ABOUT IT!
MENDY'S TAKING CARE OF IT.
WHEN YOU NEED TO KNOW, YOU'LL KNOW.
WELL, THEN I'LL JUST GET BACK TO-
ALLIE BOY.

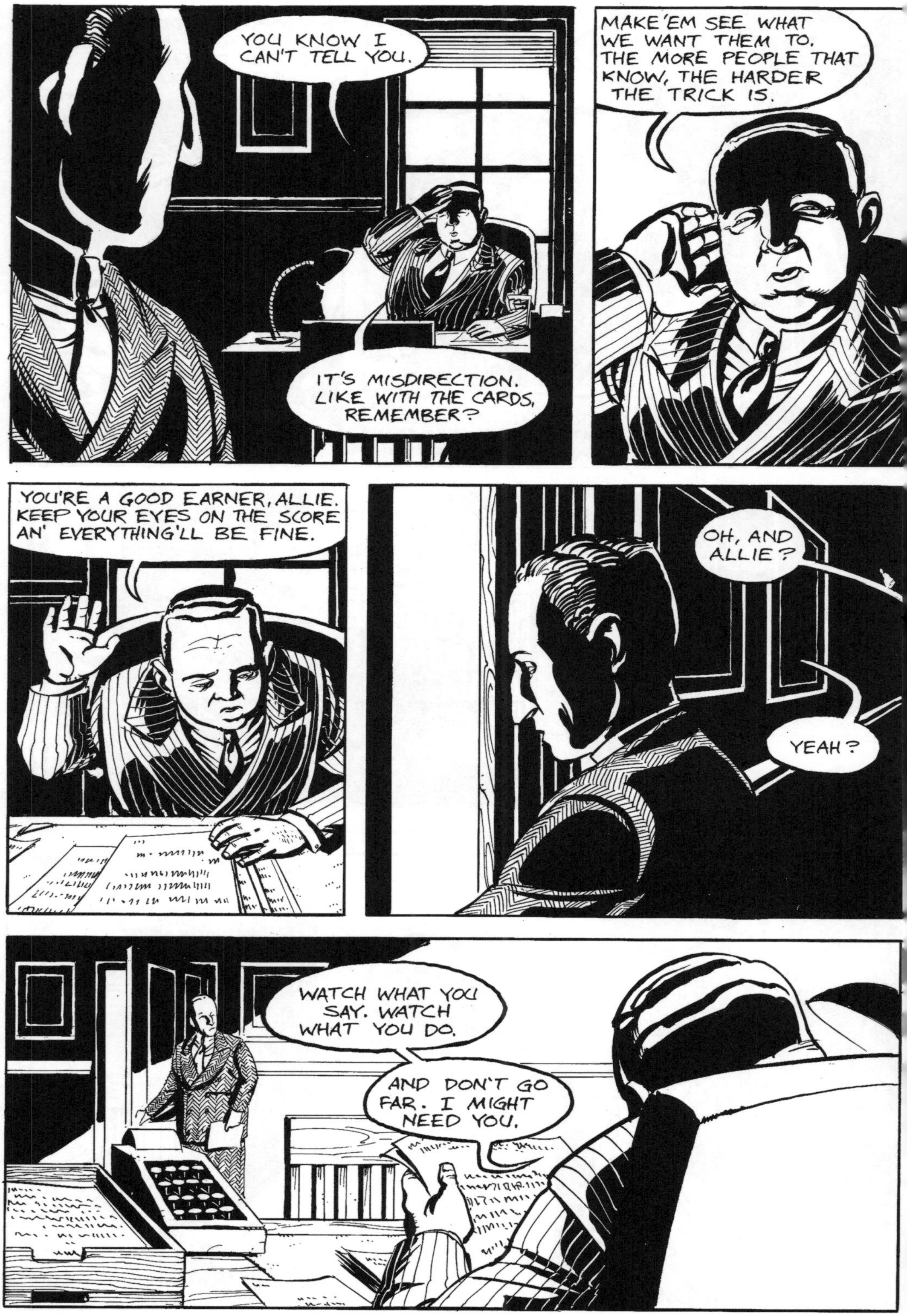
YOU KNOW I CAN'T TELL YOU.
IT'S MISDIRECTION. LIKE WITH THE CARDS, REMEMBER?
MAKE 'EM SEE WHAT WE WANT THEM TO. THE MORE PEOPLE THAT KNOW, THE HARDER THE TRICK IS.
YOU'RE A GOOD EARNER, ALLIE. KEEP YOUR EYES ON THE SCORE AN' EVERYTHING'LL BE FINE.
OH, AND ALLIE?
YEAH?
WATCH WHAT YOU SAY. WATCH WHAT YOU DO.
AND DON'T GO FAR. I MIGHT NEED YOU.

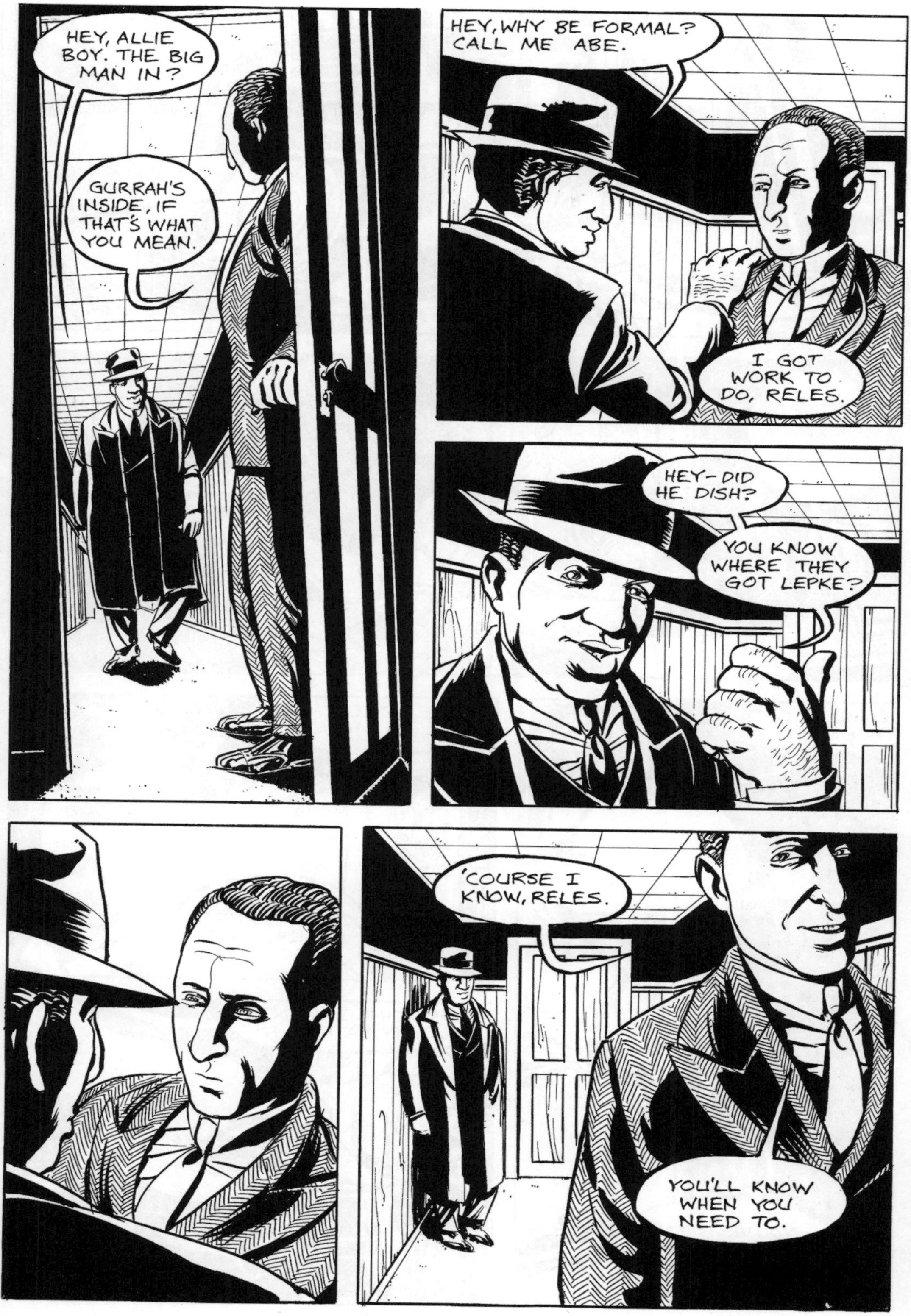
HEY, ALLIE BOY. THE BIG MAN IN?
GURRAH'S INSIDE, IF THAT'S WHAT YOU MEAN.
HEY, WHY BE FORMAL? CALL ME ABE.
I GOT WORK TO DO, RELES.
HEY- DID HE DISH?
YOU KNOW WHERE THEY GOT LEPKE?
'COURSE I KNOW, RELES.
YOU'LL KNOW WHEN YOU NEED TO.

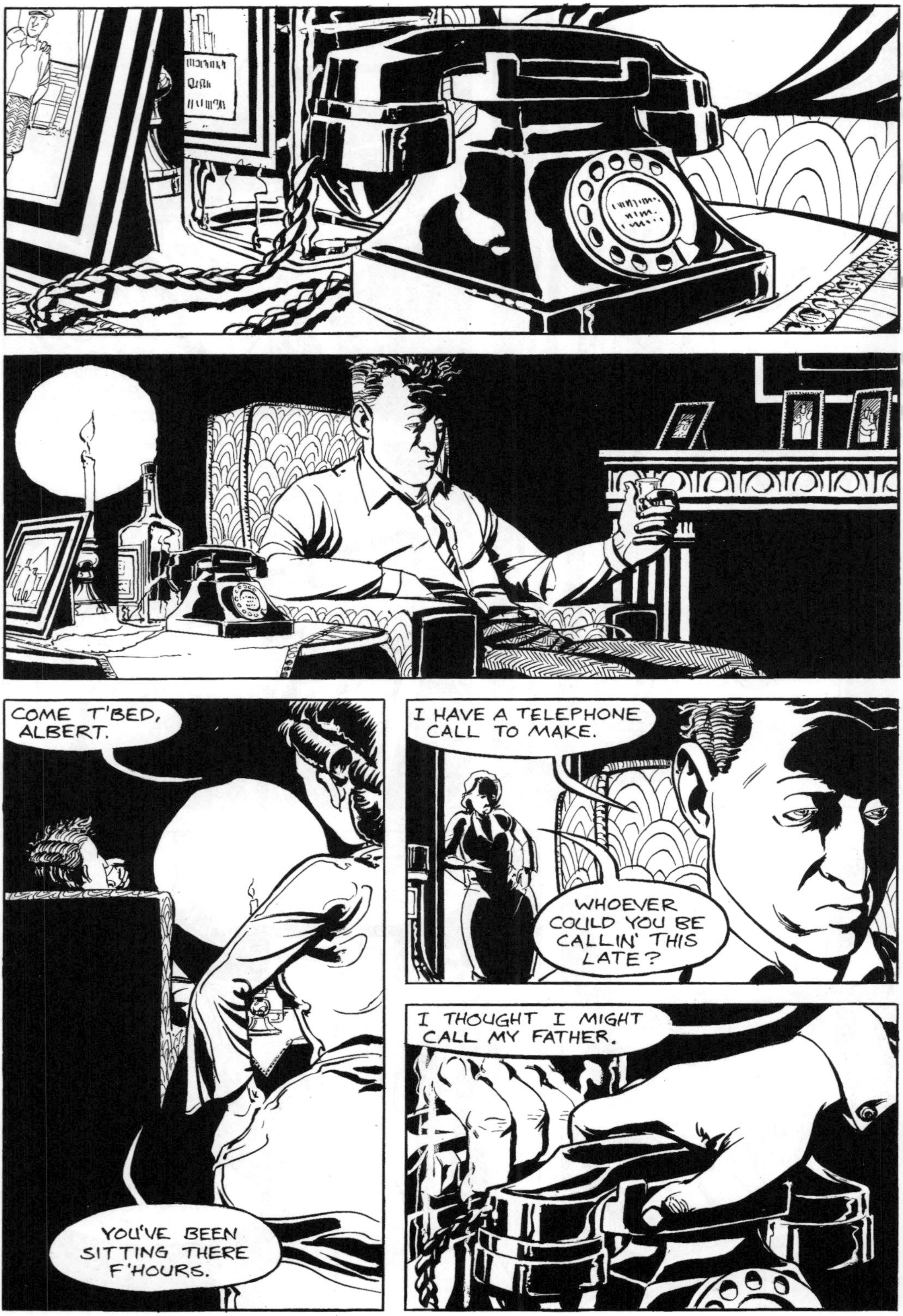
COME T'BED, ALBERT.
YOU'VE BEEN SITTING THERE F'HOURS.
I HAVE A TELEPHONE CALL TO MAKE.
WHOEVER COULD YOU BE CALLIN' THIS LATE?
I THOUGHT I MIGHT CALL MY FATHER.

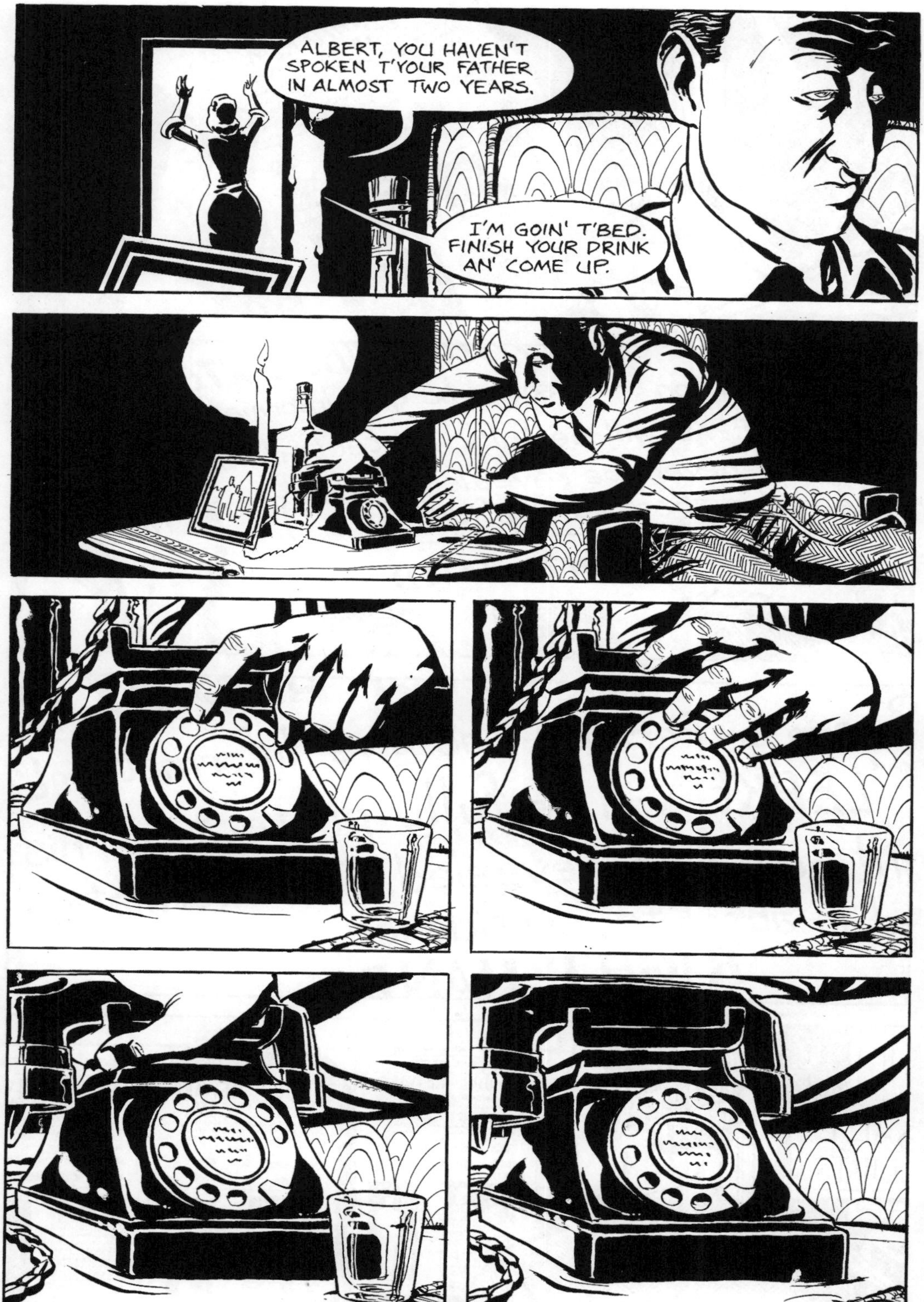
ALBERT, YOU HAVEN'T SPOKEN T'YOUR FATHER IN ALMOST TWO YEARS.
I'M GOIN' T'BED. FINISH YOUR DRINK AN' COME UP.

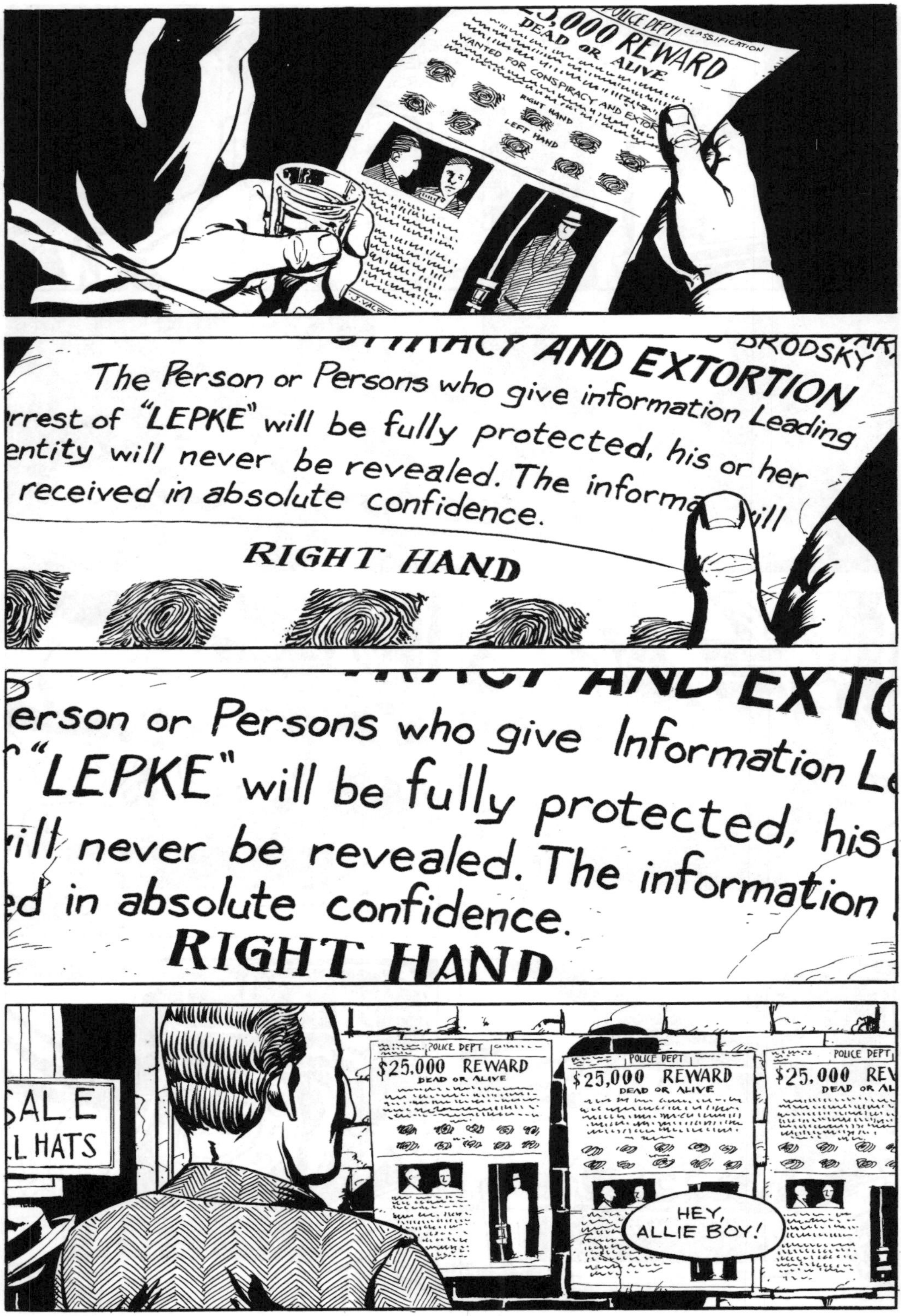
POLICE DEPT
CLASSIFICATION
5,000 REWARD
DEAD OR ALIVE
WANTED FOR CONSPIRACY AND EXTOR
RIGHT HAND
LEFT HAND
BRODSKY
AND EXTORTION
The Person or Persons who give information Leading
rrest of "LEPKE" will be fully protected, his or her
entity will never be revealed. The informa
received in absolute confidence.
RIGHT HAND
AND EXTO
erson or Persons who give Information Le
"LEPKE" will be fully protected, his
ill never be revealed. The information
ed in absolute confidence.
RIGHT HAND
SALE
LL HATS
POLICE DEPT
$25,000 REWARD
DEAD OR ALIVE
HEY, ALLIE BOY!

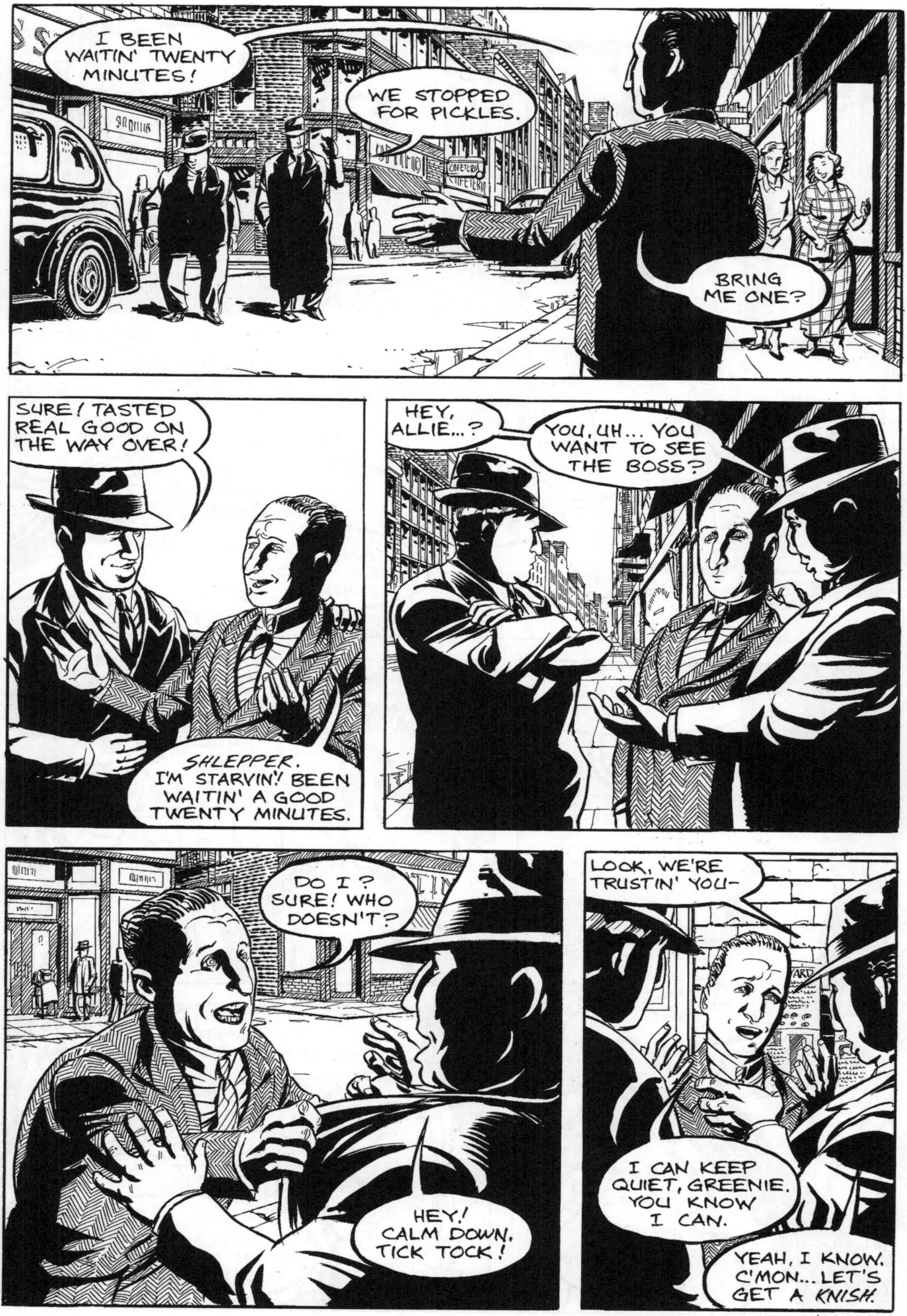
I BEEN WAITIN' TWENTY MINUTES!
WE STOPPED FOR PICKLES.
BRING ME ONE?
SURE! TASTED REAL GOOD ON THE WAY OVER!
SHLEPPER. I'M STARVIN'! BEEN WAITIN' A GOOD TWENTY MINUTES.
HEY, ALLIE...?
YOU, UH... YOU WANT TO SEE THE BOSS?
DO I? SURE! WHO DOESN'T?
HEY! CALM DOWN. TICK TOCK!
LOOK, WE'RE TRUSTIN' YOU-
I CAN KEEP QUIET, GREENIE. YOU KNOW I CAN.
YEAH, I KNOW. C'MON... LET'S GET A KNISH.

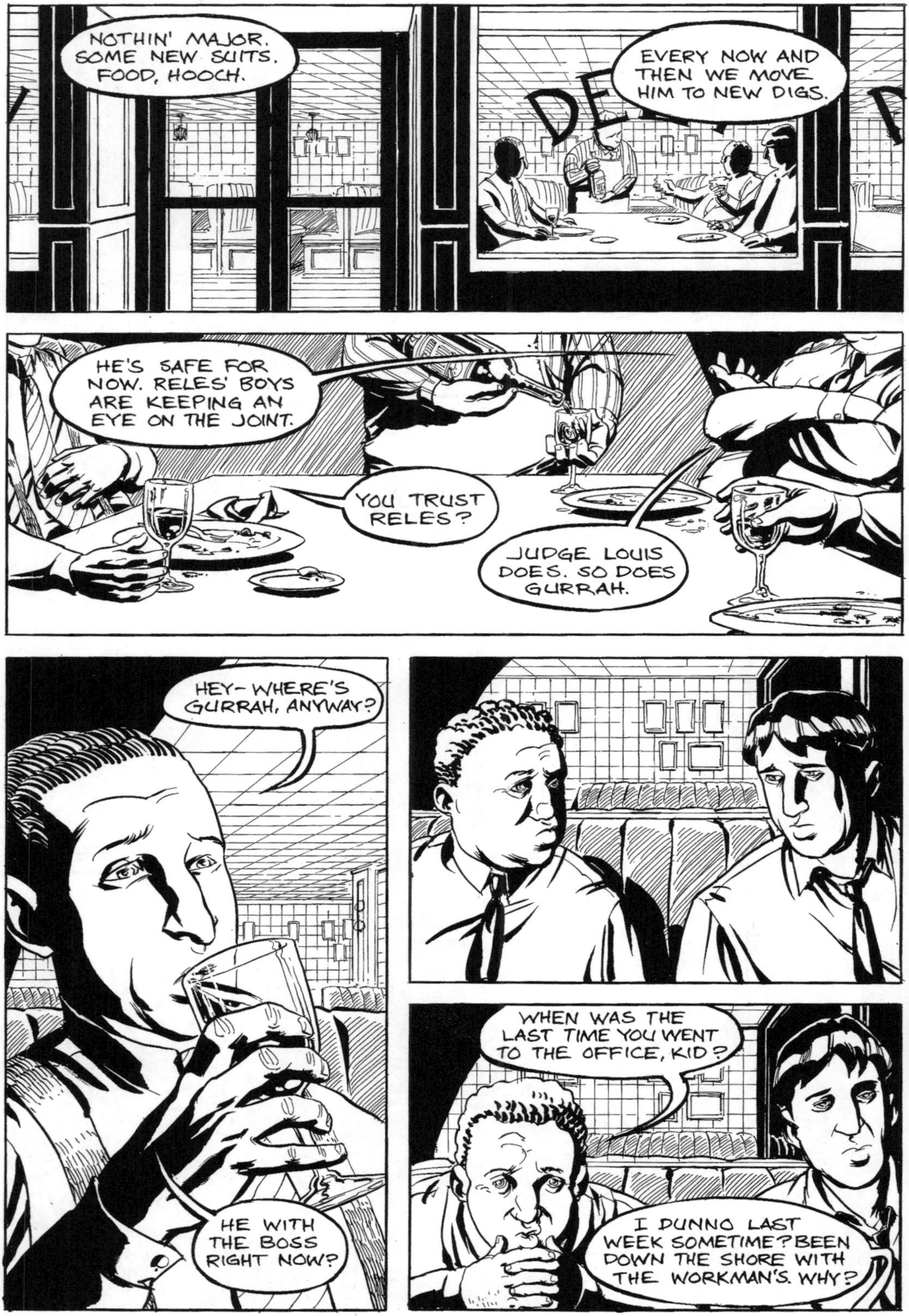
NOTHIN' MAJOR. SOME NEW SUITS. FOOD, HOOCH.
EVERY NOW AND THEN WE MOVE HIM TO NEW DIGS.
HE'S SAFE FOR NOW. RELES' BOYS ARE KEEPING AN EYE ON THE JOINT.
YOU TRUST RELES?
JUDGE LOUIS DOES. SO DOES GURRAH.
HEY- WHERE'S GURRAH, ANYWAY?
HE WITH THE BOSS RIGHT NOW?
WHEN WAS THE LAST TIME YOU WENT TO THE OFFICE, KID?
I DUNNO LAST WEEK SOMETIME? BEEN DOWN THE SHORE WITH THE WORKMAN'S. WHY?

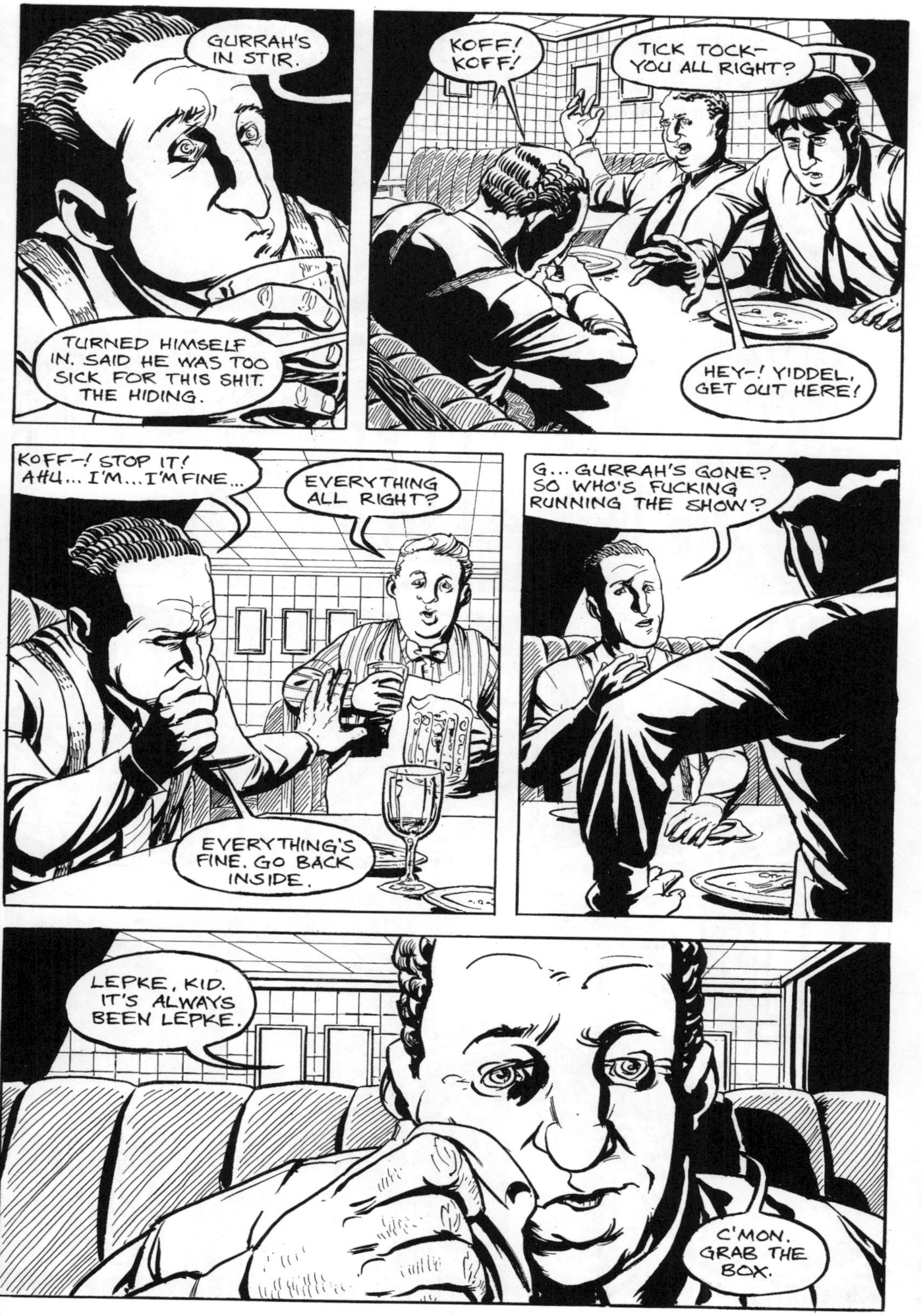
GURRAH'S IN STIR.
TURNED HIMSELF IN. SAID HE WAS TOO SICK FOR THIS SHIT. THE HIDING.
KOFF! KOFF!
TICK TOCK- YOU ALL RIGHT?
HEY-! YIDDEL, GET OUT HERE!
KOFF-! STOP IT! AHU... I'M... I'M FINE...
EVERYTHING ALL RIGHT?
EVERYTHING'S FINE. GO BACK INSIDE.
G... GURRAH'S GONE? SO WHO'S FUCKING RUNNING THE SHOW?
LEPKE, KID. IT'S ALWAYS BEEN LEPKE.
C'MON. GRAB THE BOX.

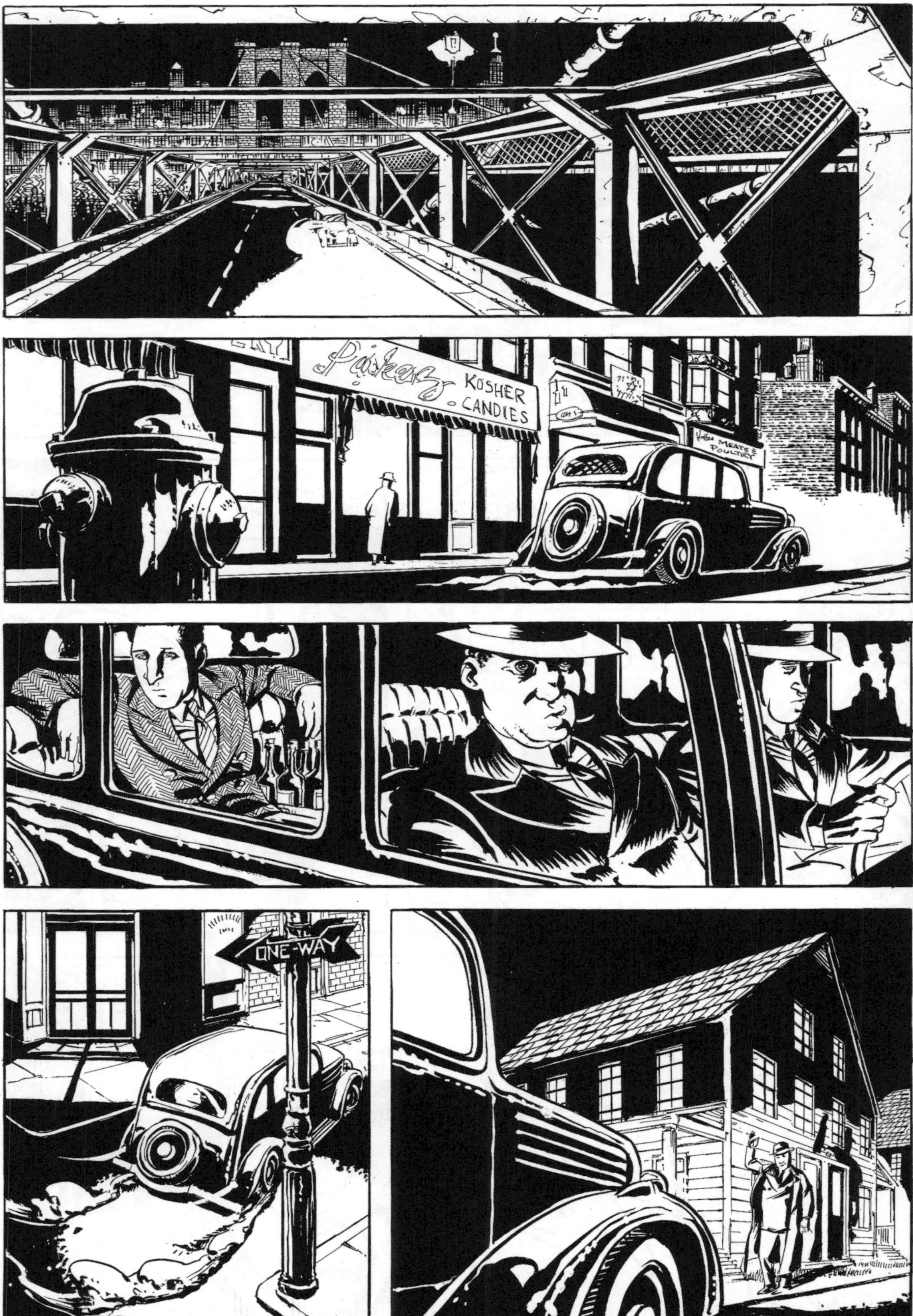
KOSHER
CANDIES
MEATS &
POULTRY
ONE-WAY

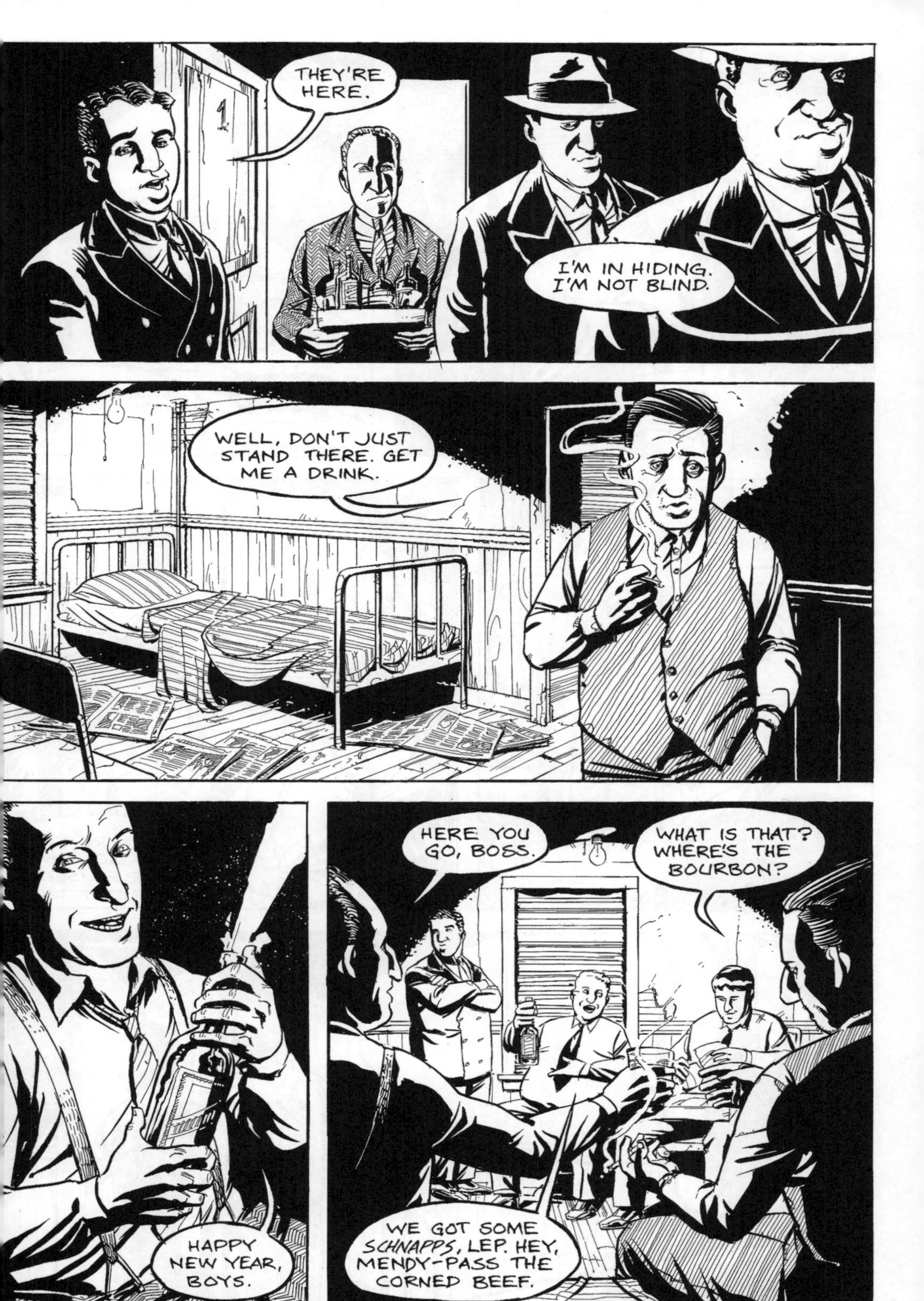
THEY'RE HERE.
I'M IN HIDING. I'M NOT BLIND.
WELL, DON'T JUST STAND THERE. GET ME A DRINK.
HAPPY NEW YEAR, BOYS.
HERE YOU GO, BOSS.
WHAT IS THAT? WHERE'S THE BOURBON?
WE GOT SOME *SCHNAPPS*, LEP. HEY, MENDY-PASS THE CORNED BEEF.

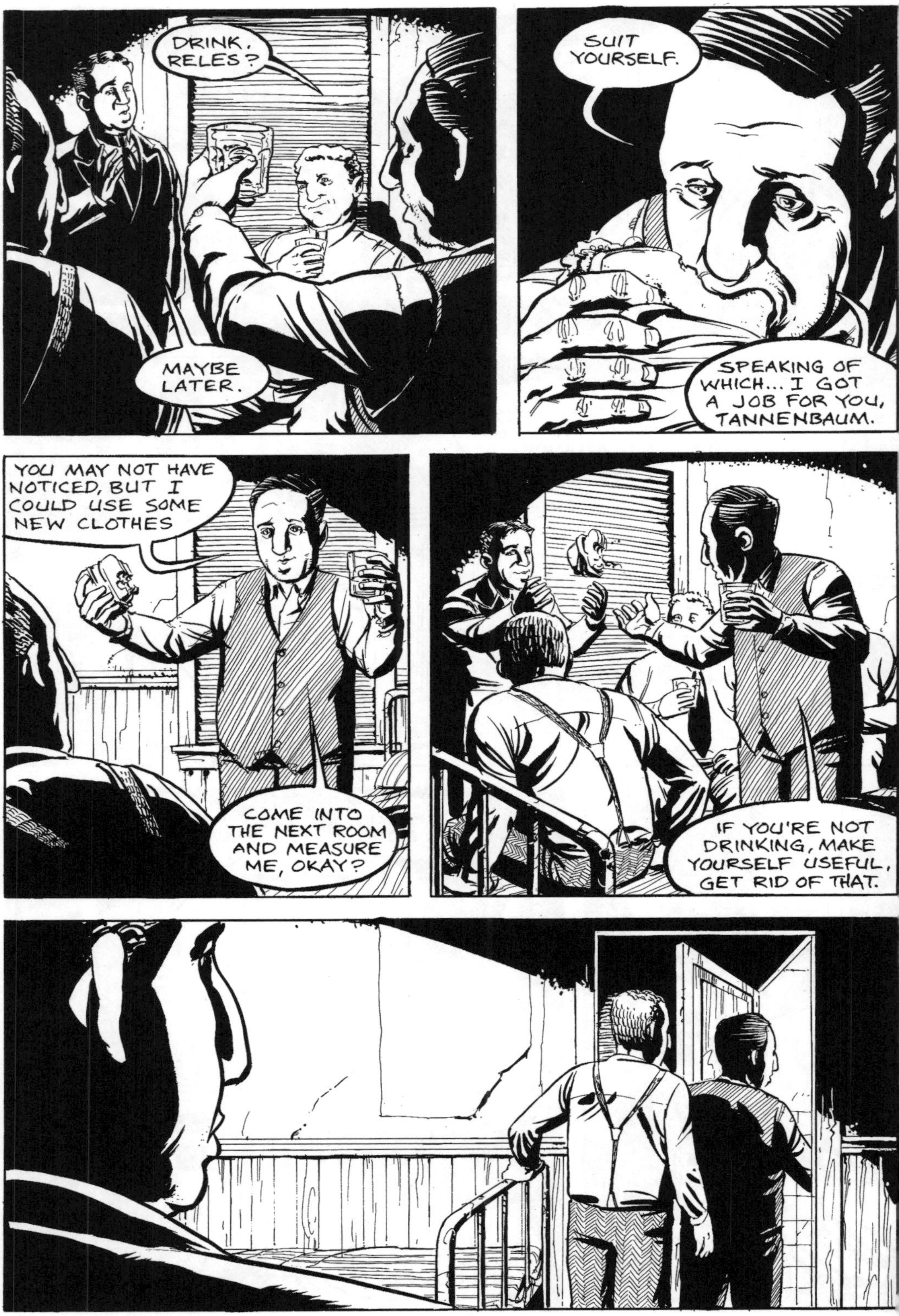
DRINK, RELES?
MAYBE LATER.
SUIT YOURSELF.
SPEAKING OF WHICH... I GOT A JOB FOR YOU, TANNENBAUM.
YOU MAY NOT HAVE NOTICED, BUT I COULD USE SOME NEW CLOTHES
COME INTO THE NEXT ROOM AND MEASURE ME, OKAY?
IF YOU'RE NOT DRINKING, MAKE YOURSELF USEFUL. GET RID OF THAT.

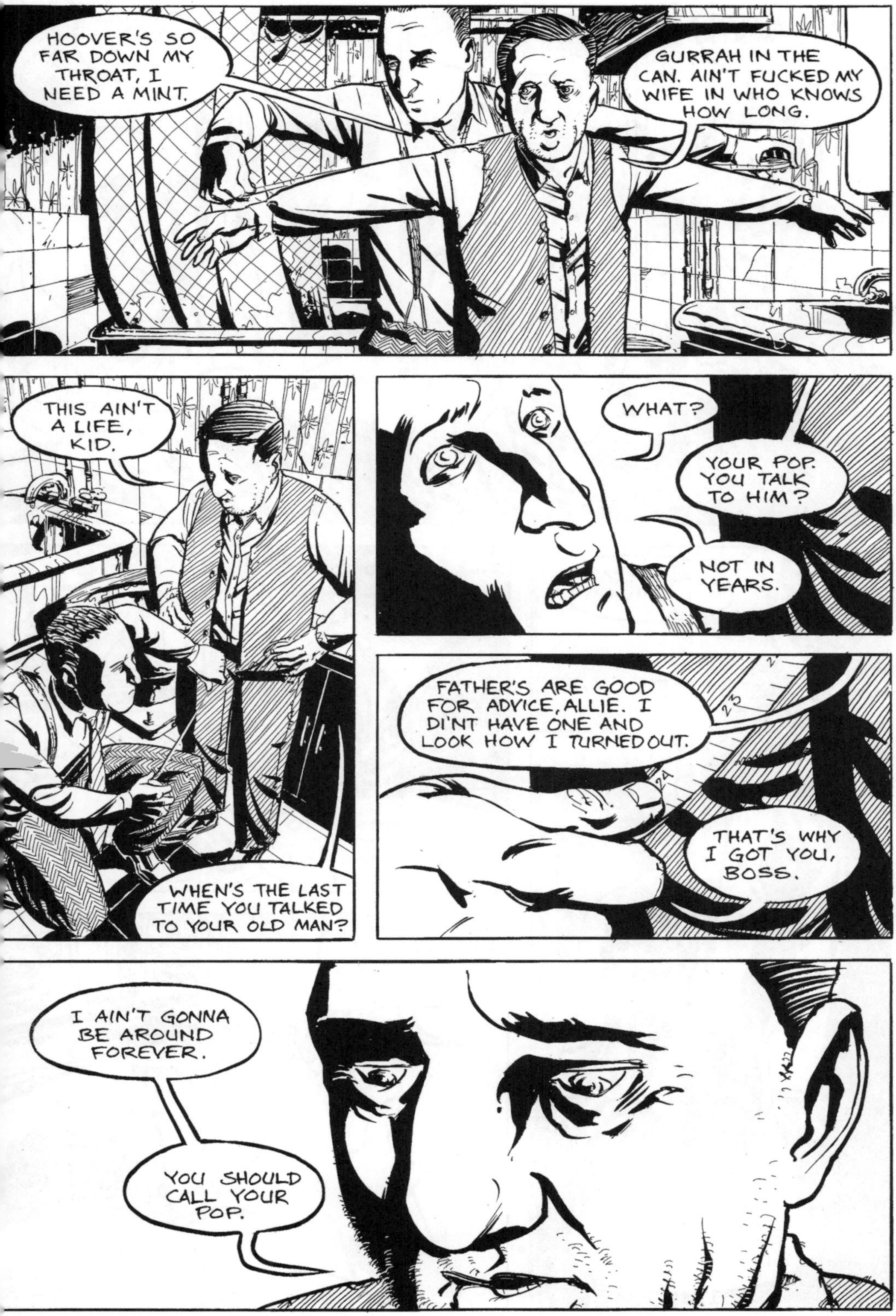
HOOVER'S SO FAR DOWN MY THROAT, I NEED A MINT.
GURRAH IN THE CAN. AIN'T FUCKED MY WIFE IN WHO KNOWS HOW LONG.
THIS AIN'T A LIFE, KID.
WHEN'S THE LAST TIME YOU TALKED TO YOUR OLD MAN?
WHAT?
YOUR POP. YOU TALK TO HIM?
NOT IN YEARS.
FATHER'S ARE GOOD FOR ADVICE, ALLIE. I DI'NT HAVE ONE AND LOOK HOW I TURNED OUT.
THAT'S WHY I GOT YOU, BOSS.
I AIN'T GONNA BE AROUND FOREVER.
YOU SHOULD CALL YOUR POP.

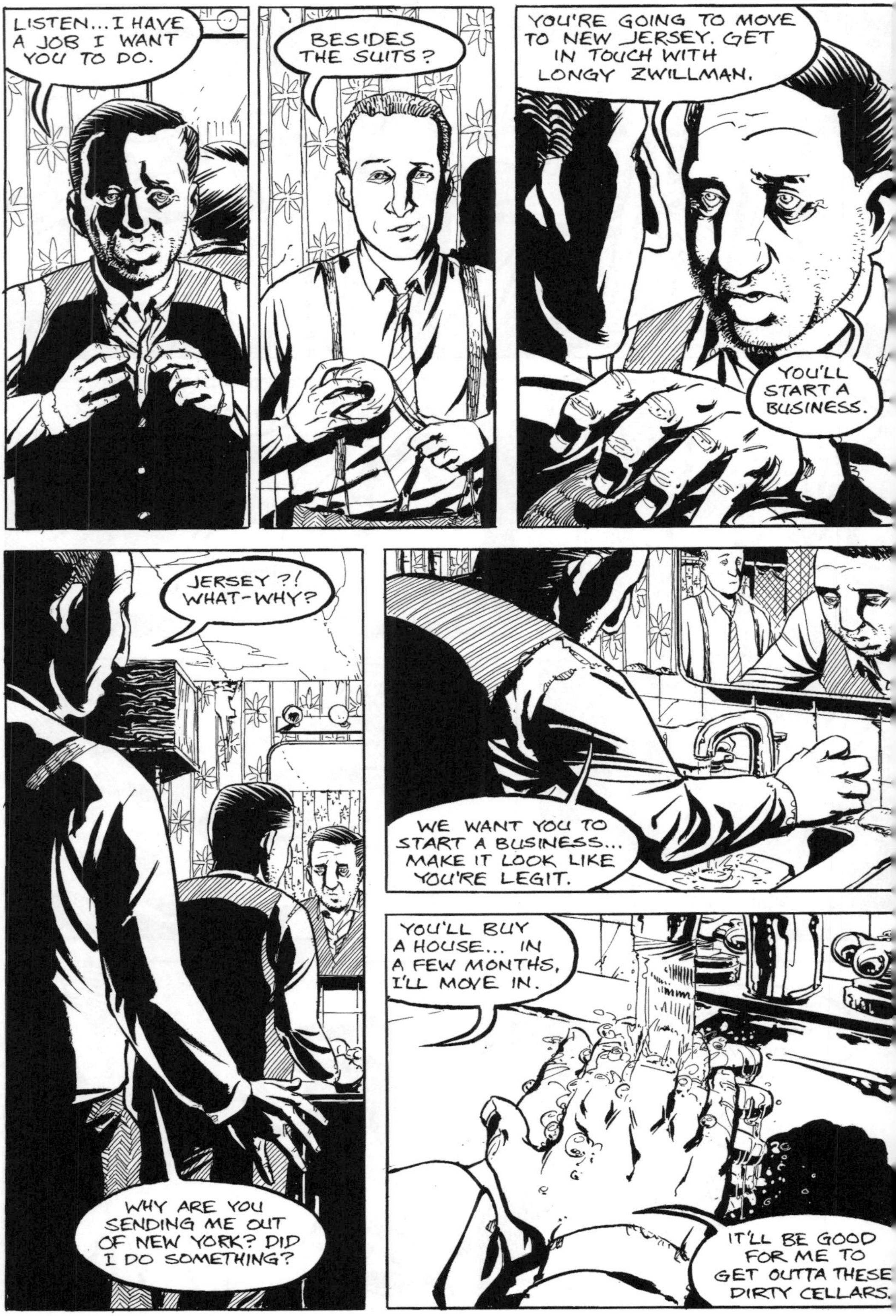
LISTEN... I HAVE A JOB I WANT YOU TO DO.
BESIDES THE SUITS?
YOU'RE GOING TO MOVE TO NEW JERSEY. GET IN TOUCH WITH LONGY ZWILLMAN.
YOU'LL START A BUSINESS.
JERSEY?! WHAT-WHY?
WHY ARE YOU SENDING ME OUT OF NEW YORK? DID I DO SOMETHING?
WE WANT YOU TO START A BUSINESS... MAKE IT LOOK LIKE YOU'RE LEGIT.
YOU'LL BUY A HOUSE... IN A FEW MONTHS, I'LL MOVE IN.
IT'LL BE GOOD FOR ME TO GET OUTTA THESE DIRTY CELLARS.

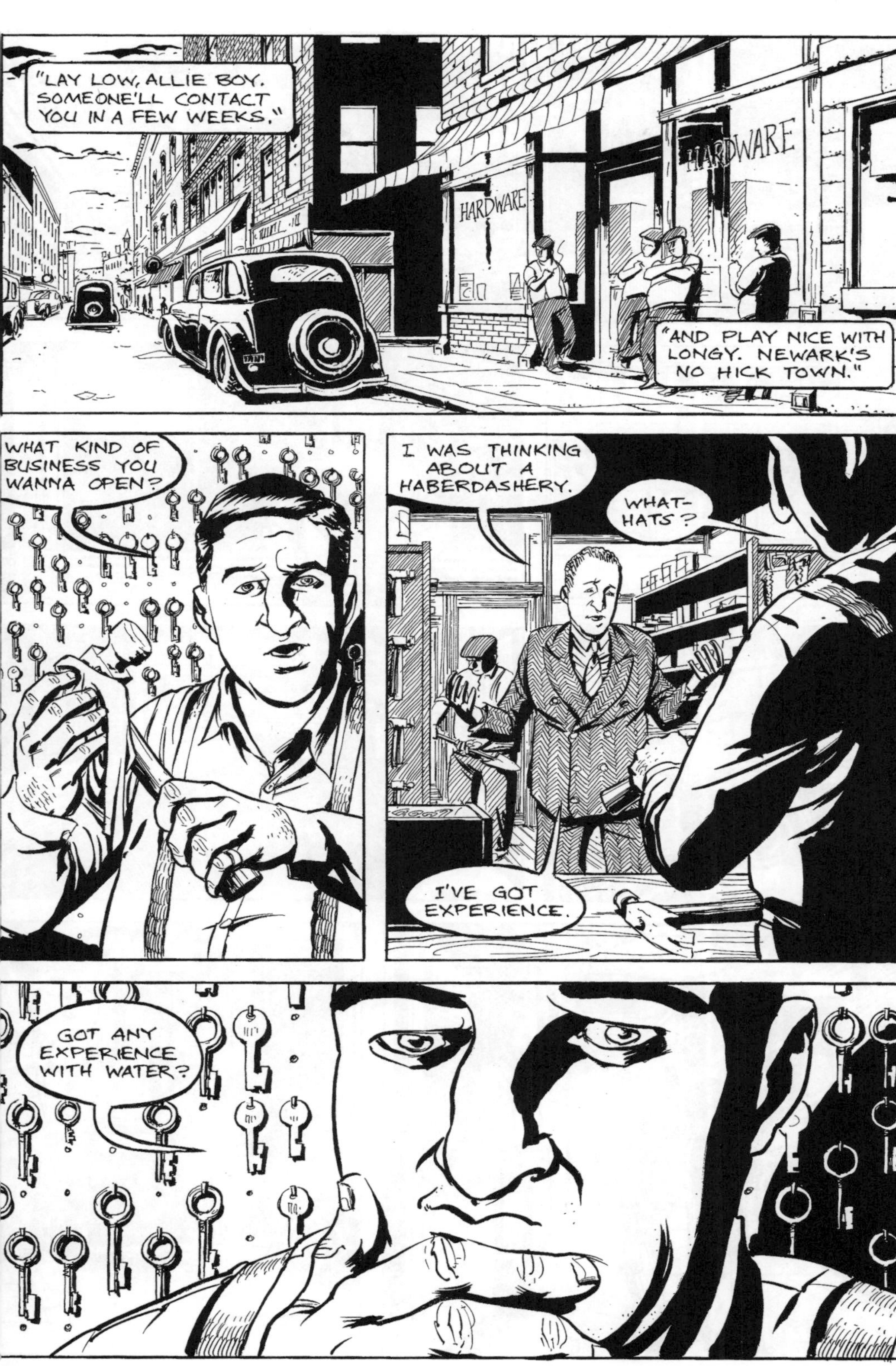
"LAY LOW, ALLIE BOY. SOMEONE'LL CONTACT YOU IN A FEW WEEKS."
HARDWARE
HARDWARE
"AND PLAY NICE WITH LONGY. NEWARK'S NO HICK TOWN."
WHAT KIND OF BUSINESS YOU WANNA OPEN?
I WAS THINKING ABOUT A HABERDASHERY.
WHAT-HATS?
I'VE GOT EXPERIENCE.
GOT ANY EXPERIENCE WITH WATER?

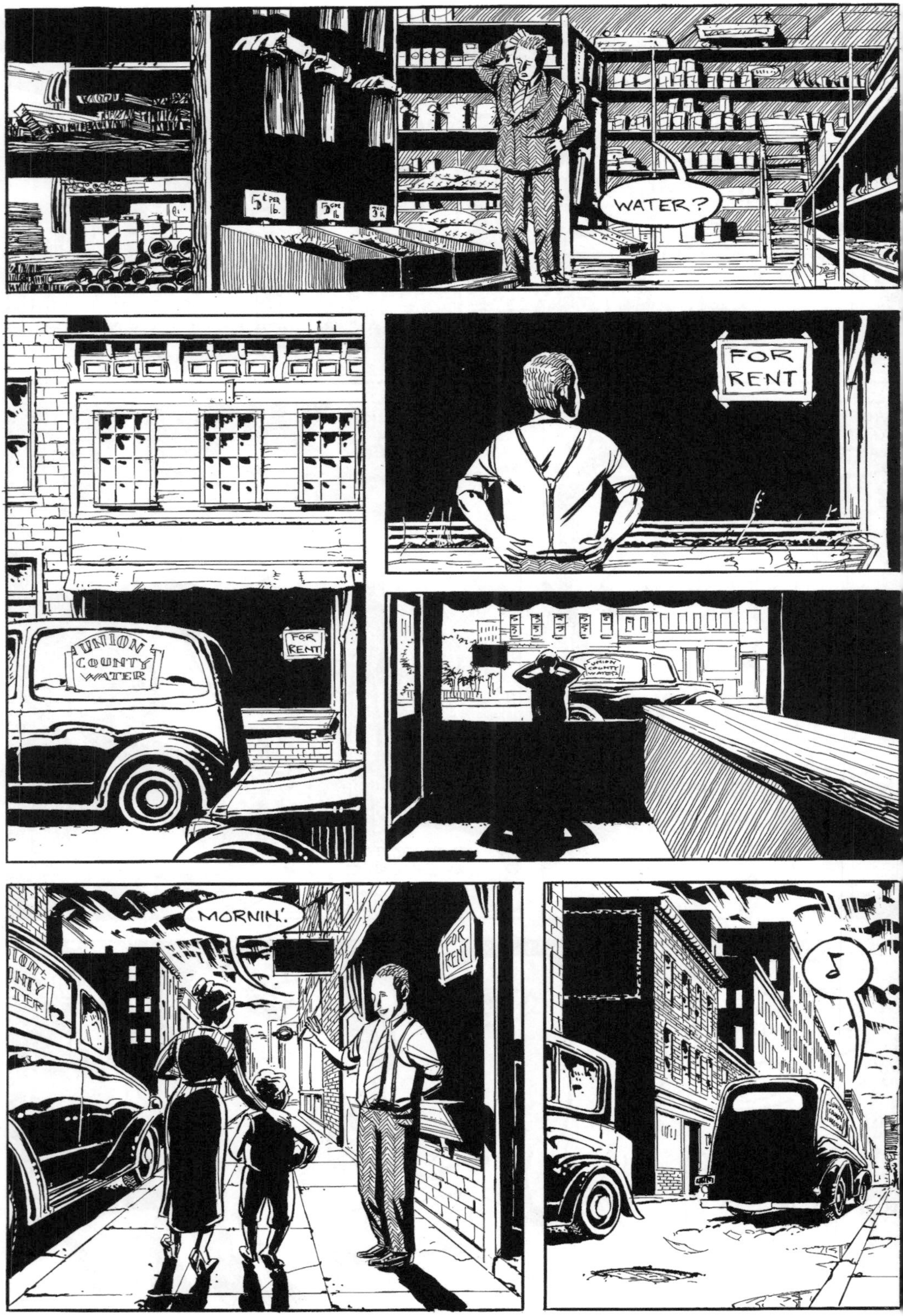
WATER?
FOR RENT
UNION COUNTY WATER
FOR RENT
MORNIN'.
FOR RENT

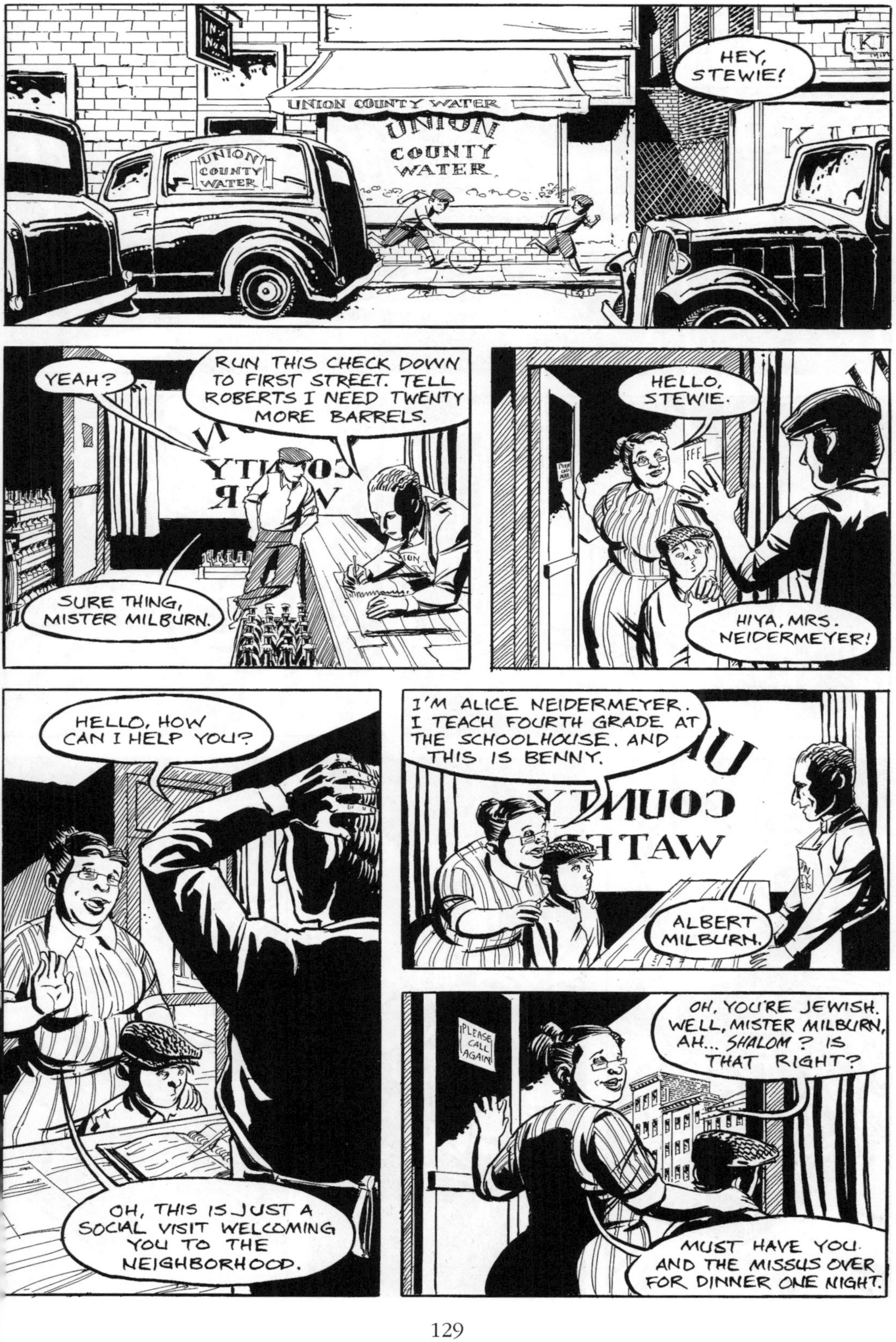
UNION COUNTY WATER
UNION COUNTY WATER
UNION COUNTY WATER
HEY, STEWIE!
YEAH?
RUN THIS CHECK DOWN TO FIRST STREET. TELL ROBERTS I NEED TWENTY MORE BARRELS.
SURE THING, MISTER MILBURN.
HELLO, STEWIE.
HIYA, MRS. NEIDERMEYER!
HELLO, HOW CAN I HELP YOU?
OH, THIS IS JUST A SOCIAL VISIT WELCOMING YOU TO THE NEIGHBORHOOD.
I'M ALICE NEIDERMEYER. I TEACH FOURTH GRADE AT THE SCHOOLHOUSE. AND THIS IS BENNY.
ALBERT MILBURN.
PLEASE CALL AGAIN
OH, YOU'RE JEWISH. WELL, MISTER MILBURN, AH... *SHALOM*? IS THAT RIGHT?
MUST HAVE YOU AND THE MISSUS OVER FOR DINNER ONE NIGHT.

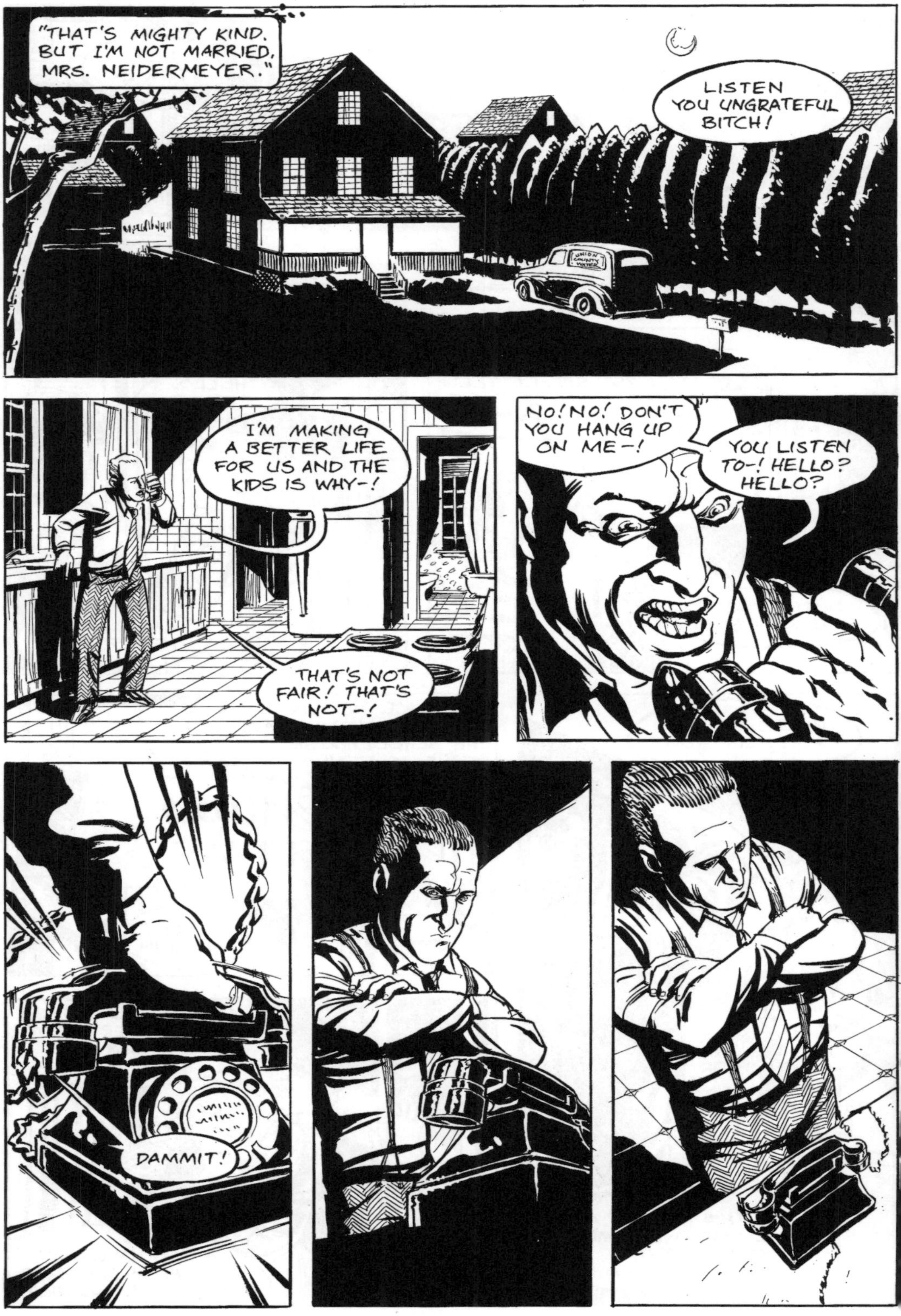
"THAT'S MIGHTY KIND. BUT I'M NOT MARRIED, MRS. NEIDERMEYER."
LISTEN YOU UNGRATEFUL BITCH!
I'M MAKING A BETTER LIFE FOR US AND THE KIDS IS WHY-!
THAT'S NOT FAIR! THAT'S NOT-!
NO! NO! DON'T YOU HANG UP ON ME-!
YOU LISTEN TO-! HELLO? HELLO?
DAMMIT!

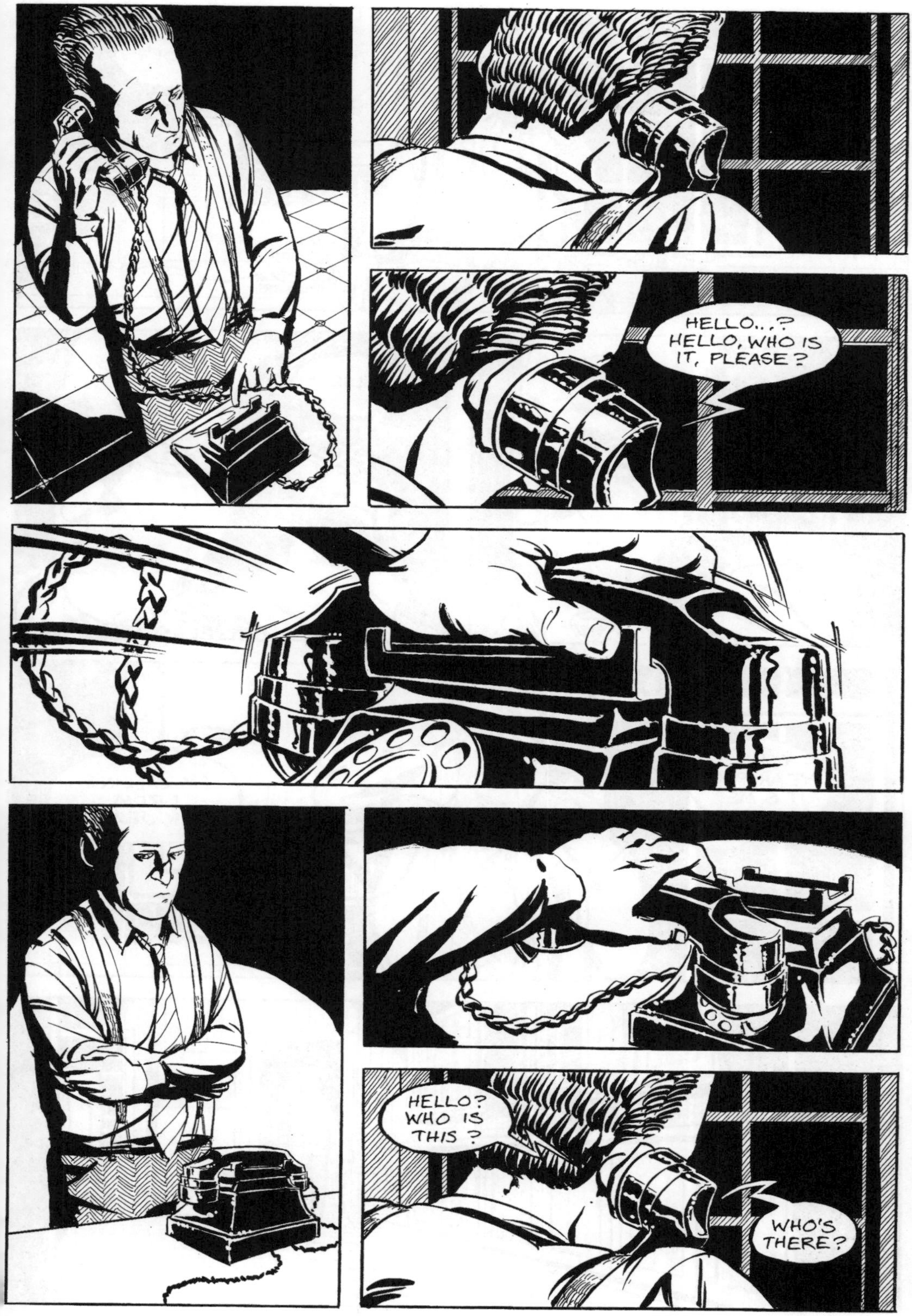
HELLO...?
HELLO, WHO IS IT, PLEASE?
HELLO? WHO IS THIS?
WHO'S THERE?

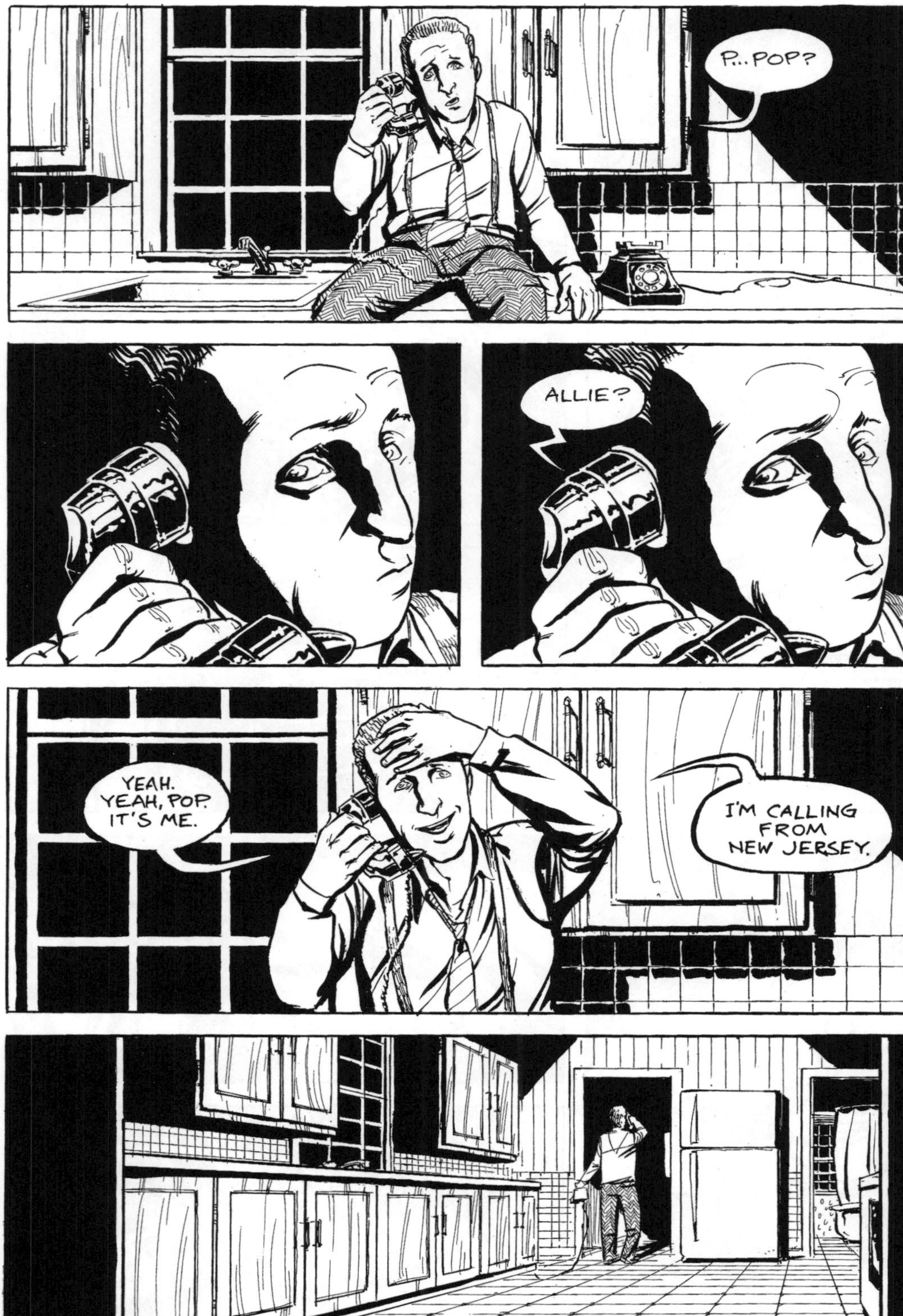
P...POP?
ALLIE?
YEAH. YEAH, POP. IT'S ME.
I'M CALLING FROM NEW JERSEY.

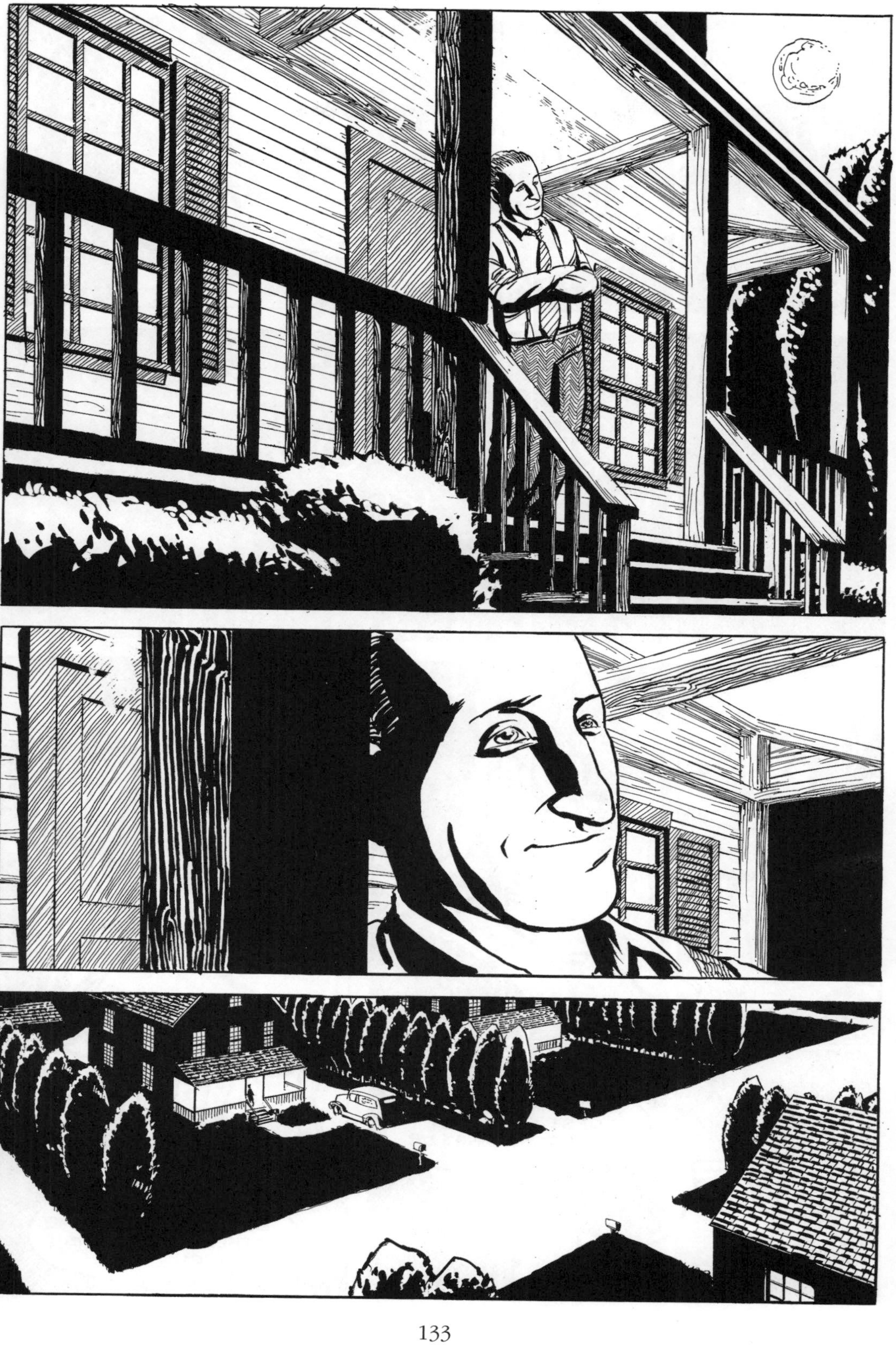

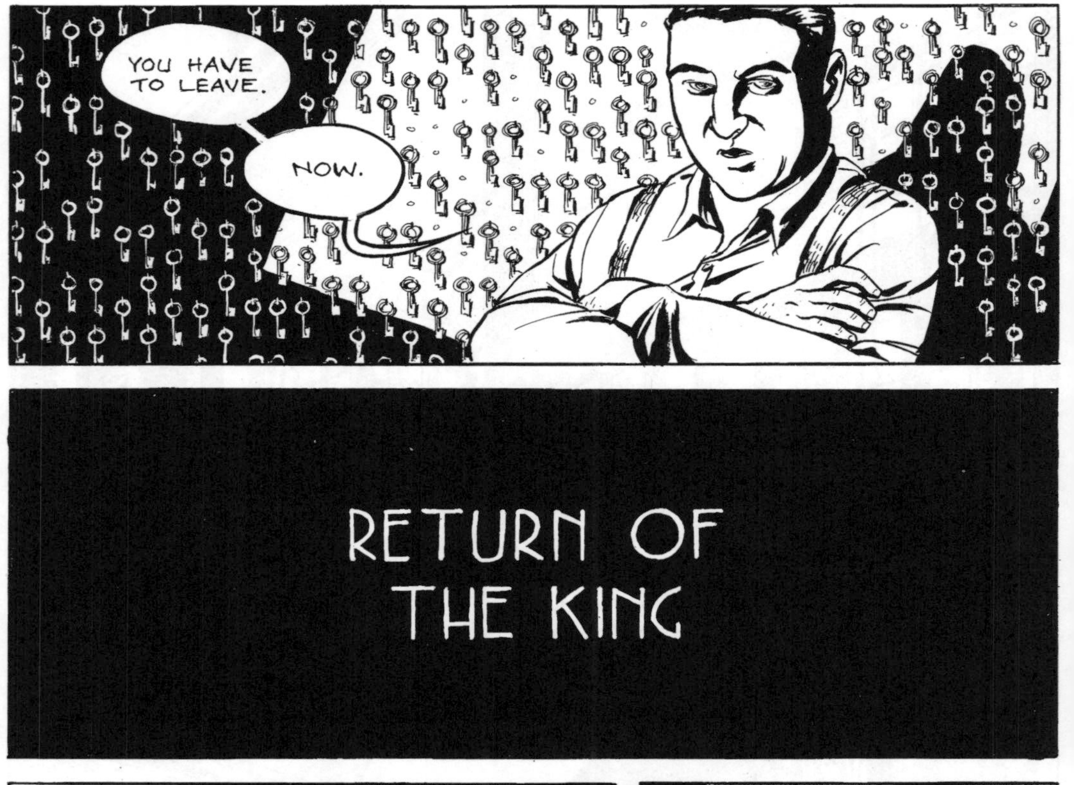
YOU HAVE TO LEAVE.
NOW.

RETURN OF THE KING

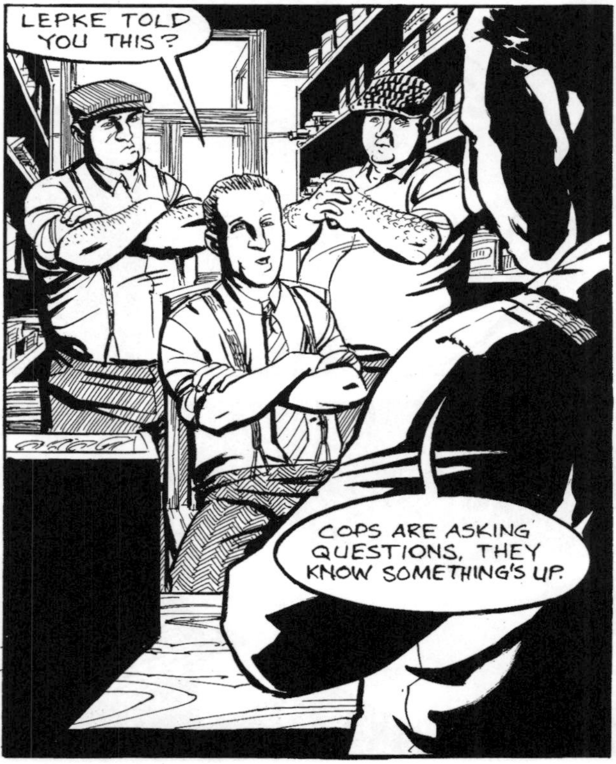
LEPKE TOLD YOU THIS?
COPS ARE ASKING QUESTIONS, THEY KNOW SOMETHING'S UP.

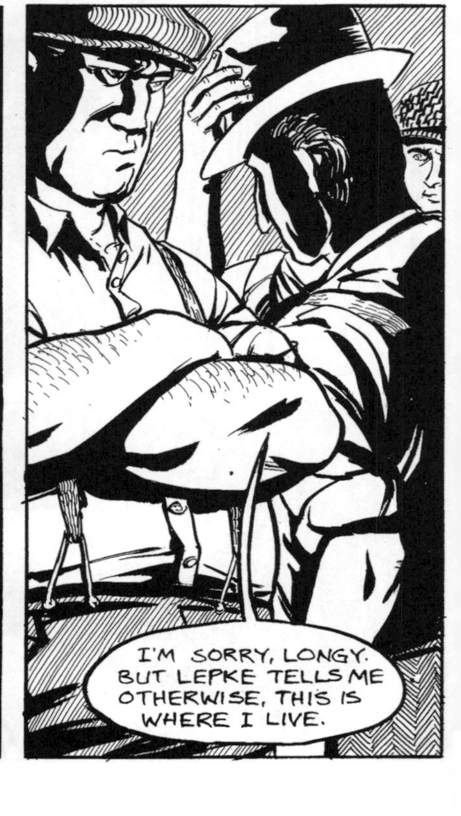
I'M SORRY, LONGY. BUT LEPKE TELLS ME OTHERWISE, THIS IS WHERE I LIVE.

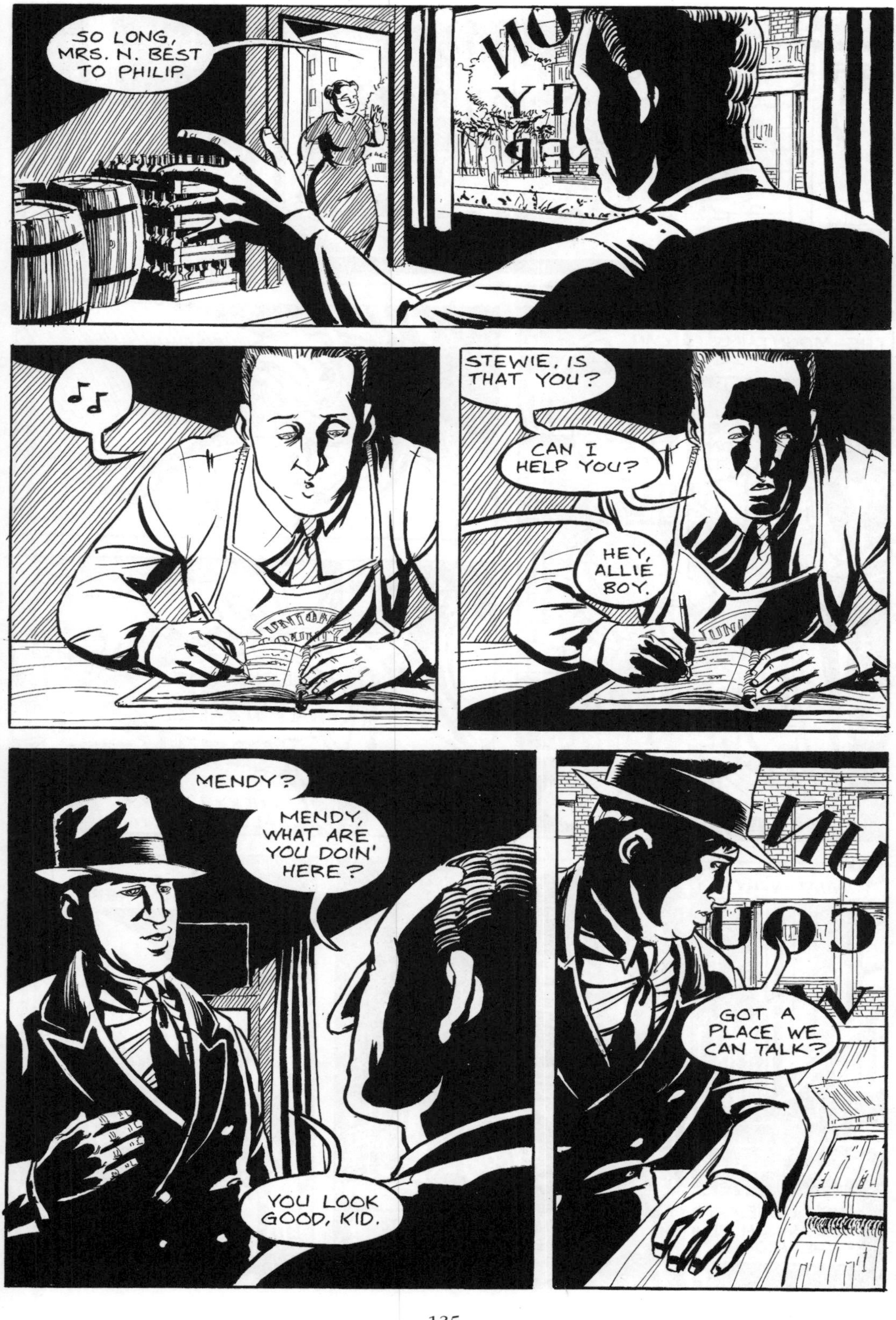
SO LONG, MRS. N. BEST TO PHILIP.
STEWIE, IS THAT YOU?
CAN I HELP YOU?
HEY, ALLIE BOY.
MENDY?
MENDY, WHAT ARE YOU DOIN' HERE?
YOU LOOK GOOD, KID.
GOT A PLACE WE CAN TALK?

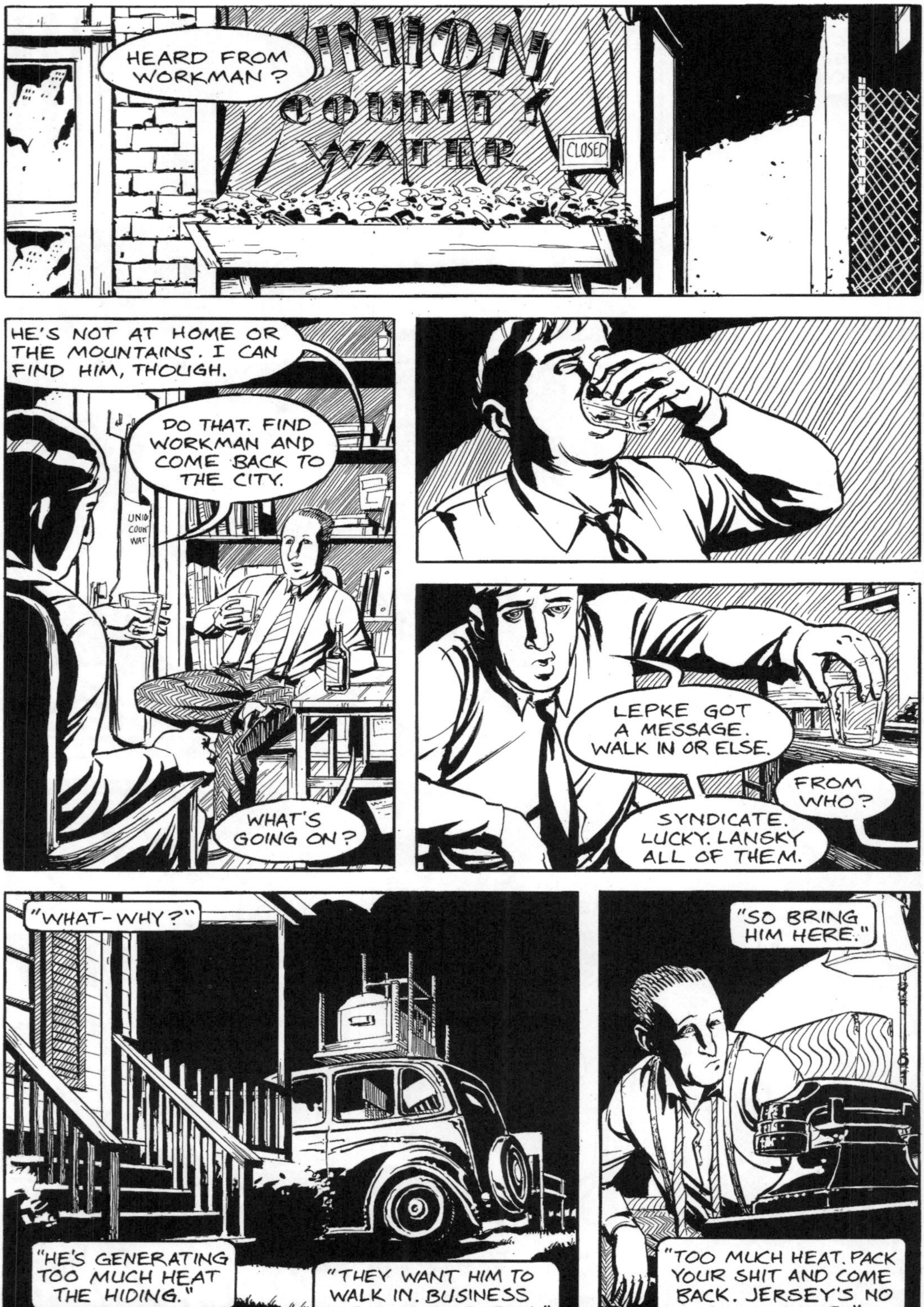
HEARD FROM WORKMAN?
UNION COUNTY WATER
CLOSED
HE'S NOT AT HOME OR THE MOUNTAINS. I CAN FIND HIM, THOUGH.
DO THAT. FIND WORKMAN AND COME BACK TO THE CITY.
WHAT'S GOING ON?
LEPKE GOT A MESSAGE. WALK IN OR ELSE.
FROM WHO?
SYNDICATE. LUCKY. LANSKY ALL OF THEM.
"WHAT-WHY?"
"HE'S GENERATING TOO MUCH HEAT THE HIDING."
"THEY WANT HIM TO WALK IN. BUSINESS IS TAKING A BEATING."
"SO BRING HIM HERE."
"TOO MUCH HEAT. PACK YOUR SHIT AND COME BACK. JERSEY'S NO GOOD, ALLIE."

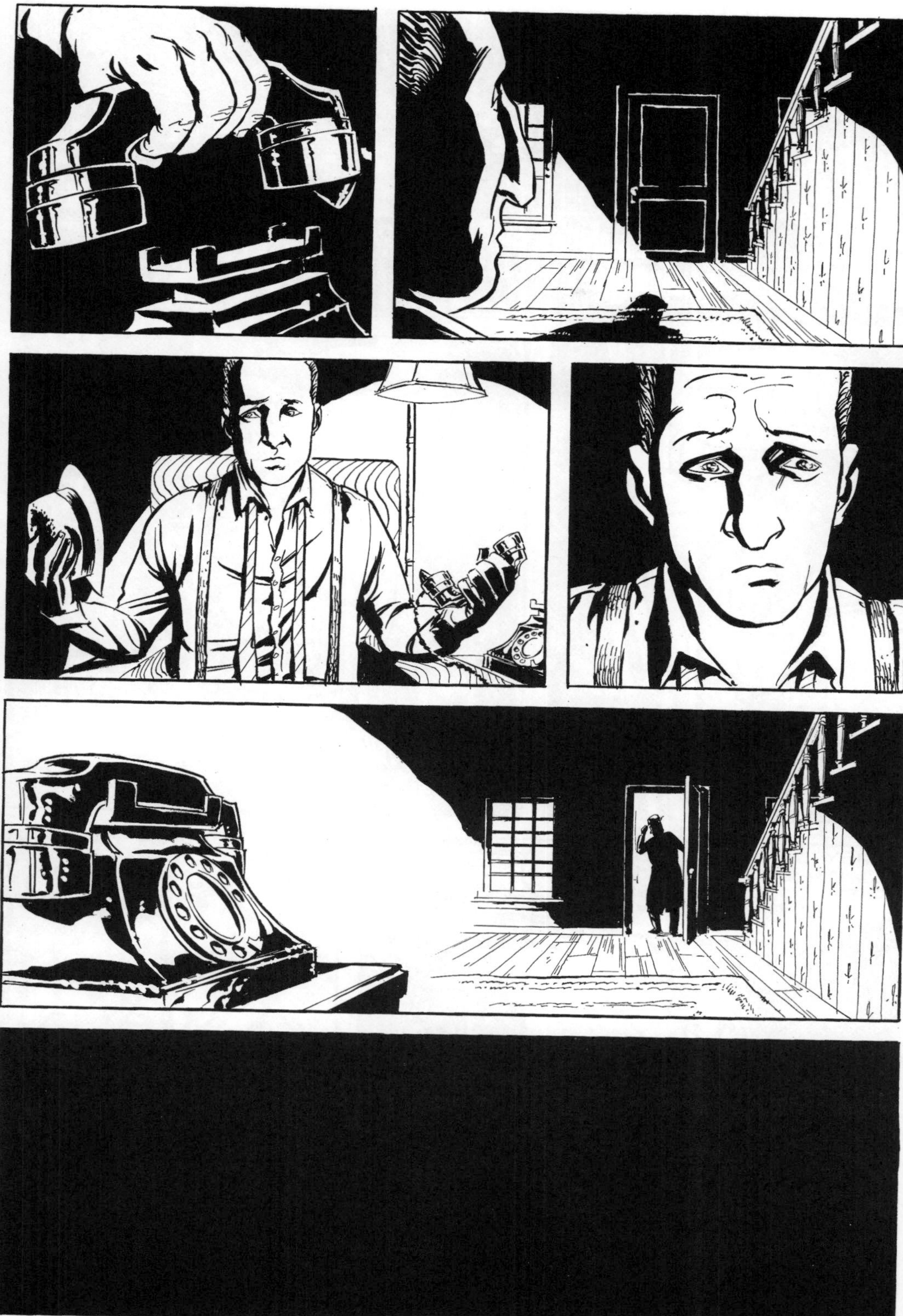

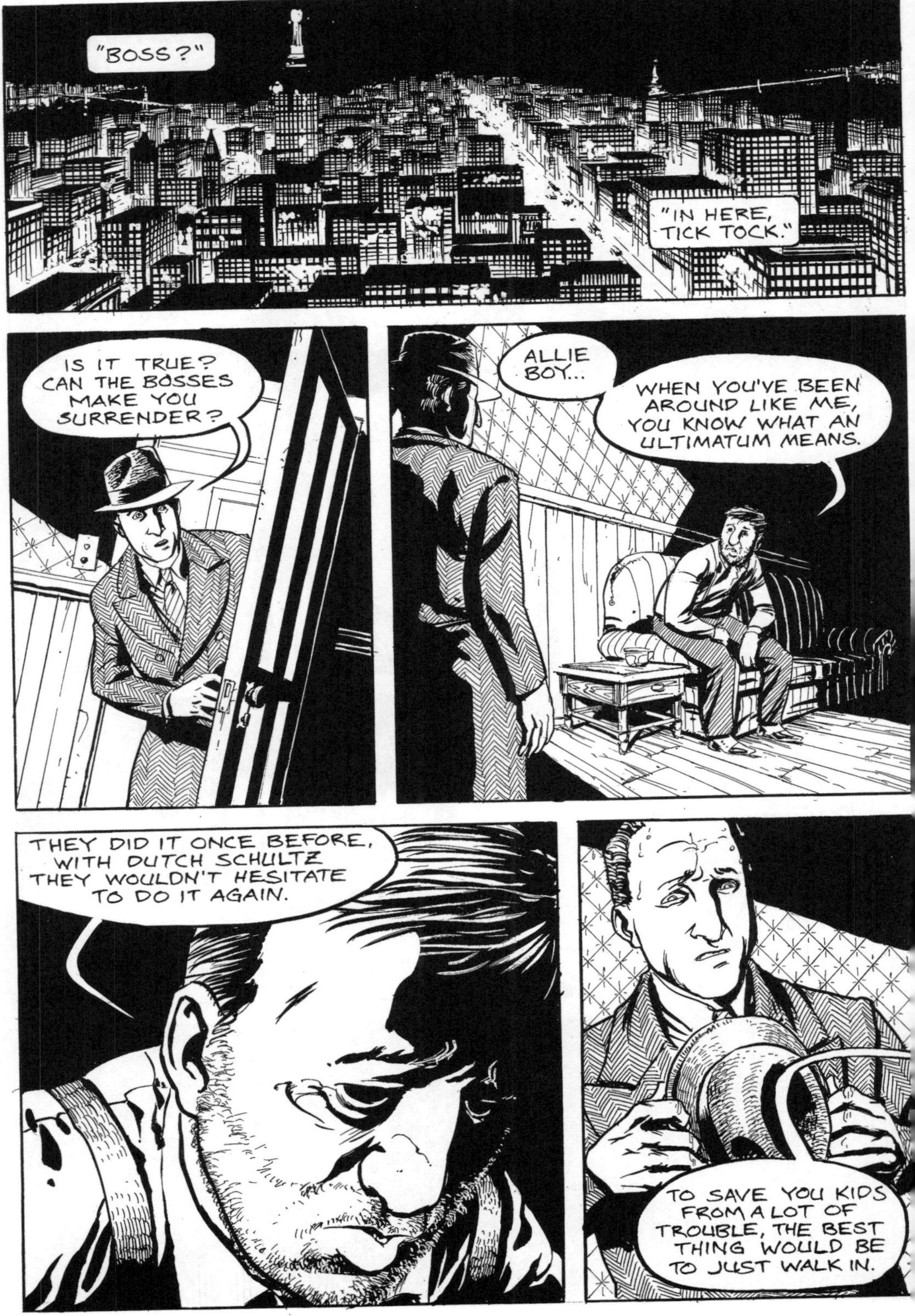
"BOSS?"
"IN HERE, TICK TOCK."
IS IT TRUE? CAN THE BOSSES MAKE YOU SURRENDER?
ALLIE BOY...
WHEN YOU'VE BEEN AROUND LIKE ME, YOU KNOW WHAT AN ULTIMATUM MEANS.
THEY DID IT ONCE BEFORE, WITH DUTCH SCHULTZ THEY WOULDN'T HESITATE TO DO IT AGAIN.
TO SAVE YOU KIDS FROM A LOT OF TROUBLE, THE BEST THING WOULD BE TO JUST WALK IN.

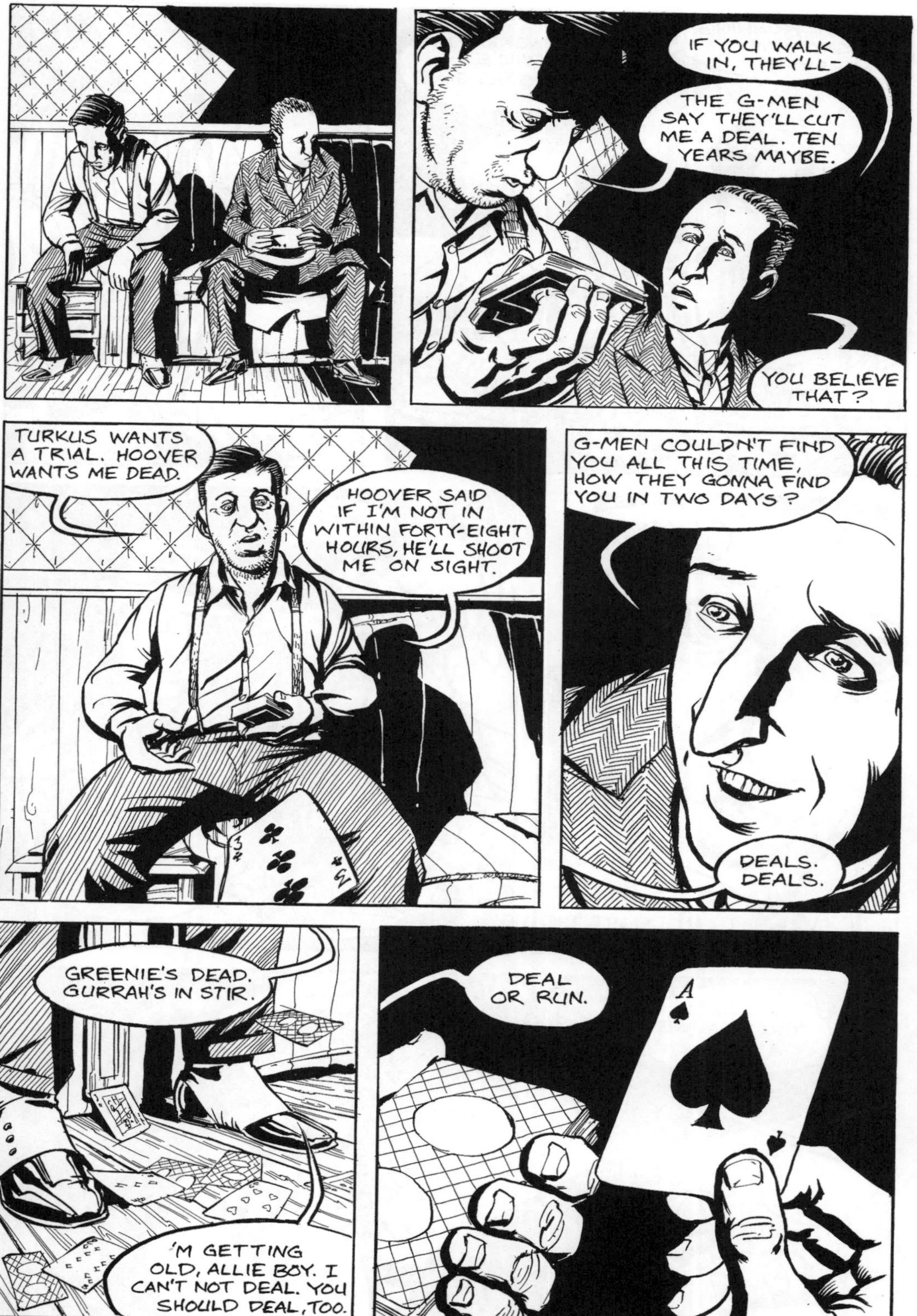
IF YOU WALK IN, THEY'LL-
THE G-MEN SAY THEY'LL CUT ME A DEAL. TEN YEARS MAYBE.
YOU BELIEVE THAT?
TURKUS WANTS A TRIAL. HOOVER WANTS ME DEAD.
HOOVER SAID IF I'M NOT IN WITHIN FORTY-EIGHT HOURS, HE'LL SHOOT ME ON SIGHT.
G-MEN COULDN'T FIND YOU ALL THIS TIME, HOW THEY GONNA FIND YOU IN TWO DAYS?
DEALS. DEALS.
GREENIE'S DEAD. GURRAH'S IN STIR.
'M GETTING OLD, ALLIE BOY. I CAN'T NOT DEAL. YOU SHOULD DEAL, TOO.
DEAL OR RUN.

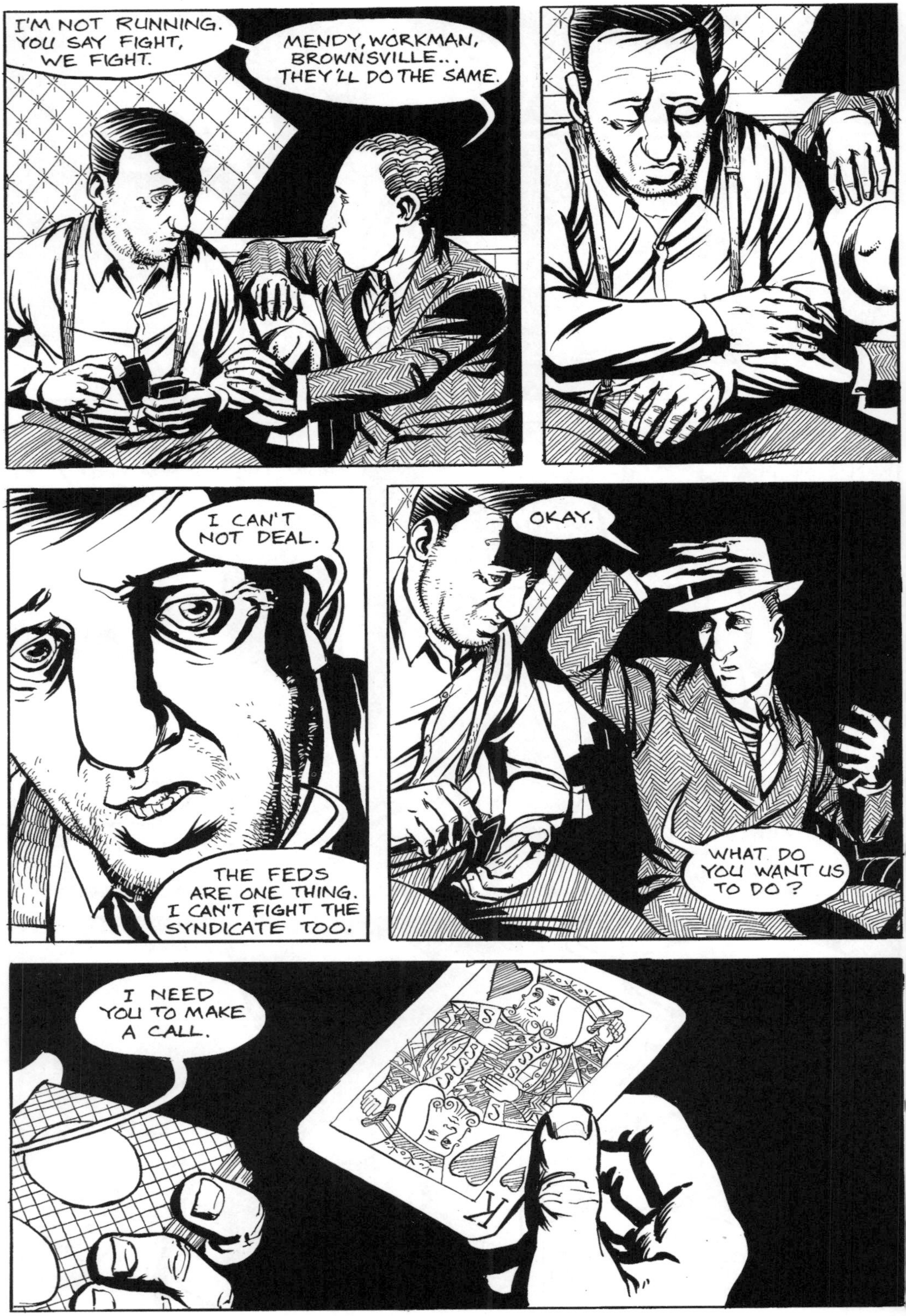
I'M NOT RUNNING. YOU SAY FIGHT, WE FIGHT.
MENDY, WORKMAN, BROWNSVILLE... THEY'LL DO THE SAME.
I CAN'T NOT DEAL.
THE FEDS ARE ONE THING. I CAN'T FIGHT THE SYNDICATE TOO.
OKAY.
WHAT DO YOU WANT US TO DO?
I NEED YOU TO MAKE A CALL.

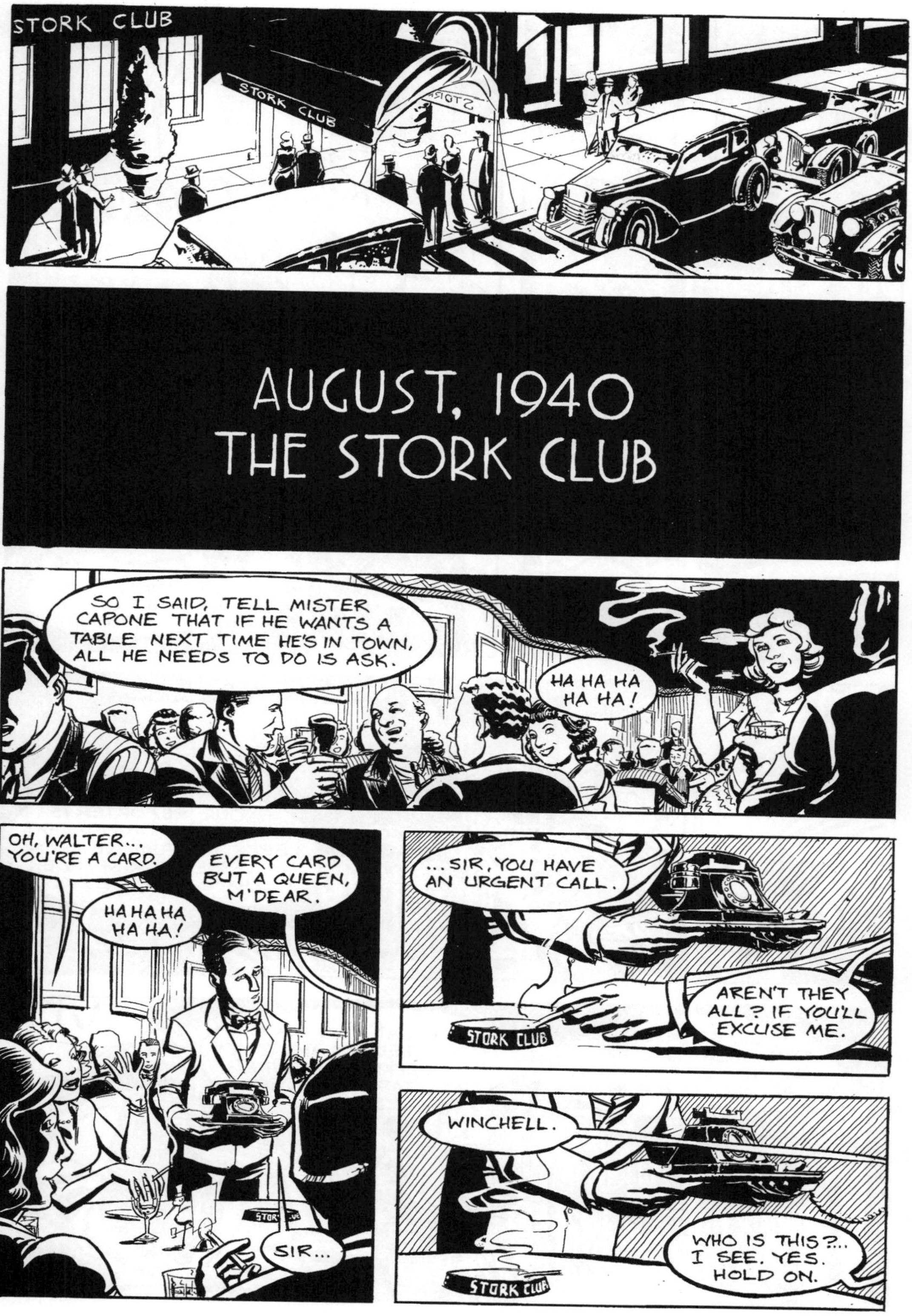
STORK CLUB
STORK CLUB
STORK
AUGUST, 1940
THE STORK CLUB
SO I SAID, TELL MISTER CAPONE THAT IF HE WANTS A TABLE NEXT TIME HE'S IN TOWN, ALL HE NEEDS TO DO IS ASK.
HA HA HA HA HA!
OH, WALTER... YOU'RE A CARD.
EVERY CARD BUT A QUEEN, M'DEAR.
HA HA HA HA HA!
SIR...
...SIR, YOU HAVE AN URGENT CALL.
STORK CLUB
AREN'T THEY ALL? IF YOU'LL EXCUSE ME.
WINCHELL.
WHO IS THIS?... I SEE. YES. HOLD ON.
STORK CLUB

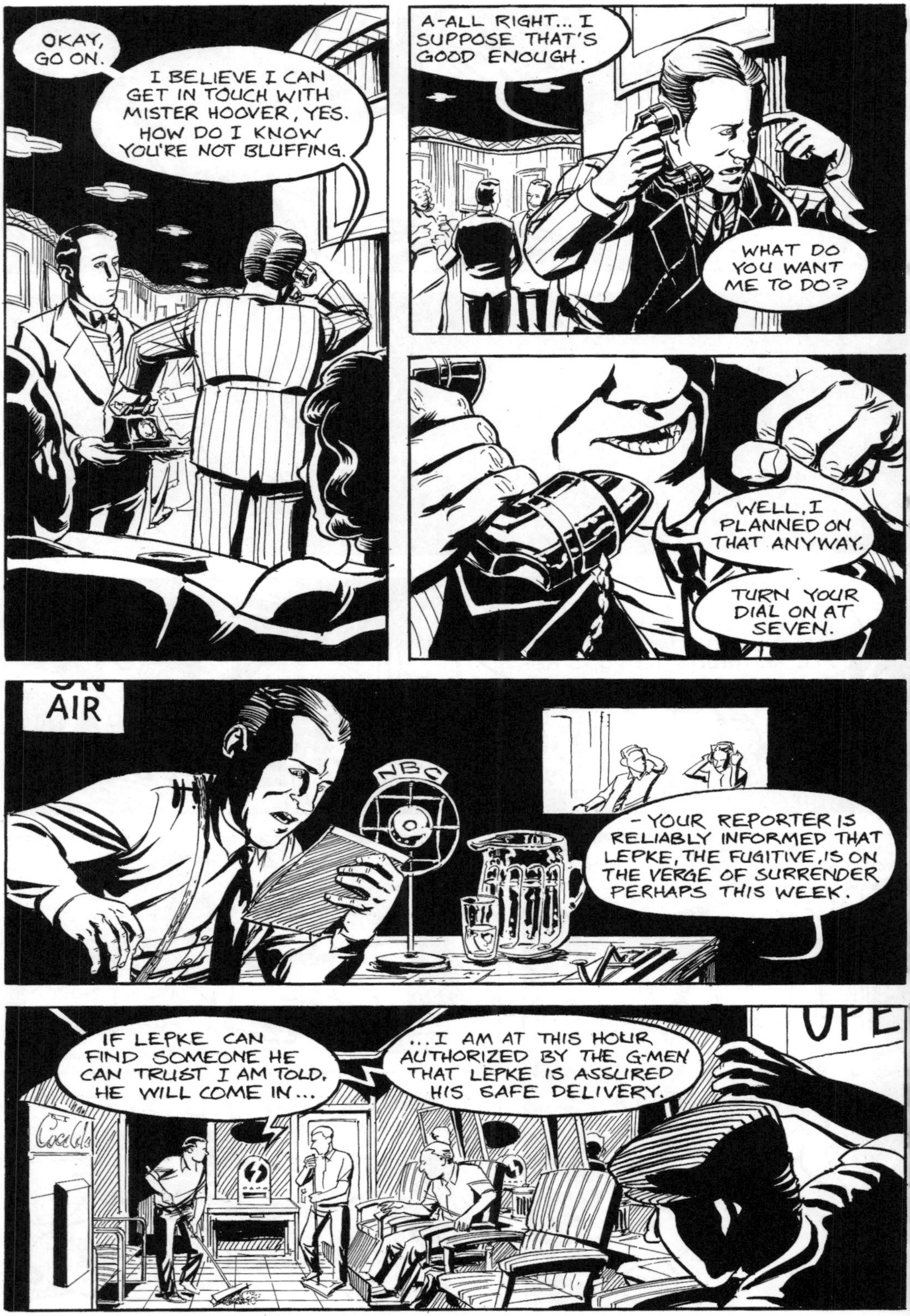
OKAY, GO ON.
I BELIEVE I CAN GET IN TOUCH WITH MISTER HOOVER, YES. HOW DO I KNOW YOU'RE NOT BLUFFING.
A-ALL RIGHT... I SUPPOSE THAT'S GOOD ENOUGH.
WHAT DO YOU WANT ME TO DO?
WELL, I PLANNED ON THAT ANYWAY.
TURN YOUR DIAL ON AT SEVEN.
AIR
NBC
- YOUR REPORTER IS RELIABLY INFORMED THAT LEPKE, THE FUGITIVE, IS ON THE VERGE OF SURRENDER PERHAPS THIS WEEK.
IF LEPKE CAN FIND SOMEONE HE CAN TRUST I AM TOLD, HE WILL COME IN...
...I AM AT THIS HOUR AUTHORIZED BY THE G-MEN THAT LEPKE IS ASSURED HIS SAFE DELIVERY.

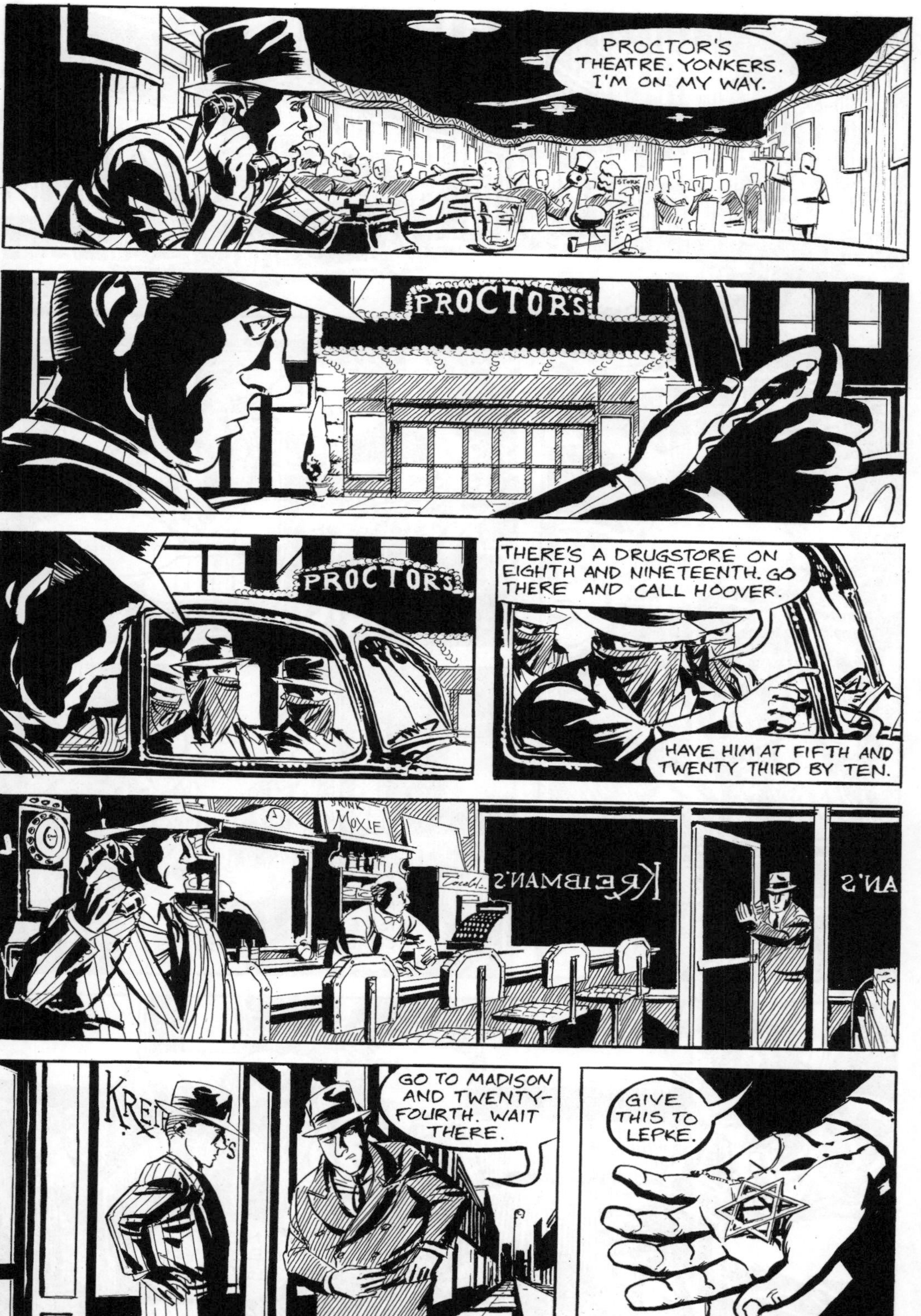
PROCTOR'S THEATRE. YONKERS. I'M ON MY WAY.
PROCTOR'S
PROCTOR'S
THERE'S A DRUGSTORE ON EIGHTH AND NINETEENTH. GO THERE AND CALL HOOVER.
HAVE HIM AT FIFTH AND TWENTY THIRD BY TEN.
MOXIE
KREIBMAN'S
GO TO MADISON AND TWENTY-FOURTH. WAIT THERE.
GIVE THIS TO LEPKE.

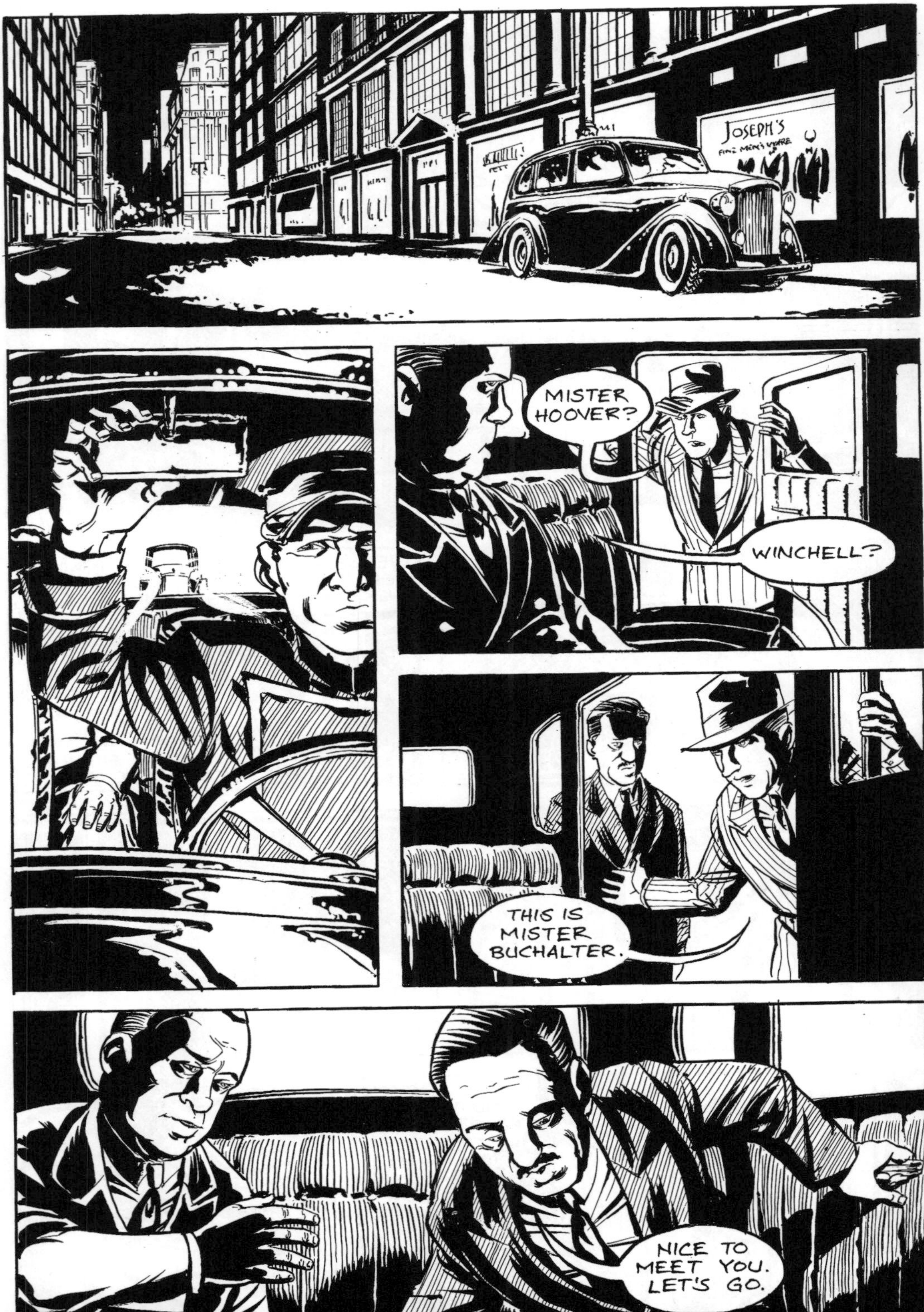
JOSEPH'S
MISTER HOOVER?
WINCHELL?
THIS IS MISTER BUCHALTER.
NICE TO MEET YOU. LET'S GO.

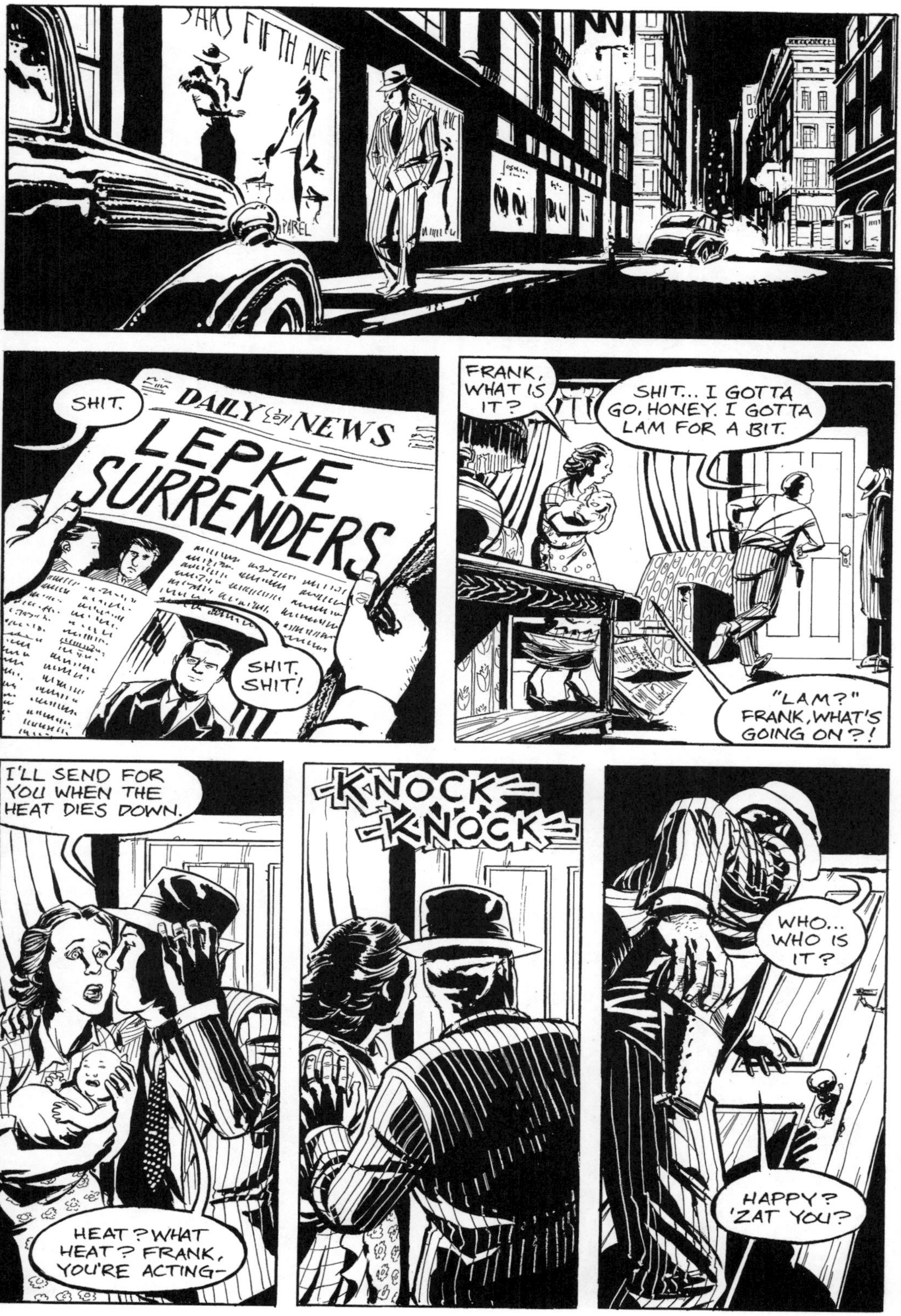
SAKS FIFTH AVE
SHIT.
DAILY NEWS
LEPKE SURRENDERS
SHIT. SHIT!
FRANK, WHAT IS IT?
SHIT... I GOTTA GO, HONEY. I GOTTA LAM FOR A BIT.
"LAM?" FRANK, WHAT'S GOING ON?!
I'LL SEND FOR YOU WHEN THE HEAT DIES DOWN.
HEAT? WHAT HEAT? FRANK, YOU'RE ACTING-
KNOCK KNOCK
WHO... WHO IS IT?
HAPPY? 'ZAT YOU?

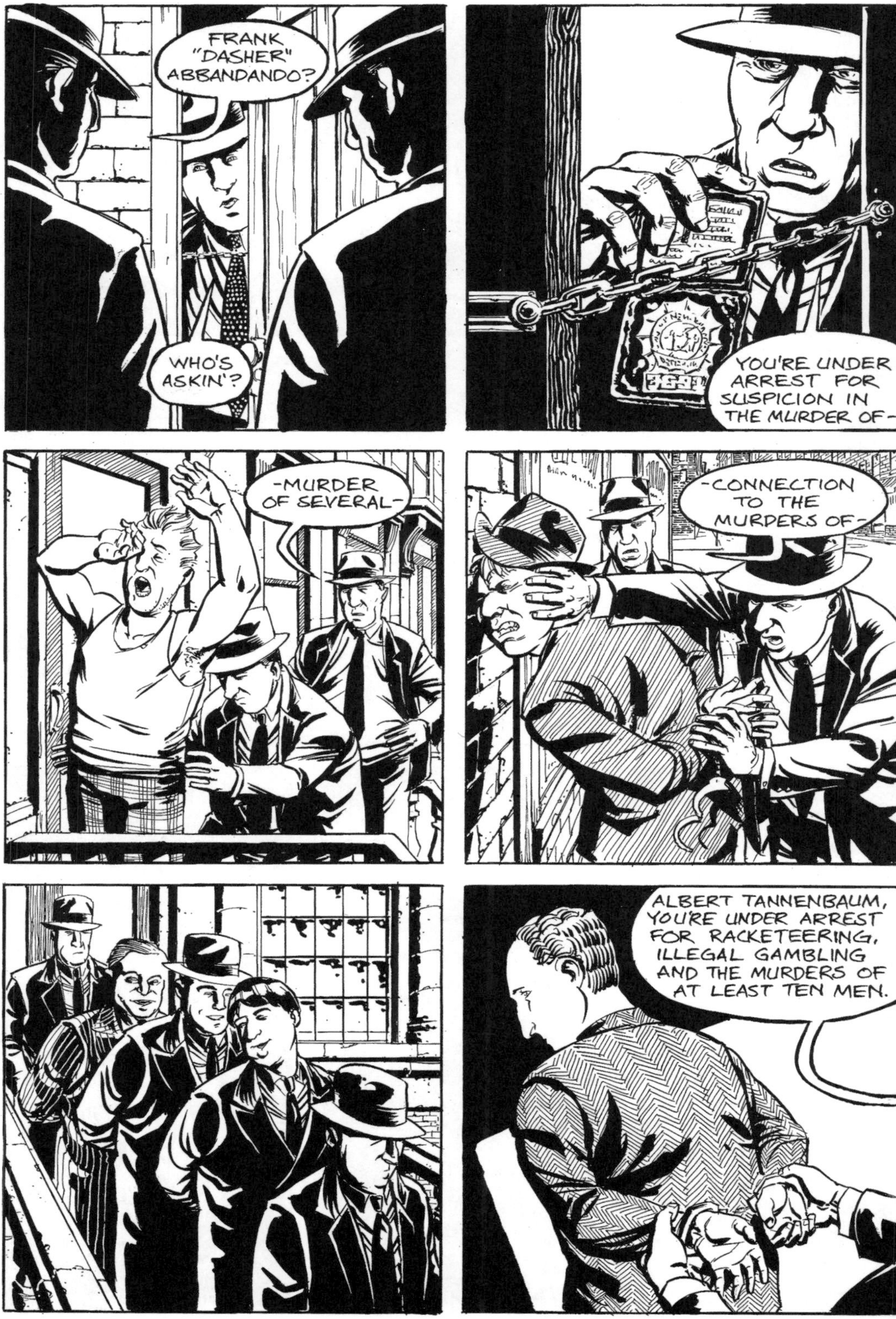
FRANK "DASHER" ABBANDANDO?
WHO'S ASKIN'?
YOU'RE UNDER ARREST FOR SUSPICION IN THE MURDER OF-
-MURDER OF SEVERAL-
-CONNECTION TO THE MURDERS OF-
ALBERT TANNENBAUM, YOU'RE UNDER ARREST FOR RACKETEERING, ILLEGAL GAMBLING AND THE MURDERS OF AT LEAST TEN MEN.

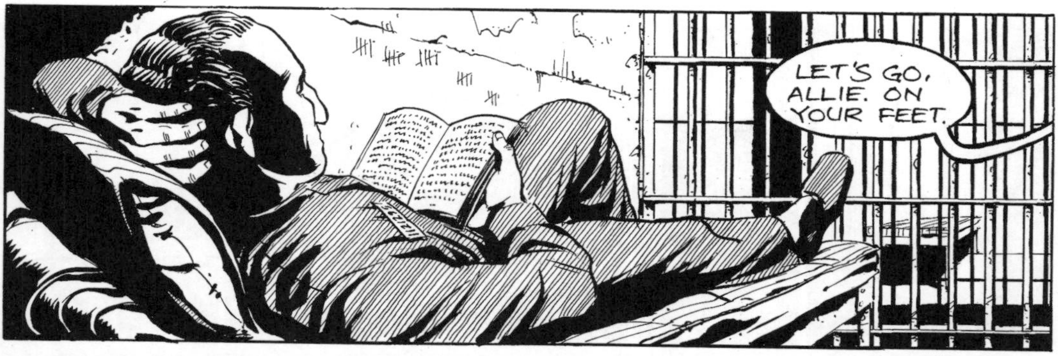
LET'S GO, ALLIE. ON YOUR FEET.

RATS

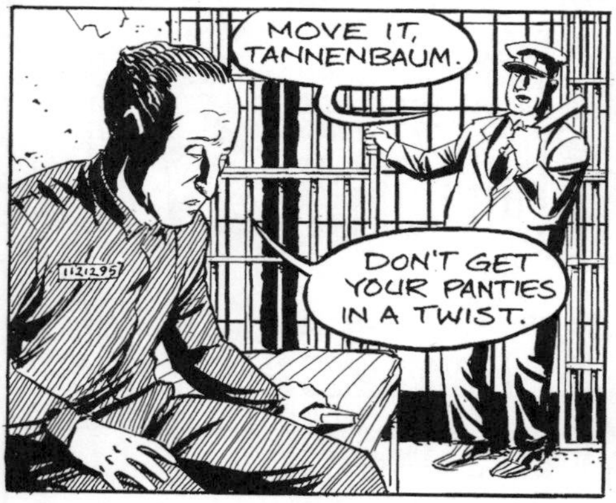
MOVE IT, TANNENBAUM.
DON'T GET YOUR PANTIES IN A TWIST.

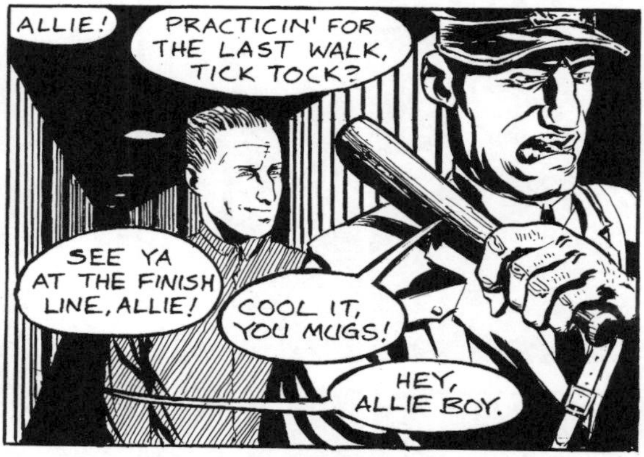
ALLIE!
PRACTICIN' FOR THE LAST WALK, TICK TOCK?
SEE YA AT THE FINISH LINE, ALLIE!
COOL IT, YOU MUGS!
HEY, ALLIE BOY.

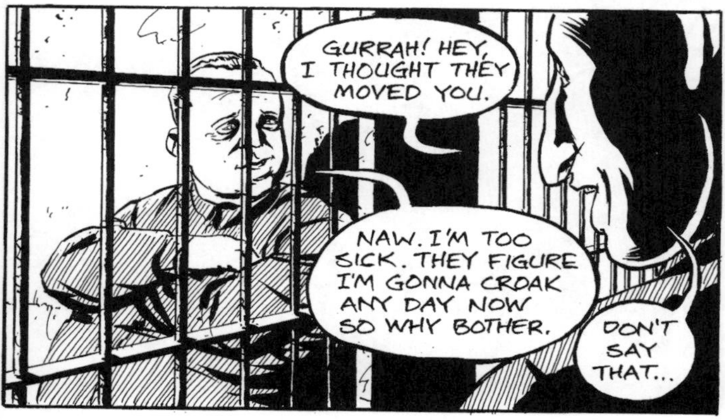
GURRAH! HEY, I THOUGHT THEY MOVED YOU.
NAW. I'M TOO SICK. THEY FIGURE I'M GONNA CROAK ANY DAY NOW SO WHY BOTHER.
DON'T SAY THAT...

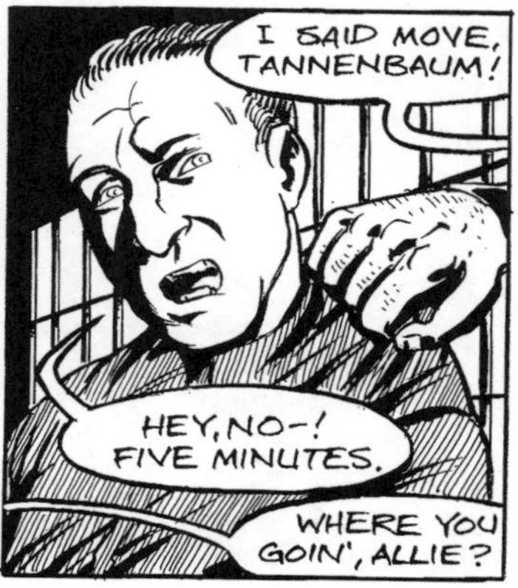
I SAID MOVE, TANNENBAUM!
HEY, NO-! FIVE MINUTES.
WHERE YOU GOIN', ALLIE?

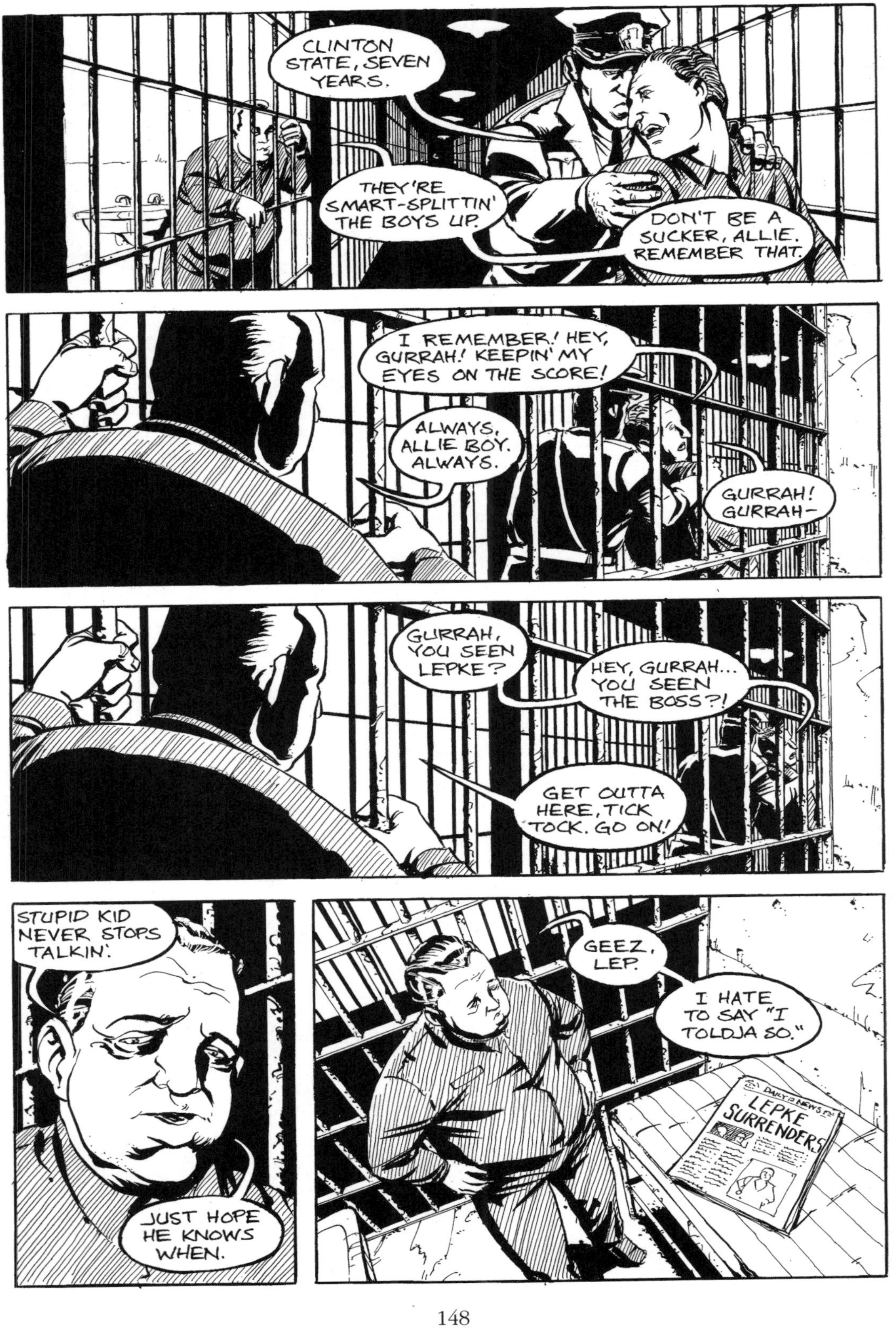
CLINTON STATE, SEVEN YEARS.
THEY'RE SMART-SPLITTIN' THE BOYS UP.
DON'T BE A SUCKER, ALLIE. REMEMBER THAT.
I REMEMBER! HEY, GURRAH! KEEPIN' MY EYES ON THE SCORE!
ALWAYS, ALLIE BOY. ALWAYS.
GURRAH! GURRAH-
GURRAH, YOU SEEN LEPKE?
HEY, GURRAH... YOU SEEN THE BOSS?!
GET OUTTA HERE, TICK TOCK. GO ON!
STUPID KID NEVER STOPS TALKIN'.
JUST HOPE HE KNOWS WHEN.
GEEZ, LEP.
I HATE TO SAY "I TOLDJA SO."
DAILY NEWS
LEPKE SURRENDERS

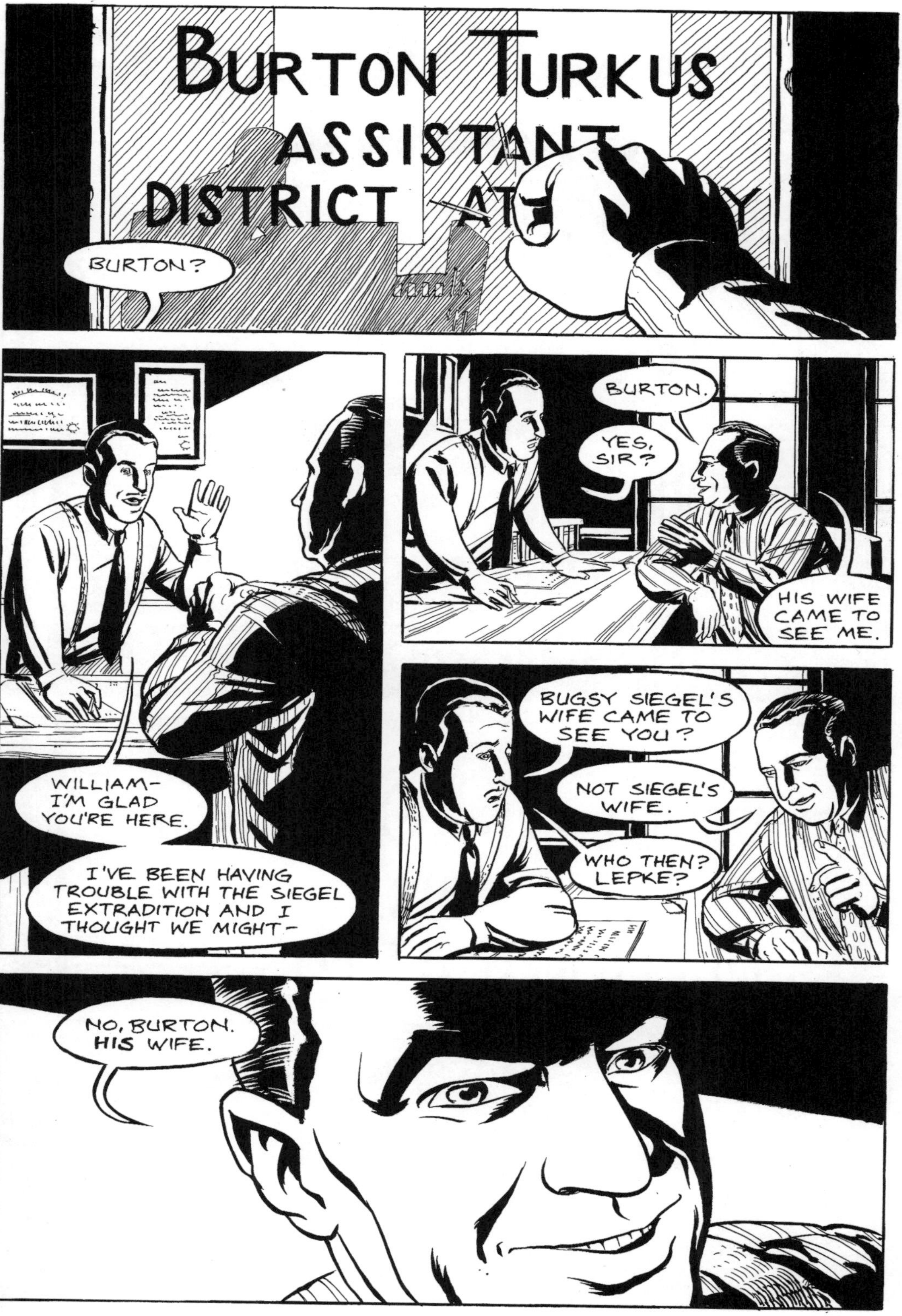
BURTON TURKUS
ASSISTANT
DISTRICT AT
BURTON?
WILLIAM- I'M GLAD YOU'RE HERE.
I'VE BEEN HAVING TROUBLE WITH THE SIEGEL EXTRADITION AND I THOUGHT WE MIGHT-
BURTON.
YES, SIR?
HIS WIFE CAME TO SEE ME.
BUGSY SIEGEL'S WIFE CAME TO SEE YOU?
NOT SIEGEL'S WIFE.
WHO THEN? LEPKE?
NO, BURTON. HIS WIFE.

I STILL DON'T— OH.

AND WHAT'S SHE SAYING?

HE WANTS TO AVOID THE CHAIR.

SIGN HIM OUT AND BRING HIM IN. WE'LL OFFER A DEAL.

"WHAT DO YOU WANT?"

"I WANNA WALK CLEAN. WHEN IT'S OVER YOU LET ME GO."

"WE COULD GET THE INFORMATION WITHOUT YOU."

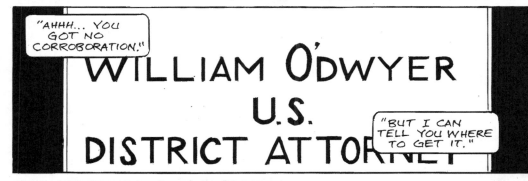

"AHHH... YOU GOT NO CORROBORATION."

WILLIAM O'DWYER
U.S.
DISTRICT ATTORNEY

"BUT I CAN TELL YOU WHERE TO GET IT."

I CAN MAKE YOU THE BIGGEST MAN IN THE COUNTRY.

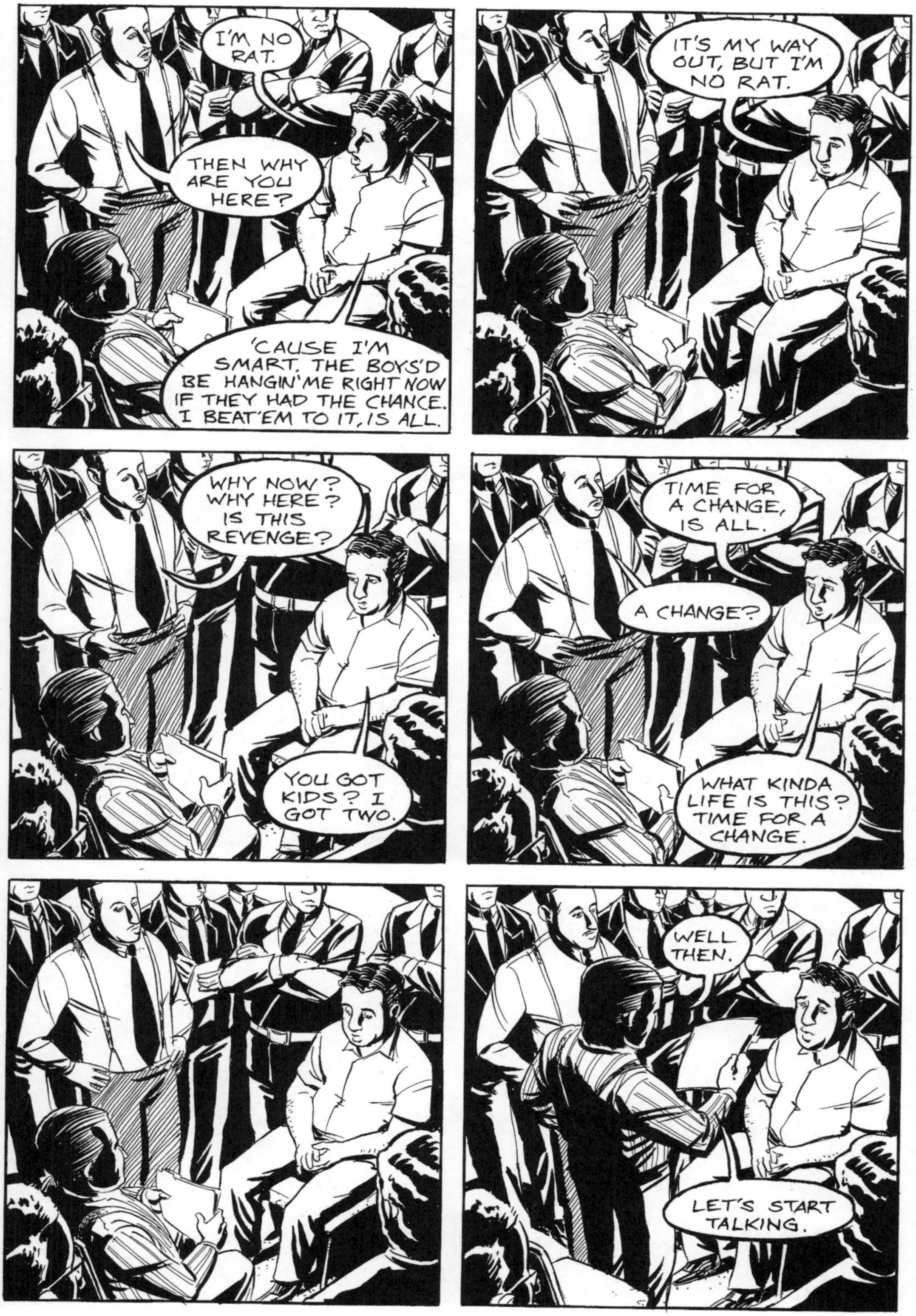
I'M NO RAT.
THEN WHY ARE YOU HERE?
'CAUSE I'M SMART. THE BOYS'D BE HANGIN' ME RIGHT NOW IF THEY HAD THE CHANCE. I BEAT 'EM TO IT, IS ALL.
IT'S MY WAY OUT, BUT I'M NO RAT.
WHY NOW? WHY HERE? IS THIS REVENGE?
YOU GOT KIDS? I GOT TWO.
TIME FOR A CHANGE, IS ALL.
A CHANGE?
WHAT KINDA LIFE IS THIS? TIME FOR A CHANGE.
WELL THEN.
LET'S START TALKING.

HOLY SHIT.

WILLIAM O'D[...] U.S. DISTRICT ATTO[...]

THIS IS BIG. KEEP THIS QUIET— I DON'T WANT HOOVER SWEEPING IN HERE AND TAKING HIM OUT OF OUR HANDS.

SET UP A HEARING RIGHT AWAY. I WANT EVERYTHING DOUBLE VERIFIED. TRIPLE.

WHERE ARE YOU GOING, SIR?

TO GET MORE!

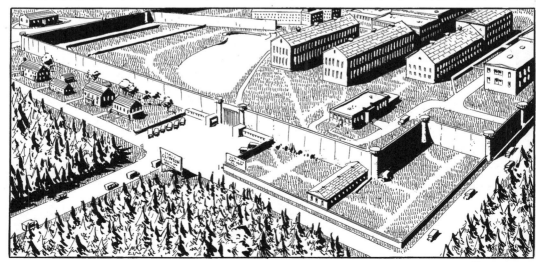

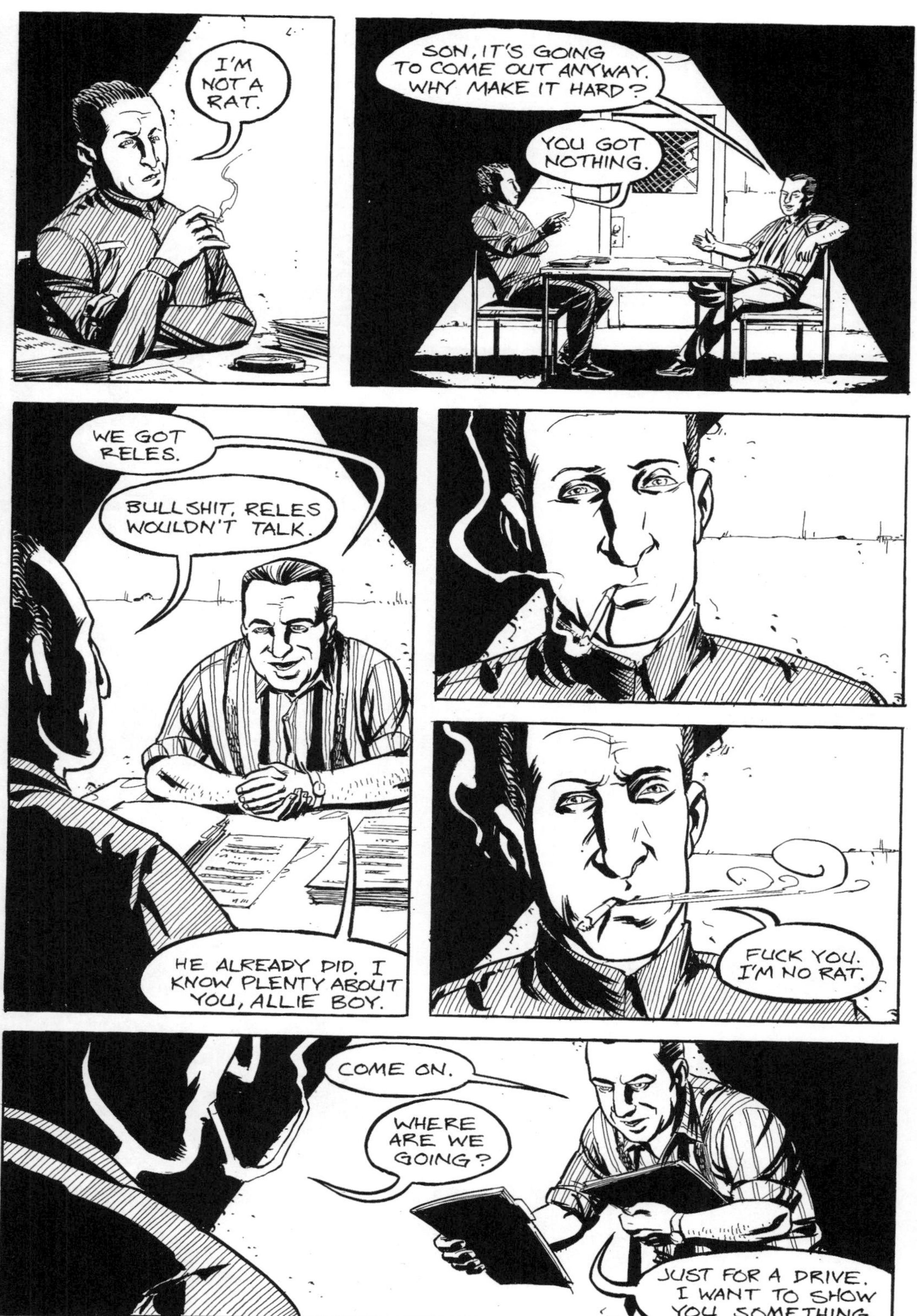
I'M NOT A RAT.
SON, IT'S GOING TO COME OUT ANYWAY. WHY MAKE IT HARD?
YOU GOT NOTHING.
WE GOT RELES.
BULLSHIT, RELES WOULDN'T TALK.
HE ALREADY DID. I KNOW PLENTY ABOUT YOU, ALLIE BOY.
FUCK YOU. I'M NO RAT.
COME ON.
WHERE ARE WE GOING?
JUST FOR A DRIVE. I WANT TO SHOW YOU SOMETHING.

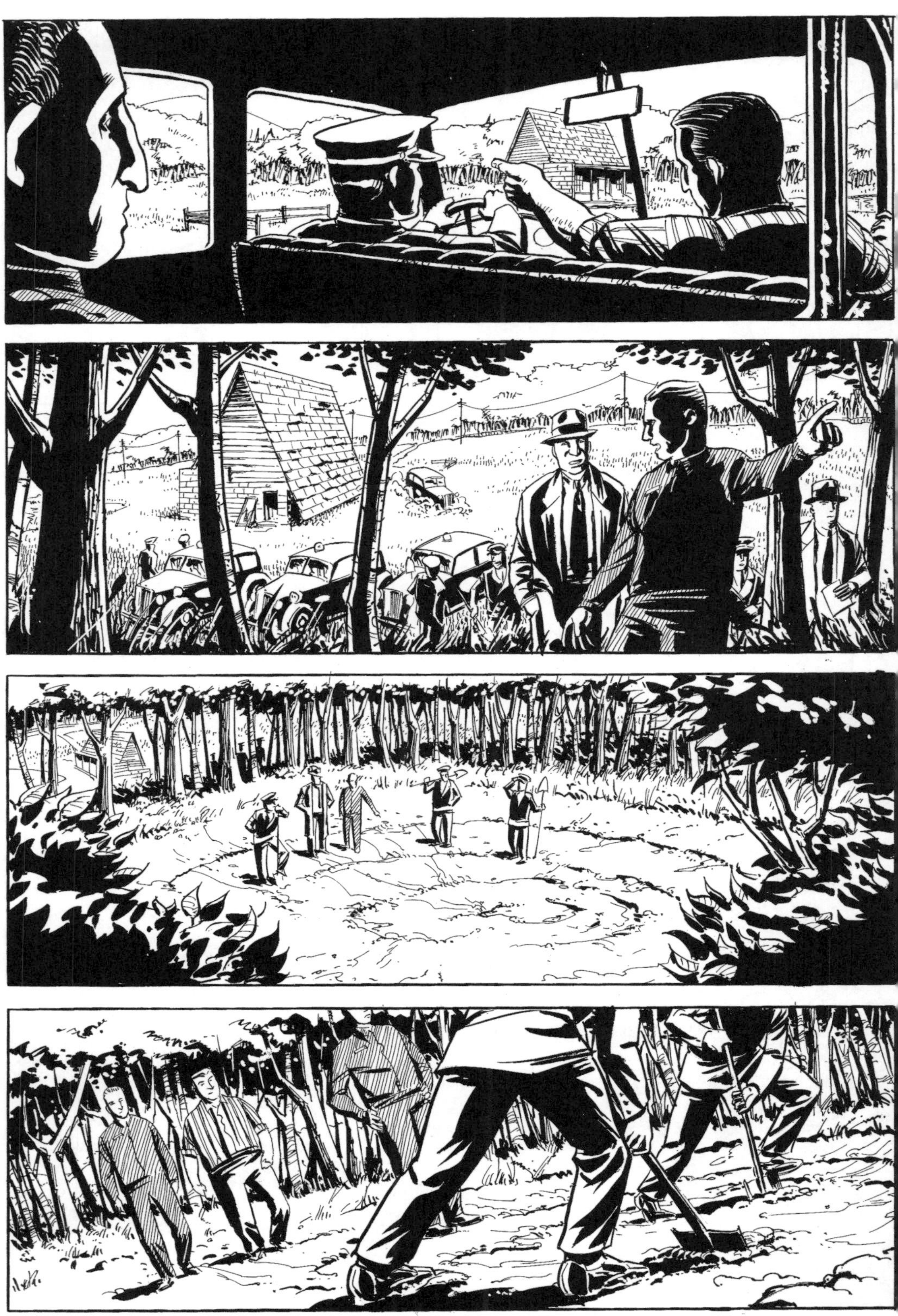

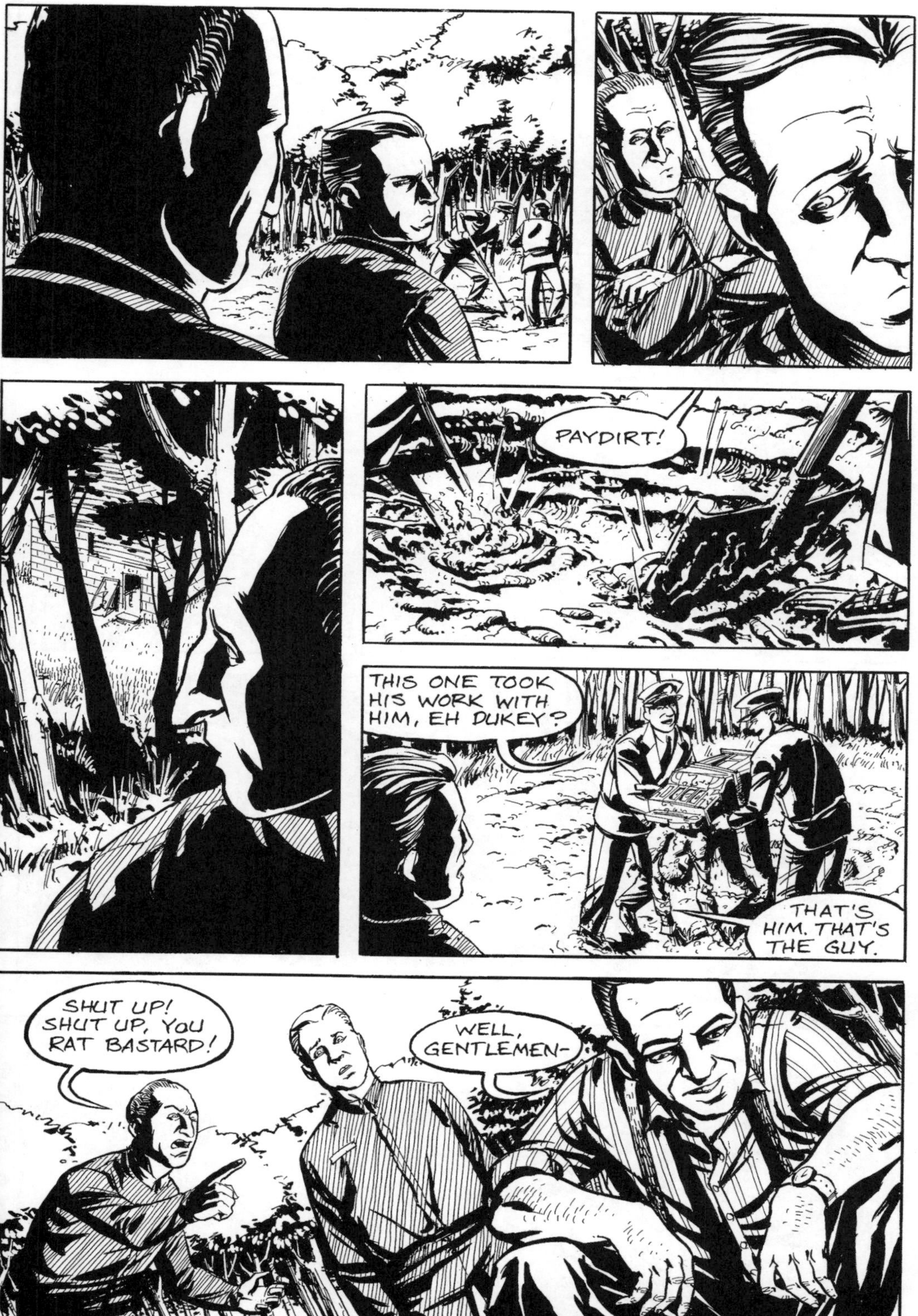
PAYDIRT!
THIS ONE TOOK HIS WORK WITH HIM, EH DUKEY?
THAT'S HIM. THAT'S THE GUY.
SHUT UP! SHUT UP, YOU RAT BASTARD!
WELL, GENTLEMEN-

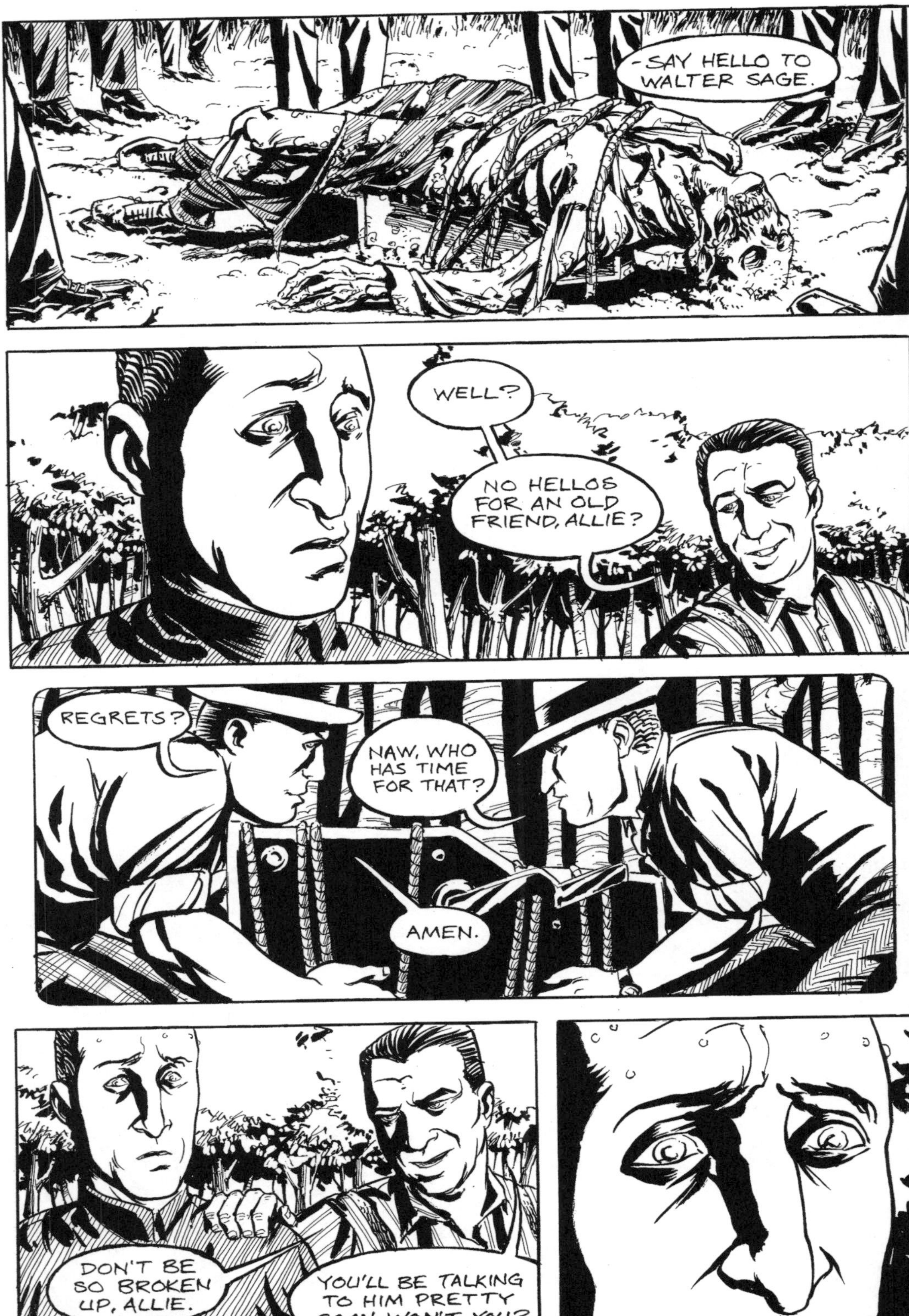
-SAY HELLO TO WALTER SAGE.
WELL?
NO HELLOS FOR AN OLD FRIEND, ALLIE?
REGRETS?
NAW, WHO HAS TIME FOR THAT?
AMEN.
DON'T BE SO BROKEN UP, ALLIE.
YOU'LL BE TALKING TO HIM PRETTY SOON, WON'T YOU?

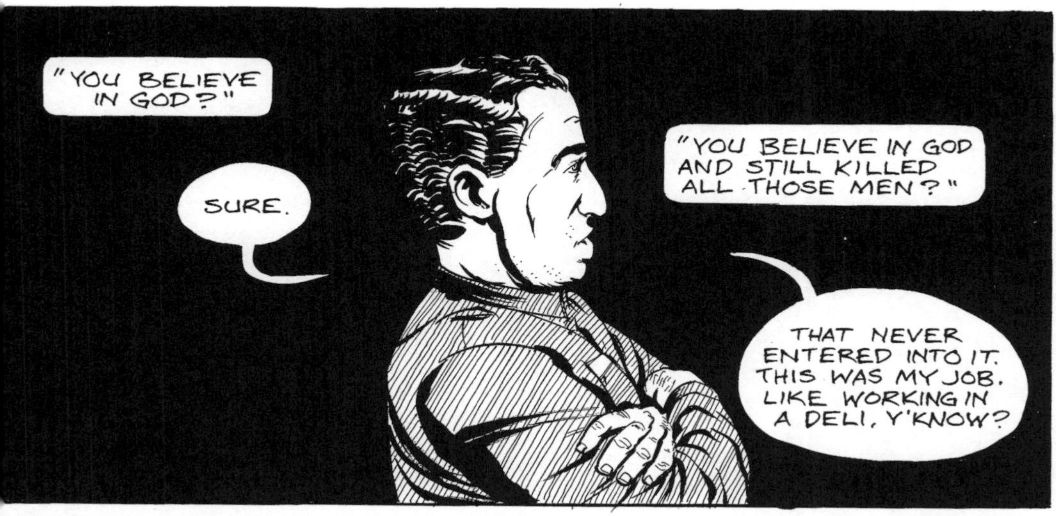
"YOU BELIEVE IN GOD?"
SURE.
"YOU BELIEVE IN GOD AND STILL KILLED ALL THOSE MEN?"
THAT NEVER ENTERED INTO IT. THIS WAS MY JOB. LIKE WORKING IN A DELI, Y'KNOW?

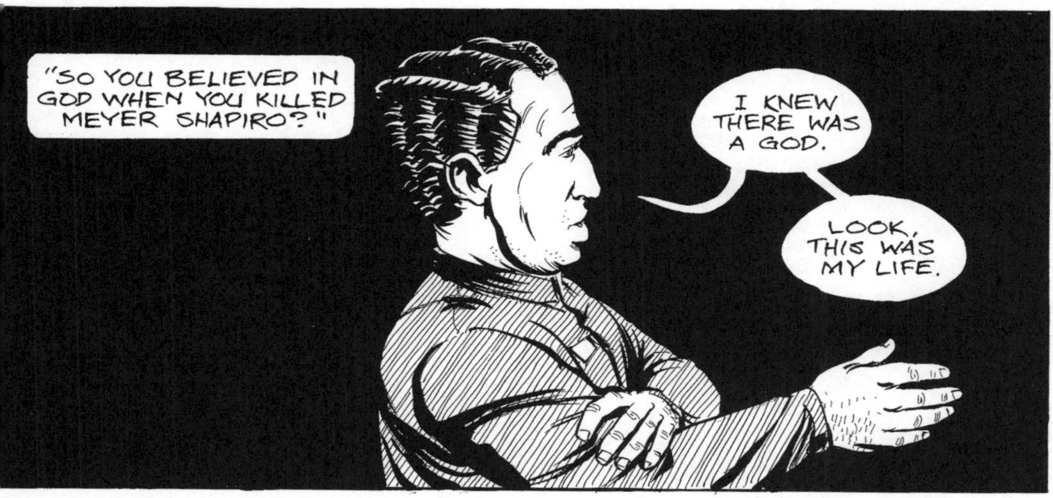
"SO YOU BELIEVED IN GOD WHEN YOU KILLED MEYER SHAPIRO?"
I KNEW THERE WAS A GOD.
LOOK, THIS WAS MY LIFE.

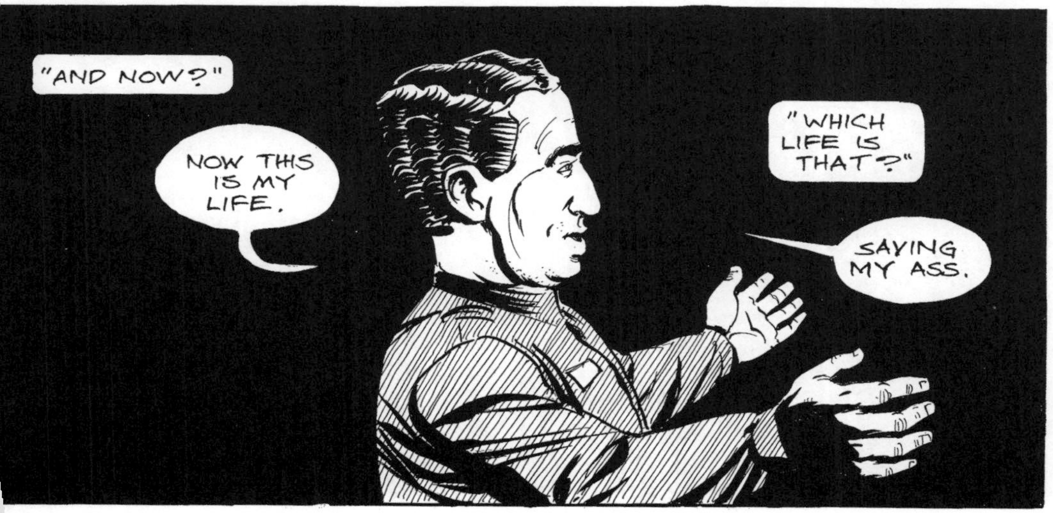
"AND NOW?"
NOW THIS IS MY LIFE.
"WHICH LIFE IS THAT?"
SAYING MY ASS.

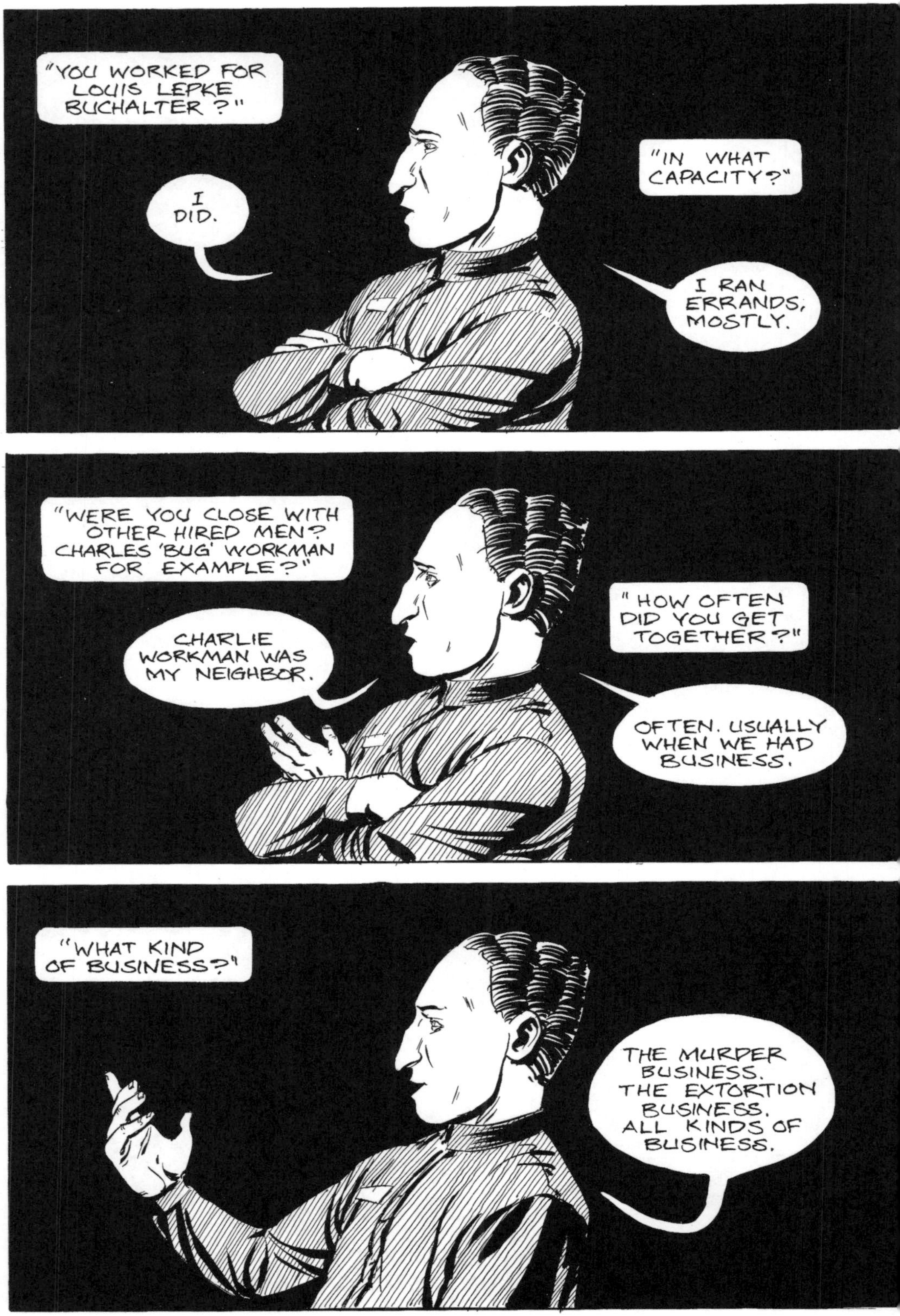
"YOU WORKED FOR LOUIS LEPKE BUCHALTER ?"
I DID.
"IN WHAT CAPACITY?"
I RAN ERRANDS, MOSTLY.
"WERE YOU CLOSE WITH OTHER HIRED MEN? CHARLES 'BUG' WORKMAN FOR EXAMPLE?"
CHARLIE WORKMAN WAS MY NEIGHBOR.
" HOW OFTEN DID YOU GET TOGETHER?"
OFTEN. USUALLY WHEN WE HAD BUSINESS.
"WHAT KIND OF BUSINESS?"
THE MURDER BUSINESS. THE EXTORTION BUSINESS. ALL KINDS OF BUSINESS.

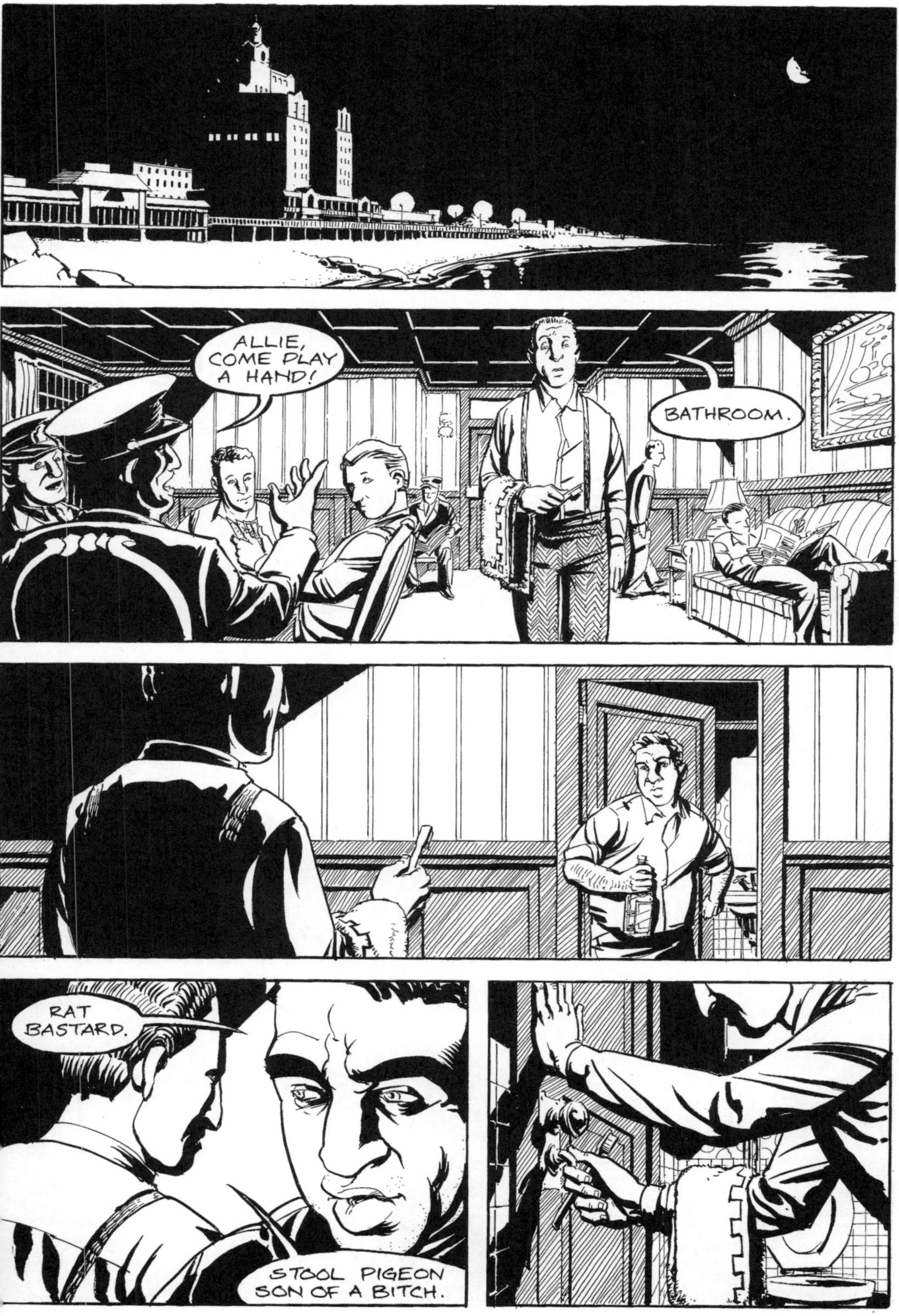
ALLIE, COME PLAY A HAND!
BATHROOM.
RAT BASTARD.
STOOL PIGEON SON OF A BITCH.

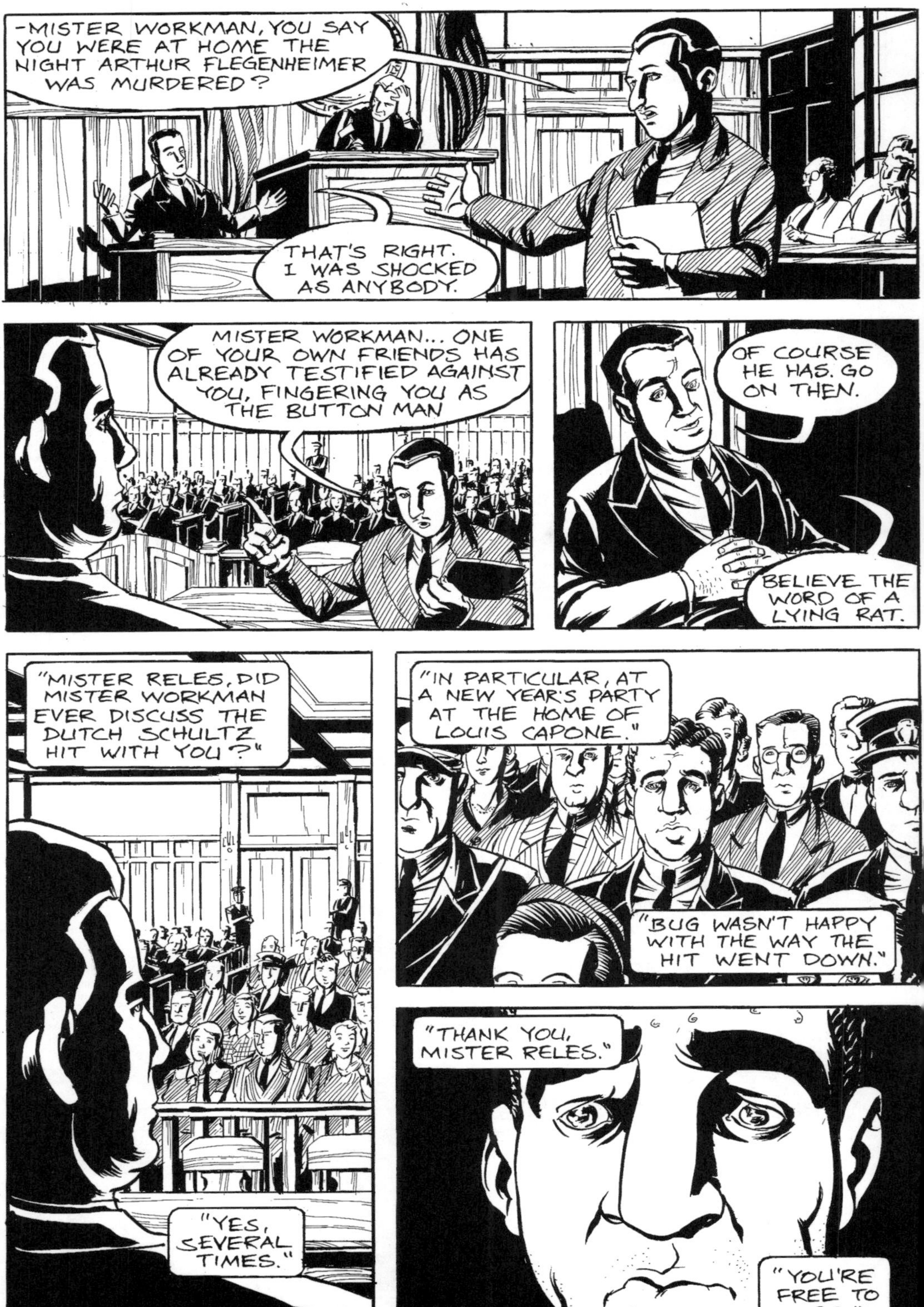

-MISTER WORKMAN, YOU SAY YOU WERE AT HOME THE NIGHT ARTHUR FLEGENHEIMER WAS MURDERED?
THAT'S RIGHT. I WAS SHOCKED AS ANYBODY.
MISTER WORKMAN... ONE OF YOUR OWN FRIENDS HAS ALREADY TESTIFIED AGAINST YOU, FINGERING YOU AS THE BUTTON MAN
OF COURSE HE HAS. GO ON THEN.
BELIEVE THE WORD OF A LYING RAT.
"MISTER RELES, DID MISTER WORKMAN EVER DISCUSS THE DUTCH SCHULTZ HIT WITH YOU?"
"YES, SEVERAL TIMES."
"IN PARTICULAR, AT A NEW YEAR'S PARTY AT THE HOME OF LOUIS CAPONE."
"BUG WASN'T HAPPY WITH THE WAY THE HIT WENT DOWN."
"THANK YOU, MISTER RELES."
"YOU'RE FREE TO GO."

BRAVO, STOOLIE.

LIFE, HARD LABOR.

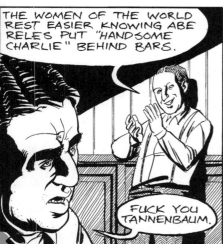

THE WOMEN OF THE WORLD REST EASIER KNOWING ABE RELES PUT "HANDSOME CHARLIE" BEHIND BARS.

FUCK YOU TANNENBAUM.

WHO'S NEXT? MENDY?

HOW ABOUT LOUIS CAPONE? OR HEY!

HOW ABOUT YOUR PAL STRAUSS?

I'M SURE HE'LL UNDERSTAND. ALL'S FAIR — RIGHT, RAT?

GOT A BIG MOUTH, ALLIE BOY.

GONNA BE HARD TO SPILL YOUR GUTS THROUGH A WIRED JAW.

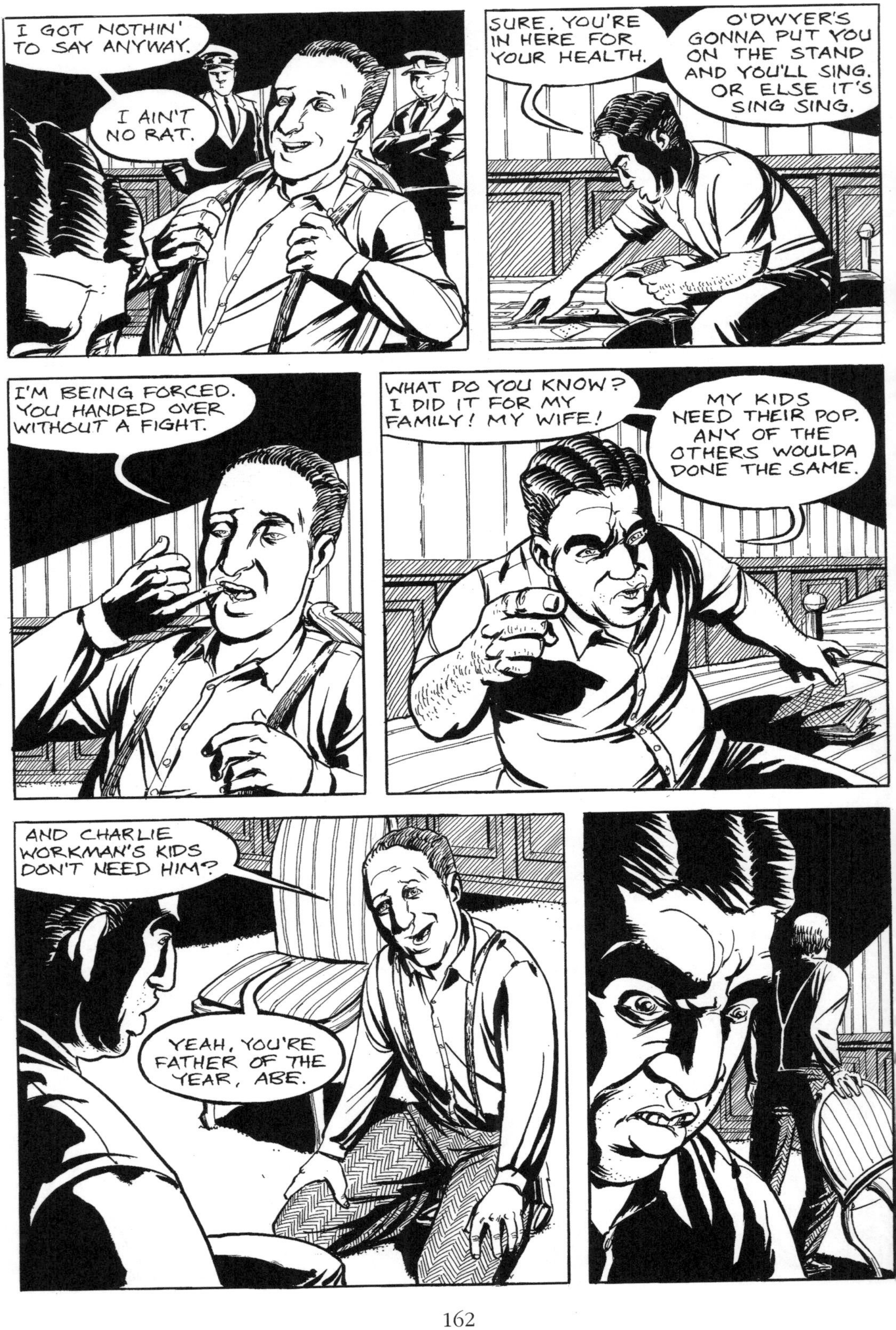
I GOT NOTHIN' TO SAY ANYWAY.
I AIN'T NO RAT.
SURE. YOU'RE IN HERE FOR YOUR HEALTH.
O'DWYER'S GONNA PUT YOU ON THE STAND AND YOU'LL SING. OR ELSE IT'S SING SING.
I'M BEING FORCED. YOU HANDED OVER WITHOUT A FIGHT.
WHAT DO YOU KNOW? I DID IT FOR MY FAMILY! MY WIFE!
MY KIDS NEED THEIR POP. ANY OF THE OTHERS WOULDA DONE THE SAME.
AND CHARLIE WORKMAN'S KIDS DON'T NEED HIM?
YEAH, YOU'RE FATHER OF THE YEAR, ABE.

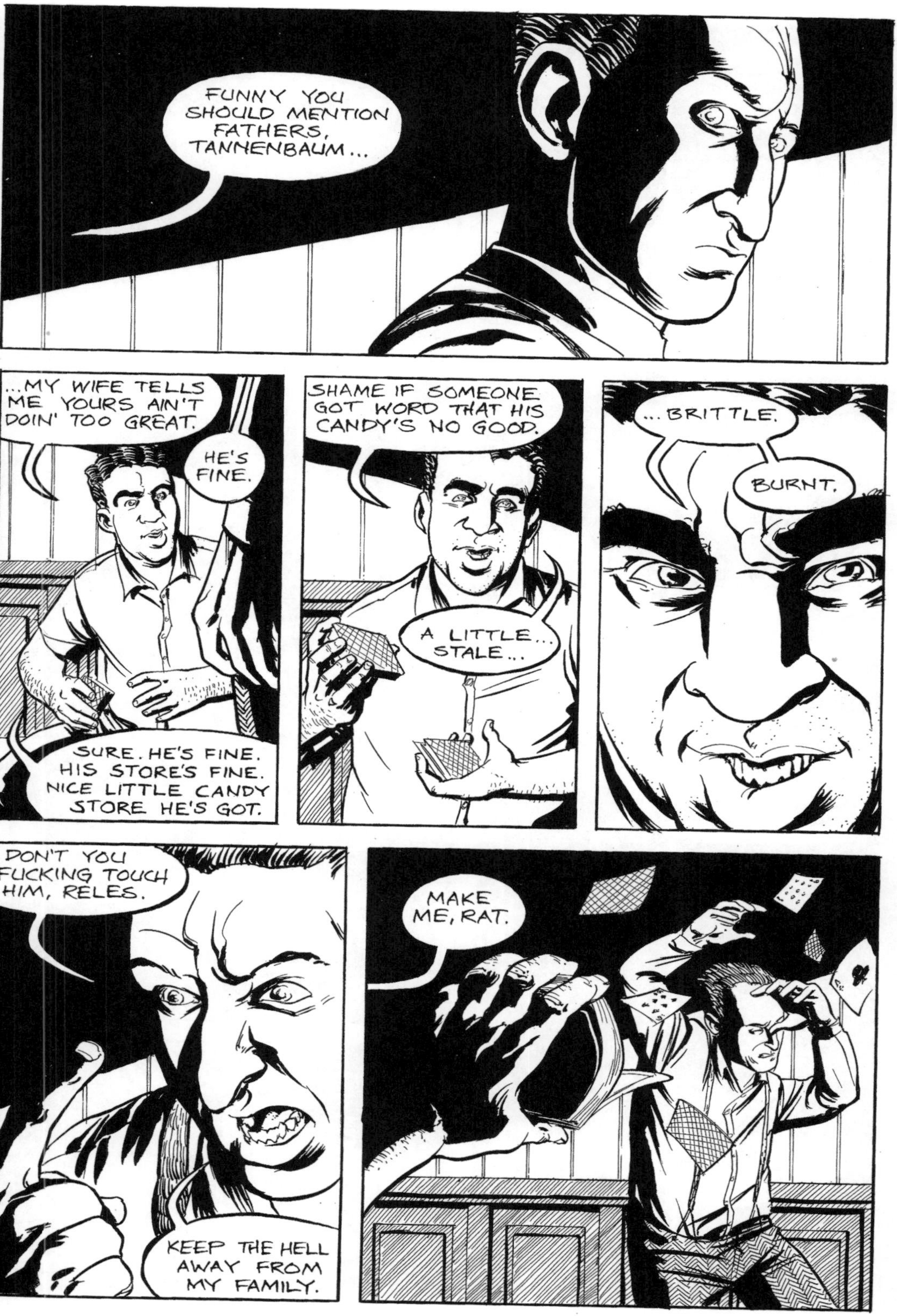
FUNNY YOU SHOULD MENTION FATHERS, TANNENBAUM...
...MY WIFE TELLS ME YOURS AIN'T DOIN' TOO GREAT.
HE'S FINE.
SURE. HE'S FINE. HIS STORE'S FINE. NICE LITTLE CANDY STORE HE'S GOT.
SHAME IF SOMEONE GOT WORD THAT HIS CANDY'S NO GOOD.
A LITTLE... STALE...
...BRITTLE.
BURNT.
DON'T YOU FUCKING TOUCH HIM, RELES.
KEEP THE HELL AWAY FROM MY FAMILY.
MAKE ME, RAT.

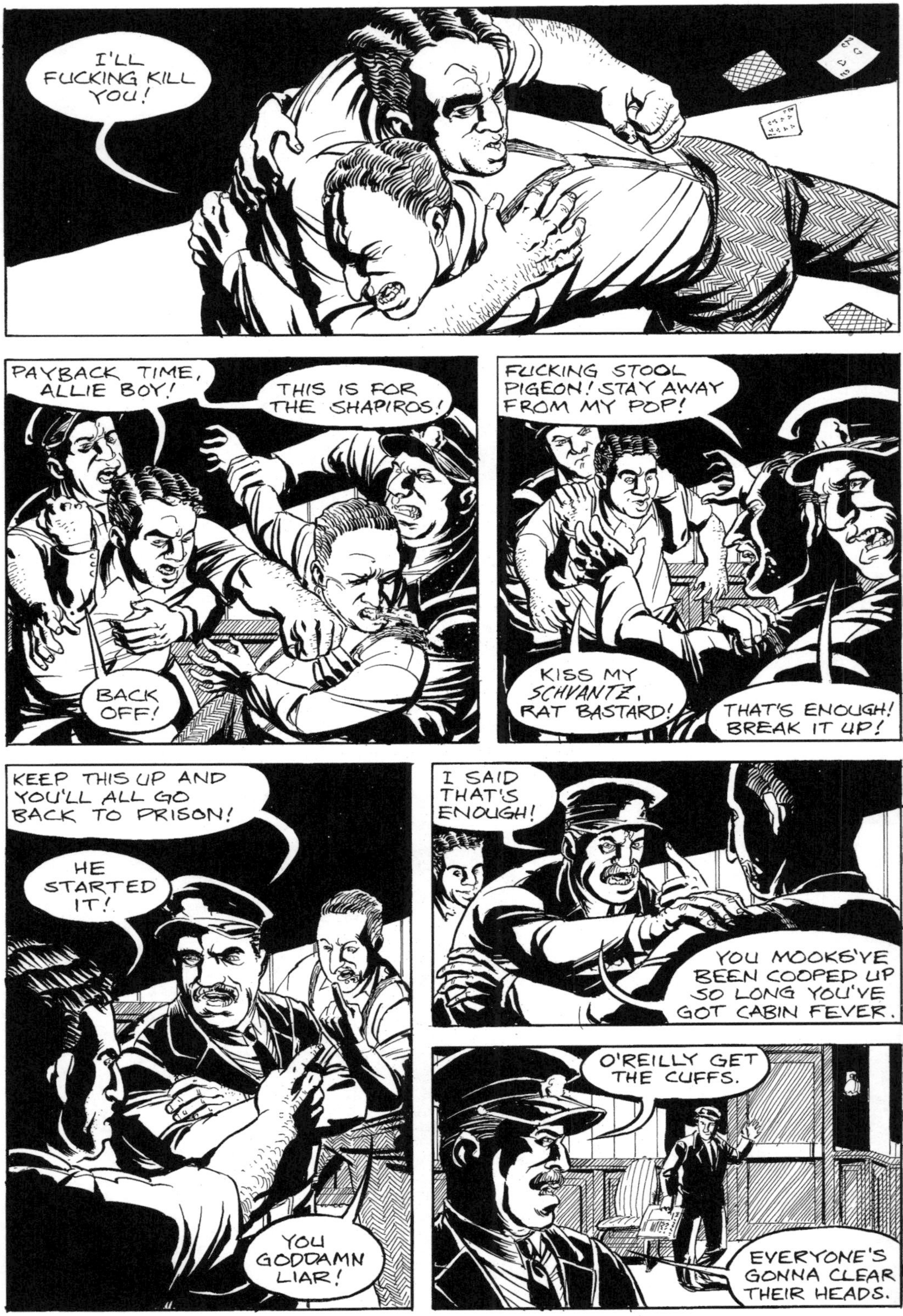
I'LL FUCKING KILL YOU!
PAYBACK TIME, ALLIE BOY!
THIS IS FOR THE SHAPIROS!
BACK OFF!
FUCKING STOOL PIGEON! STAY AWAY FROM MY POP!
KISS MY *SCHVANTZ*, RAT BASTARD!
THAT'S ENOUGH! BREAK IT UP!
KEEP THIS UP AND YOU'LL ALL GO BACK TO PRISON!
HE STARTED IT!
YOU GODDAMN LIAR!
I SAID THAT'S ENOUGH!
YOU MOOKS'VE BEEN COOPED UP SO LONG YOU'VE GOT CABIN FEVER.
O'REILLY GET THE CUFFS.
EVERYONE'S GONNA CLEAR THEIR HEADS.

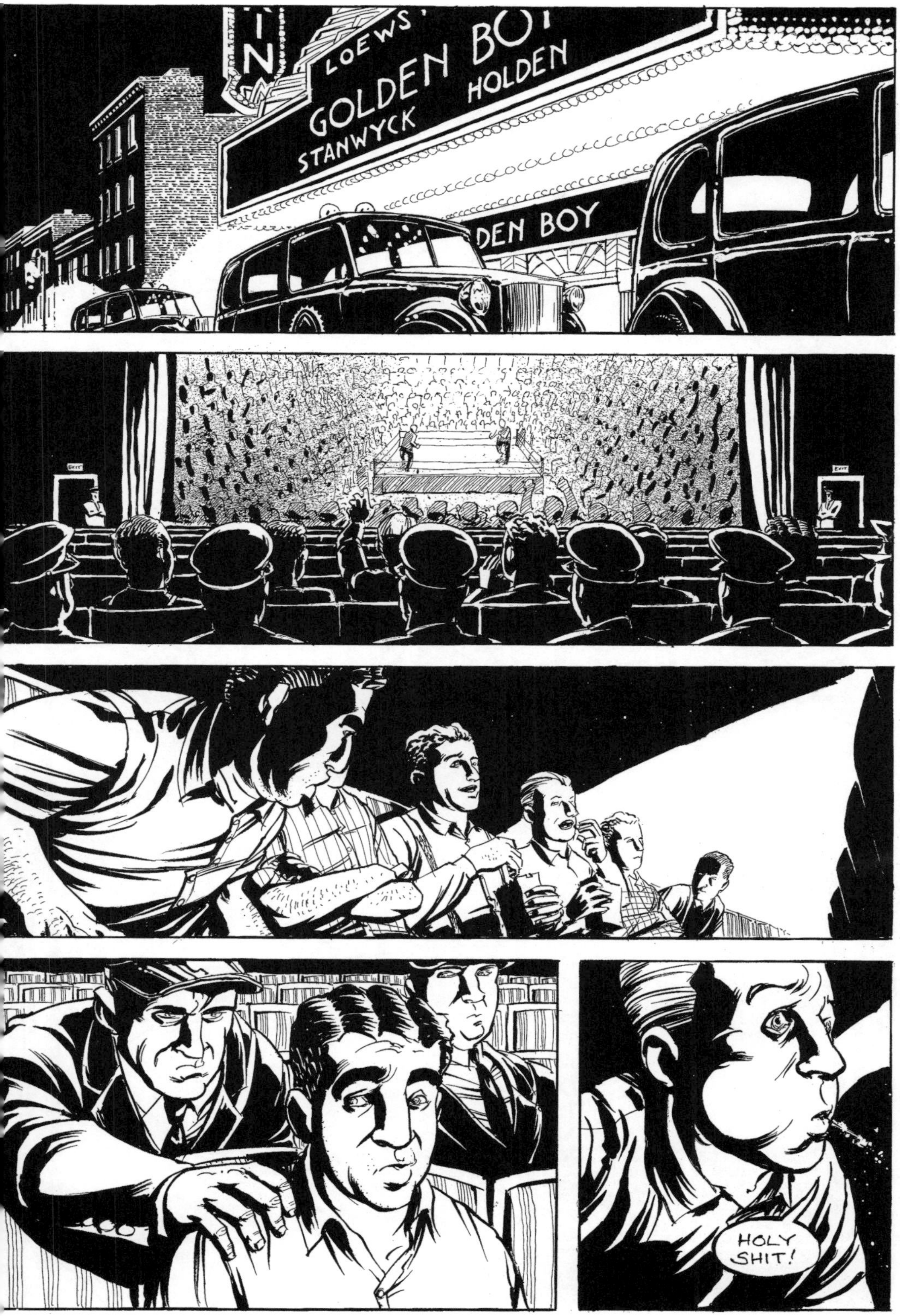
LOEWS'
GOLDEN BOY
STANWYCK HOLDEN
DEN BOY
HOLY SHIT!

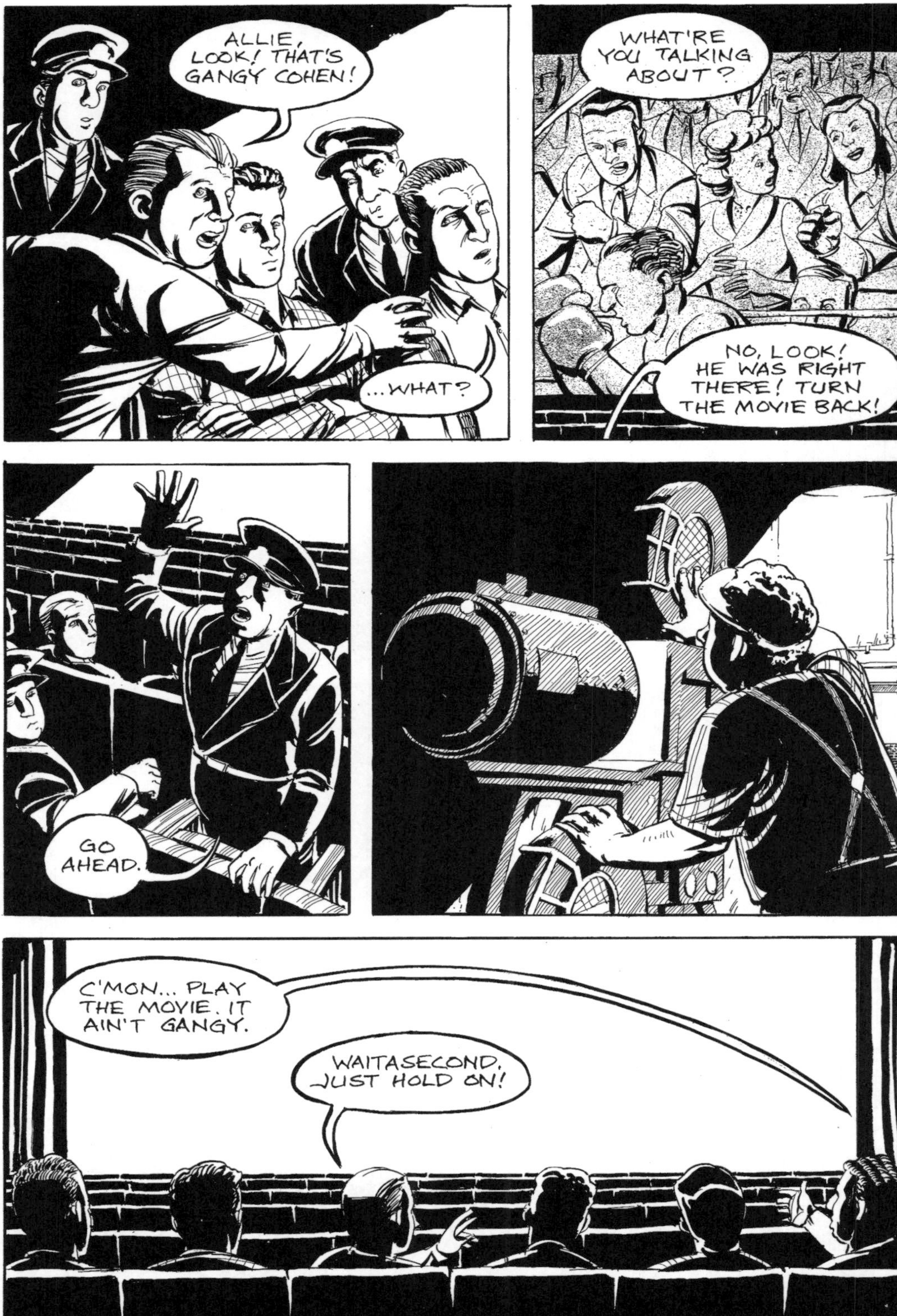
ALLIE, LOOK! THAT'S GANGY COHEN!
...WHAT?
WHAT'RE YOU TALKING ABOUT?
NO, LOOK! HE WAS RIGHT THERE! TURN THE MOVIE BACK!
GO AHEAD.
C'MON... PLAY THE MOVIE. IT AIN'T GANGY.
WAITASECOND, JUST HOLD ON!

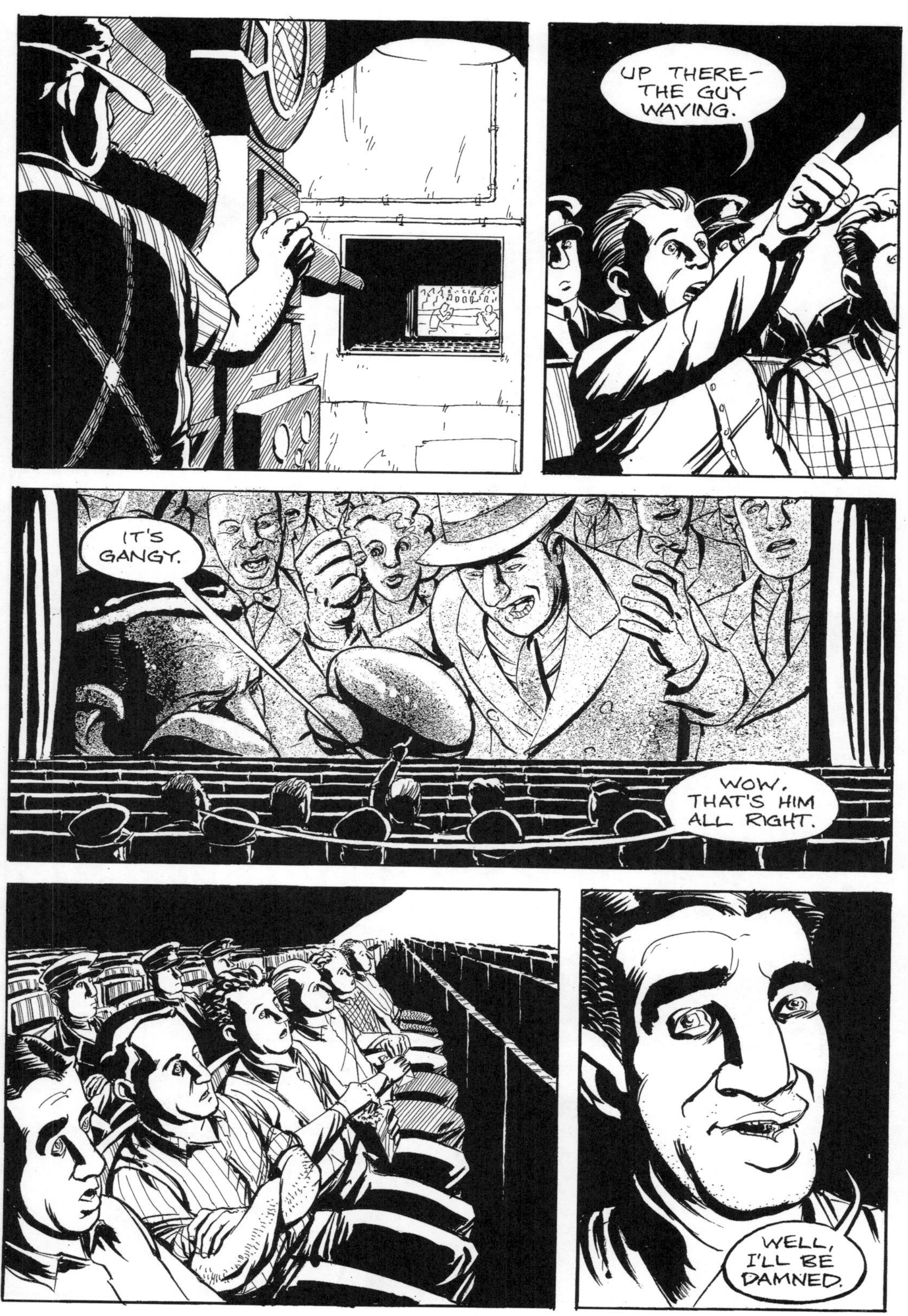
UP THERE-
THE GUY
WAVING.
IT'S
GANGY.
WOW.
THAT'S HIM
ALL RIGHT.
WELL,
I'LL BE
DAMNED.

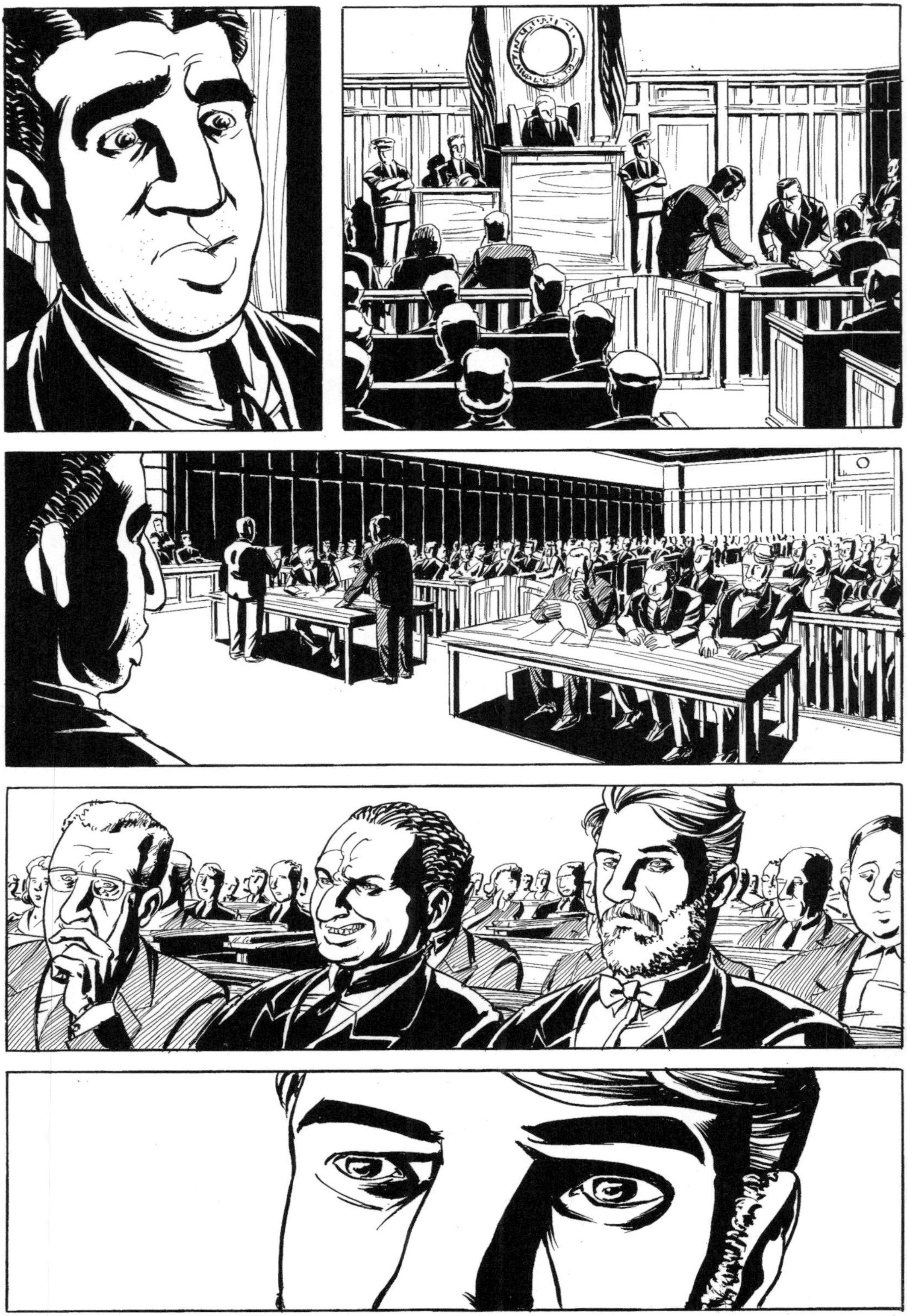

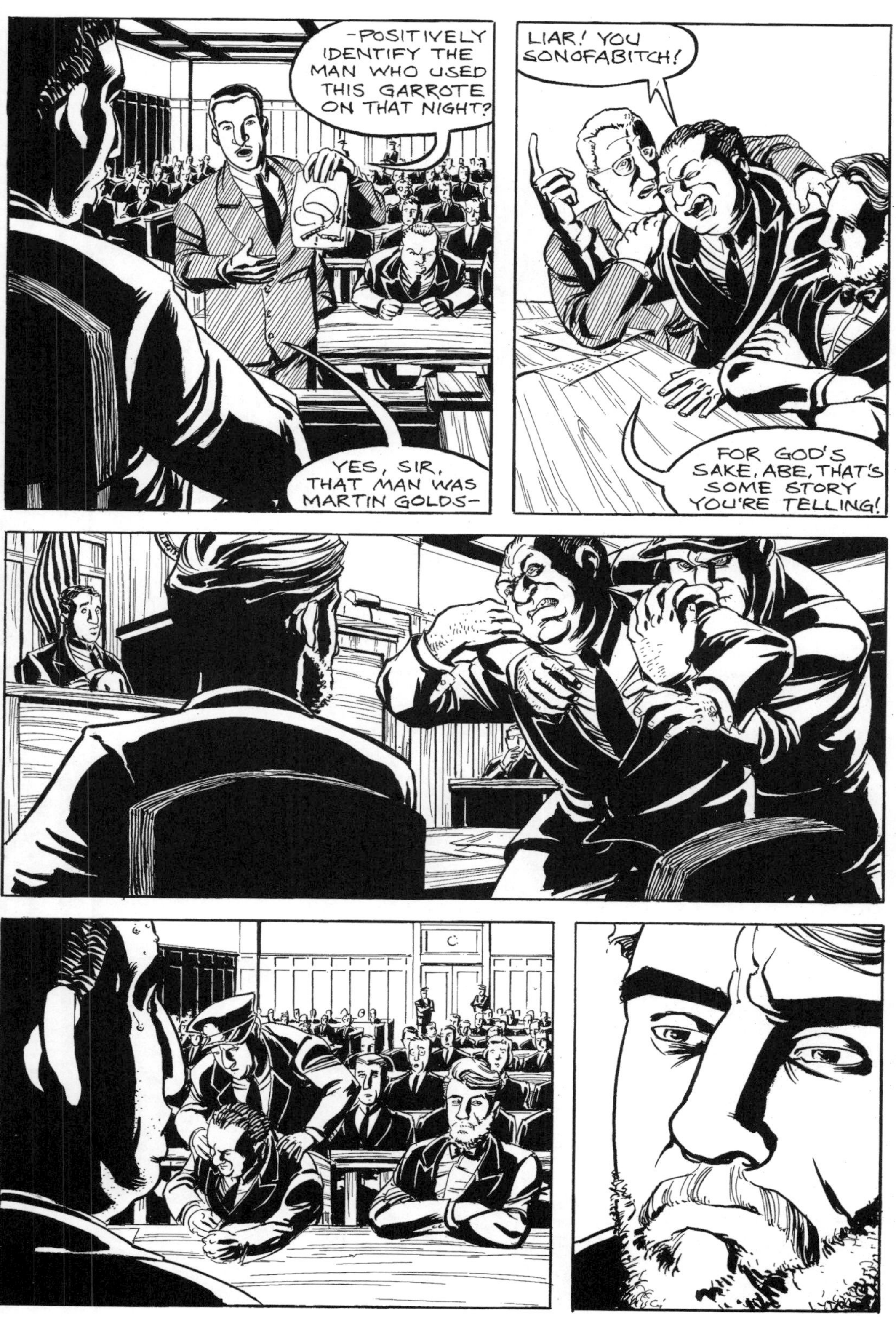
-POSITIVELY IDENTIFY THE MAN WHO USED THIS GARROTE ON THAT NIGHT?
YES, SIR, THAT MAN WAS MARTIN GOLDS-
LIAR! YOU SONOFABITCH!
FOR GOD'S SAKE, ABE, THAT'S SOME STORY YOU'RE TELLING!

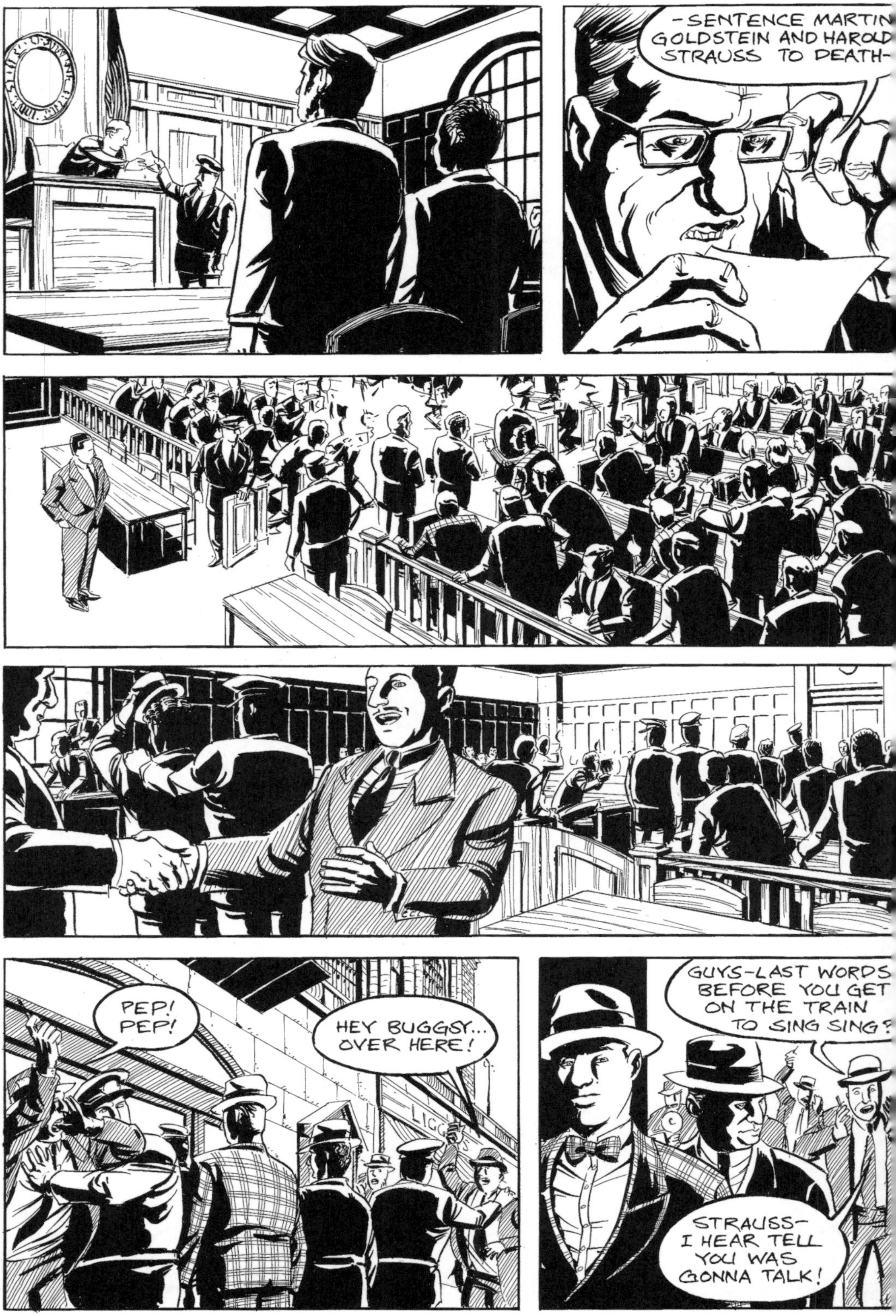

-SENTENCE MARTIN GOLDSTEIN AND HAROLD STRAUSS TO DEATH-
PEP! PEP!
HEY BUGGSY... OVER HERE!
GUYS-LAST WORDS BEFORE YOU GET ON THE TRAIN TO SING SING?
STRAUSS- I HEAR TELL YOU WAS GONNA TALK!

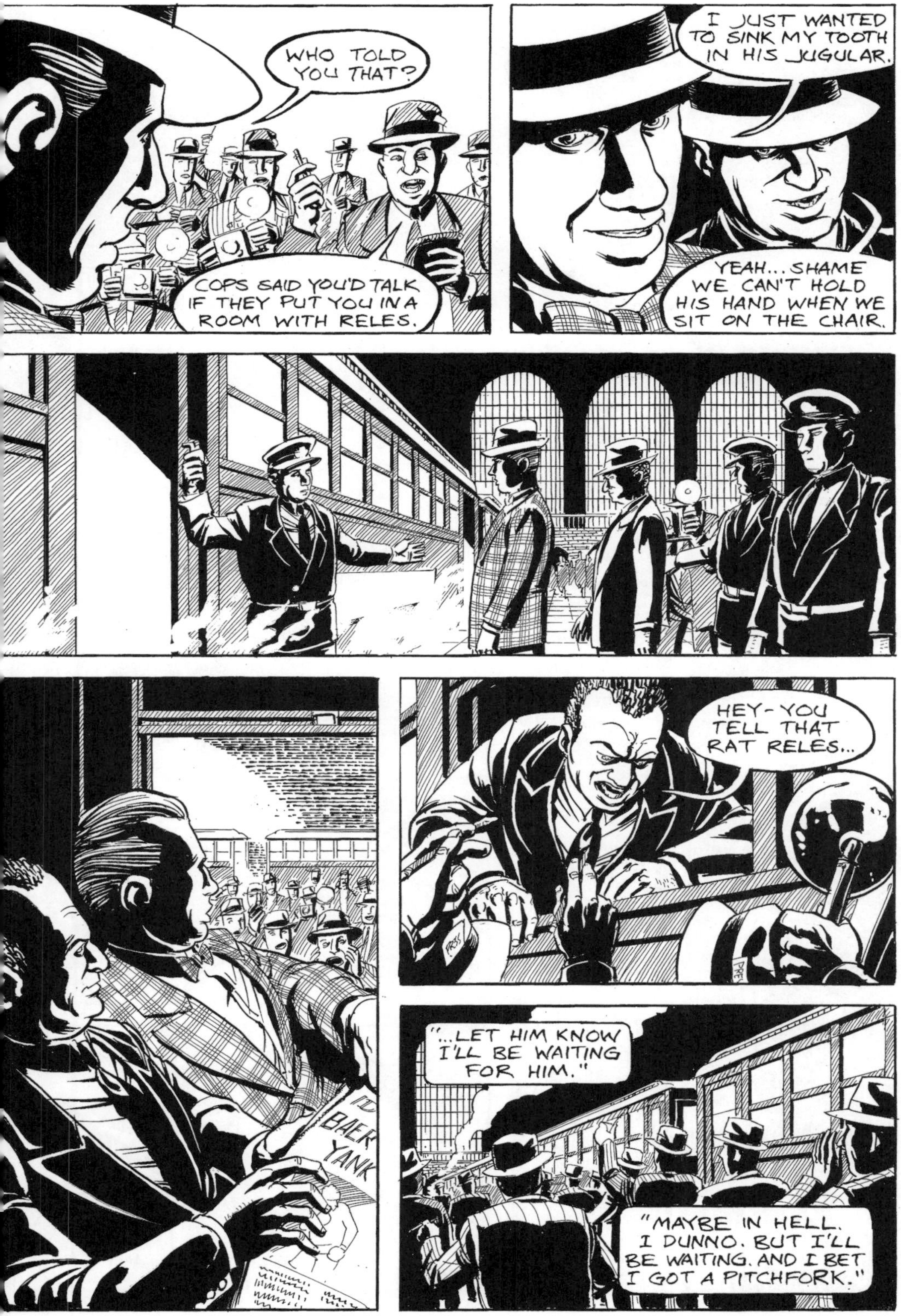
WHO TOLD YOU THAT?
COPS SAID YOU'D TALK IF THEY PUT YOU IN A ROOM WITH RELES.
I JUST WANTED TO SINK MY TOOTH IN HIS JUGULAR.
YEAH... SHAME WE CAN'T HOLD HIS HAND WHEN WE SIT ON THE CHAIR.
BAER
YANK
HEY- YOU TELL THAT RAT RELES...
"...LET HIM KNOW I'LL BE WAITING FOR HIM."
"MAYBE IN HELL. I DUNNO. BUT I'LL BE WAITING. AND I BET I GOT A PITCHFORK."

THE LAST DAYS OF THE HALF MOON

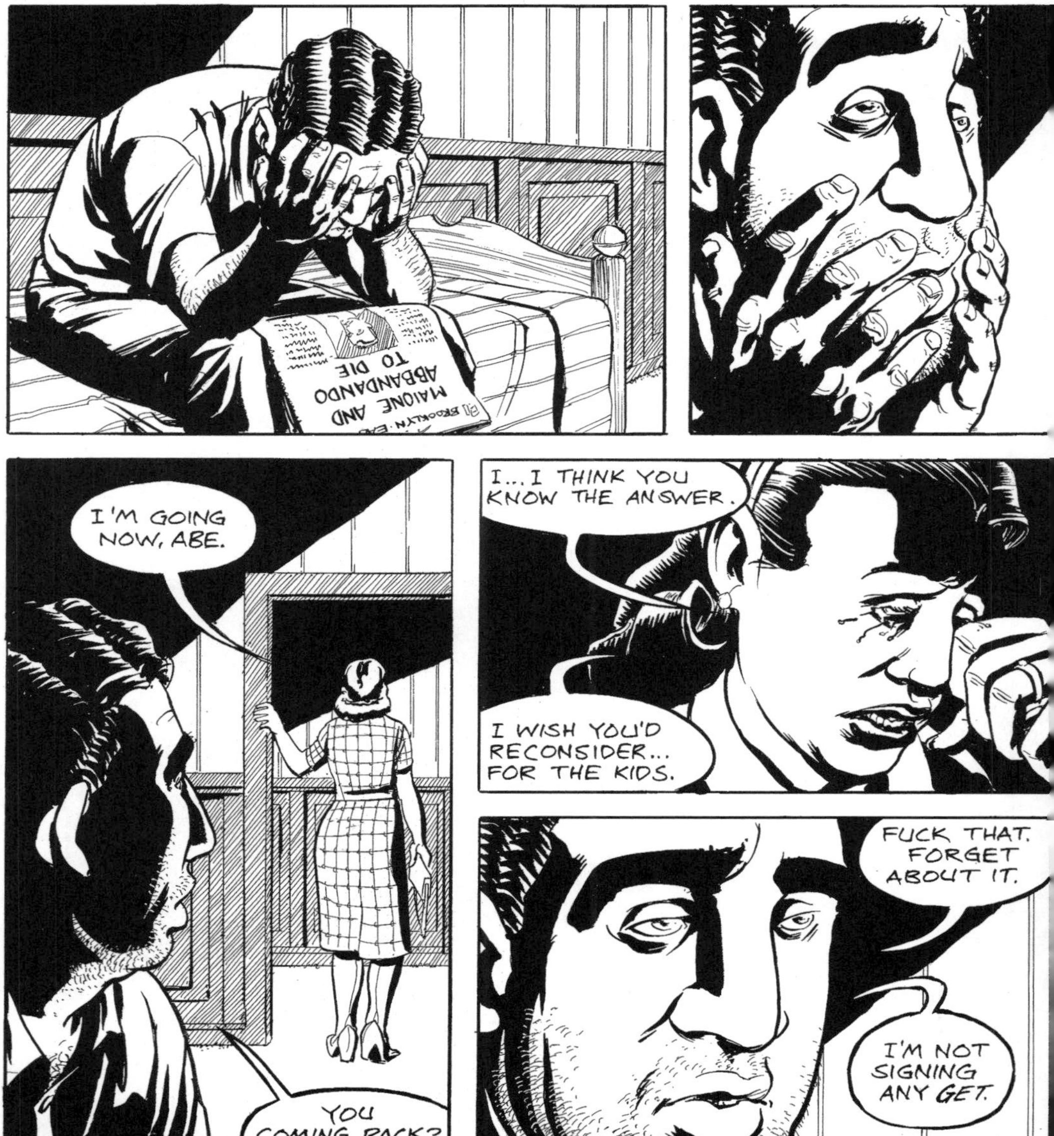
MAIONE AND
ABBANDANDO
TO DIE
I'M GOING NOW, ABE.
YOU COMING BACK?
I... I THINK YOU KNOW THE ANSWER.
I WISH YOU'D RECONSIDER... FOR THE KIDS.
FUCK THAT. FORGET ABOUT IT.
I'M NOT SIGNING ANY *GET*.

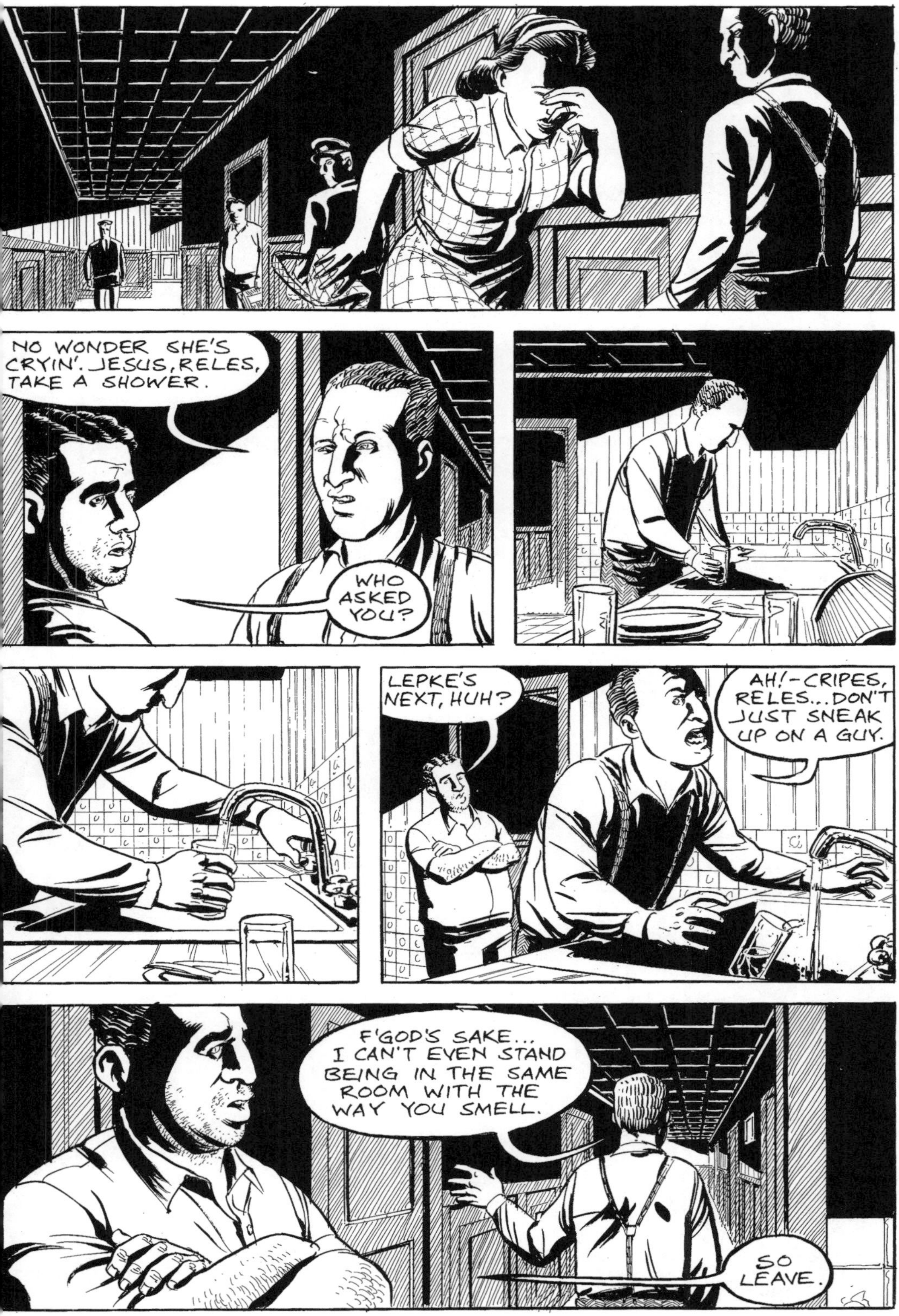
NO WONDER SHE'S CRYIN'. JESUS, RELES, TAKE A SHOWER.
WHO ASKED YOU?
LEPKE'S NEXT, HUH?
AH!-CRIPES, RELES...DON'T JUST SNEAK UP ON A GUY.
F'GOD'S SAKE... I CAN'T EVEN STAND BEING IN THE SAME ROOM WITH THE WAY YOU SMELL.
SO LEAVE.

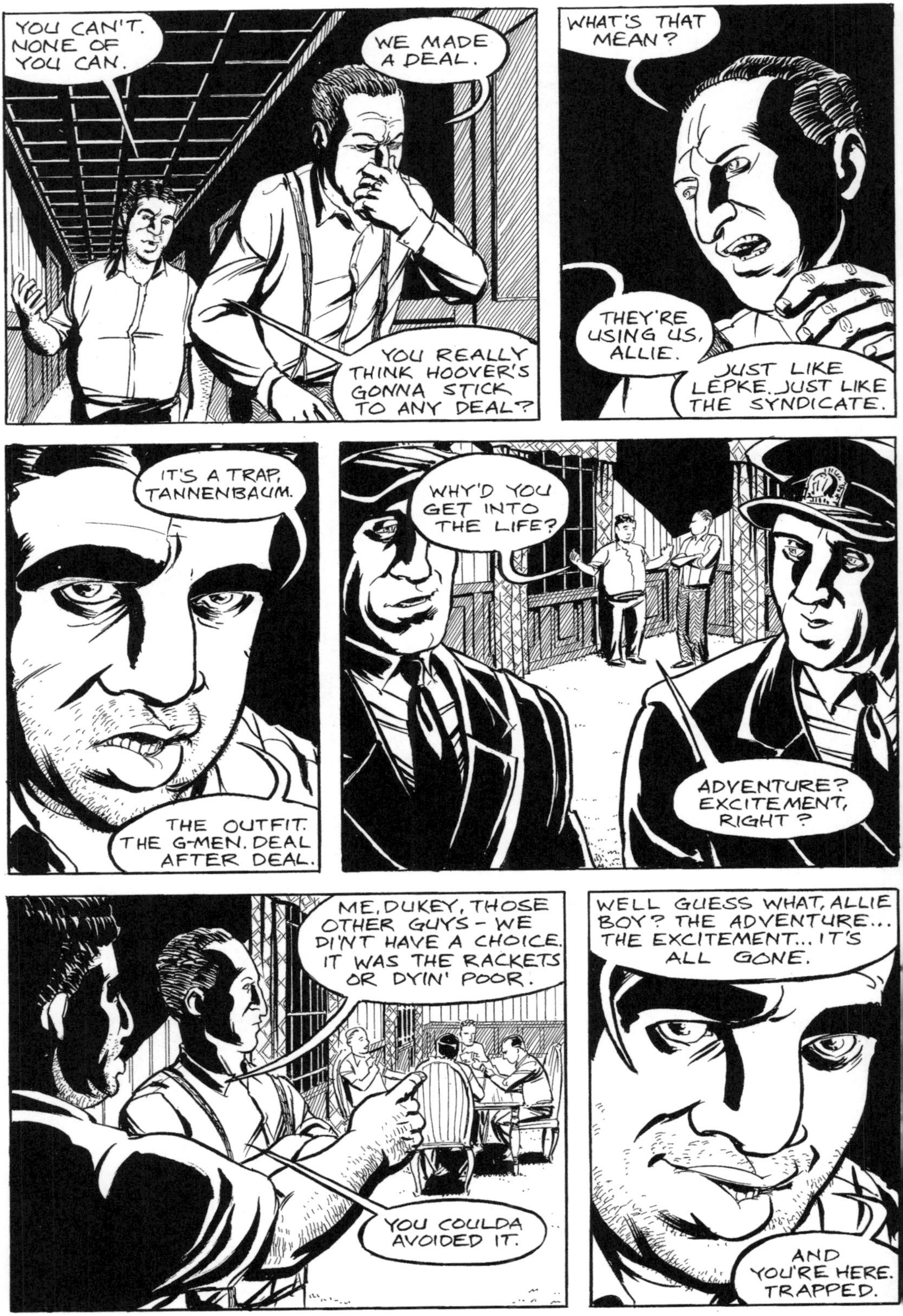
YOU CAN'T. NONE OF YOU CAN.
WE MADE A DEAL.
YOU REALLY THINK HOOVER'S GONNA STICK TO ANY DEAL?
WHAT'S THAT MEAN?
THEY'RE USING US, ALLIE.
JUST LIKE LEPKE. JUST LIKE THE SYNDICATE.
IT'S A TRAP, TANNENBAUM.
THE OUTFIT. THE G-MEN. DEAL AFTER DEAL.
WHY'D YOU GET INTO THE LIFE?
ADVENTURE? EXCITEMENT, RIGHT?
ME, DUKEY, THOSE OTHER GUYS - WE DI'NT HAVE A CHOICE. IT WAS THE RACKETS OR DYIN' POOR.
YOU COULDA AVOIDED IT.
WELL GUESS WHAT, ALLIE BOY? THE ADVENTURE... THE EXCITEMENT... IT'S ALL GONE.
AND YOU'RE HERE. TRAPPED.

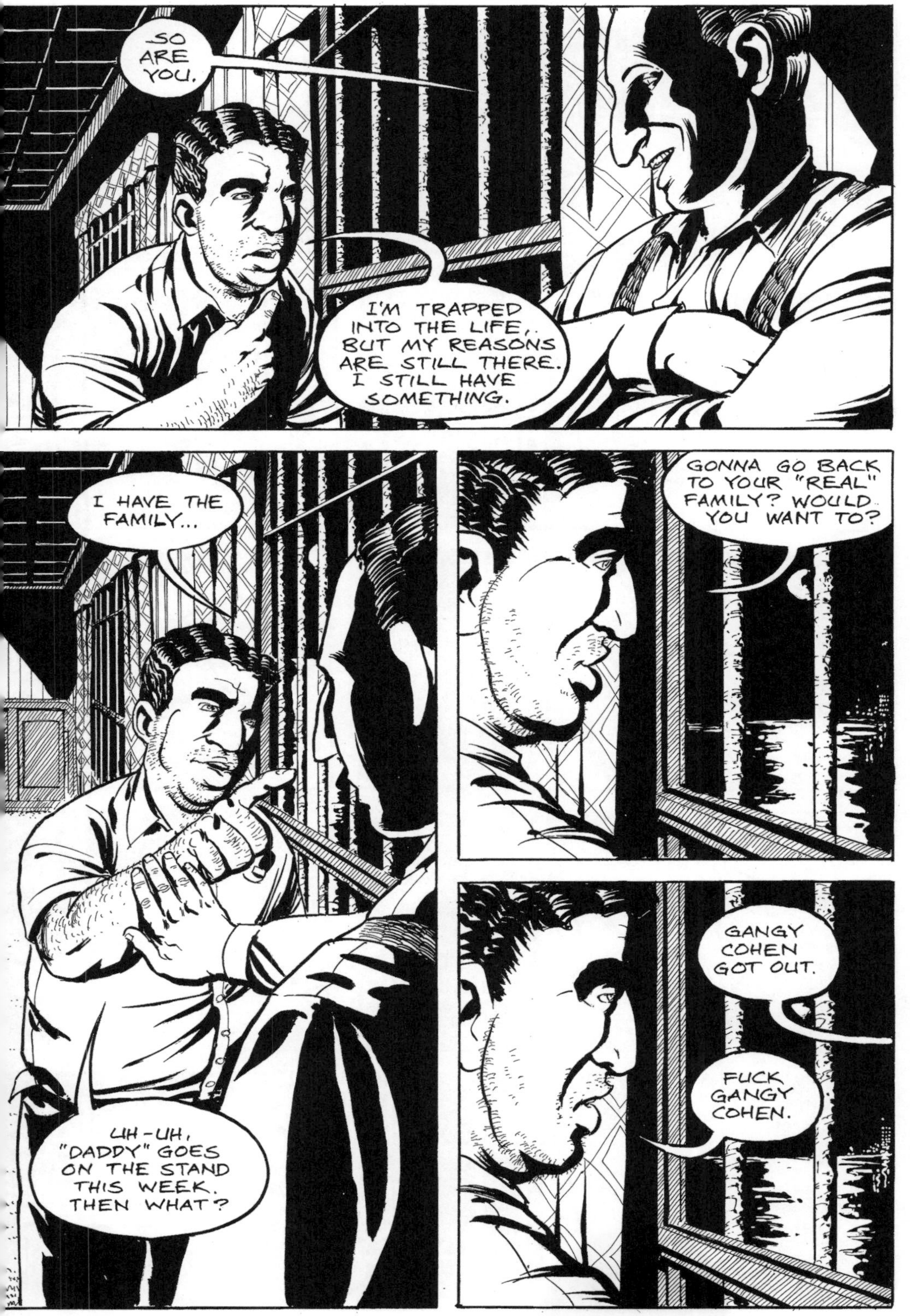
SO ARE YOU.
I'M TRAPPED INTO THE LIFE, BUT MY REASONS ARE STILL THERE. I STILL HAVE SOMETHING.
I HAVE THE FAMILY...
UH-UH, "DADDY" GOES ON THE STAND THIS WEEK. THEN WHAT?
GONNA GO BACK TO YOUR "REAL" FAMILY? WOULD YOU WANT TO?
GANGY COHEN GOT OUT.
FUCK GANGY COHEN.

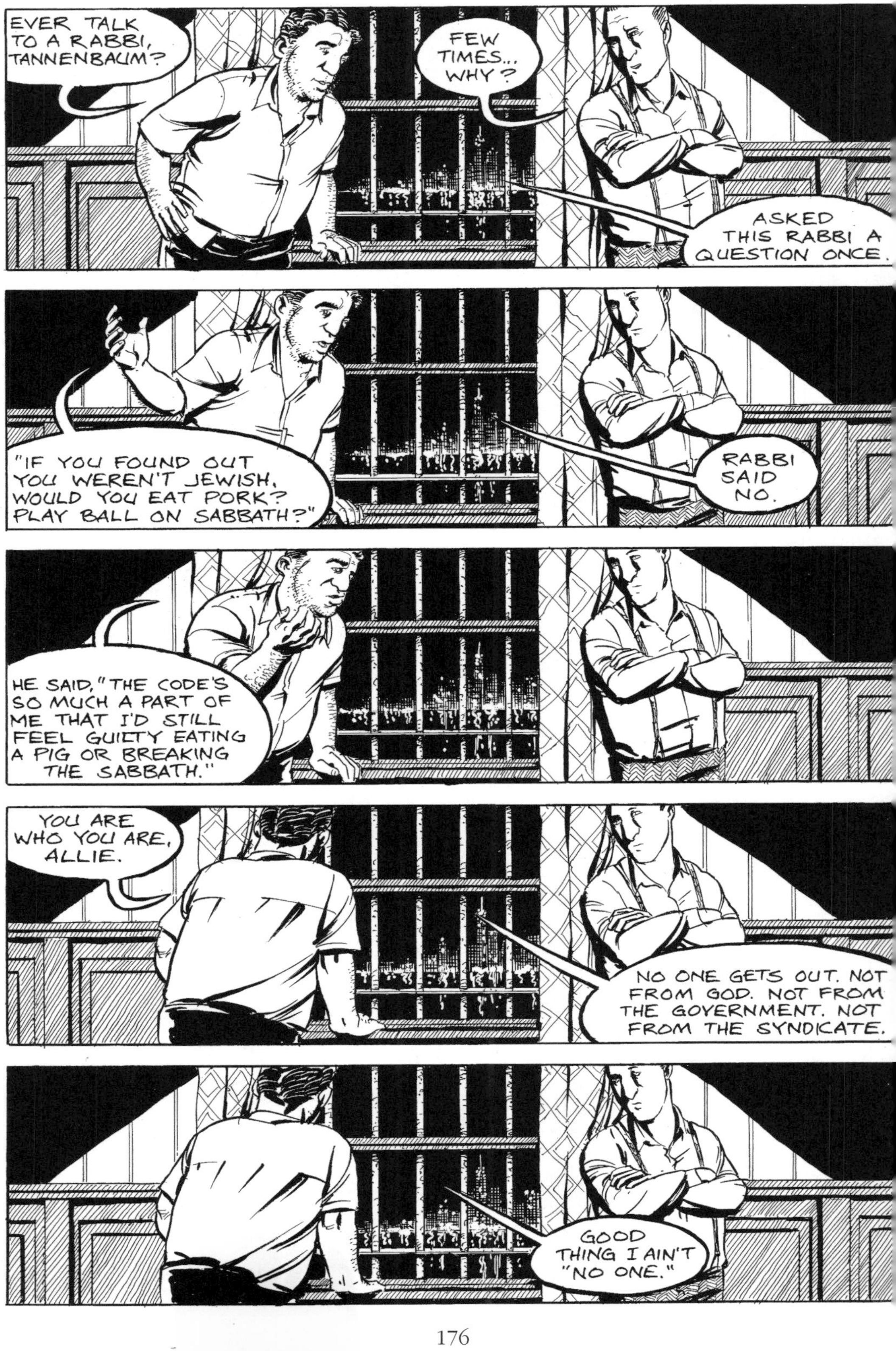
EVER TALK TO A RABBI, TANNENBAUM?
FEW TIMES... WHY?
ASKED THIS RABBI A QUESTION ONCE.
"IF YOU FOUND OUT YOU WEREN'T JEWISH, WOULD YOU EAT PORK? PLAY BALL ON SABBATH?"
RABBI SAID NO.
HE SAID, "THE CODE'S SO MUCH A PART OF ME THAT I'D STILL FEEL GUILTY EATING A PIG OR BREAKING THE SABBATH."
YOU ARE WHO YOU ARE, ALLIE.
NO ONE GETS OUT. NOT FROM GOD. NOT FROM THE GOVERNMENT. NOT FROM THE SYNDICATE.
GOOD THING I AIN'T "NO ONE."

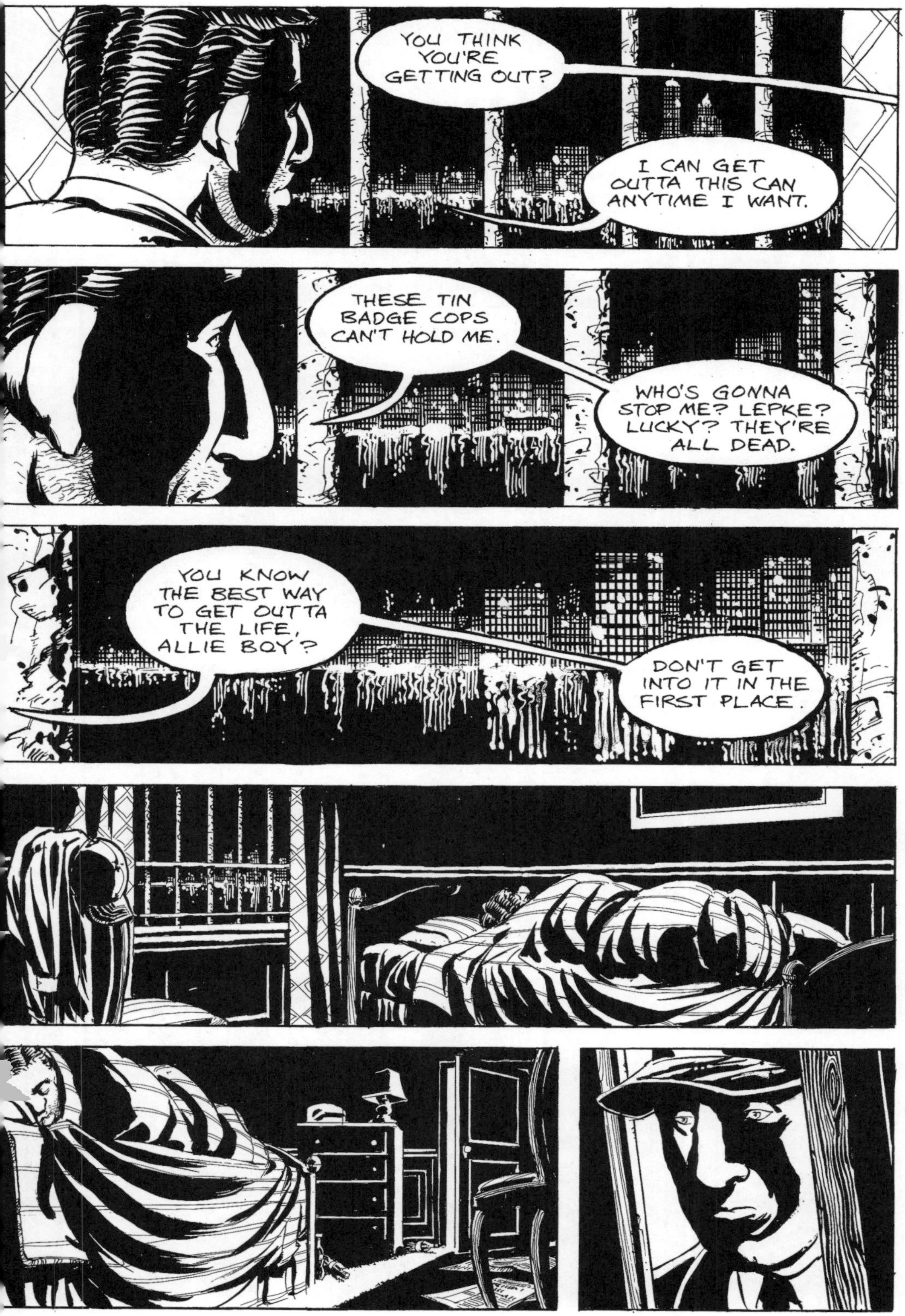
YOU THINK YOU'RE GETTING OUT?
I CAN GET OUTTA THIS CAN ANYTIME I WANT.
THESE TIN BADGE COPS CAN'T HOLD ME.
WHO'S GONNA STOP ME? LEPKE? LUCKY? THEY'RE ALL DEAD.
YOU KNOW THE BEST WAY TO GET OUTTA THE LIFE, ALLIE BOY?
DON'T GET INTO IT IN THE FIRST PLACE.

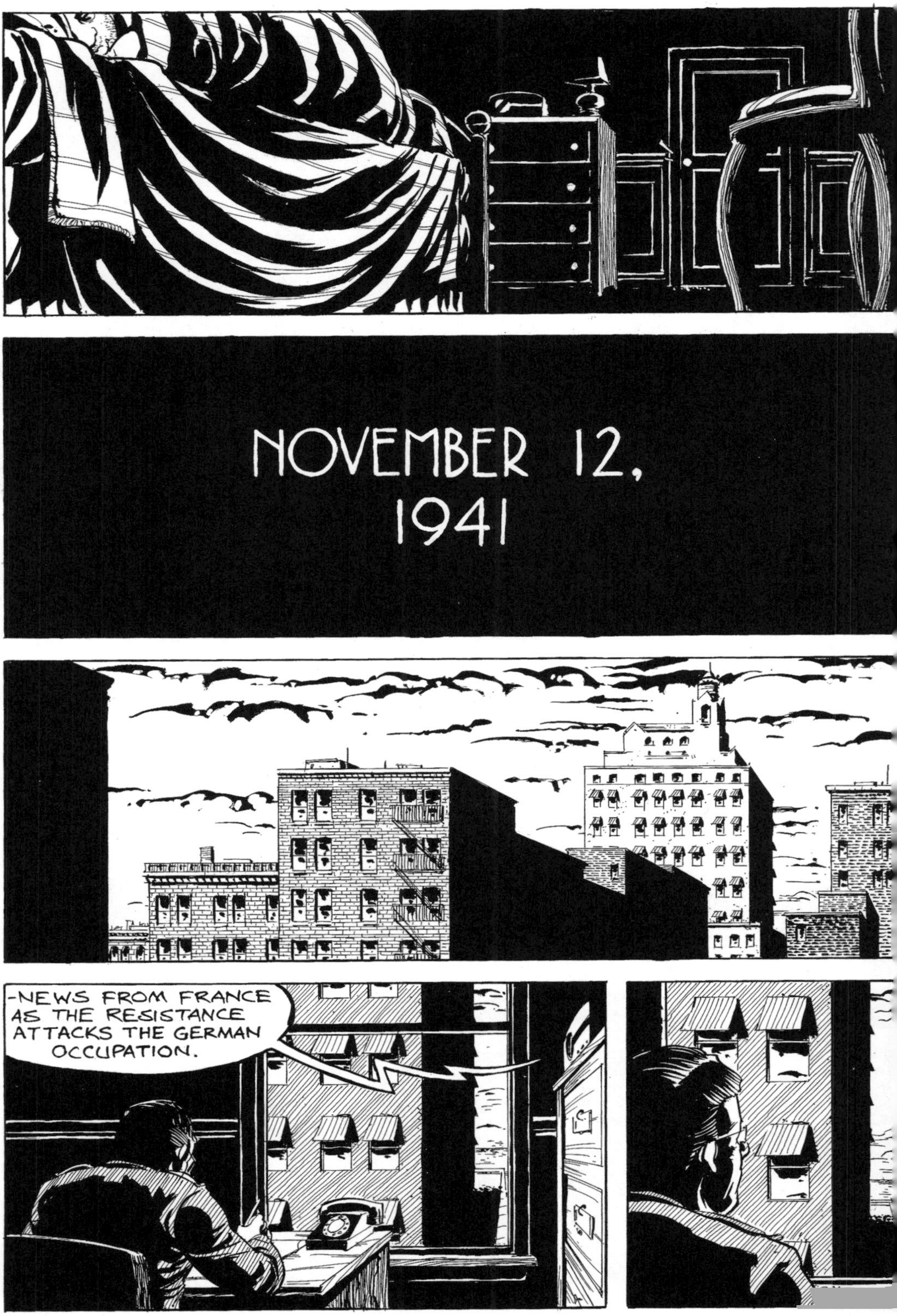
NOVEMBER 12, 1941
-NEWS FROM FRANCE AS THE RESISTANCE ATTACKS THE GERMAN OCCUPATION.

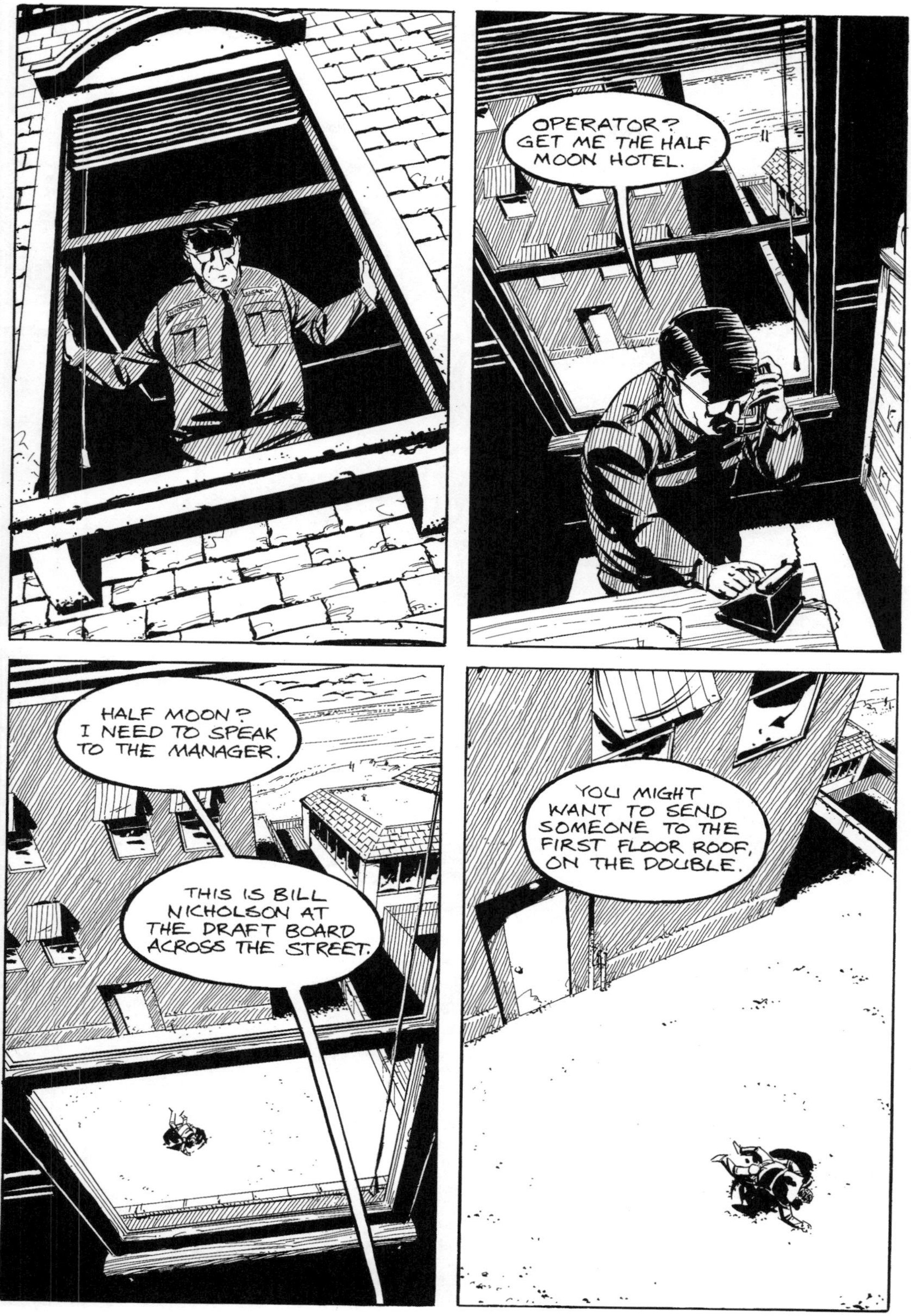
OPERATOR? GET ME THE HALF MOON HOTEL.
HALF MOON? I NEED TO SPEAK TO THE MANAGER.
THIS IS BILL NICHOLSON AT THE DRAFT BOARD ACROSS THE STREET.
YOU MIGHT WANT TO SEND SOMEONE TO THE FIRST FLOOR ROOF, ON THE DOUBLE.

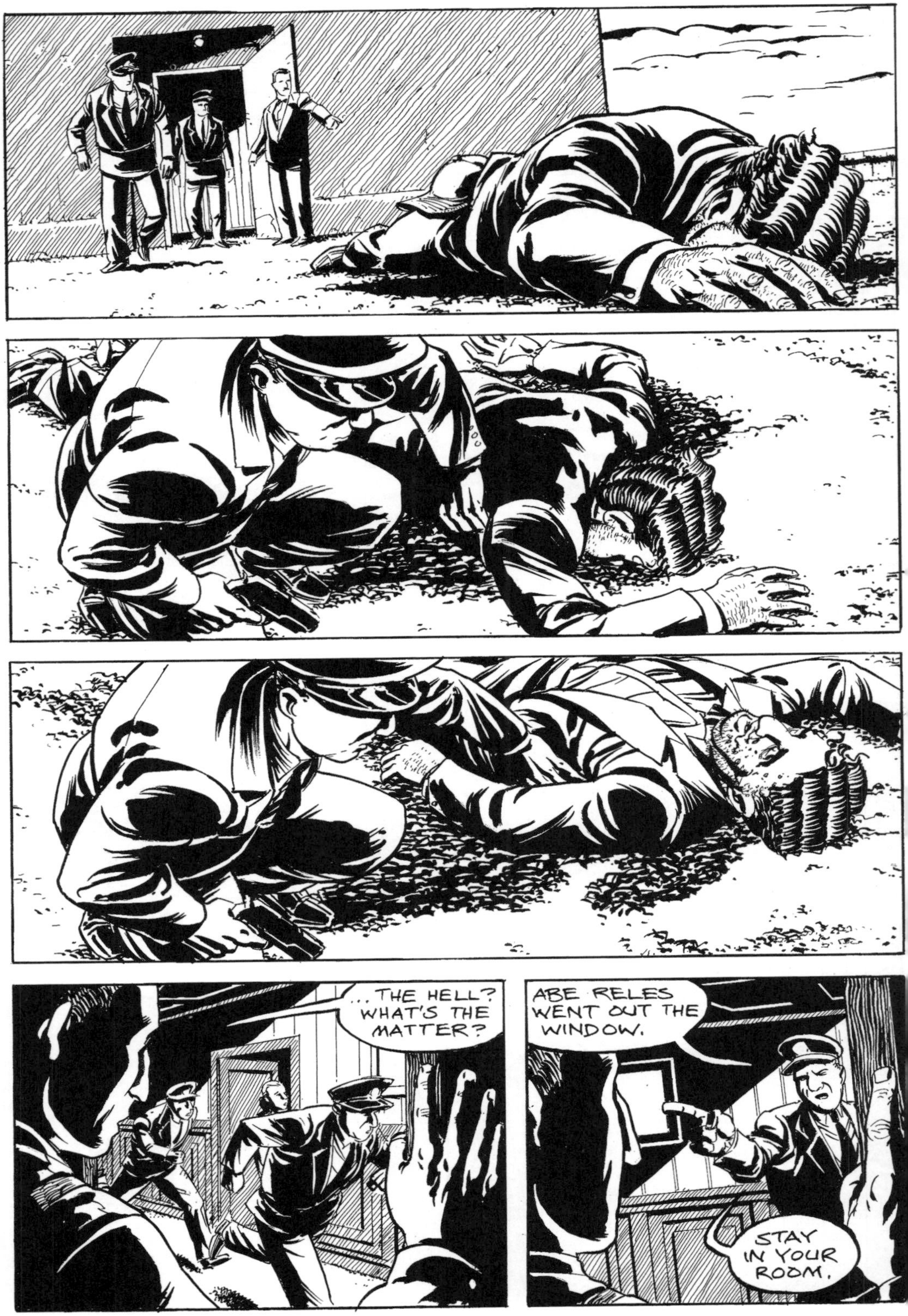
...THE HELL? WHAT'S THE MATTER?
ABE RELES WENT OUT THE WINDOW.
STAY IN YOUR ROOM.

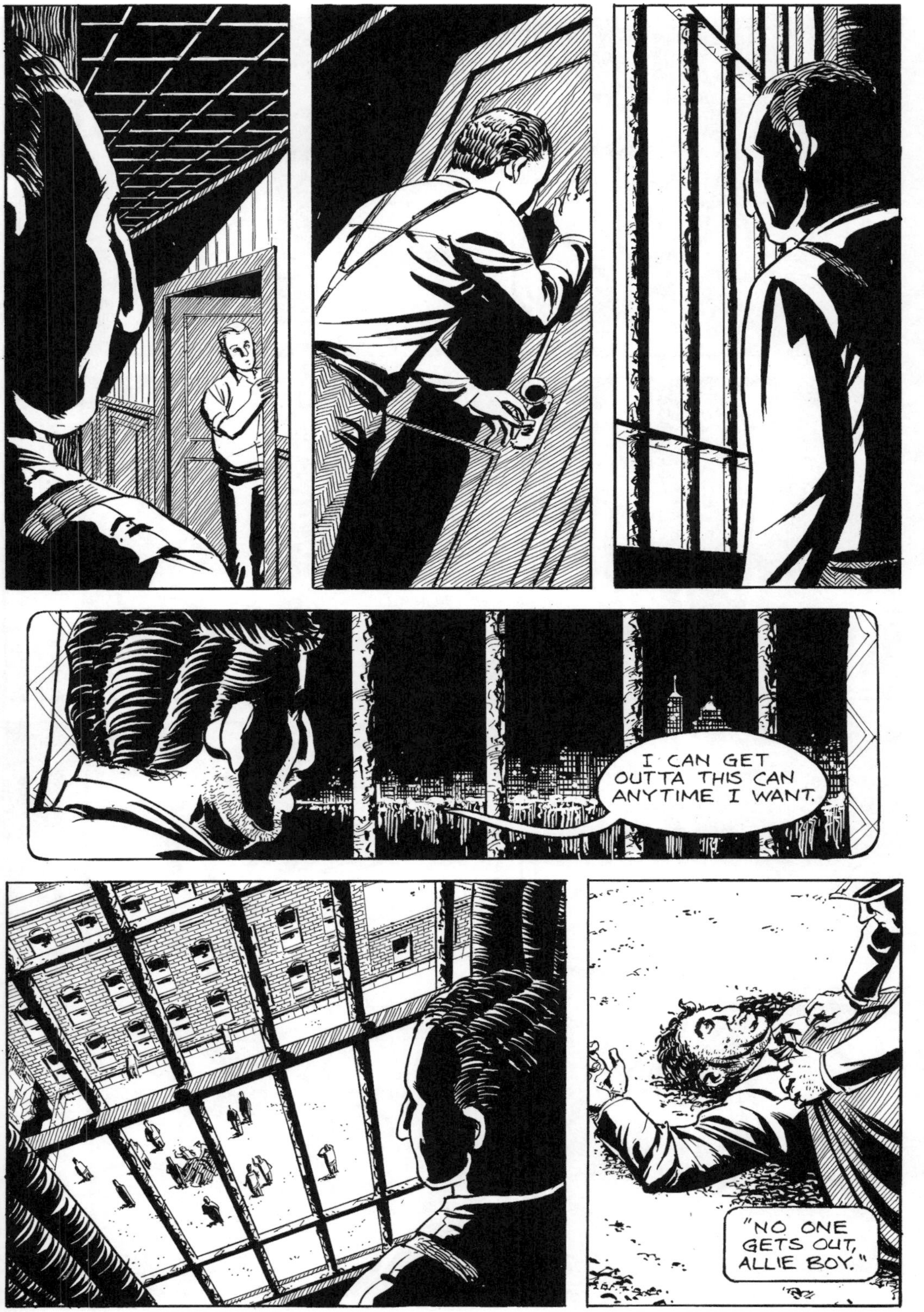
I CAN GET
OUTTA THIS CAN
ANYTIME I WANT.
"NO ONE
GETS OUT,
ALLIE BOY."

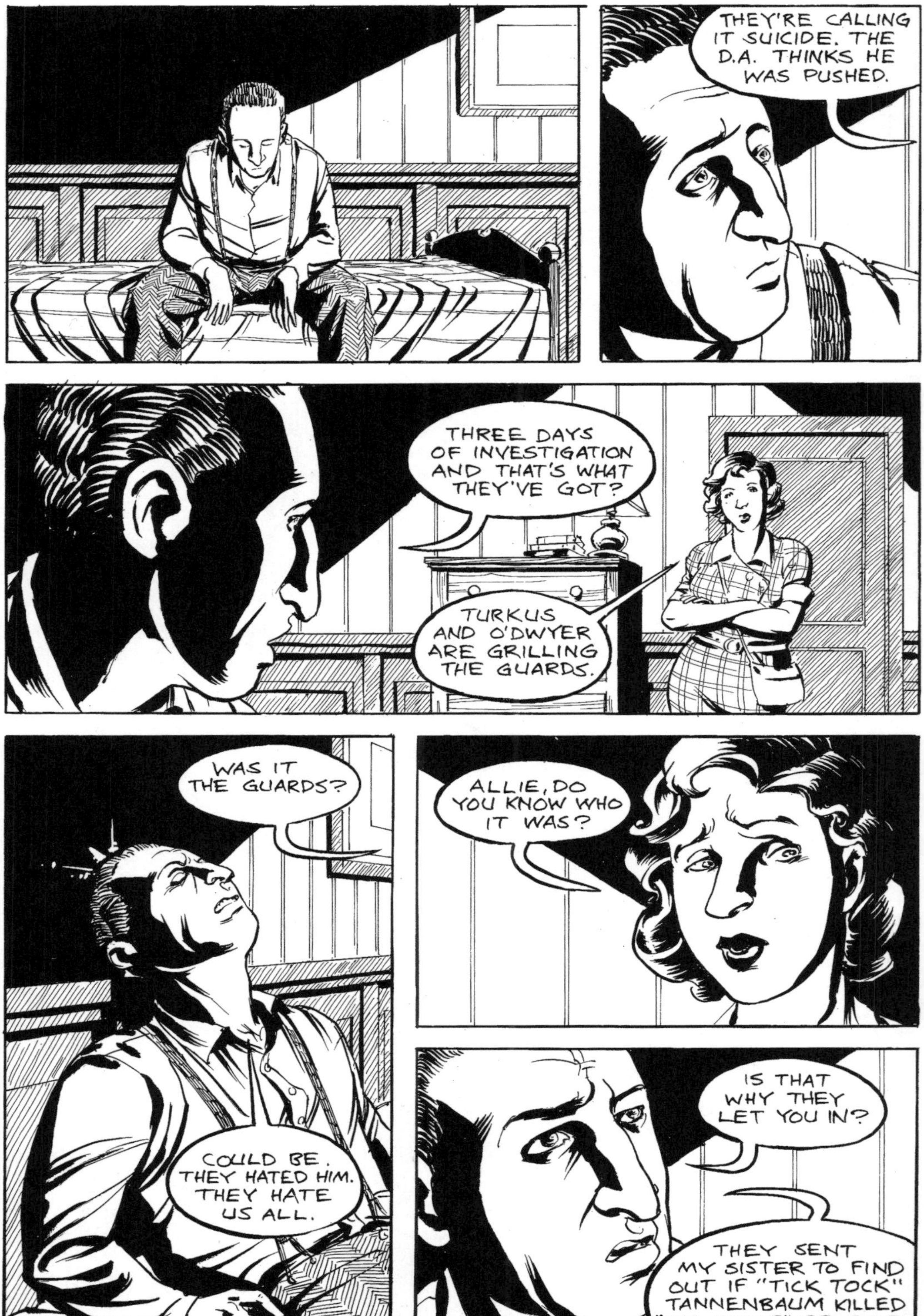
THEY'RE CALLING IT SUICIDE. THE D.A. THINKS HE WAS PUSHED.
THREE DAYS OF INVESTIGATION AND THAT'S WHAT THEY'VE GOT?
TURKUS AND O'DWYER ARE GRILLING THE GUARDS.
WAS IT THE GUARDS?
COULD BE. THEY HATED HIM. THEY HATE US ALL.
ALLIE, DO YOU KNOW WHO IT WAS?
IS THAT WHY THEY LET YOU IN?
THEY SENT MY SISTER TO FIND OUT IF "TICK TOCK" TANNENBAUM KILLED "KID TWIST" RELES?

ALLIE, NO!

I WAS SLEEPING. MY DOOR WAS GUARDED—SAME AS RELES.

COULDA BEEN THE GUARDS, COULDA BEEN ONE O' US... HELL, IT COULDA BEEN LUCKY LUCIANO, FOR ALL I KNOW!

BUT YOU DON'T.

NO. EVERYONE HATED HIM. GOD KNOWS I DID.

YOU THINK IT WAS MURDER?

HE WAS SMILING THE LAST TIME I SAW HIM. HE WAS SMILING.

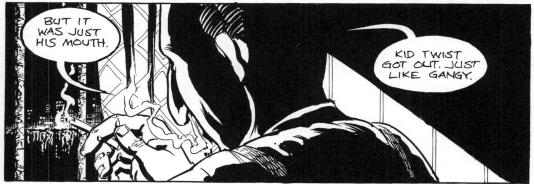

BUT IT WAS JUST HIS MOUTH.

KID TWIST GOT OUT. JUST LIKE GANGY.

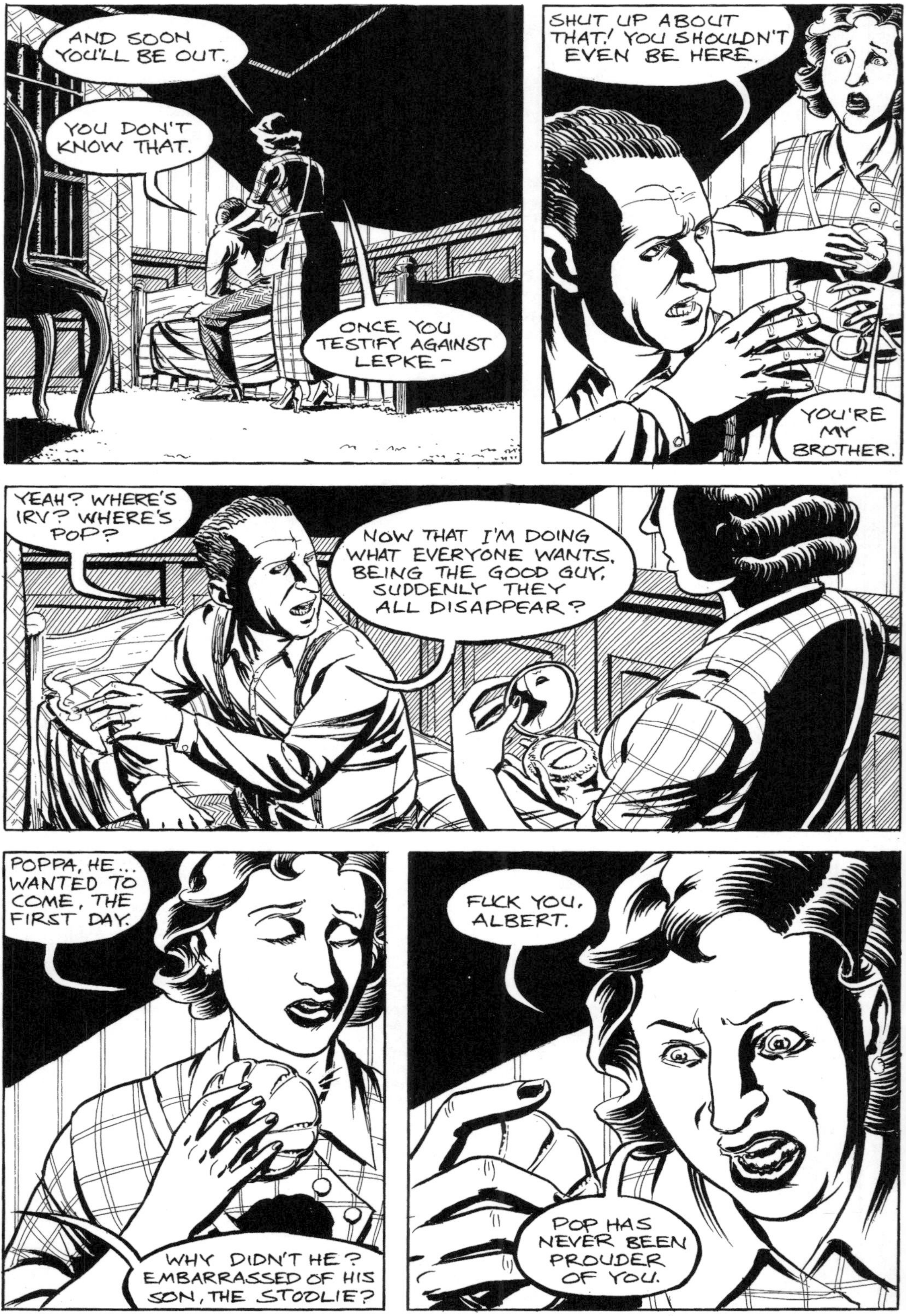
AND SOON YOU'LL BE OUT.
YOU DON'T KNOW THAT.
ONCE YOU TESTIFY AGAINST LEPKE-
SHUT UP ABOUT THAT! YOU SHOULDN'T EVEN BE HERE.
YOU'RE MY BROTHER.
YEAH? WHERE'S IRV? WHERE'S POP?
NOW THAT I'M DOING WHAT EVERYONE WANTS, BEING THE GOOD GUY, SUDDENLY THEY ALL DISAPPEAR?
POPPA, HE... WANTED TO COME, THE FIRST DAY.
WHY DIDN'T HE? EMBARRASSED OF HIS SON, THE STOOLIE?
FUCK YOU, ALBERT.
POP HAS NEVER BEEN PROUDER OF YOU.

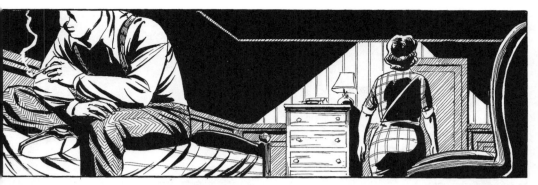

YOU HAVE TO DO THIS YOURSELF, ALBERT.

YOU HAVE TO SEE THIS TO THE END.

YOUR FAMILY WILL ALWAYS BE THERE FOR YOU.

.... YOU JUST NEED TO FINALLY CHOOSE ONE OVER THE OTHER.

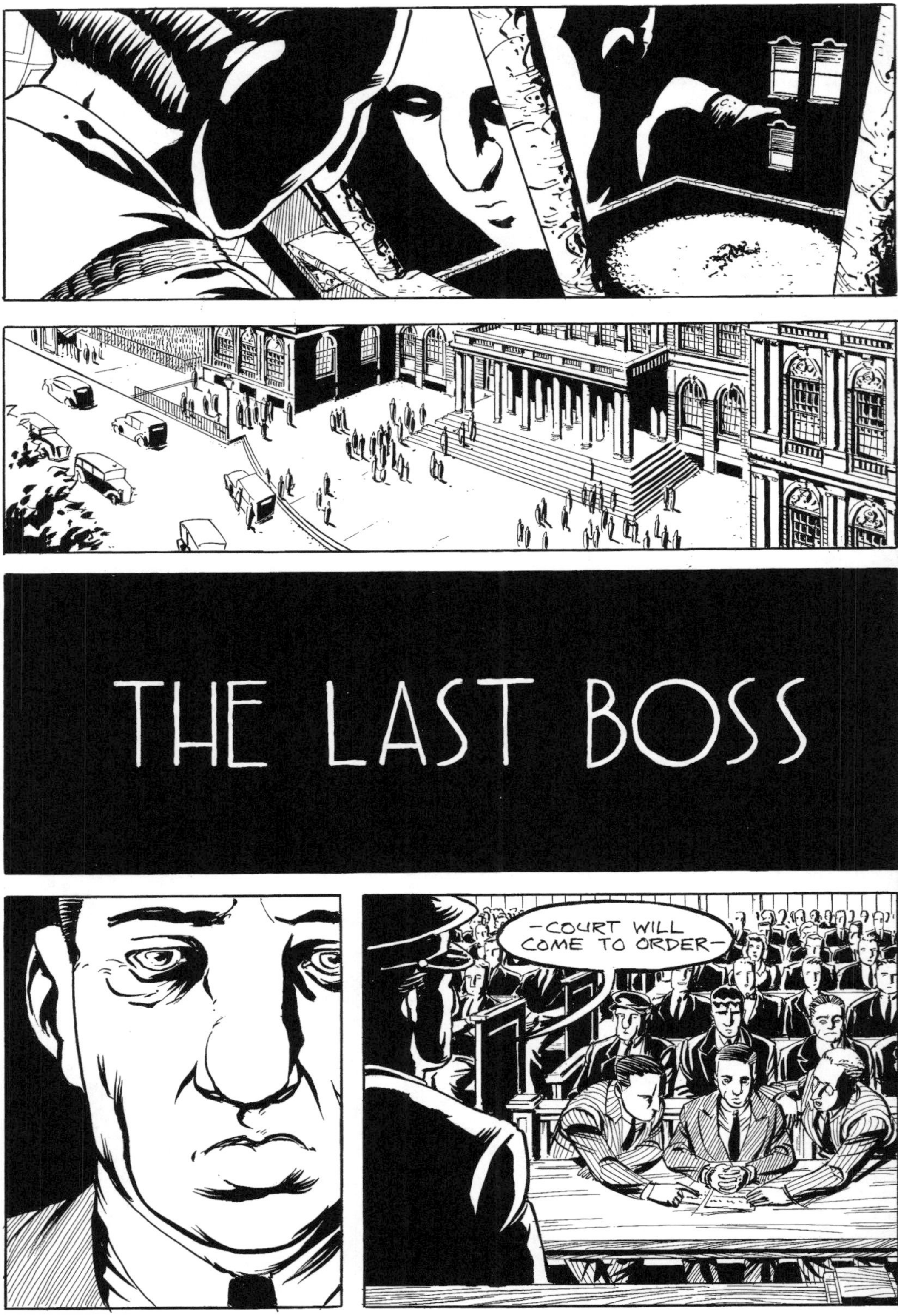
THE LAST BOSS
—COURT WILL COME TO ORDER—

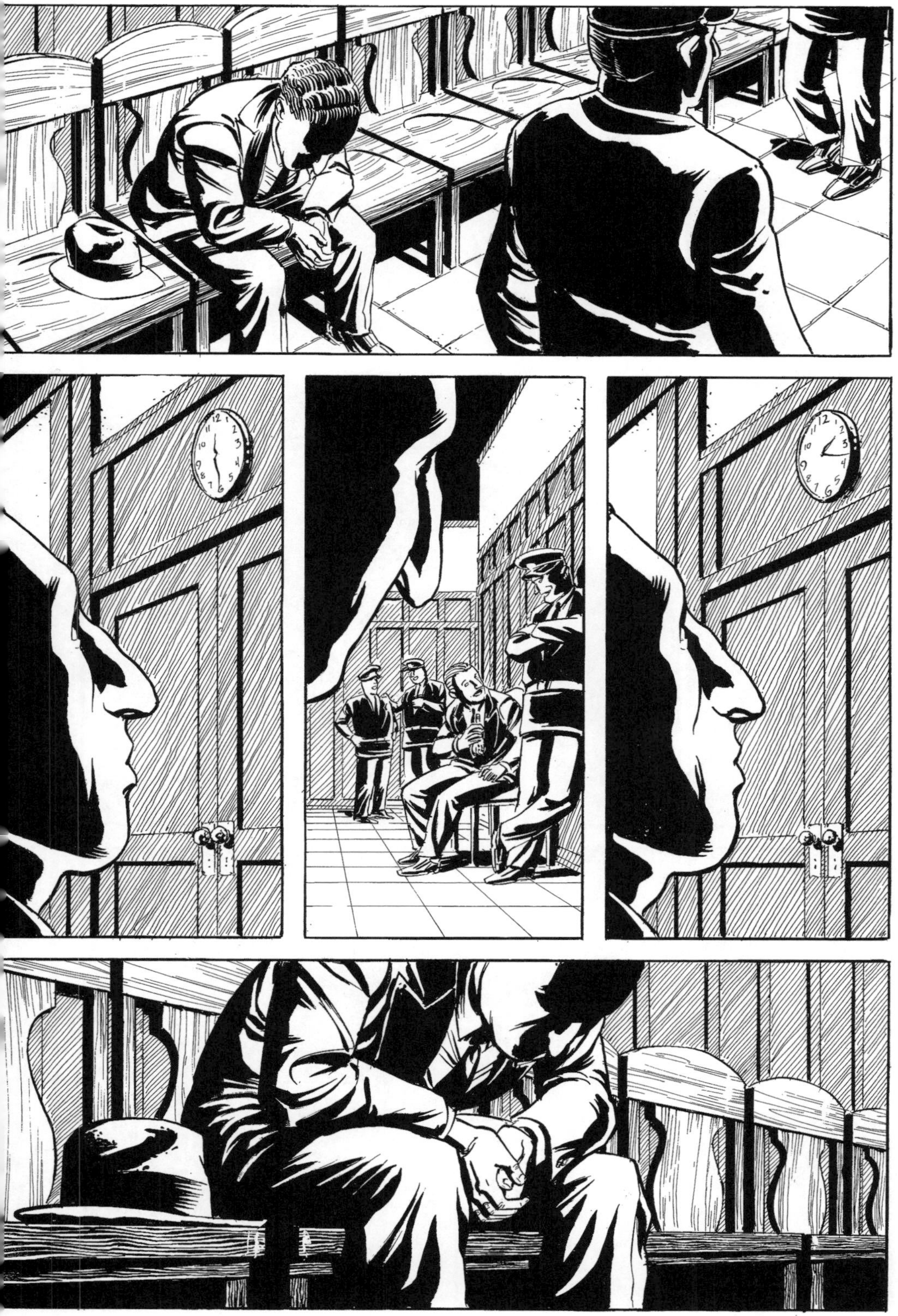

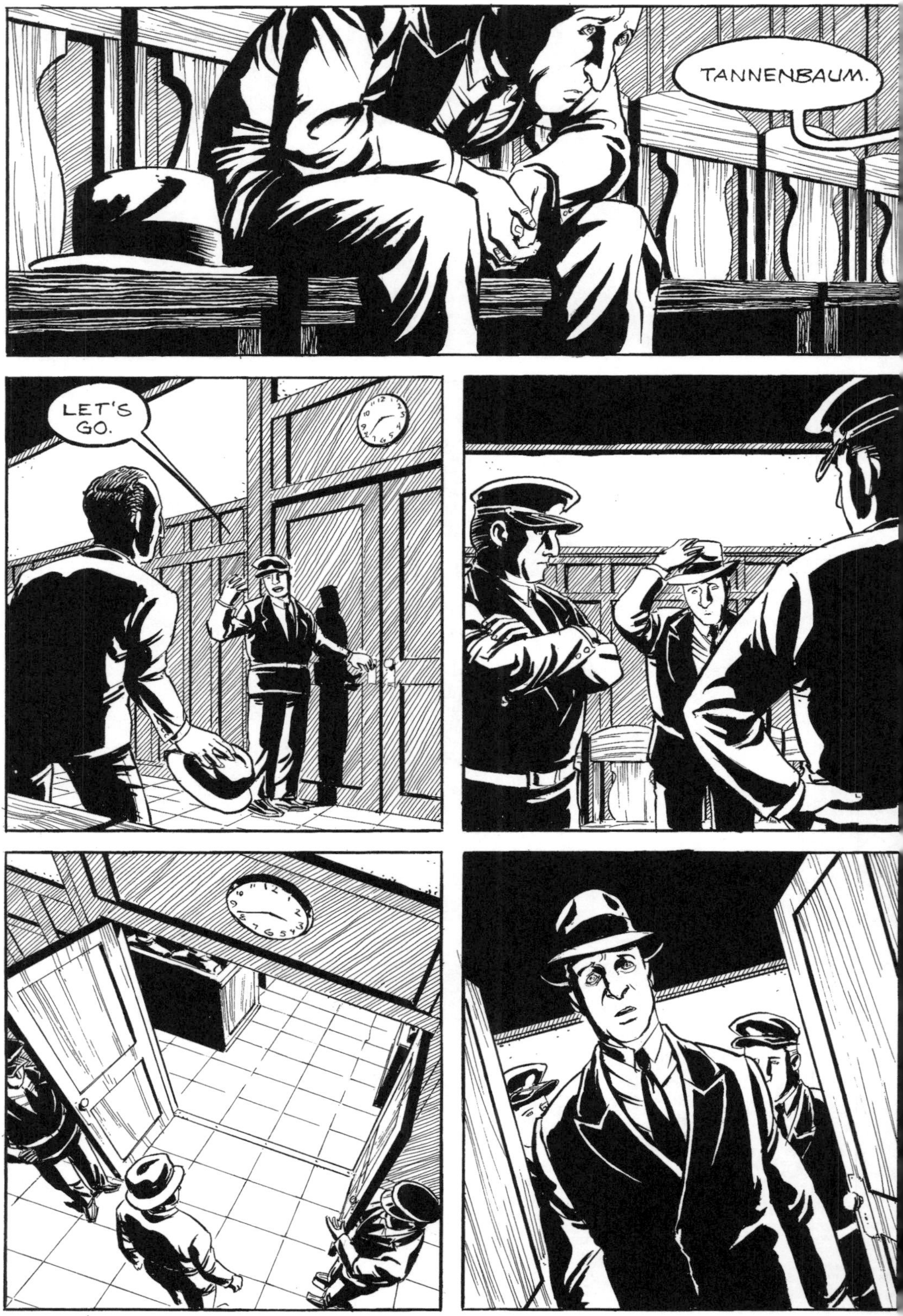
TANNENBAUM.
LET'S GO.

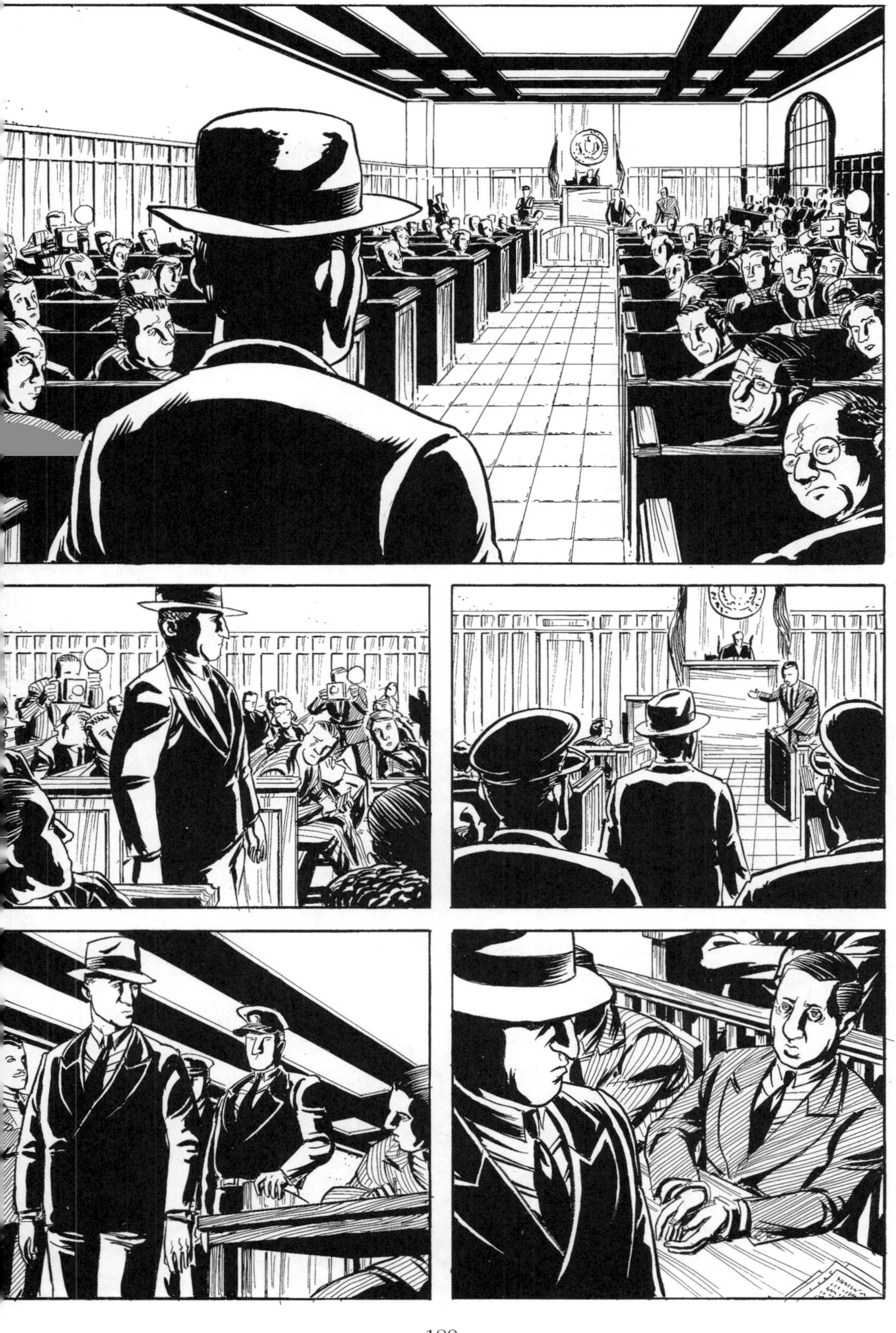

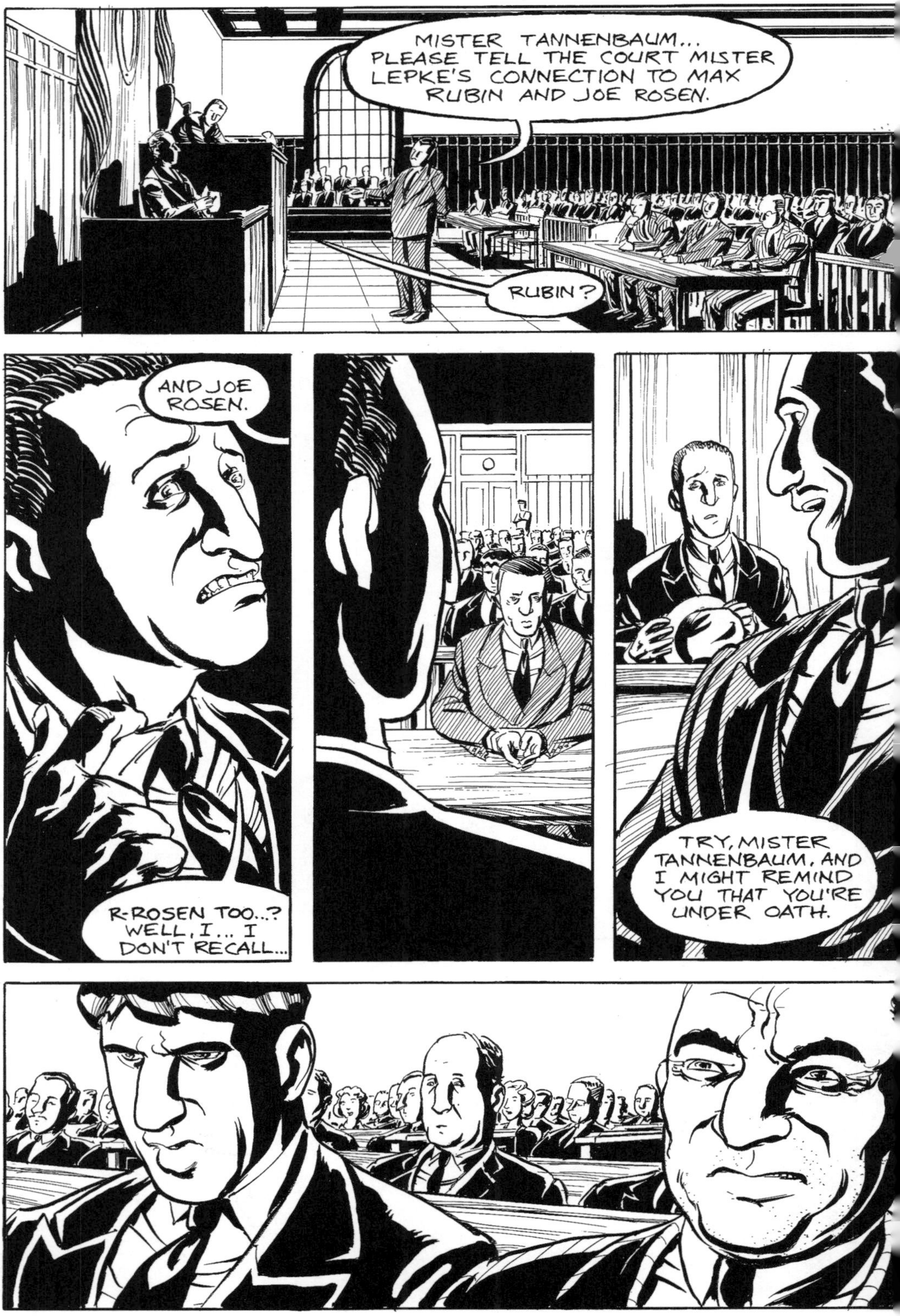
MISTER TANNENBAUM... PLEASE TELL THE COURT MISTER LEPKE'S CONNECTION TO MAX RUBIN AND JOE ROSEN.
RUBIN?
AND JOE ROSEN.
R-ROSEN TOO...? WELL, I... I DON'T RECALL...
TRY, MISTER TANNENBAUM. AND I MIGHT REMIND YOU THAT YOU'RE UNDER OATH.

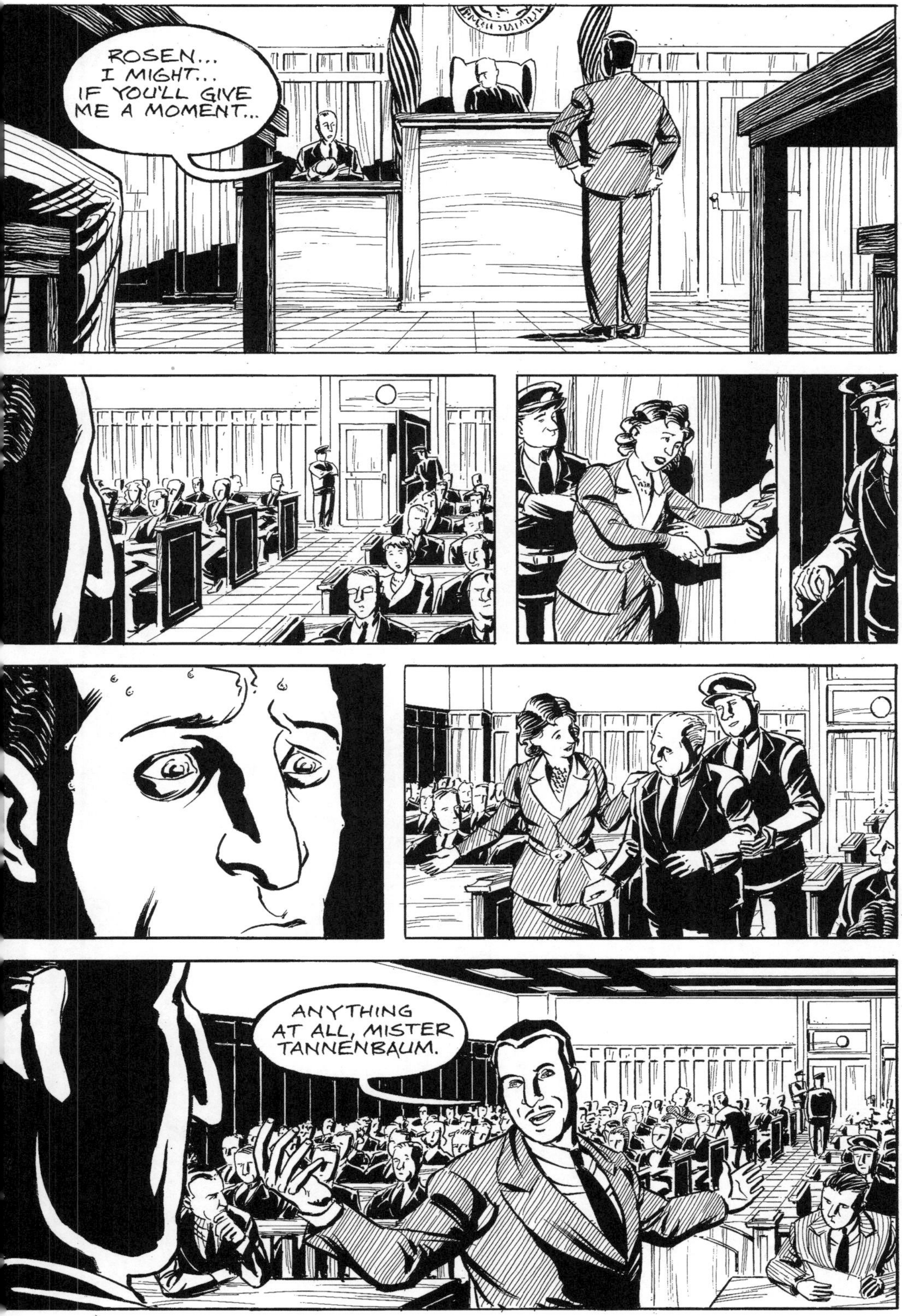
ROSEN... I MIGHT... IF YOU'LL GIVE ME A MOMENT...
ANYTHING AT ALL, MISTER TANNENBAUM.

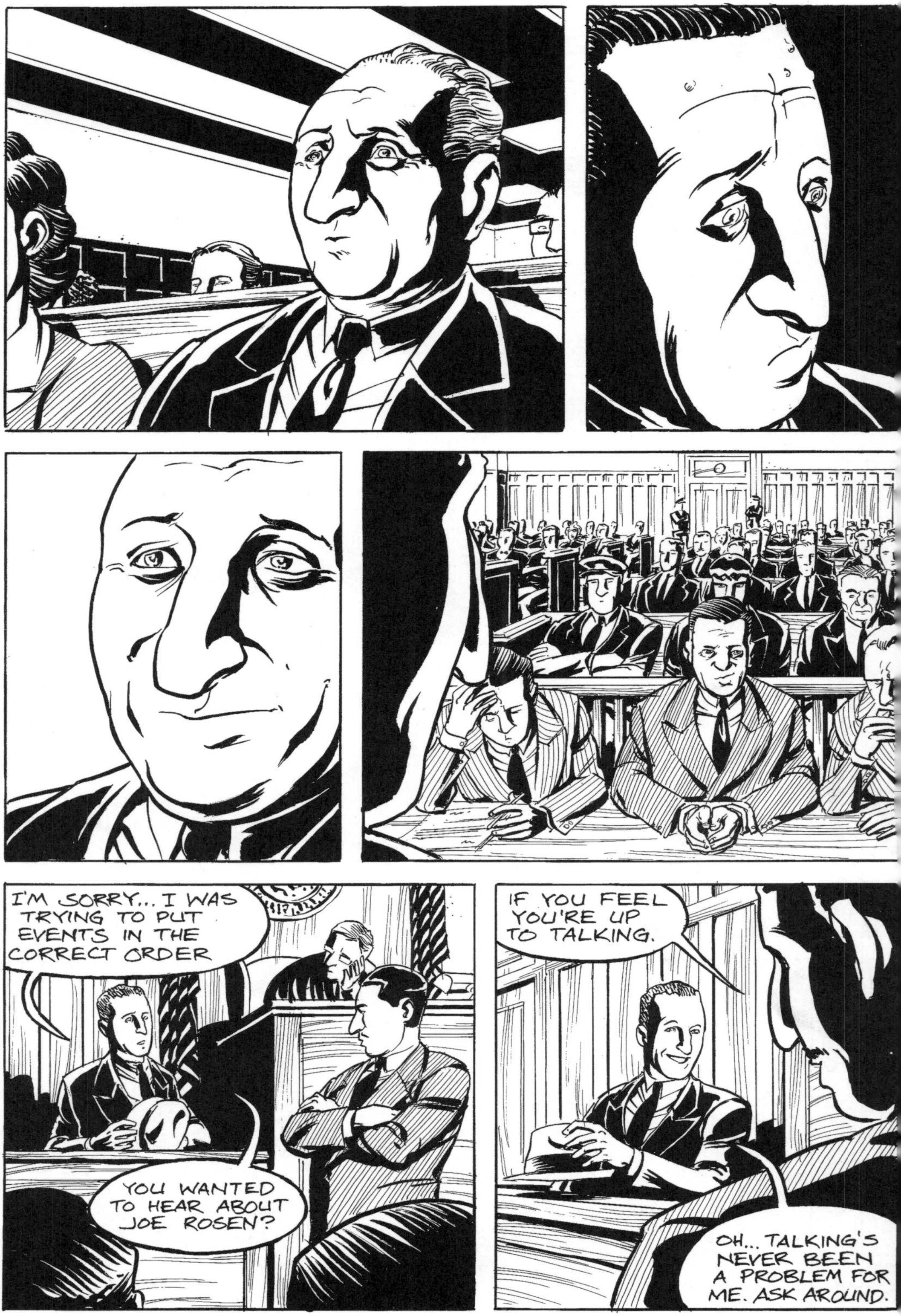
I'M SORRY... I WAS TRYING TO PUT EVENTS IN THE CORRECT ORDER
YOU WANTED TO HEAR ABOUT JOE ROSEN?
IF YOU FEEL YOU'RE UP TO TALKING.
OH... TALKING'S NEVER BEEN A PROBLEM FOR ME. ASK AROUND.

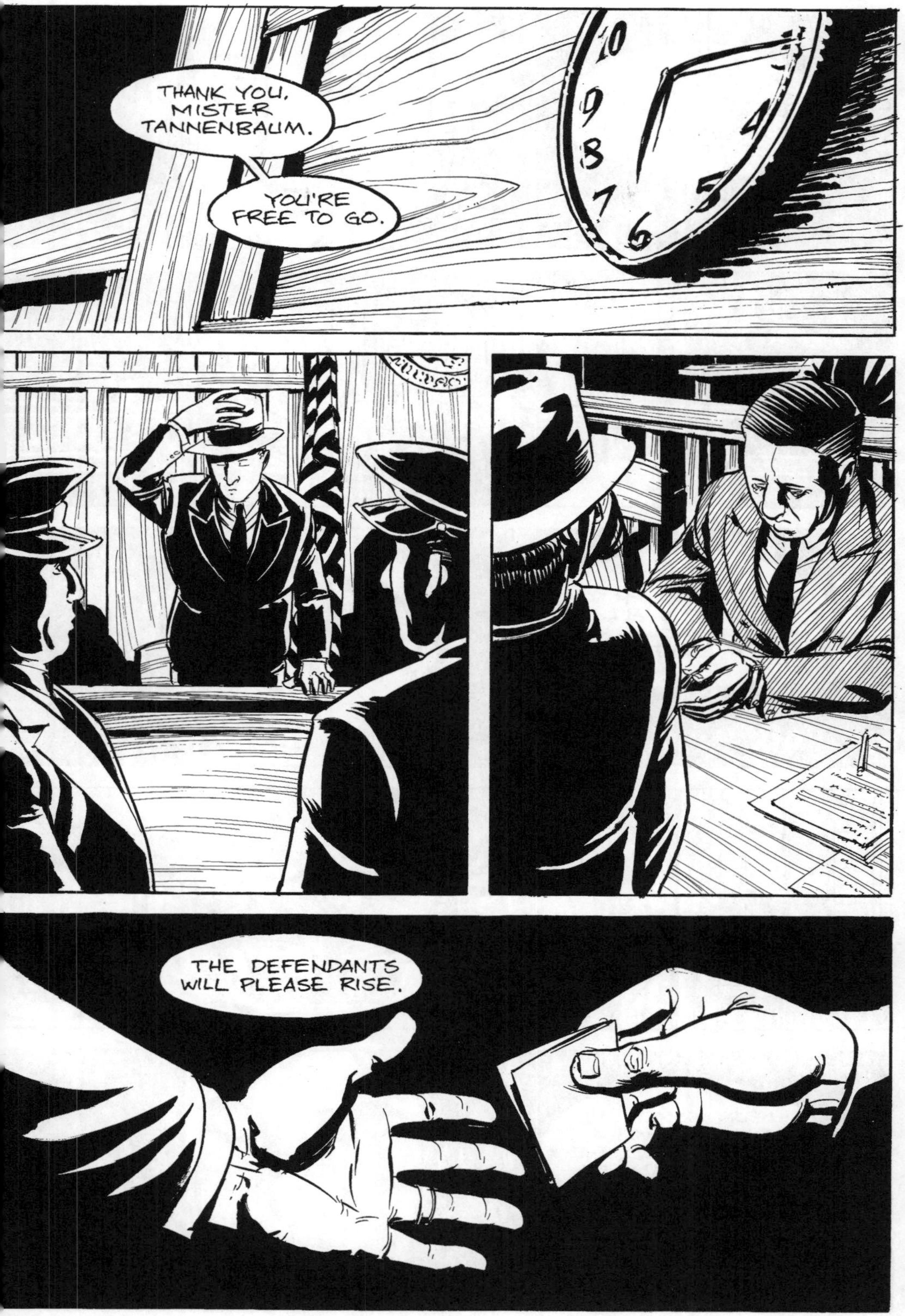
THANK YOU, MISTER TANNENBAUM.
YOU'RE FREE TO GO.
THE DEFENDANTS WILL PLEASE RISE.

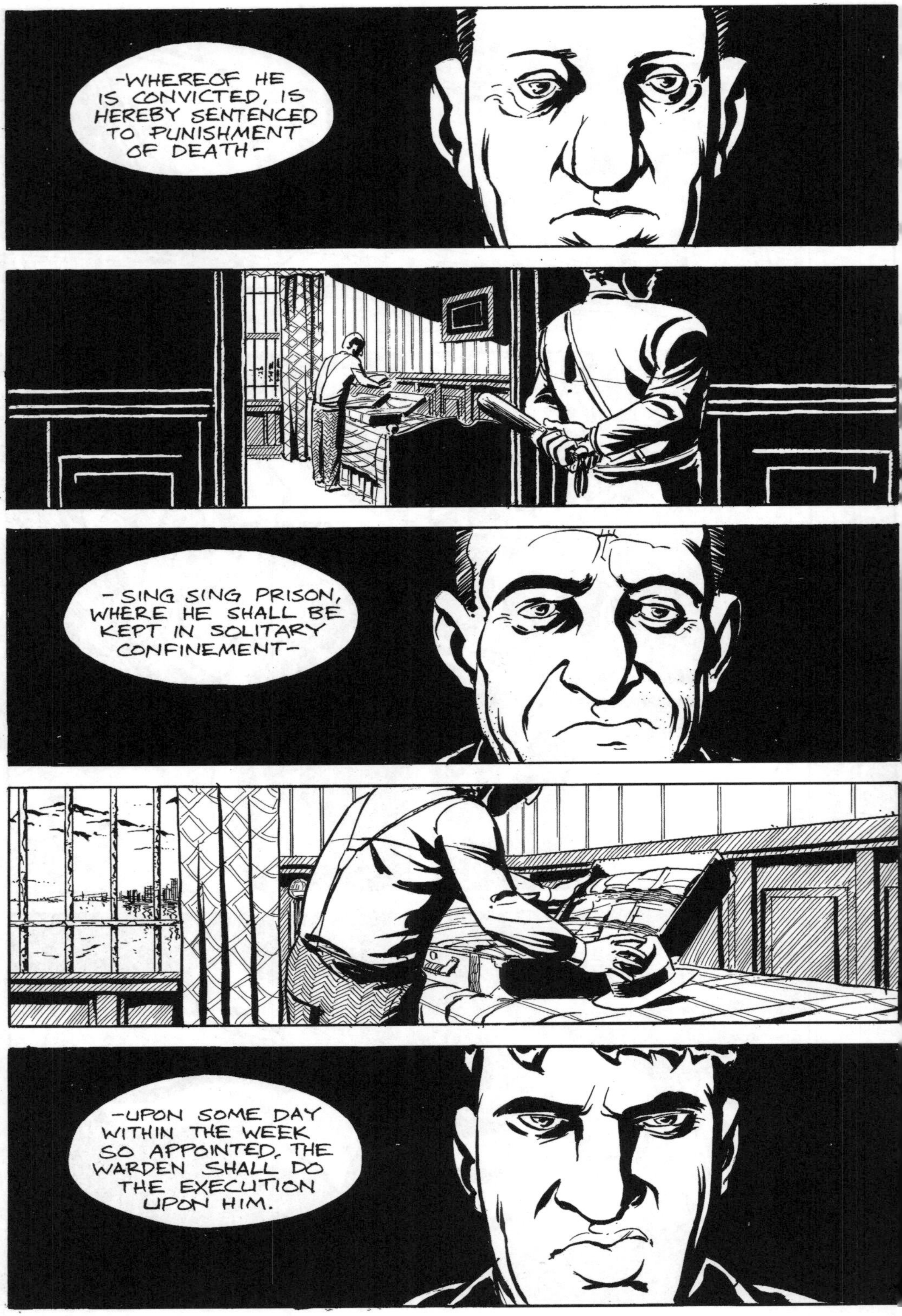
-WHEREOF HE IS CONVICTED, IS HEREBY SENTENCED TO PUNISHMENT OF DEATH-
-SING SING PRISON, WHERE HE SHALL BE KEPT IN SOLITARY CONFINEMENT-
-UPON SOME DAY WITHIN THE WEEK SO APPOINTED, THE WARDEN SHALL DO THE EXECUTION UPON HIM.

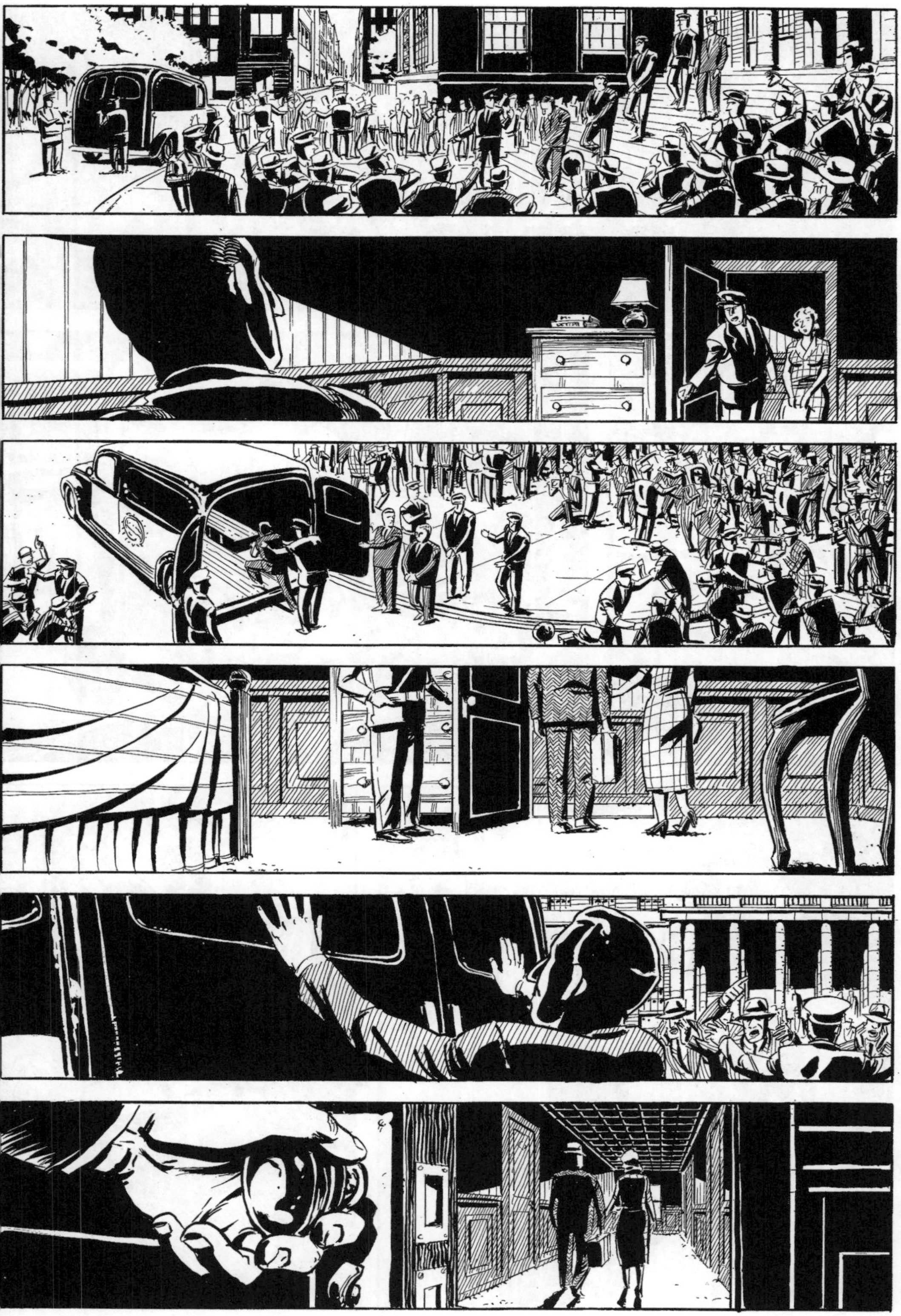

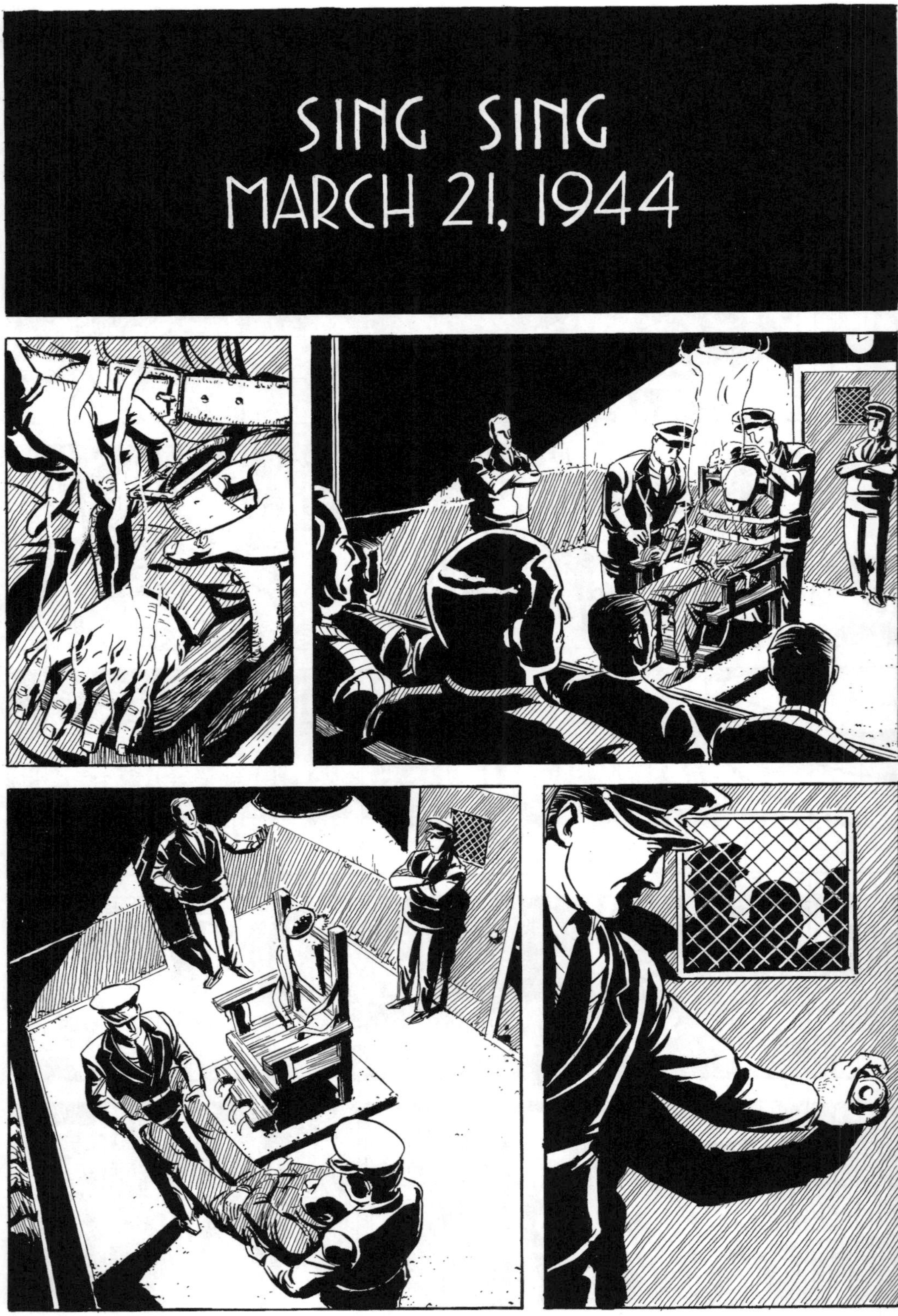
SING SING
MARCH 21, 1944

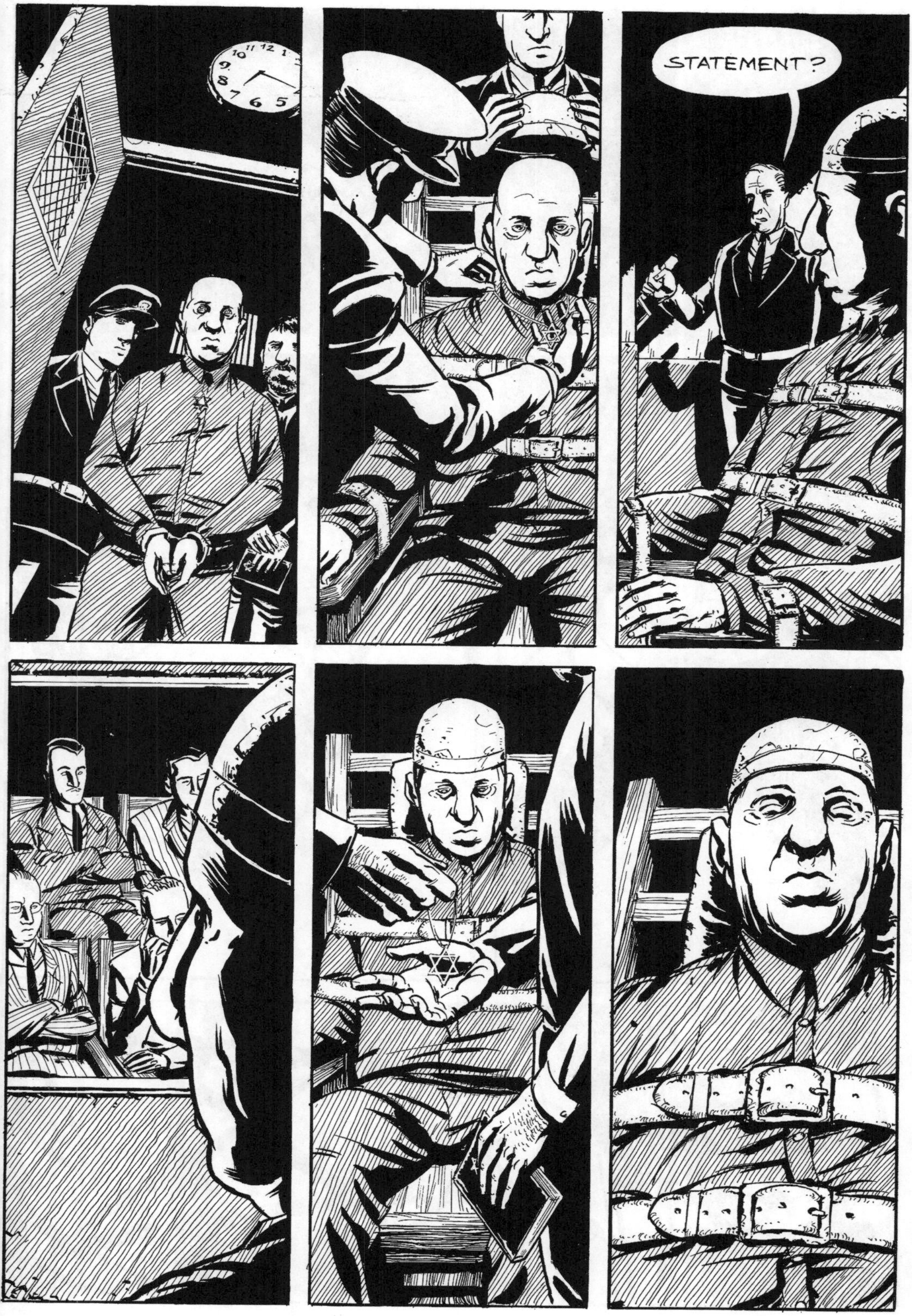
STATEMENT?

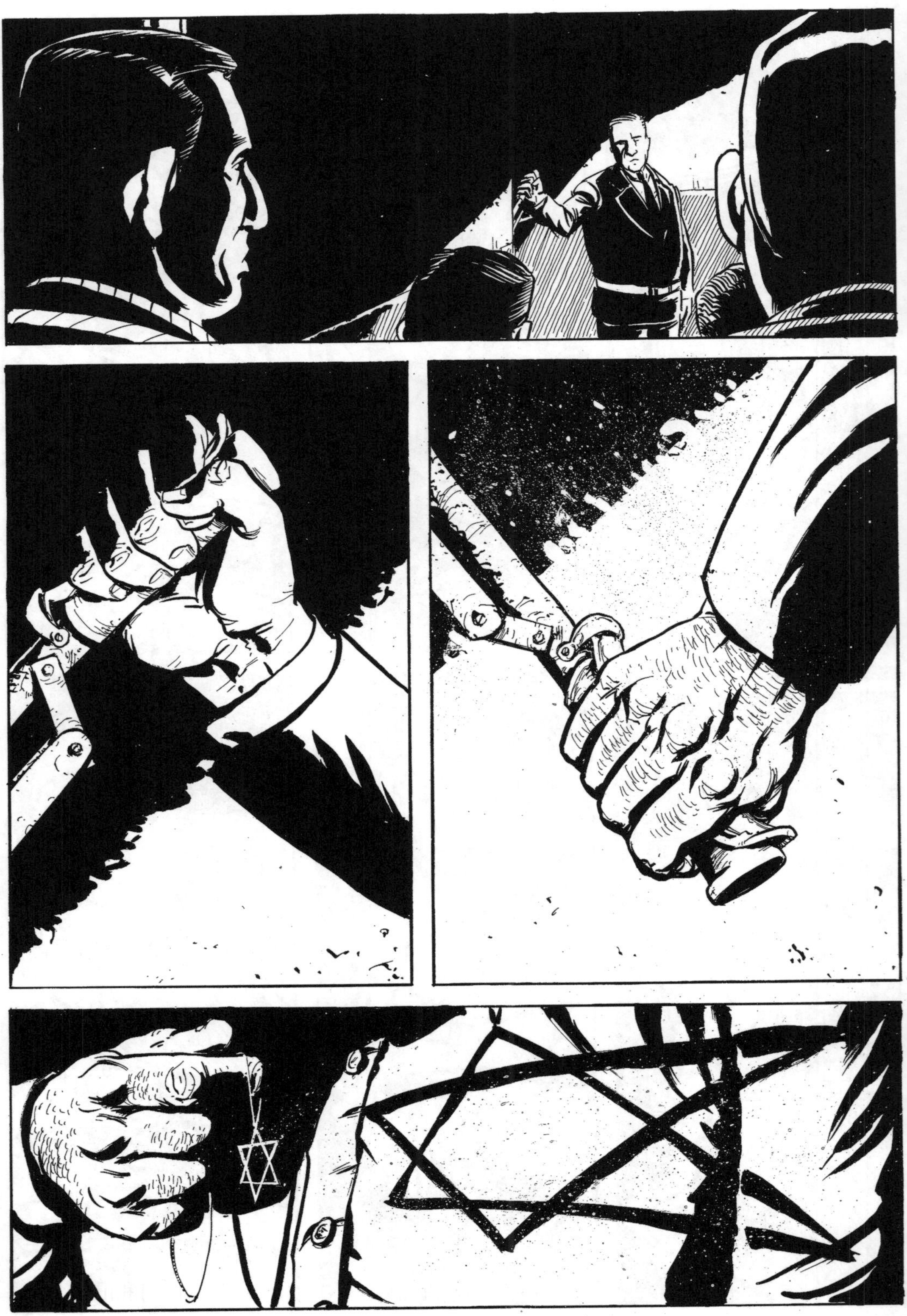

THE CORNER

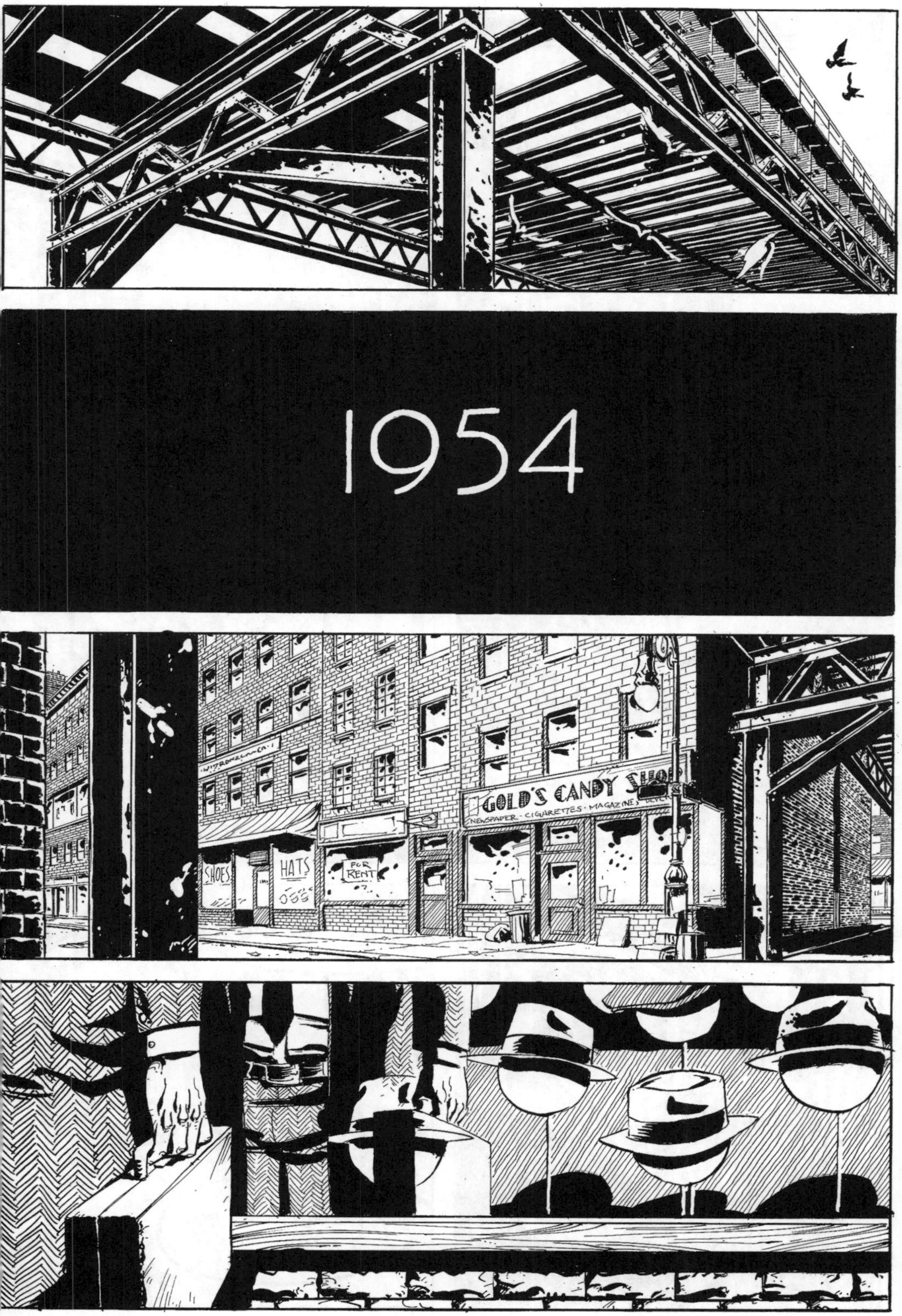
1954
GOLD'S CANDY S
NEWSPAPER · CIGARETTES · MAGAZINES
SHOES
HATS
FOR RENT

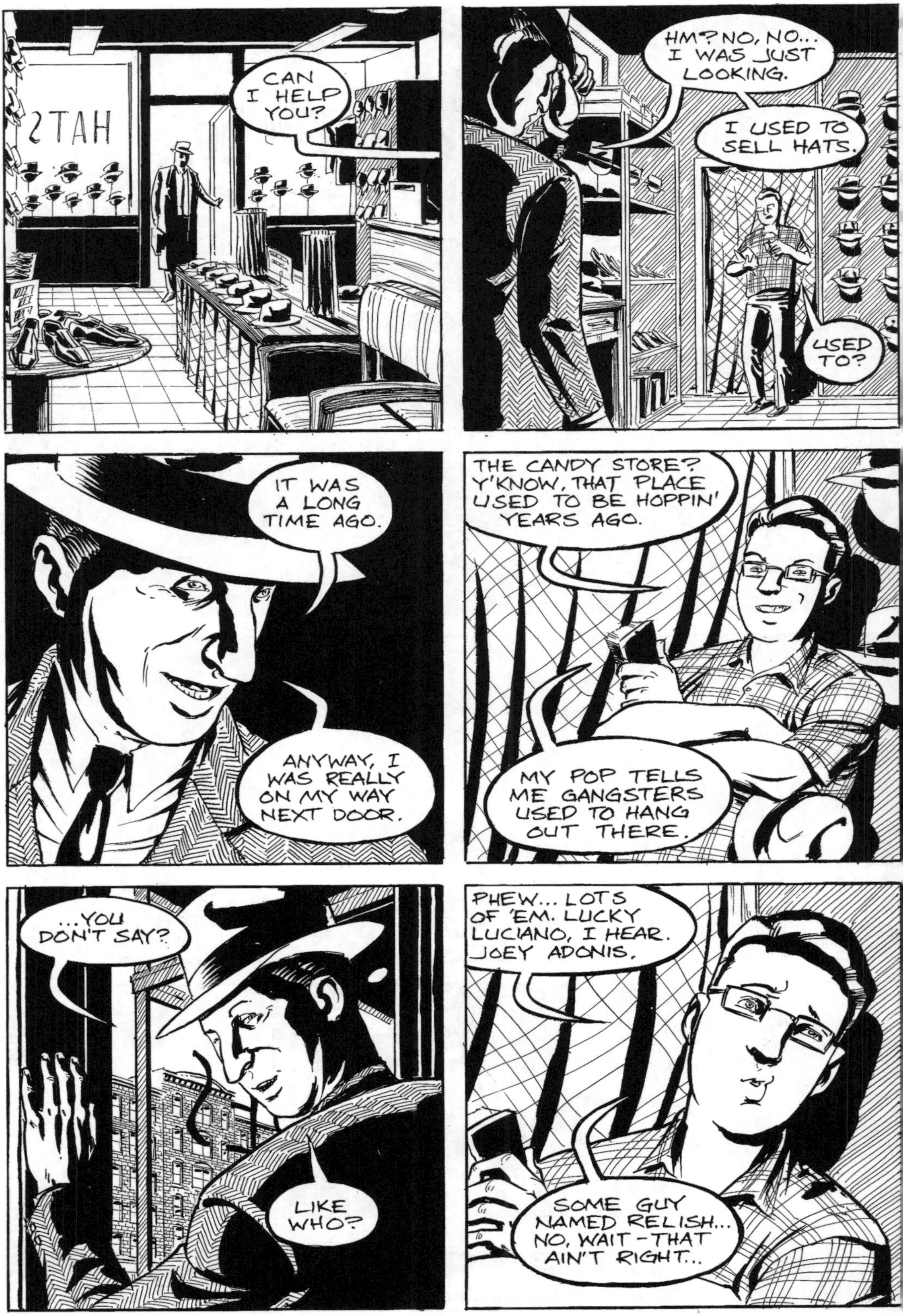
HATS
CAN I HELP YOU?
HM? NO, NO... I WAS JUST LOOKING.
I USED TO SELL HATS.
USED TO?
IT WAS A LONG TIME AGO.
ANYWAY, I WAS REALLY ON MY WAY NEXT DOOR.
THE CANDY STORE? Y'KNOW, THAT PLACE USED TO BE HOPPIN' YEARS AGO.
MY POP TELLS ME GANGSTERS USED TO HANG OUT THERE.
...YOU DON'T SAY?
LIKE WHO?
PHEW... LOTS OF 'EM. LUCKY LUCIANO, I HEAR. JOEY ADONIS.
SOME GUY NAMED RELISH... NO, WAIT-THAT AIN'T RIGHT...

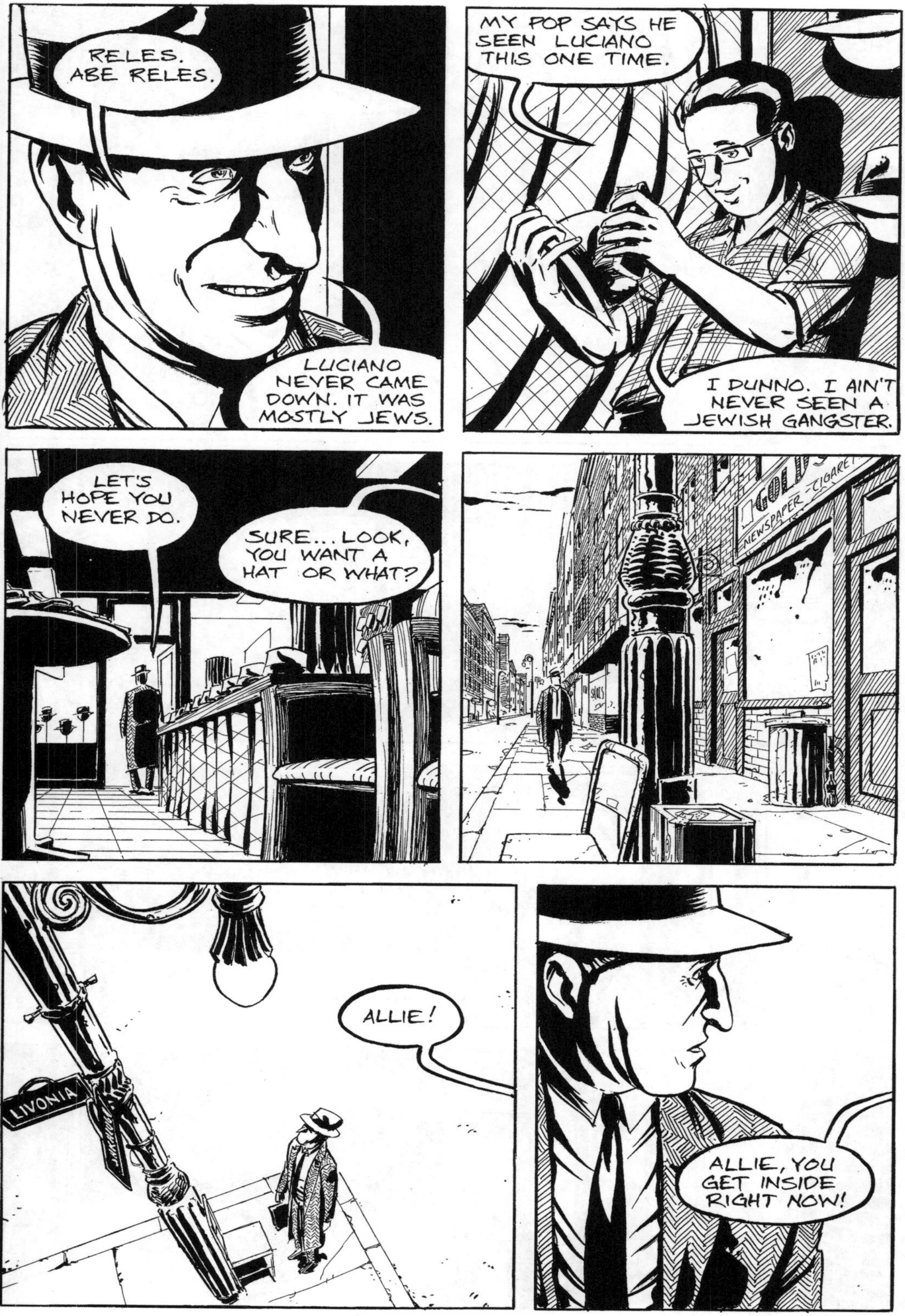
RELES. ABE RELES.
MY POP SAYS HE SEEN LUCIANO THIS ONE TIME.
LUCIANO NEVER CAME DOWN. IT WAS MOSTLY JEWS.
I DUNNO. I AIN'T NEVER SEEN A JEWISH GANGSTER.
LET'S HOPE YOU NEVER DO.
SURE... LOOK, YOU WANT A HAT OR WHAT?
NEWSPAPER - CIGARE
LIVONIA
ALLIE!
ALLIE, YOU GET INSIDE RIGHT NOW!

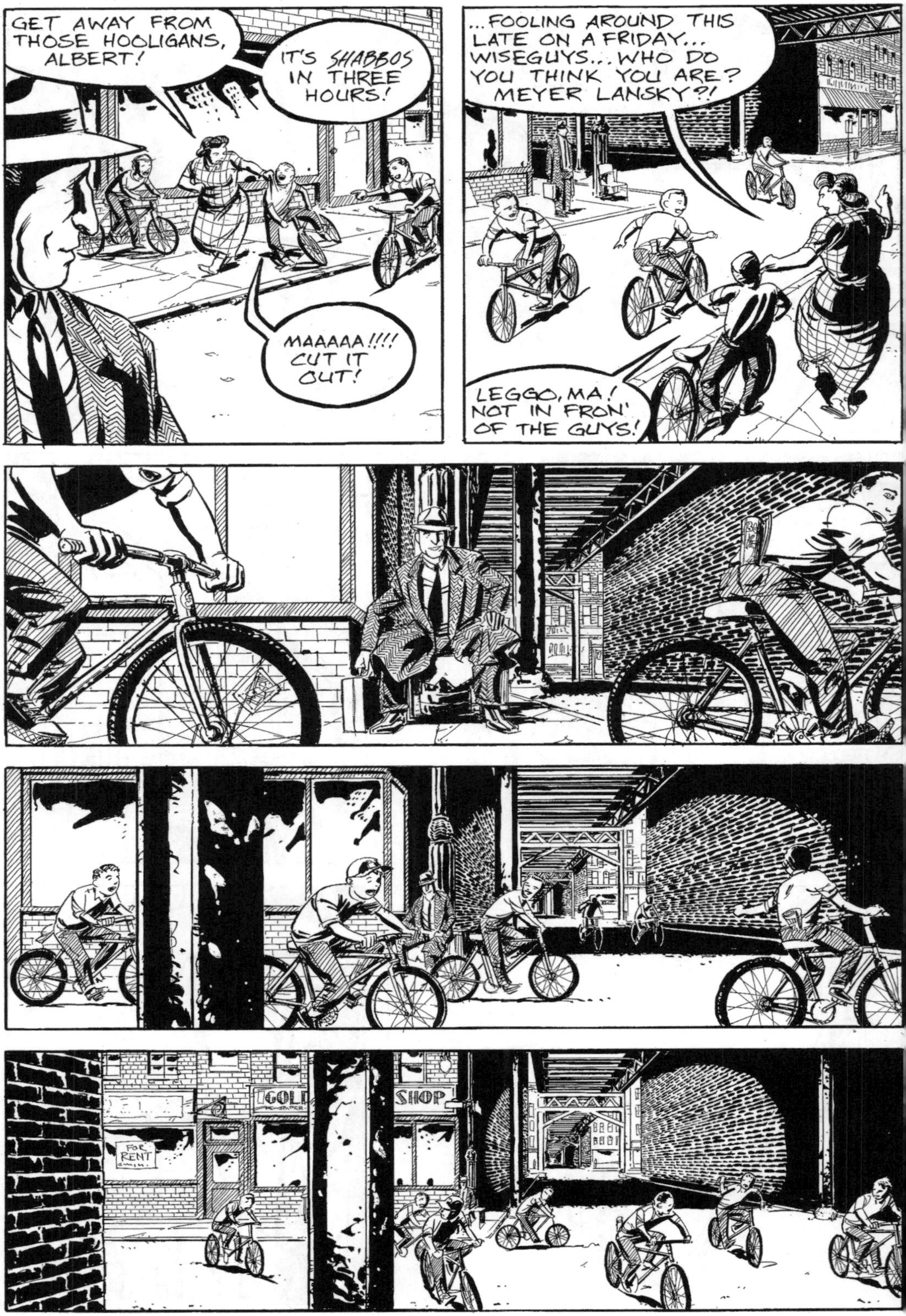

GET AWAY FROM THOSE HOOLIGANS, ALBERT!
IT'S *SHABBOS* IN THREE HOURS!
MAAAAA!!!! CUT IT OUT!
...FOOLING AROUND THIS LATE ON A FRIDAY... WISEGUYS... WHO DO YOU THINK YOU ARE? MEYER LANSKY?!
LEGGO, MA! NOT IN FRON' OF THE GUYS!
SHOP
FOR RENT

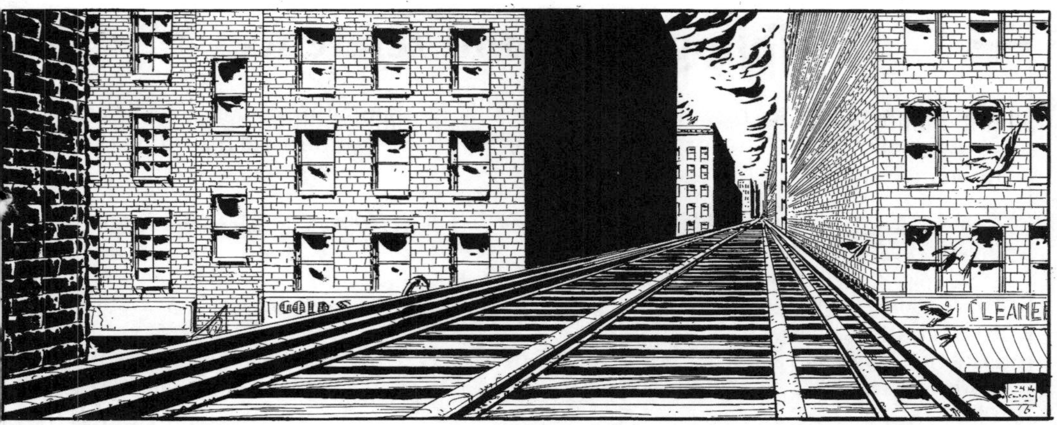
GOLD'S

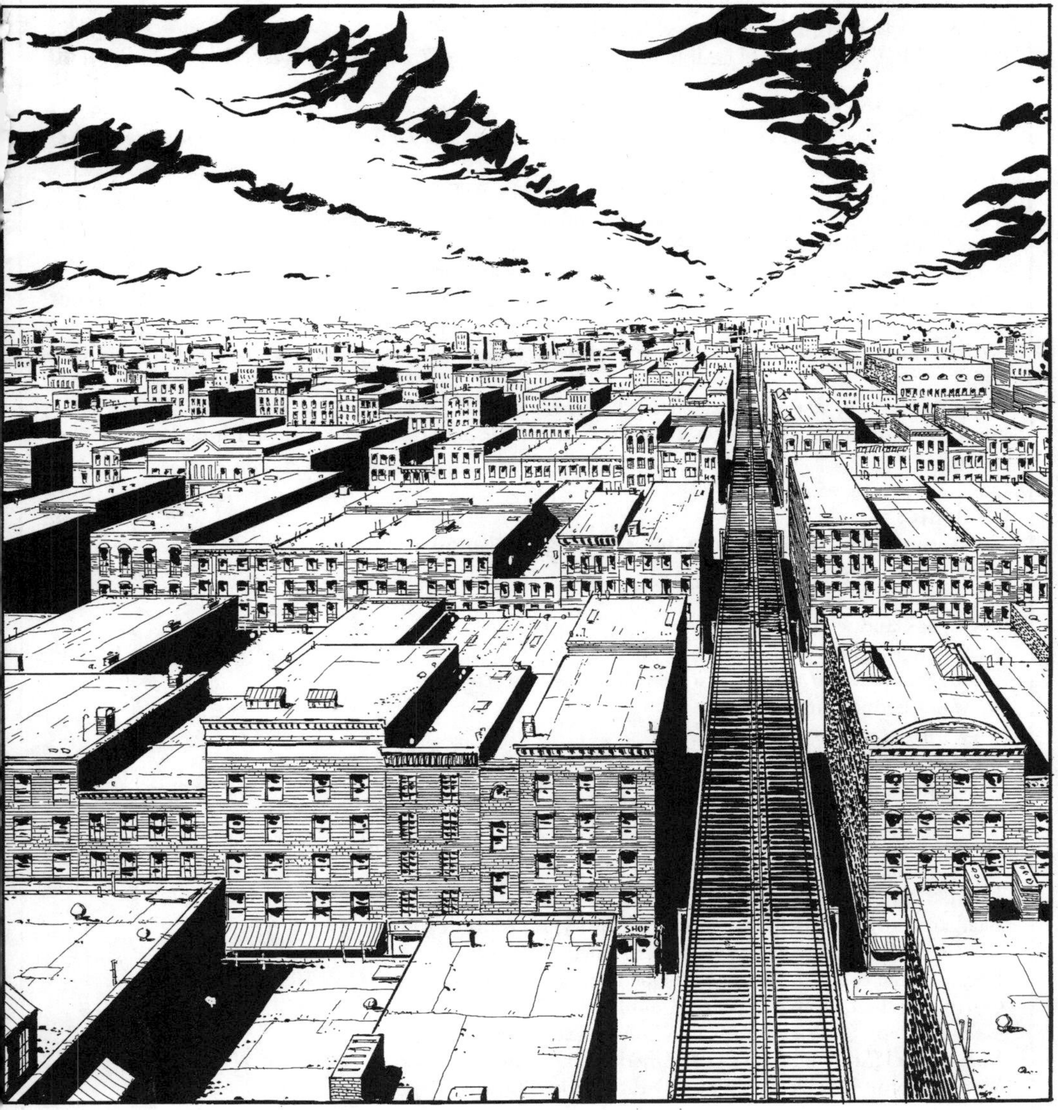
SHOP

bibliography and reference

The following books, films and internet sites were essential in researching the story of the men of Murder, Incorporated. The authors hope that they did these sources and inspirations justice.

Cohen, Rich, *Tough Jews: Fathers, Sons and Gangster Dreams.* (New York, Random House, Vintage Books, 1998)

Doctorow, E.L., *Billy Bathgate.* (New York, Harper & Row, 1989)

Downey, Patrick, *Gangster City: The History of the New York Underworld 1900-1935.* (Canada, Barricade Books, 2004)

Dargan, Amanda and Zeitlin, Steven, *City Play.* (Pircataway, NJ, Rutgers University Press. 1990)

Durham, Michael S., *The National Geographic Traveler: New York,* (National Geographic Society, 1999)

Gabler, Neal, *Walter Winchell.* (American Heritage Magazine, November 1994)

Gribben, Mark, *Murder, Inc.* (www.crimelibrary.com)

Highsmith, Carol M. and Landphair, Ted. *New York City, The Five Boroughs.* (New York, Random House Publishing, 1997)

Landesman, Alter, Brownsville: *The Birth, Development and Passing of a Jewish Community in New York.* (New York, Bloch Pub. Co., 1997)

May, Allan, *A Bug's Life.* (www.crimemagazine.com, 1999)

Opie, Robert, *The 1930's ScrapBook.* (London, New Cavendish Books, 1997)

Sann, Paul, *Kill the Dutchman.* (New York, DeCapo Press, 1971)

Sifakis, Cark, *The Mafia Encylopedia.* (New York, Facts on File, 1987)

Turkus, Burton and Feder, Sid, *Murder, Inc.: The Story of the Syndicate.* (New York, Farrar, Straus and Young, 1951)

Wright, Susan, *New York City: In Photographs 1850-1945.* (New York, Barnes & Noble Books, 1999)

Yapp, Nick, *The Hulton Getty Picture Collection: 1920's.* (Barnes & Noble Books, 1998)

Shuugar, Anthony. *New York: The City That Never Sleeps.* (New York, Smithmark Publishers, 1996)

Websites:
www.crimelibrary.com/gangsters_outlaws/gang/inc/1.html
www.crimelibrary.com
www.findagrave.com
www.ganglandnews.com
www.gangrule.com
www.geocities.com/murdersrus/index.html
www.killthedutchman.net
www.mugshots.com
www.murderinc.com
www.njhm.com/dutchschultz.ht
www.policygame.net
www.rootsweb.com/~usgenweb/ny/kings/postcards/ppcs-kings.html

Films:
Balaban, Burt & Rosenberg, Stuart. "Murder, Inc.", 20th Century Fox, 1960.
Benton, Robert. Billy Bathgate. TouchStone, 1991.
Bugsy, Dutch & Al: the Gangters. (Documentary). Rhino Home Video. 1991.
Golan, Meahen, "Lepke" Gola-Globus Filer, 1975.
Leone, Sergio. Once Upon A Time In America. Warner Bros. 1984.
Mafia: The History of the Mob in America. (Documentary). A&E, 1993.
Mendes, Sam. Road to Perdition. DreamWorks, 2002.

the writer

Xeric Award-winning cartoonist **Neil Kleid** authored NINETY CANDLES, a graphic novella about life, death, fatherhood and comic books. He moved to New York from his hometown of Oak Park, Michigan in 1999 and created minicomics and cartoons for various anthologies and magazines including 9-11: EMERGENCY RELIEF and KITCHEN SINK. He has written for NBM, Alternative Comics, Image Comics and Slave Labor Graphics. In his day job as a graphic designer, Neil has worked on campaigns for Comedy Central and Miramax Films and his work has appeared in *Variety* and the *New York Times*.

THE BIG KAHN, Neil's next book from NBM with Eisner-nominated artist Scott Chantler, spins the tale of the family of a deceased pulpit Rabbi that learns, along with his congregation, that he's been living a lie for forty years - he isn't even Jewish. visit: www.rantcomics.com

the artist

Jake Allen attended the Joe Kubert School of Cartoon and Graphic Arts for two years and took classes at Montserrat College of Art in Beverly, MA. He contributed illustrations for two shorts in Andrew Dabb's SLICES, appearing at opi8.com. Currently, Jake does graphics for 5-Star Surfboards and rock-band "Firewalk" in New Hampshire, as well as freelance projects for local companies. He is currently working on his next book, AMERICAN CAESAR, with Neil Kleid.

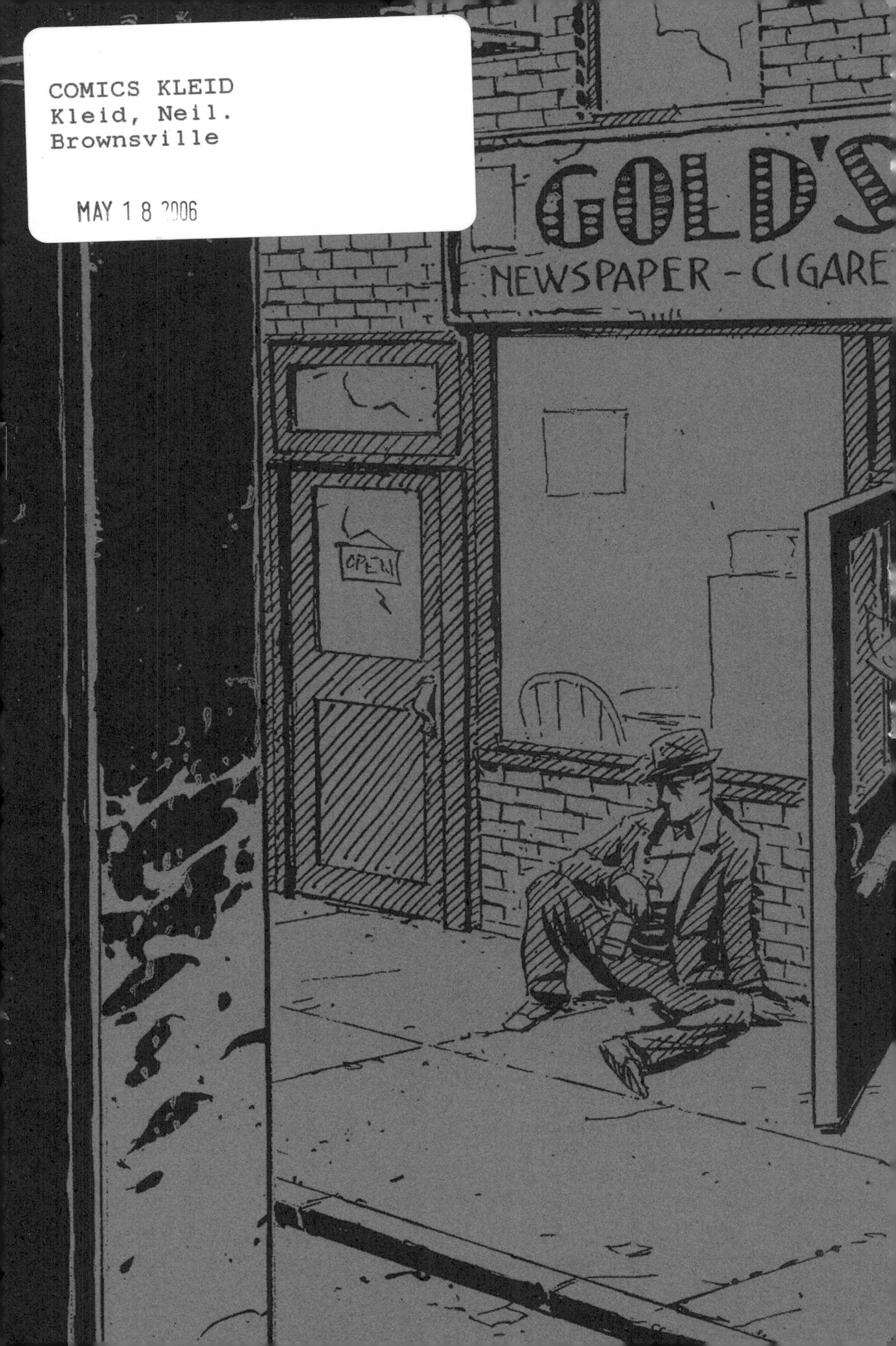
GOLD'S
NEWSPAPER - CIGARE
OPEN